Learn Microsoft Office 2021

Second Edition

Your one-stop guide to upskilling with new features
of Word, PowerPoint, Excel, Outlook, and Teams

Linda Foulkes

BIRMINGHAM—MUMBAI

Learn Microsoft Office 2021

Second Edition

Copyright © 2022 Packt Publishing

Group Product Manager: Alok Dhuri
Publishing Product Manager: Shweta Bairoliya
Senior Editor: Ruvika Rao
Technical Editor: Pradeep Sahu
Copy Editor: Safis Editing
Language Support Editor: Safis Editing
Project Coordinator: Manisha Singh
Proofreader: Safis Editing
Indexer: Rekha Nair
Production Designer: Sinhayna Bais
Marketing Coordinators: Deepak and Rayyan
Business Development Executive: Puneet Kaur

First published: May 2020

Second edition: July 2022

Production reference: 1290622

Published by Packt Publishing Ltd.
Livery Place
35 Livery Street
Birmingham
B3 2PB, UK.

ISBN 978-1-80323-973-6

www.packt.com

To my precious grandson, Caden – you are my inspiration, dedication, and the light of my life. I am so blessed to watch you grow in age and every stage. You are inscribed in my heart the way these letters are in the pages of this book. Remember to always be kind, caring, and the best version of yourself as you move through your life.

– Gran Gran, Linda Foulkes

Contributors

About the author

Linda Foulkes is a senior learning and development trainer at Knights. She is also a Microsoft Office Master Trainer, Certified Educator, and Microsoft Innovative Expert Educator with an educational and corporate background spanning 25 years. Linda is the author of the first edition of the book *Learn Microsoft Office 2019*. As well as being certified as an IT trainer, Linda represented South Africa at the Microsoft Global Forum in Redmond in 2015. She has certified students to compete at the Microsoft Office Specialist Championships in Texas, presented at conferences, and hosted webinars, TeachMeets, and MicrosoftMeets. She has a keen interest in e-learning and has developed e-learning paths and content for the Microsoft Office suite of programs.

About the reviewer

Ambarish Tarte is a Mumbai-based Microsoft Certified Professional and a globetrotter who conducts corporate training for various corporate giants/multinational companies across the globe. With Microsoft Office and Office 365 end user apps being his forte, he operates as a corporate training consultant with a team of associates in almost every major city in India. He began his corporate training stint in 2011 and has had the privilege to train delegates of over 20 nationalities in classroom and online sessions. Being able to add a bit of humor and always keep participants engaged during training is a unique selling point that Ambarish has achieved over the years. Ambarish is also a YouTuber and runs various social media pages.

I thank my parents for their continued support during my stint so far as a corporate training consultant. Quitting a full-time job and moving into freelancing requires support from your family and my parents left no stone unturned in doing so. I would also like to thank Mr. Saiesh G Tripathi, my colleague, for his input. Thanks to Ms. Neha Sikka, my protégé, for the initial screening of the chapters in this book.

Table of Contents

3

Styles, Referencing, and Media

4

Managing Professional Documents

Part 2: Learning PowerPoint 2021

5

The PowerPoint Interface and Presentation Options

6

Formatting Slides, Charts, and Graphic Elements

7

Photo Albums, Sections, and Show Tools

8

Mastering Best Practices with Presentations

Part 3: Learning Excel 2021

9

New Features, Filters, and Cleaning Data

10

Exploring New and Useful Workflow Functions

11

Date -Time Functions and Enhancing PivotTable Dashboards

12

Useful Statistical and Mathematical Functions

Part 4: Outlook 2021 and Useful Communication Tools

13

Creating and Attaching Item Content

14

Managing Mail and Contacts

15

Calendar Objects, Tasks, Notes, and Journal Entries

16

Creating and Managing Online Meetings

17

Presenting and Collaborating Online

Index

Other Books You May Enjoy

Preface

This book is a comprehensive journey through Office 2021 applications, which includes visual and detailed explanations of concepts and the opportunity to practice using relevant workplace examples. In addition to imparting new and updated skills for Word, Excel, PowerPoint, and Outlook, we explore Microsoft Teams to effectively collaborate and present. Also included is a topic on best practices.

This book is a progressive broadening of skills from our previous edition, and addresses the most up-to-date, efficient, and streamlined features of the Office 2021 applications. This edition includes a section on presenting with PowerPoint, Teams channel top tips, collaborating, and learning all about presenting during meetings.

Who this book is for

This second edition of the book is tailored to those working with Microsoft Office applications and wanting to broaden their skillset and learn about new technologies. It would be of value to those working in any industry and for students who are moving into the workplace, or for certification. The book introduces real-world practical workplace skills applicable to beginners through to power users, helping to make the most of the most recent application features.

Although there are no prerequisites, an understanding of the applications would be beneficial, as covered in the previous edition of the book, *Learn Microsoft Office 2019*.

What this book covers

Chapter 1, *Exploring the New Interface and Managing OneDrive*, firstly discusses what Microsoft Office 2021 offers within the single-user license compared to the Microsoft 365 online version, and then progresses to upskill you on the new interface features. Throughout, we will explore many new tools applied to the office standalone and web apps. The final topic will concentrate on managing the OneDrive experience in the cloud and desktop connections and teach you how to troubleshoot sync errors.

Chapter 2, Dictation, Co-Authoring, and Embedding, focuses on features new to Office 2021 and the latest versions (and revisions) of the Office 365 offering. You will learn about the new transform feature to integrate amazing presentations with Microsoft Sway. We will discuss the new dictation tools in Word 2021, and also investigate co-authoring requirements and learn about modern commenting. The last topic introduces several new embedding features.

Chapter 3, Styles, Referencing, and Media, touches on enhancements to existing features and teaches you how to become more comfortable when working with styles by refining the layout. We will troubleshoot more than one table of contents within a document and take a look at cross-referencing. There is also a section on working with media content and drawing elements.

Chapter 4, Managing Professional Documents, a new-edition chapter, revisits some of the features with updates applicable to the Office 2021 interface and teaches some new features. We'll teach you how to construct a form using content controls and generate an online form within Word desktop and online to collect information from others. You will also recap adding headers and footers to a document, tracking, and the compare/combine tools, as well as learning how to automate processes when using Word 2021.

Chapter 5, The PowerPoint Interface and Presentation Options, introduces new PowerPoint 2021 features and recaps skills to personalize and navigate the interface to perform tasks such as creating, saving, printing, and viewing presentations. New features covered here will include Presenter Coach, Stock Images, Transparency, Link to Slide, Ink Replay, and the Immersive Reader, and we will cover even more over the next few PowerPoint chapters.

Chapter 6, Formatting Slides, Charts, and Graphic Elements, teaches you how to set up a presentation, order a sequence of slides, apply a presentation theme and slide layout, and reuse slides. You will also learn how to manipulate slide elements using the Auto Fix feature, insert an agenda, and work with charts, which make data much easier to present and explain, thus adding to the impact of a presentation. We will also investigate the new drawing features and how to create and insert captions into a video, as well as exploring playback options for audio and video.

Chapter 7, Photo Albums, Sections, and Show Tools, teaches you how to create stunning photo albums with captions and define presentation sections and motion effects. We will also run through animations, transitions, and how to control slide timings and the playback of audio narration. You will learn about the new Record feature, work with Presenter View, Inking, and advanced morph, and cover a topic on the new feature to set the reading order and rehearse presentations using a body language and presenter coach.

Chapter 8, Mastering Best Practices with Presentations, discusses how the strength of a PowerPoint presentation not only relies on your ability to utilize powerful tools that are housed within the application when creating presentations but also depends on your ability to design and communicate well. This chapter of the book focuses on useful design and presentation principles to consider when creating professional presentations.

Chapter 9, New Features, Filters, and Cleaning Data, takes you on a journey through essential updates and new features of Excel 2021. You will learn all about Advanced Filter and the new **FILTER** function and explore conditional formatting rules further. We will focus on cleaning data and learning how to import, clean, join, and separate data, learning about some new features along the way, such as the **UNIQUE** function.

Chapter 10, Exploring New Functions and Useful Workflow Functions, concentrates on the latest functions, helping you to learn the syntax and construction of a formula, such as **XLOOKUP**, **LET**, and **XMATCH**, and focuses on **IFs**. We will learn how to combine formulas, such as **IFERROR** and **VLOOKUP**, explore the term **ARRAYS**, and look at the new dynamic array functions in Excel 2021. Also included is a topic on database functions and a final topic exploring **COUNTIFs**.

Chapter 11, Date-Time Functions and Enhancing PivotTable Dashboards, explores date functions and looks at how to work with time. We will explore **DATEDIF()**, **YEARFRAC()**, **EDATE()**, **WORKDAY()**, and many more functions to become more productive in the workplace. In addition, a large part of this chapter will explore a host of PivotTable customizations and a walk-through on creating dashboards. We will also learn how to construct the **GETPIVOTDATA** function to reference cells in a PivotTable report.

Chapter 12, Useful Statistical and Mathematical Functions, builds on prior skills to work with math, trig, and statistical functions using Excel 2021 and introduces some additional functions to the mix. We will explore how to generate random numbers using the **RANDBETWEEN** and **RAND** functions. In addition, we will work through examples of **PRODUCT** functions, including the **SUMPRODUCT**, **MROUND**, **FLOOR**, **TRUNC**, **AGGREGATE**, and **CONVERT** functions. We will also investigate the **MEDIAN**, **COUNTBLANK**, and **AVERAGEIFs** statistical functions.

Chapter 13, Creating and Attaching Item Content, takes you through Outlook 2021 enhancements, where we will explore and configure objects such as mail, contacts, tasks, notes, and journals. You will set some advanced options and language options in the interface and learn how to manipulate item tags and arrange the content pane. We will learn how to search and filter and attach content to an email and will cover email best practices.

Chapter 14, Managing Mail and Contacts, introduces you to best practices while working with message attachments, to keep your mailbox clean and streamlined. You will learn how to set up rules and manage junk mail options and how to create or modify signatures within the Outlook application. This chapter will also teach you how to be proficient at creating business cards for contacts, and you will learn how to set up and manage contacts and contact groups.

Chapter 15, Calendar Objects, Notes, Tasks, and Journal Entries, teaches you how to work with calendars, appointments, and events, as well as setting meeting response options and arranging calendars and calendar groups. You will also learn how to work with tasks and how to assign them to other Outlook users, as well as tracking them via the status report tool.

Chapter 16, Creating and Managing Online Meetings, introduces you to all the significant features to communicate and collaborate using online tools such as Microsoft Teams and Zoom. We will look at how to set up, join, and manage meetings within the Outlook 2021 environment, learning about the different methods to present content using the Share icon within Teams and Zoom. There is also a topic on meeting notes and we will discover many useful apps in the Teams space.

Chapter 17, Presenting and Collaborating Online, is where we will discover the Teams app's useful features and understand the different locations we save to in the online space. The best methods to share and present PowerPoint slides using PowerPoint Live will be explored, as well as the new Presenter modes. We will look at important features, such as spotlight, attendance reports, raising a hand, recording video, and meeting notes. The final topics will address collaborating and file sharing using Teams and you will learn about versions and sheet view.

To get the most out of this book

Software/hardware covered in the book	Operating system requirements
Microsoft Office 2021 (Word, Excel, PowerPoint, and Outlook)	Windows 10 or 11
Microsoft 365 and Office web apps SharePoint and OneDrive	
Teams app and meeting add-on	
Zoom meeting add-on	

The main focus of this second edition of the book is Microsoft Office 2021 desktop applications, but we do make reference to Microsoft 365 web apps for comparison when explaining certain features.

If you are using the digital version of this book, we advise you to access the files from the book's GitHub repository (a link is available in the next section).

Download the example code files

You can download the example files for this book from GitHub at `https://github.com/PacktPublishing/Learn-Microsoft-Office-2021-Second-Edition`. If there's an update to the code, it will be updated in the GitHub repository.

We also have other code bundles from our rich catalog of books and videos available at `https://github.com/PacktPublishing/`. Check them out!

Download the color images

We also provide a PDF file that has color images of the screenshots and diagrams used in this book. You can download it here: `https://packt.link/NjcRa`.

Conventions used

There are a number of text conventions used throughout this book.

`Code in text`: Indicates code words in text, database table names, folder names, filenames, file extensions, pathnames, dummy URLs, user input, and Twitter handles. Here is an example: "Open the workbook named `MattsWinery.xlsx`."

Bold: Indicates a new term, an important word, or words that you see onscreen. For instance, words in menus or dialog boxes appear in **bold**. Here is an example: "Make sure you are on the **General** category on the left of the **Settings** screen. Scroll down to select **Calls** on the left, then locate the **Voicemail** heading and select **Configure voicemail**."

> **Tips or Important Notes**
> Appear like this.

Get in touch

Feedback from our readers is always welcome.

General feedback: If you have questions about any aspect of this book, email us at `customercare@packtpub.com` and mention the book title in the subject of your message.

Errata: Although we have taken every care to ensure the accuracy of our content, mistakes do happen. If you have found a mistake in this book, we would be grateful if you would report this to us. Please visit `www.packtpub.com/support/errata` and fill in the form.

Piracy: If you come across any illegal copies of our works in any form on the internet, we would be grateful if you would provide us with the location address or website name. Please contact us at `copyright@packt.com` with a link to the material.

If you are interested in becoming an author: If there is a topic that you have expertise in and you are interested in either writing or contributing to a book, please visit `authors.packtpub.com`.

Share Your Thoughts

Once you've read *Learn Microsoft Office 2021*, we'd love to hear your thoughts! Scan the QR code below to go straight to the Amazon review page for this book and share your feedback.

`https://packt.link/r/1803239735`

Your review is important to us and the tech community and will help us make sure we're delivering excellent quality content.

Part 1: Learning Word 2021

Microsoft Word 2021 is included in Microsoft's latest Office desktop productivity suite, Microsoft Office 2021. This part of the book introduces you to Word 2021, identifying its new features and demonstrating how to use it to create, format, and work with documents. You will cover everything you need to know to start using Word 2021 productively, in the workplace, at home, or for certification purposes.

Beyond the basics, you will cover a range of tasks, from learning about the new features, understanding OneDrive, and getting to grips with adding references and multiple tables of contents to a single document to real-time collaboration and dictation techniques. Throughout, you will be introduced to new features of the application and learn how to work with long documents. Once you reach the end of this part, you will have gained advanced-level knowledge and skills to be a pro at creating professional Word 2021 documents.

This part contains the following chapters:

- *Chapter 1, Exploring New Features and Managing OneDrive*
- *Chapter 2, Dictation, Co-Authoring, and Embedding*
- *Chapter 3, Styles, Referencing, and Media*
- *Chapter 4, Managing Professional Documents*

1

Exploring the New Interface and Managing OneDrive

Welcome to the first chapter of *Learn Microsoft Office 2021*. This chapter will highlight the difference between the standalone and subscription versions of Office 2021. In our previous edition of this book, *Learn Microsoft Office 2019*, we provided an in-depth explanation of all the Office applications and covered the very basic to advanced skills. In this book, we will build on the skills that were presented in the first edition.

First, we will look at what Microsoft Office 2021 offers within the single-user license compared to that of the Microsoft 365 online version, then progress to upskill you on the new interface features. We will also become familiar with the importance of OneDrive when working with Office 2021, learn how to manage OneDrive, and learn how to save files in Office 365. Lastly, we'll point out any new formatting elements, as well as quick ways to control attributes and ways to speed up the document formatting process.

The following topics will be covered in this chapter:

- Exploring standalone versus online 365 apps

- Highlighting the new interface features

- Managing OneDrive
- Saving and renaming files in Office 365

The skills mentioned in this chapter will help build your confidence so that you can work on the later chapters in this book.

> **Note**
>
> Some of the interface features we will talk about span all the Microsoft Office suite applications and can be accessed and applied using the same method shown for Word 2021.

Technical requirements

To benefit from the contents of this book, you must be able to follow along with and work through the examples provided in each chapter. The examples for this chapter can be found at `https://github.com/PacktPublishing/Learn-Microsoft-Office-2021-Second-Edition`.

Exploring standalone versus online 365 apps

In this section, we will discuss the difference between the latest release of Office 2021 versions. Microsoft Office 2021 is offered as a one-time purchase, which grants you a lifetime license for the software.

The Microsoft 365 plans include online apps and can be purchased as subscription services (monthly or yearly) with regular updates to features. Apps that are included with Microsoft 365 can be shared to your devices, as well as within your family unit.

With the Office 2021 standalone desktop version, you are limited to one installation per user. You will need to purchase any further upgrades for the software when they're released. However, security updates will be pushed out to both platforms (standalone desktop and online apps).

> **Reference**
>
> More information regarding Microsoft 365 can be found here:
>
> `https://support.microsoft.com/en-us/office`.

There are various purchase options for the desktop version of Office 2021 and your requirements will determine the best option. The following applications are always included as a standard:

- Word 2021

- Excel 2021

- PowerPoint 2021

Other applications such as Access 2021, Outlook 2021, Publisher 2021, Teams, and OneNote 2019 form part of the offering, depending on the plan you choose:

Figure 1.1 – Microsoft Office 2021 plans

The Microsoft 365 contribution (2021 apps) is divided into **Home** and **Business** plans, with a range of different options under each. Visit the following website for details: `https://www.microsoft.com/en-gb/microsoft-365/buy/compare-all-microsoft-365-products-b?`. Regarding the operating systems that Office 2021 requires, it can run on Windows 10 and 11 (as well as macOS).

In this chapter, we will refer to **OneDrive** and **SharePoint**. It is important to note the difference between these two online storage apps. OneDrive is a personal online storage and sharing tool that is provided, along with other apps, when you sign up for a Microsoft account. As a personal user with OneDrive, you can grant others access to files, known as **file sharing**. Note that some plans are free, while some must be paid. SharePoint is used to collaborate on files via a team within an organization. SharePoint offers a higher level of security and access to files is managed by the Admin team.

Let's move on to the next section, where we will look at what changes have been made to the Microsoft Office 2021 interface.

Highlighting the new interface features

In this section, you will learn how to recognize some of the new features that have been incorporated into the latest update of the desktop versions of the 2021 applications. You will also learn whether they are available within the Microsoft 365 apps.

Although most interface features and explanations are identical in some classic applications, any features that can be applied solely to an application will be addressed in the relevant chapter going forward. Let's browse the environment and learn about the different elements that make up Office 2021 applications.

Overall look and feel

Office 2021 has a much clearer interface, with tabs and groups being so much cleaner and crisper. The icons (buttons) are much less complex, with icon graphics represented using single lines. The edges seem softer and easier on the eye – you can locate features much quicker at a glance.

The following screenshot shows the **Microsoft Word 2021** interface, as well as the **Microsoft 365 – Word 2021** app interface:

Figure 1.2 – Difference between the desktop and online app versions

Some features have been enhanced in the new version of Office 2021. Let's highlight a few of the cosmetic changes.

The title bar

As you may already know, the title bar is located at the very top of each program that's launched in the Windows app and macOS environment.

Microsoft Word 2021 includes an **AutoSave** button, which can be found on the left-hand side of the title bar, as well as an **Editor** button.

The area of the title bar that houses the **AutoSave** button is named the **Quick Access Toolbar** (**QAT**) and is where you can add any program manipulation icons. The **AutoSave** and **Editor** buttons have been added to the QAT by default:

Figure 1.3 – The title bar showing the QAT, which includes the AutoSave and Editor features

The title bar also includes the file's description (filename), along with a drop-down list where you can see the version history of your document, move it to another location, and rename the description of the file.

By default, the **AutoSave** button is set to **Off**, and the filename drop-down list is deactivated unless the document is saved to the cloud. Normally, the online cloud service of choice would be OneDrive (or SharePoint).

Customizing the QAT

There are two ways to customize the QAT, as follows:

1. Use the **Customize Quick Access Toolbar** drop-down menu located to the top left of the title bar:

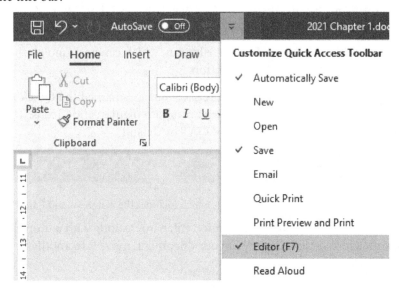

Figure 1.4 – The QAT drop-down list

> **Note**
> Icons that already display a checkmark to the left indicate that the icon is already an option on the QAT. You simply have to click on the name of the shortcut that you want to add to the QAT.

2. Click on the **File** tab, then select **Options**. From the **Word Options** dialog box, choose **Quick Access Toolbar**. From the right-hand side of the dialog box, you will notice the features that are currently visible on the QAT. To add additional features to the QAT, simply double-click on the relevant feature on the left-hand side to add it. Click on **OK** to confirm this:

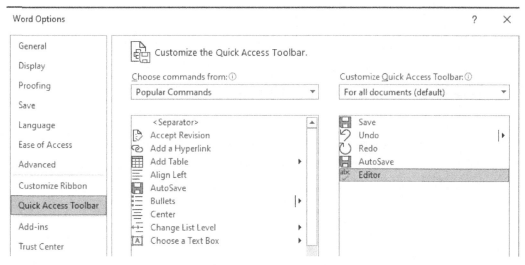

Figure 1.5 – The Word Options dialog box displaying the QAT customization options

In the next section, we will learn how to use the new **Search** facility in Office 2021.

Using Microsoft search

Toward the center of the title bar of your Office 365 apps or standalone Office 2021 applications, you will notice the **Search** facility. This facility is available when you're using Word, Excel, PowerPoint, Outlook, and OneNote:

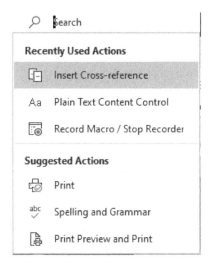

Figure 1.6 – New Search feature in Office 2021

This tool is extremely useful as it lets you do the following:

- Search for contacts (people) and locate text within the document
- Search for common features without going through all the tabs
- Locate documents you have used in the office environment
- Look up definitions
- Opens the task pane to the right-hand side of the application after entering search terms to locate information from the web, media, and help
- Find relevant features after typing in search criteria:

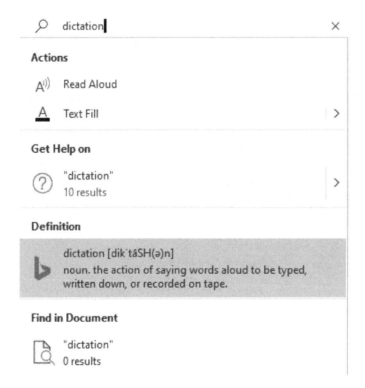

Figure 1.7 – Using the Search facility to locate a feature

The **Accessibility** feature lives on the status bar and watches you while you work on documents. We will discover this new feature in the next section.

Checking a document using the Accessibility feature

The **Accessibility** checker is included in Word, Excel, and PowerPoint 2021.

As we know, the status bar displays information about the current file we are working on and provides quick access to some tasks. The **Accessibility** checker is one of the default features along the status bar. The checker runs in the background while you work (by default) and offers you recommendations on various accessibility enhancements you can apply to a document:

Figure 1.8 – Status bar showing the new Accessibility feature

If we click on the **Accessibility: Investigate** feature on the status bar, the **Accessibility** pane will open to the right of the document. This pane contains the **Inspection Results** area:

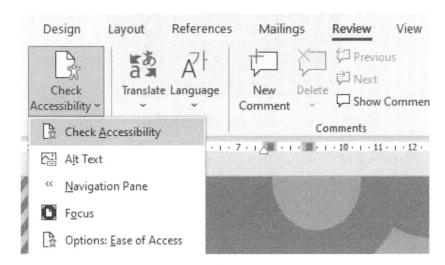

Figure 1.9 – The Accessibility checker in Word, PowerPoint, and Excel

Applying dark mode (enhanced)

Changing the visual display of the **Office Theme** was available in the previous versions of Office, but the document's background remained white. This feature has now been enhanced to display the document's background in dark mode too. Some enjoy this feature as it is easy on the eye and provides less strain and improved light sensitivity. To access this feature, go to **File | Options | General | Office Theme**:

Figure 1.10 – Change the Office Theme to Black (dark mode)

We can change the canvas's mode back to display the background of the Word document in white while the rest of the display is in dark mode:

1. Click on the **View** tab.

2. Select **Switch Modes** from the **Dark Mode** group. Note that the **Switch Modes** feature only appears as a button on the ribbon when the Office background is set to **Black**.

3. As you can see, the document's background appears white while the rest of the window remains in dark mode:

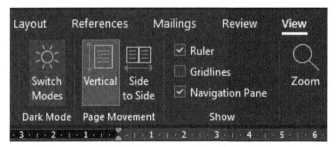

Figure 1.11 – Switching modes

While dark mode is activated, we can explore **Focus** mode.

Exploring Focus mode

Focus mode can be accessed through the **View** tab on the ribbon, or via the **Focus** button on the status bar. Focus mode hides all the unnecessary parts of the screen so that you concentrate on the document in question only.

While in **Focus** mode, move your cursor to the center top of the screen. Click on the three dots (**…**) to pull down the Word 2021 ribbon. Make sure you are on the **View** tab, then select a color from the **Background** button dropdown:

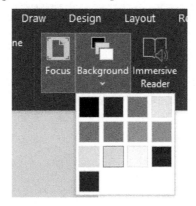

Figure 1.12 – Changing the background's color while in Focus mode

In the next section, we will look at the immersive reader. It is a brilliant tool with several benefits.

Using the immersive reader

The immersive reader is located under the **View** tab on the ribbon and contains several really useful tools, from reducing eye stress and removing distractions from a document, to reading the text out loud while you proofread your documents:

Figure 1.13 – Immersive reader contextual menu

Once you activate the immersive reader in Word 2021 on desktop or on the online app, your screen will open in much the same view as Focus mode to begin with (explained previously), showing a less complex view of the document.

Let's see what the immersive reader has to offer.

Column width

The width of the margin to the left and the right can be adjusted to suit you in terms of comprehension and concentration. This is especially beneficial when you're working on a smaller screen:

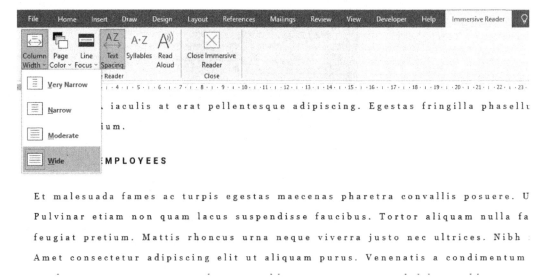

Figure 1.14 – Immersive reader column width options

As we mentioned previously, we can also set the page's color when using **Focus** mode. Let's learn how.

Page color

Selecting a page color here will create a softer reading experience for the reader and reduce strain on the eyes.

Line Focus

The third button on the immersive reader is the **Line Focus** dropdown. Dependent on the number of lines that are selected from the drop-down list, the reader will navigate through the document while reading only the number of lines that you've chosen to focus on:

Figure 1.15 – The Line Focus option showing three lines of the document at a time

Although **Line Focus** is a great tool to aid concentration, increasing the text's spacing (covered in the next section) can also make a big difference.

Text spacing

The fourth option on the **Immersive reader** contextual tab is the ability to set the text spacing. Using this option will expand the spacing between lines, characters, and words. Click the button once to expand, and then again to reduce the spacing.

Syllables

The syllables option allows you to focus more on pronouncing words as it adjusts words to include breaks, which helps you recognize words. This is a brilliant tool for children who wish to gain command of a language:

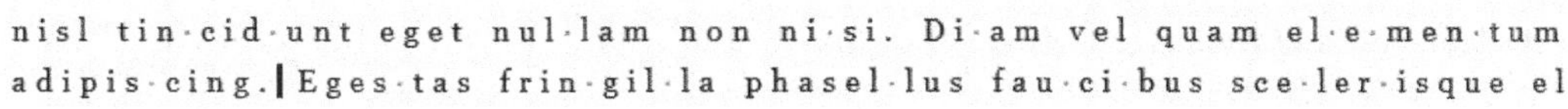

nisl tin·cid·unt eget nul·lam non ni·si. Di·am vel quam el·e·men·tum adipis·cing.|Eges·tas frin·gil·la phasel·lus fau·ci·bus sce·ler·isque el

Figure 1.16 – A paragraph showing syllable breaks when using the immersive reader

This tool can be used in conjunction with others in the immersive reader. Now, let's focus on the last option – the **Read Aloud** feature.

Read Aloud

This tool will highlight each word as it reads it back to you, one word at a time. Once you have activated the tool, use the buttons to the top-right-hand side of the window to rewind, play, forward, or set reading speed customizations. If you do not enjoy Microsoft David as the voice narrator, you can select Microsoft Zira or Microsoft Mark instead:

Figure 1.17 – The Read Aloud feature's playback buttons and settings

Once you get to grips with the **Read Aloud** feature, you may wish to experiment with the following shortcut keys:

Ctrl + Spacebar	To play or pause the Read Aloud feature
Alt + right arrow *Alt + left arrow*	To speed up or slow down the reading pace
Ctrl + right arrow *Ctrl + left arrow*	To read either the previous or next paragraph
Ctrl + Alt + Spacebar	To start or exit the Read Aloud feature

Table 1.1 – Read Aloud shortcuts

Now that we have explored some of the new features within the Word 2021 environment, let's learn about OneDrive features and understand what is meant by the term OneDrive.

Managing OneDrive

OneDrive is the online file storage area that you can access once you have signed up for a Microsoft account. It provides you with a means to access services and devices and was previously known as **Windows Live ID**. You can use OneDrive if you have a Microsoft account or Microsoft 365 Work/School account access. OneDrive is free to use if you are happy to only have 5 GB of storage space. If not, you can choose from a range of paid plans.

OneDrive is important as the service allows you to add (save) documents directly from within the Microsoft Office 2021 applications to the online storage facility.

Many features within the new version of Office will only be activated once you've done this. Previously, we could upload files to OneDrive and/or save them directly to OneDrive. This feature is now integrated so that we can move files and see version history directly within the Office applications, instead of having to open OneDrive to achieve this.

Like many other plans, OneDrive offers Home and Business plan options. The differences between them relate to the amount of storage quota, your monthly or annual subscription, whether you need the storage free for personal use or Microsoft 365 apps, or whether you want business use with access to Office apps.

In the next section, we will learn how OneDrive is integrated into Word 2021.

Saving documents to OneDrive

As we mentioned previously, for the **AutoSave** feature to be enabled within Office 2021 applications, you need to ensure that your file is saved to OneDrive. One of the pros of using OneDrive as the preferred storage location for documents is that you will not lose any work as the document is updated constantly in the background. Having files stored in the OneDrive app also means that you can access them at any time on any device that's logged into the Office 365 service.

Follow these steps to save documents to OneDrive:

1. Click the **File** tab.
2. Choose **Save As** from the list on the left.

3. If you are connected to OneDrive, you will see your accounts already listed here. We are already associated with **OneDrive – Personal**, as shown in the following screenshot:

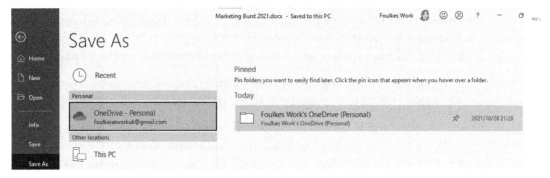

Figure 1.18 – The Save As options in Word 2021 showing the connection to OneDrive – Personal

4. If the OneDrive connection is not readily available, click the **Add a Place** option:

Figure 1.19 – Available locations when saving documents

5. Finally, choose from either the **OneDrive** or **OneDrive for Business** option:

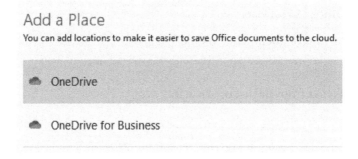

Figure 1.20 – Selecting OneDrive or OneDrive for Business as a document location

6. After selecting the location, you may be asked to sign in to your OneDrive account if you have not already done so:

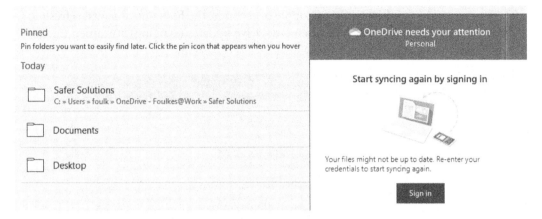

Figure 1.21 – Dialog box prompting you to sign in to OneDrive to sync files

7. Add or amend the **File name:** description, if necessary:

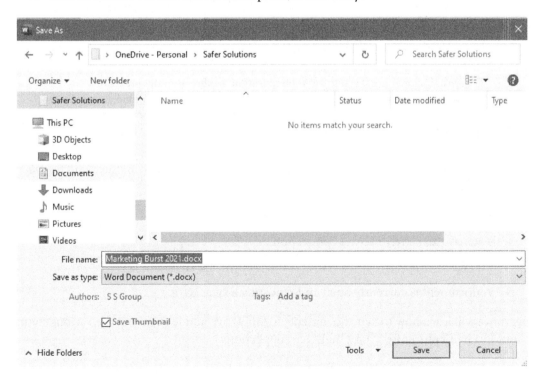

Figure 1.22 – Adding or amending the File name: description

8. Click the **Save** button to confirm your choice.

The document will now be saved to the cloud and the title bar will display **Saved...** just after the description of the file. Every couple of seconds, the filename area will refresh to display **Saving...**. This will happen when OneDrive updates (syncing) any amendments you've made to the cloud automatically:

Figure 1.23 – The title bar indicating when the document is updated and saved to the cloud

> **Note**
>
> When a document is saved to an online location, as shown in the preceding screenshot, the **Save** button to the left of the QAT will display a double arrow to the bottom right of the button. Click that button to refresh the document with amendments from other authors.

Note that documents will not sync automatically to the cloud, nor from the cloud to your devices, unless the following is true:

- Sync is activated on your device.
- You have an active internet connection.
- You have set up your OneDrive account and you are signed in.
- A document is currently open and reporting a sync error.

Next, we will learn how to sync documents to OneDrive and learn about the various status icons in **File Explorer** for your OneDrive connections.

Syncing a document to OneDrive

When we create documents in Office 365, they are stored in OneDrive's online storage area. These documents are only available online if you're not synced to other devices. The same would happen to documents that have been created locally within Microsoft Word 2021, for instance. Although documents exist in the OneDrive location on the local computer's **File Explorer** area, they may not be available online until certain sync conditions have been met.

To sync documents to the cloud or from the cloud to a OneDrive-connected folder location, you will need to set up OneDrive and have sync active. To understand this better, let's look at a scenario.

The following screenshot shows an example of the contents of the **Safer Solutions** folder on OneDrive online:

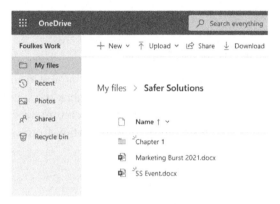

Figure 1.24 – The contents of the Safer Solutions folder on OneDrive

> **Tip**
> The three blue stripes at the top left of the filename (as shown in the preceding screenshot) indicate that the file has recently been updated.

Now, let's go to the same OneDrive folder that exists in **File Explorer** on our local computer. Notice the **Status** column in the following screenshot. Not all the status icons are the same. The **SS Event** document's status indicates that it only exists online, although we can see the file in the OneDrive-connected folder locally. This means that we can see the file in OneDrive and that on opening the file from this area, it will only open in the browser.

The **Marketing Burst 2021** document was saved locally and synced to OneDrive online (which means that the document can be accessed online and locally). We will discuss why the folder and document are pending sync here:

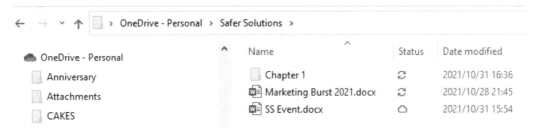

Figure 1.25 – OneDrive folder connection showing the status of documents

Next, we will discuss the different statuses so that you know how to manage your online and local environments better.

Understanding OneDrive icons

In the previous section, the OneDrive-connected folder on my local computer indicates that two of the folder items are pending sync. We can check the status of a document by placing our cursor over the status icon in the **Status** column (see the following screenshot). There are several status icons, so it is important to recognize the differences between them:

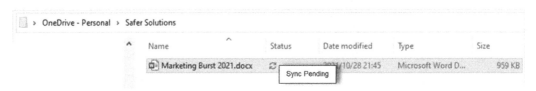

Figure 1.26 – Explorer showing the OneDrive sync pending status

The following table outlines the most common status icons:

Indicates the document is available online and shared with others.	○ ♁
Indicates the document is available online (you can only access the document when connected to the internet).	○
Indicated the document's sync is pending.	⟳
Indicates that the document/folder is only available on the local device – note that these status types take up hard drive space.	◉
Indicates the folder / file has been downloaded to your local device. Access to it is available, even if you're not connected to the internet.	◎

Figure 1.27 – OneDrive-connected folder status meanings

To ensure that a file/folder remains only on the local device, right-click on the file/folder in the OneDrive folder on the computer and select **Always keep on this device**. The status icon will display a green circle with a white checkmark:

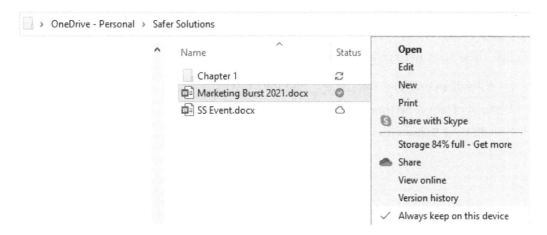

Figure 1.28 – The Always keep on this device option after right-clicking a document

There are several reasons why we may receive sync errors when working with the OneDrive folder locally. Let's learn how to troubleshoot such sync issues.

Troubleshooting sync errors

Once you have set up OneDrive on your computer, you can check its status by clicking the **OneDrive** icon to the right of the Windows taskbar. This icon will indicate whether you are online, offline, or if sync has been paused:

Figure 1.29 – The OneDrive taskbar's icons displaying paused, offline, and online

When you visit the OneDrive folder location within your **File Explorer** area, you will notice the sync status next to the document or folder. It is important to keep an eye on both these status areas so that you can ensure your documents are being synced, are accessible on all devices, and contain the latest amendments.

Depending on several factors, OneDrive could slow down your system considerably if you're syncing all the time. You can change this setting so that you only sync manually or pause syncing for a certain period.

To pause syncing

Follow these steps to learn how to pause syncing:

1. Click the **OneDrive** icon on the Windows taskbar.
2. Select **Help & Settings**.
3. Click the **Pause syncing** drop-down arrow:

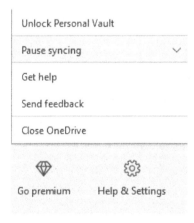

Figure 1.30 – OneDrive's Pause syncing option

4. Choose to pause for 2, 8, or 24 hours.

5. The **OneDrive** icon on the taskbar will indicate that OneDrive is paused.

Now, let's learn how to specify which online folders are available on your computer.

Choosing folders

Folders from OneDrive's online storage can be made available on your local computer. If we use OneDrive as our primary storage area, we may need to make a few of these folders accessible locally:

1. Click the **OneDrive** icon on the Windows taskbar.

2. Select **Help & Settings**.

3. Click **Settings**.

4. Be sure to select the **Account** tab at the top of the dialog box that populates.

5. Click the **Choose folders** button (sign in to OneDrive if required), then select the folders by clicking on them:

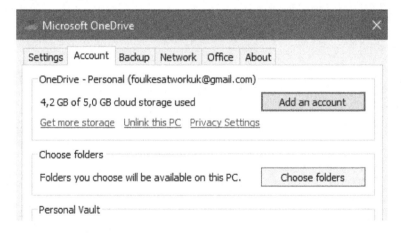

Figure 1.31 – The Account settings dialog box for OneDrive

6. Select **OK** to confirm this.

> **Note**
> OneDrive accounts can also be unlinked from your PC using the respective **Unlink this PC** option on the **Account** tab. Go to the **Settings** tab to choose options related to starting OneDrive and customizing notifications.

Saving and renaming files in Office 365

Files are automatically saved to the cloud when you're using Office 365 plans. The cloud platform that can be accessed through Office 365 is OneDrive, as we explained previously.

Saving documents in Office 2021

Saving a document when you're working in the Word 2021 online application is a simple process:

1. Locate the document's description on the title bar of the application.

2. Select the drop-down arrow to the right of the document's description.

3. The **File Name** area, as well as the **Location** areas, can be amended here.

4. After typing in the filename's description, click the OneDrive location to tell OneDrive to choose an online folder to save the document to.

5. Notice that **Save status** and **Version History** are also part of this drop-down list:

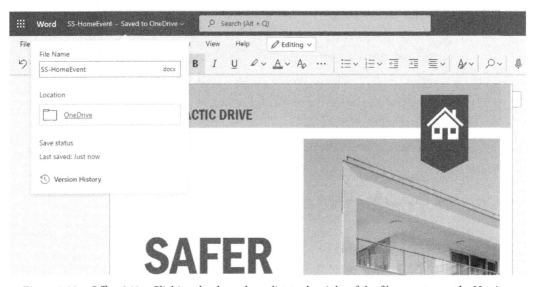

Figure 1.32 – Office 365 – Clicking the drop-down list to the right of the filename to see the Version History and save options

Renaming documents in Office 2021

In this section, we will learn how to rename documents without having to use the **Save As...** command or navigate back to **File Explorer** to rename the document. It is now possible to rename a document directly within the Office 2021 environment, without creating a copy.

If a document has been saved using the specified OneDrive location, you can edit the filename directly within the title bar area of the application, as follows:

1. Open a document that's been saved to your OneDrive location or create a new document and save it to OneDrive. We are using the `Invoice.docx` document for this demonstration.

2. Click into the document filename area, located on the title bar:

Figure 1.33 – Renaming a document that's been saved to OneDrive

3. Rename the document by editing the filename directly.

4. The document will be updated and renamed.

When we save documents to our local personal computer, we will not be able to rename the document directly within Word. Upon accessing the dropdown to the right of the filename on the title bar, we will see that the ability to edit the filename is grayed out. We would need to upload the document to OneDrive first.

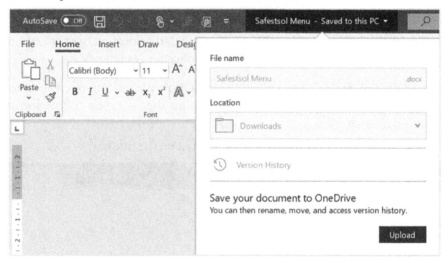

Figure 1.34 – When the File name field is grayed out, we will need to use the Upload button to save our document to OneDrive first

With that, we hope you are confident in managing OneDrive and saving files using the desktop app of OneDrive, as well as using the various online plans for Office 365.

Summary

In this chapter, we learned about the new interface features of Office 2021 and discussed the differences between the online and desktop plans. We explored the immersive reader tools such as **Read Aloud** and looked at ways to enhance the users' experience when proofreading documents on-screen and renaming documents. The final section concentrated on managing the OneDrive experience in the cloud and on the desktop. We also learned how to troubleshoot sync errors.

The next chapter will focus on more of the new features that Office 2021 offers, as well as the latest revisions that have been made to the Office 365 offering. We will concentrate on dictation, co-authoring, and embedding.

We will also focus on a few more features that are new to Office standalone and web applications. You will learn how to access the new Transform feature so that you can integrate amazing presentations with Microsoft Sway. Then, you will learn how to dictate directly within Word 2021, where we will discuss all the options around the new Dictate feature.

Commenting and working in real time with others is also discussed here. There, we will look at co-authoring and investigate modern commenting, embedding, and converting.

2
Dictation, Co-authoring, and Embedding

In this chapter, we will focus on a few more features that are new to Office 2021 and the latest versions (and revisions) of the Office 365 offering. You will learn how to access the new Transform feature to integrate amazing presentations with Microsoft Sway. You will also learn how to dictate directly within Word 2021, where we will discuss all the options around the new Dictate feature. Although the first two chapters of this book focus on skills that have been separated for ease of reading, we often use more than a couple together in applications when working on a document.

Commenting and working in real time with others is greatly enhanced in the new version. We will also be investigating co-authoring requirements and learning about modern commenting. Finally, we will introduce several new embedding features.

The following topics will be covered in this chapter:

- Investigating the new transform feature
- Dictating enhancements in Word for the web
- Commenting and co-authoring
- Embedding and converting using Word

Technical requirements

Before you complete this chapter, you should be able to navigate the Word 2021 interface and have knowledge of different parts of the screen, such as the ribbon, groups, tabs, and icons. Being able to select the relevant ribbon icons and being familiar with using the right-click shortcut menu to access formatting options is also a prerequisite.

The examples in this chapter can be found at the following GitHub URL: `https://github.com/PacktPublishing/Learn-Microsoft-Office-2021-Second-Edition`.

Investigating the new transform feature

Microsoft Sway is located at `https://sway.office.com` and has been available since August 2015 within Office 365 plans. Before 2015, it was released as a preview on iOS apps. It allows users to create exciting and engaging presentations in a couple of seconds from new or existing documents (reports, books, writing, CVs, stories, and so on) using a specific design and layout. You can edit, share, and check analytics on your sways. Animations are automatically applied alongside design elements. Three options are available for creating sways:

- Creating a sway from scratch
- Basing the new sway on an existing topic
- Creating a sway from an existing document that you must upload via the website

In the latest Word version of Office 365, we can send a document from within the application using the **Transform** feature. Follow these steps to transform your Word document into a Sway presentation:

1. Open the document you wish to create the Sway presentation from. For this example, we will be using the `Safest Solutions.docx` file. You can find this document by going to the GitHub repository link mentioned in the *Technical requirements* section.

2. Click on the **File** tab.

3. Choose **Transform** from the list provided.

4. The **Transform to Web Page** pane will open to the right of the Word document:

Figure 2.1 – The Transform to Web Page pane to the right of the Word document

> **Note**
>
> If you haven't signed in to your Microsoft account, you will need to sign in.
> Details of you signing in will be evident at the bottom of the **Transform to a
> Web Page** pane.

5. Notice the **Style** area at the bottom of the pane. Click through the style types
   using the scroll bar to the right of the style's area to navigate through the list of
   styles. Click each style type to see a snapshot of how the design will modify your
   document's design once applied.

6. Click the **Transform** button to continue.

7. The web browser will open and the sway will be presented:

Figure 2.2 – Browser displaying the Word document transformed into a Sway

8. Click the **Edit** button to make changes to the sway. Alternatively, click the **Share** button to allow others to view the sway via a link or send the sway to your social media channels directly.

9. Once you click the **Edit** button, several cards will appear in the **Storyline** window, all of which you can customize. At the top of the screen, you will see two buttons, namely **Storyline** and **Design**.

10. Click the insert content button (the green circle with a white cross inside it) to add another card.

11. Once it's created, click on the card's background to select it. Then, use the buttons along the top of the card to apply and format accents, elements, links, and many more features:

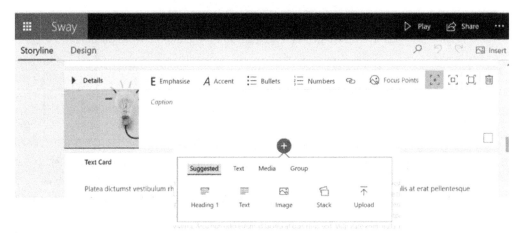

Figure 2.3 – Sway storyline view displaying new content and card buttons to format elements

12. Click on **Design**, then the **Styles** button to open the **Styles** pane to apply a different style set and customize colors, typography, and texture:

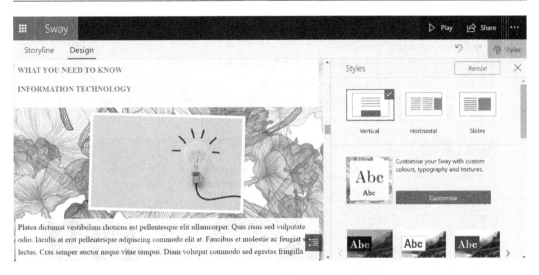

Figure 2.4 – The Sway Design screen displaying the Styles pane

Using the **Transform** to **Sway** feature is a great way to visually display documents creatively instead of using the normal "go-to" PowerPoint presentation. The best way to get to grips with Sway is to create a new sway from scratch and build your content using the card elements.

Access to the transform feature will differ, depending on the Office version you have installed or released through the Office 365 environment. If you cannot locate the **Transform** option on the **File** tab, then visit the **Export** option to locate the **Transform to Web Page** option:

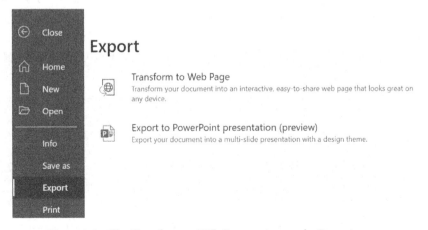

Figure 2.5 – The Transform to Web Page option on the Export menu

The following screen will appear, where you can select a **Style** to base the sway on. Select the **Transform** button to continue:

Figure 2.6 – Accessing Transform to Web Page from the Export option using Word online

The sway is then displayed in the browser, where you can edit it. We explained this previously.

Remember that there are other options for transforming a Word document into a web page. If you do not have access to the features described previously, go to the `https://sway.office.com` web page directly and click on **Start from a document**:

Figure 2.7 – Clicking the Start from a document button on sway.com to upload a document to transform into a web page

In the next section, we will learn how to use the Dictate feature.

Dictation enhancements within Word

Dictation has been deployed on the desktop, iPad, and web versions of Office 2021. One thing you need to ensure is that you are signed into either your Microsoft account or Office 365 account. The icon (button) is located on the **Home** tab of the Word ribbon:

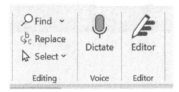

Figure 2.8 – The Dictate feature on the Home tab of the Word ribbon

Now that you know where to locate the **Dictate** feature, let's learn how to record our voice. We will look at various commands you can use when dictating and then explore the **Transcribe** feature.

Activating Dictate

Before you record within Word, make sure that you have a new blank document open or have positioned your cursor over the existing document. The dictation will start at the cursor's position in the document:

1. Click the **Dictate** icon that's located in the **Voice** group of the **Home** tab.

2. A dialog box will appear on the document's window (as shown in the following screenshot). Move the dialog box by dragging it with your cursor to relocate it to the Word environment:

> **Note**
> If you have not used a microphone before with Word, the system will prompt you to select or confirm your microphone's type.

Figure 2.9 – The Dictate dialog box shows the Settings, Start Recording, and Help buttons

3. Click the **Dictate** button to start recording your voice.

4. To stop recording, click the **Dictate** button once more.

When dictation is active, the recording button will be shown on the Microsoft Word browser tab. In the following screenshot, you can see Microsoft Edge on a Windows 11 operating system. While recording is active, a *red dot* (with a red circle line) appears on the tab:

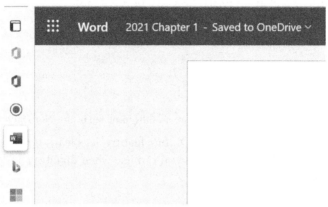

Figure 2.10 – Dictation showing as active in the Windows 11 Microsoft Edge browser

Now that we know how to start and stop our recording, let's look at the settings and commands we can use when dictating within Word.

Setting options when recording

Before recording, we may need to check that everything is working correctly in terms of the microphone settings and set any language options we may need to customize. Let's get started:

1. Click the **Dictation Settings** button on the dictation dialog box.

2. Use the **Spoken language** drop-down list to choose the language for speech-to-text. Language types are added often in this area:

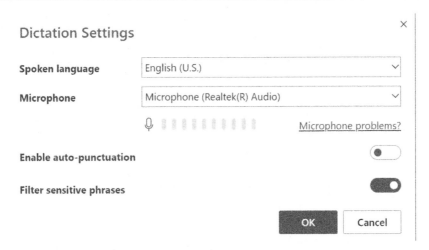

Figure 2.11 – The Dictation Settings dialog box displaying Microphone and other language settings

3. In this dialog box, we can also alter the **Microphone** settings and **Enable auto-punctuation**. This feature is great as it will automatically work out where it should punctuate by adding full stops, commas, and question marks (for example).

When we dictate, we must be able to control and speed up the recording process. There are various built-in voice actions that we can use to command the dictation process. Let's look at some of these commands.

Using dictation commands

Just like most popular dictation services on the market today (Dragon Dictate and BigHand are two that come to mind here), we can use voice commands instead of having to interact using the keyboard. For a comprehensive list of commands, click on the **Help** button on the dictation dialog box to visit the **Help** task pane, which will appear to the right of the document's window:

Figure 2.12 – The Help button located on the dictation dialog box

The commands shown in the following table are just a few voice actions you can perform while recording. Remember to visit the **Help** task pane to try these out. You will soon get to grips with how you and the **Dictate** feature can work together efficiently:

Command	Action
What can I say?	Saying this command while dictating will open the **Help** task panel to the right of the document window, where you can visit all the available command types.
New line	This is the same as pressing *Enter* on your keyboard to move down a line. If you would like to enter two lines while dictating, you should say "new line new line."
Full stop	Here, you can dictate "full stop" or "period."
Comma	Punctuation dictation work as if we were to normally describe the item; for example, "question mark," "exclamation point," and so on.
Delete or delete that	Voicing "delete" will remove the previous word that was spoken, while "delete that" will remove the previously spoken words.
Open quotes/close quotes	Use these commands to start and end quotation marks (speech marks), respectively.
Bold, italics, underline	The formatting commands are exactly as they are shown on the menu in Word. To apply bold formatting to a word, say "select," then say the word you wish to select "dictate," and then say "bold that." The word "dictate" in this example would then appear as dictate.
Go to previous paragraph or Go to previous page	Moving around in the document is easy. Simply use the "go to previous paragraph" or "go to next paragraph" commands when working with paragraphs. To move to the previous or next page, substitute "paragraph" with "page."

Table 2.1 – Dictation commands

Transcribing meetings

In this section, we will take a brief look at the **Transcribe** feature as it is an important tool when you need to produce a transcript from an existing meeting recording or to create a new meeting recording between individuals. Once you are done with the meeting, the recording will be transcribed in OneNote and produce an editable recording of the meeting's dialog. The editable recording will be readily available so that you can import it back into Microsoft Word.

> **Note**
> The **Transcribe** tool is only available through the Microsoft 365 platform.

1. Locate **Transcribe** by clicking on the drop-down arrow next to the **Dictation** button once you've signed into Microsoft 365:

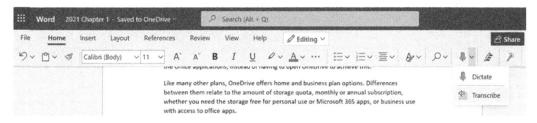

Table 2.13 – The Transcribe tool in Word 365

2. Start a new meeting recording between meeting participants by clicking on the **Start Recording** button from the **Transcribe** task pane to the right of the window. Alternatively, use the **Upload audio** feature to locate a previous meeting recording (either in .mp4, .m4a, .mp3, or .wav format).

3. Once you start a recording, you can pause and resume it whenever you want. If you have finished recording the meeting, click the **Save and transcribe now** button to save the recording to OneDrive, after which the recording will appear at the top of the **Transcribe** task pane alongside the transcription. You can make amendments to the transcription as well as add the individual speaker transcriptions using the + button to the right of each speaker transcription. Alternatively, click the **Add to document** button for more options to insert the transcription directly into the current Word document:

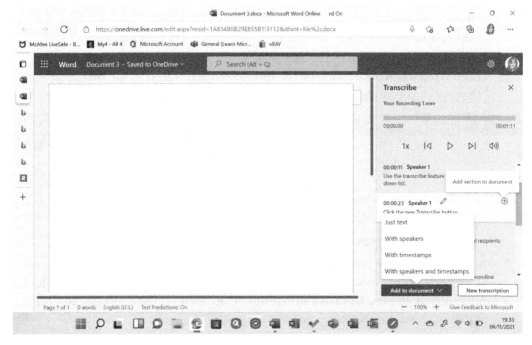

Figure 2.14 – The Transcribe panel detailing the transcription, individual speaker scripts, and the Add section to document and Add to document options.

> **Note**
>
> When you create a new transcription in the same document, the current transcription will be overwritten in OneDrive. If you wish to keep the transcription in the current document, you will need to open another document to start a new transcription.

Now that you know how to create and upload using the **Transcribe** tool, let's have a look at the **Editor** tool in Word. Note that the **Editor** tool sometimes takes a while to appear in your Office accounts, so you may not see it straight away in your Outlook or Word environments, especially if you signed up for a new account when purchasing the plan.

Refining writing using the Editor tool

The **Editor** tool is available when you're using the Word app, but it is also available when you're signed into Microsoft 365 apps. While you work, the editor checks the following aspects of your document:

- Extension accessibility to gain assistance when writing content
- Access to document statistics such as word count (words, paragraphs, characters, and so on) and the time it takes to speak/read the document
- Overall document score, corrections, refinements, and enhancements
- Plagiarism instant check against online sources with feedback on likenesses
- Ability to add text prediction

These tools, in combination with the **Accessibility** tool (discussed in *Chapter 1, Exploring the New Interface and Managing OneDrive*), are a huge benefit to authors. The following screenshot shows the placement of both the **Editor** drop-down options (the **Review** tab) and the **Editor** button (located on the **Home** tab, which opens the **Editor** task pane to the right of the document window).

We can use the **Editor** drop-down list to access options relating to **AutoCorrect** and **Proofing Language** and to change the default options for the editor:

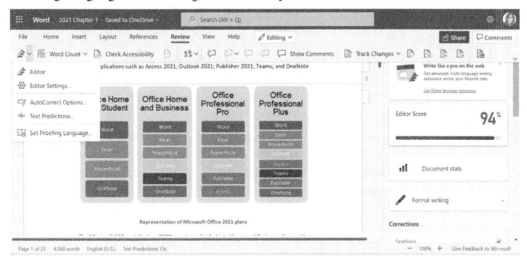

Figure 2.15 – The Word app displaying the Editor tab from the Review tab, as well as the Editor pane, which can be accessed from the Home tab

These tools are worth a second glance as they let you inspect the document and offer suggestions on how to improve your writing. They also prompt you to give your document a final once-over.

Editor Score, which is located on the **Editor** task pane, indicates the document's overall score. In the following screenshot, we can see that we can achieve an outstanding 6% improvement by scrolling through the suggested refinements and accepting or ignoring the issues that have been found:

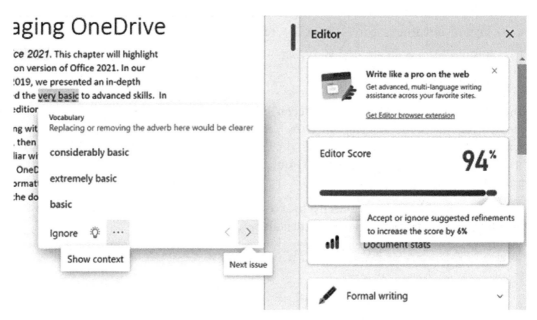

Figure 2.16 – The Editor pane highlighting the overall score and the ability to move through suggested changes in the document

We can also use the **Editor** task pane to look at suggested changes by using its built-in grammar checker. Simply click on the underlined word in the document, after which the drop-down suggestions will populate. The **Editor** button is located in the bottom right-hand corner of the suggestion area:

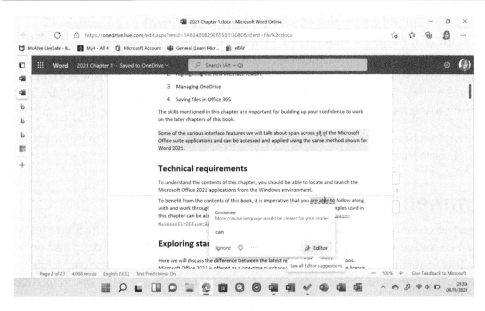

Figure 2.17 – The Editor button can be accessed from the grammar suggestion drop-down list

Text prediction has become a popular feature for text services on our mobile phones and, as such, this feature has been added to the newest version of Word. Let's take a look.

Using the Text Predictions feature

The **Text Predictions** feature can be accessed via the **Editor** drop-down list on the **Review** tab, or via Word's status bar:

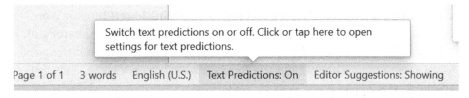

Figure 2.18 – Switching the Text Predictions feature on and off via the status bar

When active and you start typing in a document, the **Text Predictions** feature will assume the next words you may type, depending on the user interaction. It will highlight any assumed text in light gray. To ignore any suggestions, just keep typing as you would normally do on your mobile device, or press the *Tab* key (or the right arrow key) on your keyboard to grab the suggested words. This feature aids those who may have dyslexia or find it difficult to express themselves and need a little help using accessibility features in Word.

In the next section, we will learn how to collaborate within the Word environment as many of these features have been improved upon.

Commenting and co-authoring

It is easy to collaborate within Word desktop and the Word app using the **Share** feature. We can co-author with over 30 individuals in real time on both the desktop and online apps. This feature is also available when you need to collaborate on files in a Teams channel. This feature has been updated so that you can comment using the contextual view or the **@mention** tool, and then resolve any comments.

> **Note**
> These updates are also available in PowerPoint and Excel.

Let's look at each of these updates.

Commenting using the new contextual view

The main requirement that needs to be met for co-authoring in real time in Word, PowerPoint, or Excel 2021 is that files need to be saved to OneDrive or SharePoint. It is possible to share files from your desktop and online applications.

Sharing a document with others

1. Open the document you wish to share or create a new document. For this example, we will open `Safest Solutions.docx`.

2. Save the document either to **OneDrive** or **SharePoint** so that you can collaborate with others in real time.

3. Click the **Share** button at the top right-hand side of the window. When you click on the **Share** button, the options will differ, depending on the application you are working in and where the document is saved. The **Share** pane may populate or the **Share Link** dialog box may appear. As we are sharing a document that's been saved to OneDrive from the Word 2021 desktop app, we will see the **Share** task pane:

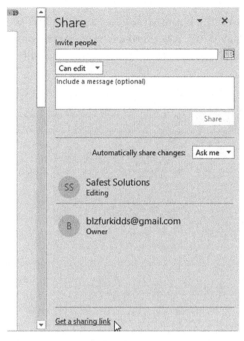

Figure 2.19 – Clicking on Share, after which the Share task pane will open to the right-hand side of the document

4. Add the recipients into the **Invite people** area. For this example, we have added one recipient.

5. Make sure that the permission is set to **Can edit** if you wish the author to make amends to the document. Alternatively, select the drop-down list to set the permission to **Can view** only.

6. Add a message or instructions for the author in the white space provided below the edit options.

7. Click the **Automatically share changes:** option (next to the heading) to share changes with co-authors. Here, you have the options of **Always**, **Never**, and **Ask me**.

8. Finally, click the **Share** button to share the document.

Note

There is also a **Get a sharing link** icon at the bottom of the task pane to help you obtain an edit or view shareable link.

---

9. Once you have shared the document, you will see a link to the co-authors that have been listed in the task pane. If you are working on the online app, you can identify whether a document has any collaborators next to the filename in the title bar:

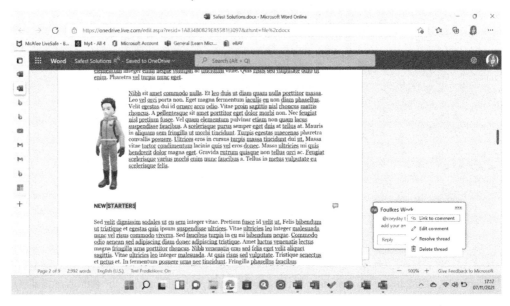

Figure 2.20 – The Safest Solutions filename showing that the document has collaborators (it's been shared with others)

Now that you know how to share a document, let's learn how to work with comments.

Adding comments to a shared document

In addition to editing a document with others in real time, we can add and delete comments, and then resolve them when necessary. Comments and collaboration amendments are automatically saved, so you don't have to continuously worry that you have not updated the changes. Follow these steps:

1. Place your cursor over the paragraph, line, or text you wish to comment on.

2. Click the **Review** tab and select the **New Comment** button from the **Comments** group. You can also right-click inside the document and select **New Comment** from the drop-down list.

3. Add a comment inside the comment area that's provided in the commenting pane to the right of the document window. If you have shared the document with collaborators, the authors will see the comments too:

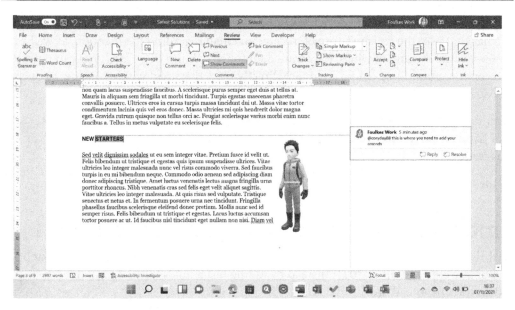

Figure 2.21 – Word showing the Review tab and the New Comment and Comment panes

4. If you are working in the Office apps online, click the three dots (…) to the right of a comment to view the available options. Here, you can create a link to a comment, edit a comment, delete the comment's thread, or resolve the thread by agreeing to the suggested changes:

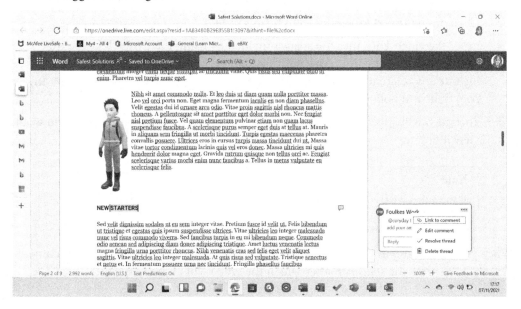

Figure 2.22 – Commenting options in Word 2021

We can use the **@mention** feature to tag someone in a comment, just like we can on social media. That way, the collaborator will receive an email regarding the mention, as well as a snippet of the document where they were mentioned. Within this email, you can reply to the comment by adding a new comment directly from the email without having to open the document in OneDrive.

Now that you know how commenting and sharing works within Word, PowerPoint, and Excel for Microsoft 365, have some fun collaborating with others to get the gist of this feature.

In the next section, we will look at ways to embed content within Word.

Embedding and converting using Word 2021

In this section, we will learn how to embed and convert documents within the desktop and online apps for Office 2021. Instead of adding just a link's URL, we can now embed videos directly into Word.

Embedding videos into Word

1. Open a Word document either from the desktop or online app.

2. Copy the video link you wish to use into your Word document by selecting the link in the browser. Then, press *Ctrl + C* to copy the link into memory.

3. Click on the **Insert** tab and select **Online Videos**.

4. Enter the video URL into the space provided by using the *Ctrl + V* keyboard shortcut to paste the link. Alternatively, right-click and select **Paste**. Be sure to include any reference credits to the video once inserted so that you abide by any copyright and policy requirements.

5. The video will appear in the document with the relevant controls, just as you would view it online.

> **Note**
> If the video URL you have provided is set to private, you won't be able to embed the video.

When you're working in the Word app, you can simply paste the link into the document directly, then press the *spacebar*, after which the video will embed directly.

In the next section, we will learn how to embed forms into Word. However, these are not the only links we can embed. Microsoft continues to add more and more sources to the list of embed links.

Embedding forms into Word

Instead of sending customers outside of the Word environment to fill out a feedback form, for instance, we can now have this happen directly in the Word document by embedding interactive forms. Follow these steps:

1. Open the document that you need to add a form to. The best way to insert the form is to make sure you have the document open in Word for the web.

2. Open **Microsoft Forms** by visiting `https://forms.microsoft.com/`. Log in, if required, then locate the form you have designed or use one of the existing form templates.

3. Copy the link to the form you wish to embed into the Word document using the **Copy** button to the right of the form:

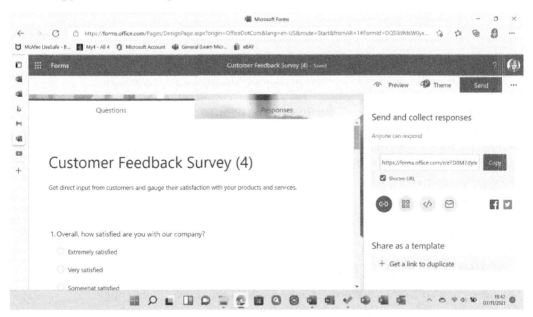

Figure 2.23 – Microsoft Forms showing the Send and collect responses pane so that you can copy the form link

4. Position your cursor where you would like the form to reside in the document.

5. Press the *Ctrl + V* shortcut on your keyboard to paste the form's link into the document.

6. Press the *spacebar* to unfold the form into the document, creating an interactive, accessible form directly in Word:

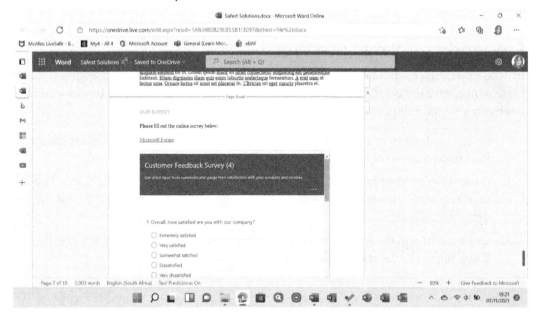

Figure 2.24 – Microsoft Forms embedded into a Word document

7. The user can answer the survey directly within the Word environment.

We can also embed **Sways** into a document directly. This procedure is the same as what we covered previously – that is, by copying the link of the Sway from the `https://sway.office.com/` website, then pasting the link into the Word app directly. Pressing the *spacebar* will ensure that the Sway behaves in the document exactly as it would in the browser. Interactivity at your fingertips!

Now, let's learn how to convert a Word document into PowerPoint slides. Although this isn't an entirely new feature, it has been enhanced in Word's online interface.

Converting Word documents into PowerPoint slides

Let's learn how to convert a Word online document into PowerPoint slides:

1. Open a Word document that you would like to convert. Make sure you open it in Word for the web.
2. Click the **File** tab, then select **Export**.
3. Choose the **Export to PowerPoint presentation (preview)** option from the list provided:

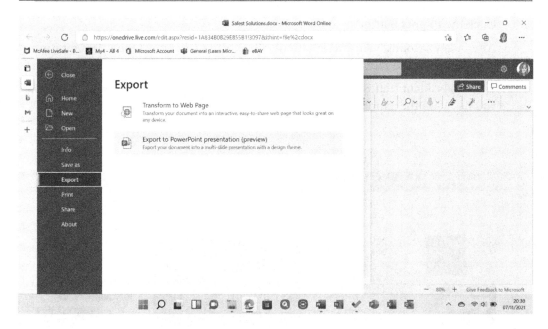

Figure 2.25 – The Export option on the File tab in Word for the web

4. Choose a design theme to apply to the presentation:

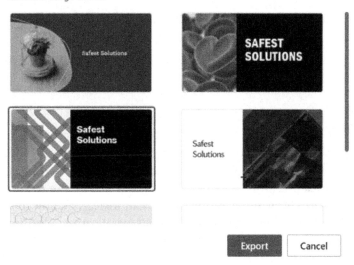

Figure 2.26 – The Export to presentation design theme options

5. Click the **Export** button.

6. After a few seconds, your presentation will be ready. Click the **Open Presentation** button to view the slides in PowerPoint for the web.

7. This is a brilliant feature! All the formatting, text, and elements will be inserted for you based on the template you chose:

Figure 2.27 – Exported document turned from a Word document into a presentation in PowerPoint for the web

8. The presentation is automatically named the same as the Word document and saved to OneDrive.

Summary

In this chapter, we focused on a couple of new features, in addition to those discussed in *Chapter 1*, *Exploring the New Interface and Managing OneDrive*. We learned how to use the **Transform** feature, as well as Microsoft Sway, which we can use to send Word documents directly to a Sway presentation. After that, we learned how to activate dictation and set options when recording. We learned about several common commands in dictation "speak" and how to transcribe meetings.

The **Editor** pane was discussed in detail and we mentioned the **Text Predictions** tool. While learning about real-time document co-authoring, we learned how to embed content such as videos, forms, and sways into Word documents directly.

In the next chapter, we will touch on making enhancements to existing features and learn how to become more comfortable when working with styles by refining the layout. Building on your existing knowledge is key to this chapter, where we will troubleshoot more than one table of contents within a document, generate cross-references, work with media content, and draw elements.

3

Styles, Referencing, and Media

In this chapter, we will touch on making enhancements to existing features and learn how to become more comfortable when working with styles by refining the layout. After that, we will cover some tips and tricks. Building on your existing knowledge from the previous chapters is key to this chapter, where we will troubleshoot more than one table of contents within a document and look at cross-referencing. A section on working with media content and drawing elements will also be provided.

The following topics will be covered in this chapter:

- Managing the styles environment
- Word referencing features
- Creating media and drawing elements

Technical requirements

To complete this chapter, you should be able to work with and create styles. Knowledge of the basics related to inserting and generating a table of contents, as well as working with graphical elements, is encouraged – these features were dealt with in detail in the first edition of this book.

The examples for this chapter can be found at the following GitHub URL: `https://github.com/PacktPublishing/Learn-Microsoft-Office-2021-Second-Edition`.

Managing the styles environment

In the previous edition of this book, *Learn Microsoft Office 2019*, we learned how to create and edit styles. In this section, we will build on our skillset by looking at ways to manage the Word environment so that we can work with styles more efficiently.

To set the **Style** pane, we need to be in the **Draft** or **Outline** view. Let's do this so that we can see the **Style** pane.

Viewing a document in the Draft view

By default, a document will open in the **Print Layout** view. We can change the view to the **Draft** view when we need to see any additional marks in the document and when we would like to view document styles (marks such as paragraph markers, spaces, and tabs). When working in the **Draft** view, we won't able to see any images, only text.

If you would like to follow the steps provided in the next section to view a document in the **Draft** view and add the **Style** pane, open the `Butterfly Agreement.docx` file. Click the **View** tab, then select **Draft** from the **Views** group.

Once the document is in **Draft** view, we can add the **Style** pane.

Adding the Style pane

When we work with long documents that contain several built-in or custom styles, it is sometimes necessary to see the style names that already exist in lines or paragraphs in the document. This is especially relevant when you're receiving documents from outside your organization as you may need to make amends, but then continue using the same style set throughout the document to maintain uniformity. Adding the **Style** pane to the left-hand side of the document window allows you to see all the styles that have been applied to a document:

1. Click the **File** tab.
2. Select **Options**.
3. Click the **Advanced** category from the left-hand side of the dialog box.
4. Scroll down until you locate the **Display** heading.

5. Locate the **Style area pane width in Draft and Outline views:** option.

6. Enter 2 cm into the space provided:\

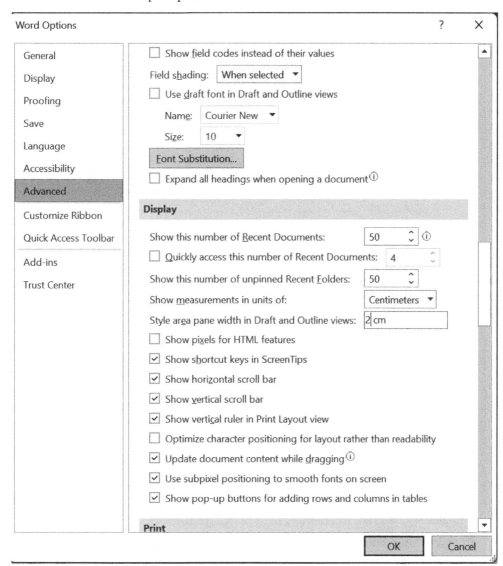

Figure 3.1 – The Word Options dialog box displaying the Style pane's width in the Draft and Outline views

7. Click **OK** at the bottom of the dialog box to confirm your selection.

8. To the left-hand side of the document window (in the margin area to the left-hand side of the document), you will now see the **Styles** pane. This pane contains all of the styles that have been applied throughout the document:

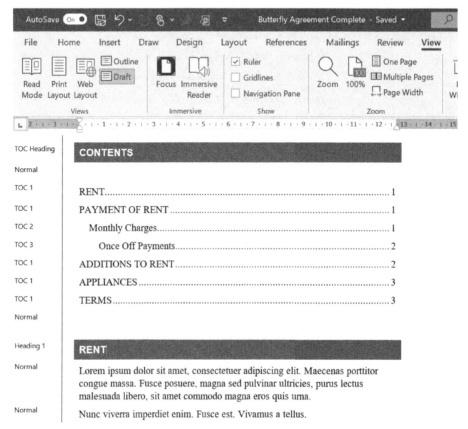

Figure 3.2 – The Styles pane's width of 2 cm to the left-hand side of the document window

9. Now that we have the **Styles** pane on the left, we can add it to the right of the document window. This way, you can see all the existing styles on the left and all the available style sets to the right.

10. Click the **More** button to the right of the **Styles** group on the **Home** tab:

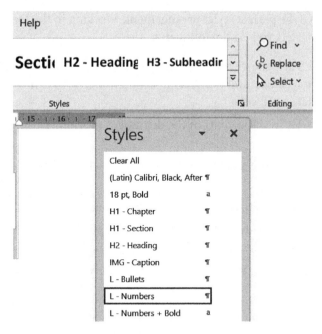

Figure 3.3 – Using the More button to launch the Styles pane

11. Double-click the **Styles** pane's header area to dock the **Styles** pane to the right-hand side of the Word document:

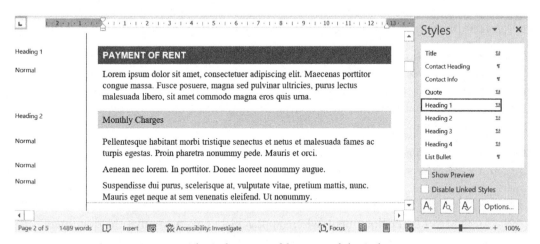

Figure 3.4 – The Styles area width pane and the Styles pane

12. Now, you have the perfect styles arrangement. Working in the **Draft** view with both panes available lets you do the following:

   A.   See styles at a glance that have already been applied to different headings, paragraphs, lines, and numbering throughout the document. This can be seen on the left-hand side.

   B.   Copy styles from one part of the document to another using the Format Painter button.

   C.   Select parts of the document and visually see the style that's been applied in the right pane.

   D.   Apply new styles to selected paragraphs using the right pane.

   E.   Add the **Show/Hide** button (via the **Paragraph** group on the **Home** tab) to display spaces, tabs, indents, and paragraph markers throughout the document.

   F.   Have quick access to create new styles, modify existing styles, or update existing styles.

Now that you can arrange your environment more efficiently when working with styles, let's learn how to keep styles intact when sharing outside our organization, for instance.

Making sure styles are not updated

When we have a set of styles that have been customized for a company brand, we may need to "protect" those styles from being updated if the document is shared with other parties.

In the previous edition of this book, we learned how to create, modify, and update styles. When we create a set of styles that can be applied to our organization, we want these styles to remain intact, even if we send the document for review to others outside of our organization. This could be a lengthy contract or agreement that has been formatted using our specific company style set.

Once you have applied styles to a document, you need to ensure the document template does not allow your styles to be automatically updated. Let's learn how to do this:

1.   To follow these steps, make sure the `Butterfly Agreement.docx` file is open.

2.   Apply styles to the document, where applicable, then ensure that the document has been saved. Once you are ready to share the document with others, click the **Developer** tab of the ribbon.

> **Note**
>
> If the **Developer** tab is not visible, click the drop-down list at the end of the **Quick Access Toolbar (QAT)**, then select **More Commands…**. Navigate to the **Customize Ribbon** category on the left. On the right-hand side of the window, make sure that the **Developer** option is selected. Click **OK** to confirm this. The **Developer** tab should now be visible on the ribbon.

3. Remove the tick from the default **Automatically update document styles** option that's located on the **Templates** tab:

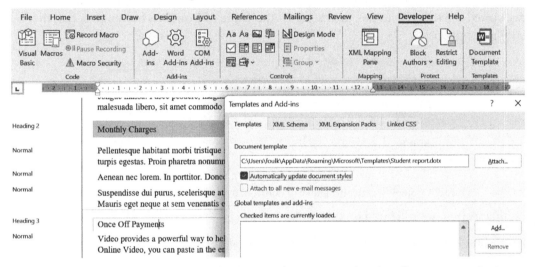

Figure 3.5 – The Automatically update document styles option needs to be off to preserve styles in a document

4. Click **OK** to confirm this, then save the document to update it.

Now, you can feel confident when you're sharing documents that have a specific style set you wish to keep intact. The document will be returned to you without any changes being made to your brand style set.

In the next section, we will learn how to create multiple **tables of contents (ToCs)** in one document.

Referencing features using Word 2021

In this section we will go through the steps to add multiple Table of Contents to a Word document.

Working with multiple ToCs

When you're working with a long document that contains two or more sections, you may want to add a ToC per section. In the previous edition of this book, we learned how to create a ToC using Microsoft Word 2019. To insert a ToC in the previous edition, we visited the **References** tab, then selected the **Table of Contents** button to access the available options:

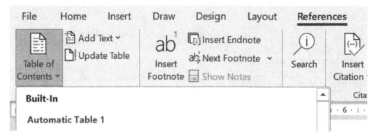

Figure 3.6 – Steps to generate a table of contents from the Reference tab in Word 2021

In this section, we will build on this skill.

To add multiple ToCs to a document, follow these steps:

1. Open a document that contains multiple sections. We will be using the `BestBean Coffee Plan TOC.docx` file here. Open this document if you wish to follow along.

2. This document consists of two sections – **BestBean Coffee Business Plan** and **BestBean Coffee Startup Costs**. We would like to add a ToC for each of these sections within the same document.

3. Before we use this method to add the ToCs to the document, it is important to note that the document headings are formatted using **Heading 1 style**. Format your headings to the **Heading 1** style. You can change the format of the **Heading 1** style to suit your font attributes before or after you have applied the style. This was explained in the first edition of this book, *Learn Microsoft Office 2019*.

4. Locate the first section heading (**INTRODUCTION**) that you wish to add to the first ToC page. Click before the heading.

5. Visit the **Insert** tab, then click the **Explore QuickParts** button. From the drop-down list, click **Field…**:

Figure 3.7 – Adding the \f switch using the Explore QuickParts button to access the Field... options

6. In the dialog box that populates, we will add the **\f** switch, which will allow us to create multiple ToCs in a single document.

7. Click on **TC** from the **Field names:** list.

8. In the **Text entry:** field, enter the name of the first heading for the first ToC.

    Check the **Field options** checkboxes so that the **TC entry in doc with multiple tables** option is enabled and **Outline level:** is set to **1**. Selecting **1** here will format the ToC using the TOC1 style:

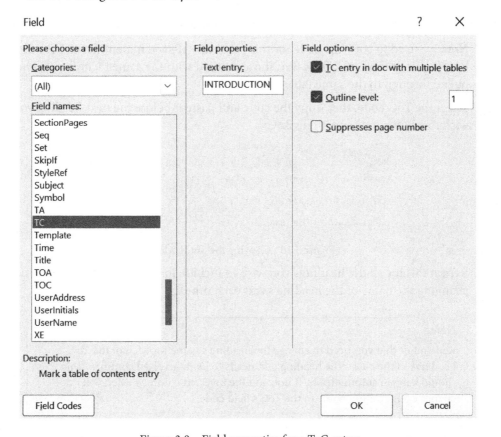

Figure 3.8 – Field properties for a ToC entry

9. Click **OK** to confirm this.
10. To see the ToC's field code to the left of the **INTRODUCTION** heading in the document, click on the **Show/Hide** button on the **Home** tab.
11. You will see the field code in the document. This code consists of the **\f** switch, as mentioned previously.
12. We need to amend this code slightly so that we add an identifier to the **\f** switch. By amending the code, we can identify which ToC we are assigning the relevant headings to.
13. Click to the right of the letter **f**, add a space, and type `a`. The identifier does not need to be any specific letter; it can be any identifier you wish:

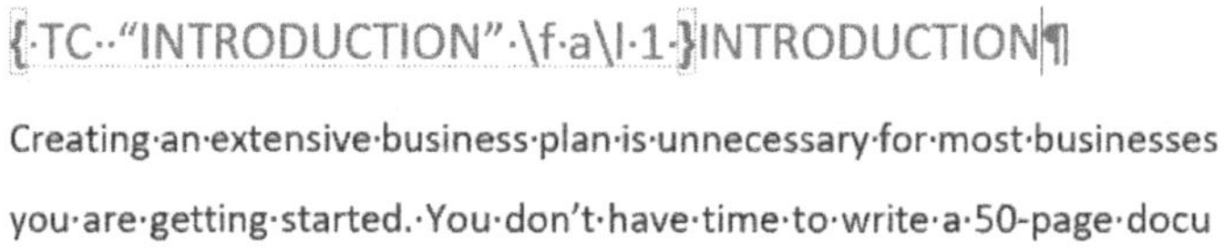

{·TC··"INTRODUCTION"·\f·a\l·1·}INTRODUCTION¶
Creating·an·extensive·business·plan·is·unnecessary·for·most·businesses
you·are·getting·started.·You·don't·have·time·to·write·a·50-page·docu

Figure 3.9 – The \f switch code added before the first heading

14. Now, we need to copy the code for this particular **\f** switch identifier to the other headings in this section. This way, those marked with the same identifier will be pulled through to the same table of contents.
15. Select the ToC code, then copy the code and paste it before the next heading you wish to include in the section's ToC:

{·TC··INTRODUCTION·\f·a·\l·1·
Creating·an·extensive·business·plan·is
you·are·getting·started.·You·don't·ha
either.·However,·the·exercise·of·cre
Cut
Copy
Paste Options:

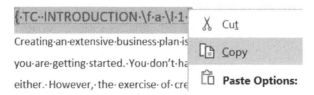

Figure 3.10 - Copying the ToC code

16. Repeat this for all the headings you wish to include in the first section's ToC, changing the name of the heading's text each time.

> **Note**
>
> Remember that you need to change the heading's name for each of the ToC headings in the code. The heading text needs to be in inverted commas. This should happen automatically. If not, add the inverted commas when you change each heading name in the ToC's field code.

17. Once you have copied the code to all the headings, click where you would like the first section's ToC to be placed inside the document.

18. Click the **References** tab, then click the **Table of Contents** button.

19. Select **Custom Table of Contents…** from the list provided.

20. Click the **Options…** button.

21. At the bottom of the **Table of Contents Options** dialog box, ensure that **Table entry fields** is selected. **Outline levels** should be unchecked:

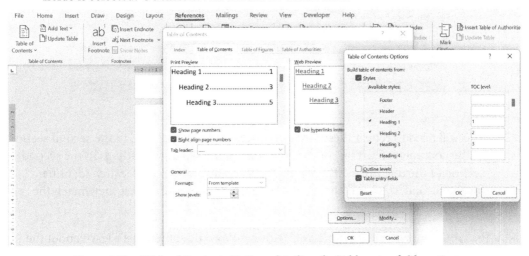

Figure 3.11 – Table of Contents Options detailing the Table entry fields option

22. Click **OK** to confirm this.

23. The ToC field code will be inserted into the document, but the table headings won't be pulled through yet. The code states that **No table of contents fields found**.

24. Press *Alt + F9* to update the code.

25. The identifier reference needs to be added so that it can pull the correct headings into the ToC. Type **a** after the \f switch, as shown in the following screenshot:

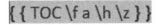

Figure 13.12 – The \f switch code displaying the addition of the a identifier

26. Press *Alt + F9* to update the ToC code. The first section's ToC will appear. If you make any changes in the document at some point, remember to update the ToC again by right-clicking and selecting **Update Field**. The shortcut key to update a ToC is *F9*:

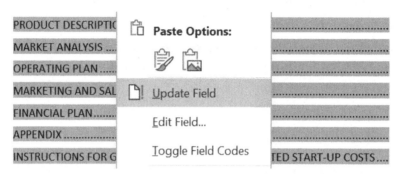

Figure 3.13 – The ToC when changes are made

27. You will need to repeat these steps to populate the second ToC in the second section of the document. Start by copying the code to the separate headings in the second section of the document. Then, remember to add a different **\f** switch identifier for the second TOC and change the headings in the code so that they match the relevant headings throughout.

Now that you can generate multiple ToC within a Word document, let's learn about the new **Table of Contents** feature for Word for the web.

The Table of Contents feature in Word for the web

The ability to create a ToC is a great additional feature for Word for the web users. To create a ToC online, position your cursor inside the document where you would like the ToC to be situated. Then, follow these steps:

1. Click the **Reference** tab.

2. Select **Table of Contents**. Then, from the drop-down list, choose **Insert Table of Contents**:

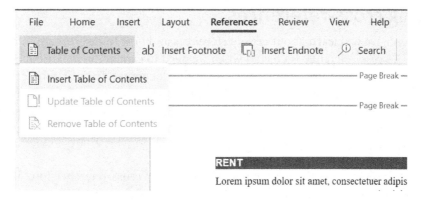

Figure 3.14 – The Table of Contents feature in Word for the web

3. The ToC will be generated automatically based on the heading styles within the document:

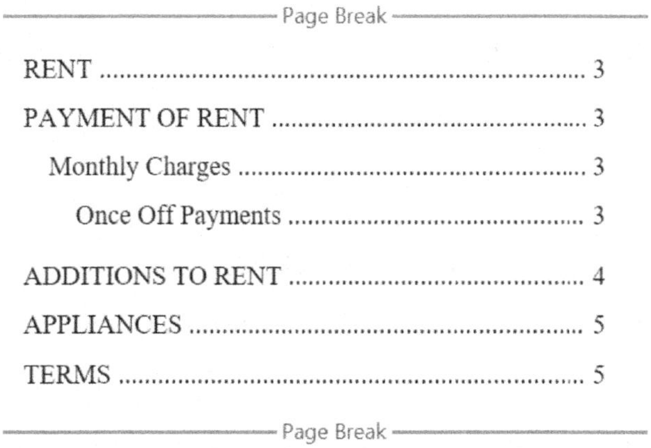

```
———————————————— Page Break ————————————————

RENT ..................................................................... 3

PAYMENT OF RENT ............................................... 3

    Monthly Charges ....................................... 3

    Once Off Payments .............................................. 3

ADDITIONS TO RENT ............................................. 4

APPLIANCES ........................................................... 5

TERMS ..................................................................... 5

———————————————— Page Break ————————————————
```

Figure 3.15 – Table of Contents on Word for the web

4. We can update or remove the ToC using the buttons that are available in the **Table of Contents** drop-down list.

This section concentrated on just one method of creating multiple ToCs in a single document. There are a few methods you can apply to achieve the same result, but I find this method the most logical. In the next section, we will focus on generating cross-references.

Creating cross-references

In this section, we will learn about **cross-references** and how to insert them into a document. A cross-reference is created when we need to expand on a particular part of a document by denoting a link somewhere else in the document. Cross-references are often used in legal documents, where we click to navigate to another part of the document to expand on a particular clause, for example. We can create cross-references to headings, numbered items, tables, footnotes, and endnotes, to name a few. Follow these steps to create a cross-reference:

1. Open the document that you would like to insert a cross-reference into. If you want to follow along, open the `Safest Solutions Plan.docx` file.

2. Navigate to the bottom of page 1 and locate the sentence **Please refer to point for more information and the car allowance policy**.

3. As we would like to insert a cross-reference to the point on the car allowance policy mentioned in this sentence, we need to click in-between the words **point** and **for**.

4. Click on the **Insert** tab, then select **Cross-reference** from the **Links** group.

5. In the **Cross-reference** dialog box that populates, make sure that **Reference type:** is set to **Numbered item** and **Insert reference to:** is set to **Paragraph number (full context)**.

6. Click on the **CAR ALLOWANCE / COMPANY CAR** numbered item to make sure it's selected for the **For which numbered item:** option.

   This ensures that the number of the **CAR ALLOWANCE / COMPANY CAR** item's location is inserted where your cursor is in the sentence. The user can then click on the numbered item referenced in the sentence to jump directly to that link for more information:

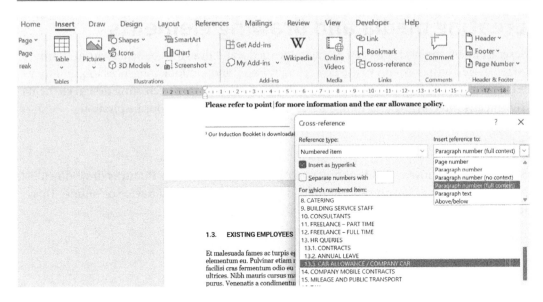

Figure 3.16 – The Cross-reference dialog box detailing various options

If a link that you have inserted a cross-reference for changes location, when you're amending the document, you do not need to redo the cross-reference. Use the *Ctrl + A* shortcut to select the entire document, then press **F9** to update the references. You can also right-click on an existing cross-reference, then choose **Update Field**.

If, however, the reference no longer exists in the document, you will need to update the reference by manually reinserting the cross-reference.

If the reference cannot be located in the document, it should display **Error! Reference source not found.**:

Please refer to point Error! Reference source not found. **for more information and the car allowance policy.**

Figure 3.17 – Cross-reference error text in the document

> Tip
>
> Use the **Find** tool to locate all the instances of the word **error** once you have applied cross-referencing to your document. This method will alert you to the cross-references that need attention throughout the document.

7. Once the cross-reference has been inserted, *Ctrl + click* to move to the reference item in the document.

Now that you know how to apply multiple ToCs to one document and can generate and update cross-references, let's look at some new drawings and media elements.

Creating media and drawing elements

Several enhancements have been made to the media and drawing elements within Word 2021. These features extend to the PowerPoint, Excel, and Outlook interfaces too, and they lean toward improving your document's presentation when you're creating design elements. This means you don't have to look outside the Office environment for inspiration.

Stock Images

Stock Images is now available as an extra option from within the **Pictures** drop-down list. Normally, we would only be able to upload images from our local device or online. This feature is really exciting as it contains the following categories:

- Images
- Icons
- Cutout People
- Stickers
- Illustrations

The new **Stock Images** feature is available in Word, Excel, PowerPoint, and Outlook 2021's standalone and online applications. Let's take a look:

1. In your document, click where you would like to insert a stock image. For this example, we will be working on the `ColorfulTabs.docx` file.

2. Go to the **Insert** tab and click **Pictures** to access the drop-down list.

3. Select **Stock Images…**:

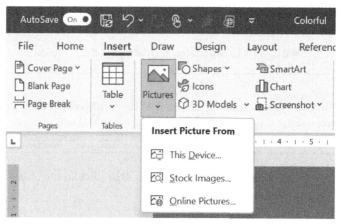

Figure 3.18 – The Pictures drop-down list displaying the Stock Images… option

4. Select a category from the top of the dialog box:

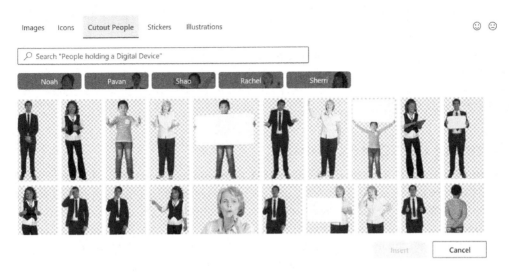

Figure 3.19 – The Stock Images… option displaying the available categories

5. Click on a picture to select it. If you would like to insert more than one picture, simply select the pictures you wish to include by clicking on them. The number of pictures you've chosen will be displayed in brackets within the **Insert** button:

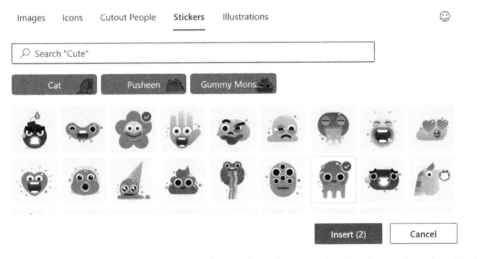

Figure 3.20 – The Stickers category displaying the number of pictures that have been selected within the Insert button

6.   Click on **Insert (2)** to add the chosen pictures to the document.

7.   Move the pictures to place them in the document, and then resize or format them as necessary.

The **Cutout People** picture category is extremely useful for e-learning assets as you can create engaging learning materials via Word, Excel, Outlook, and PowerPoint. In the next section, we will look a little closer at color shades when working with elements in Word 2021.

Coloring using Hex values

Previously, we could only use the **RGB** or **HSL** color models to enter specific color shades in the **Custom colors** dialog box. We can now type in **Hex** codes when applying color to objects, shapes, lines, or text. A hex code is a combination of six numbers or letters and is prefixed with the # symbol (hashtag). An example of a Hex code is *#8A2BE2*. There are lots of websites on the internet that can help you convert RGB into Hex codes, and vice versa, to find that perfect shade you require. Follow these steps:

1.   Open the document that contains the elements you wish to change. For this example, we will be working with the `ColorfulTabs.docx` file.

2.   Select an image, shape, or text to alter its color. We would like to change the color of the circle shape at the top-left corner of the second page of the document.

3.   Double-click to select the circle.

4.   The **Shape Format** tab will appear at the end of the ribbon.

5.   Select the **Shape Fill** drop-down arrow, which can be located via the **Shape Styles** group.

6.   Click on **More Fill Colors…**:

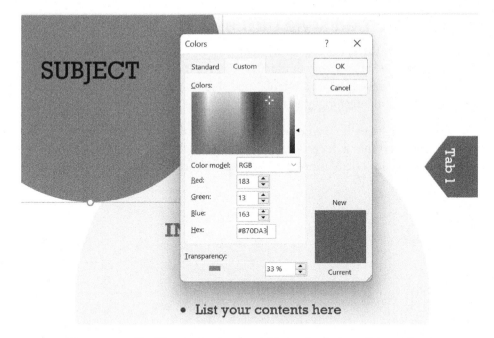

Figure 3.21 – The Hex: option is now visible on the Custom Colors palette

7. The **Colors** dialog box will populate. At the bottom of the dialog box, you will notice a new option named **Hex:**.

8. Type in the Hex code you wish to format your shape with by replacing any text that's already been entered into the area provided to the right of **Hex: text**. For this example, we will use Hex code **#8A2BE2**.

9. Click **OK** to confirm this. Now, your shape will be a new bright color.

10. We have learned a new skill to apply different shades of color to elements within Word. Let's have some fun on the next topic looking at ways to jazz up our drawing shapes.

Applying sketched style outlines

The **sketched style outlines** are one of my favorite new features. They can be found by going to the **Shape Styles** group of the **Shape Format** contextual menu. Instead of inserting computer-drawn perfect straight-lined shapes, you can now insert shapes and turn them into fun and engaging graphics.

The following screenshot shows an example of a standard straight-lined rectangle that we would normally insert into a document. Below the straight-lined rectangle are examples of the three new sketched style outlines – that is, **curved**, **freehand**, and **scribble**:

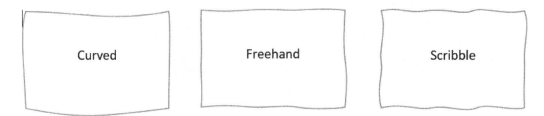

Figure 3.22 – Representation of the standard rectangle and the three new sketched line styles – curved, freehand, and scribble

Now that you are familiar with the names of the new sketched shape styles, let's apply them:

1. Open a Microsoft Word 2021 desktop document.
2. Click the **Insert** tab, then locate the **Illustrations** group.
3. Select the **Shapes** option, then choose a shape from the categories listed.
4. A **cross-hair** (+) will now appear as your cursor.
5. Click inside the document and drag with your cursor until you have drawn the shape size you require. Release your cursor to view the shape.
6. Double-click the outside border of the shape to select it.
7. Notice that the **Shape Format** tab has appeared at the end of the existing tabs of the ribbon:

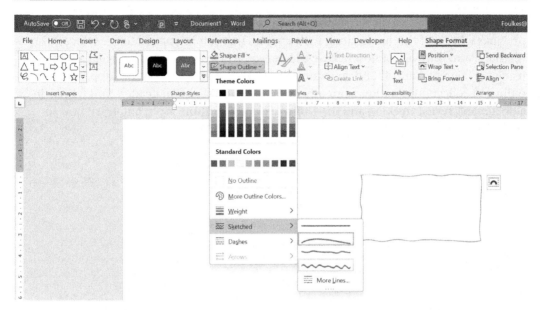

Figure 3.23 - New Sketched style options in Word, PowerPoint, and Excel 2021 (desktop)

8. While the shape is still selected, locate the **Shape Styles** group.

9. Select the **Shape Outline** option.

10. From the drop-down list, select **Sketched**. Then, navigate to the right, where you will see the three new sketched shape styles. Select from **curved**, **freehand**, or **scribble**.

Note

Sketched line options are available in the Word, Excel, and PowerPoint 2021 desktop versions.

Summary

This chapter built on the previous edition's skills and introduced some of the new features of Office 2021. We focused on ways to manage the styles environment to make amending long documents an easy task and keeping styles intact when working with external collaborators. You now know how to apply more than one ToC to a document and be more creative with shapes, color shades, and stock images.

In the next chapter, we will revisit some of the features that were explained in the previous edition of this book, along with updates that can be applied to the Office 2021 interface, and learn about new features. Here, you will learn how to construct a form using the content controls and generate an online form within Word desktop, as well as online, to collect information from others. We will also recap on headers and footers in a document, revisit tracking and the **Compare** and **Combine** tools, and learn how to automate processes when using Word 2021.

4

Managing Professional Documents

Word 2021 includes an array of features that aid in creating attractive and professional documents. In the previous edition of this book, we concentrated on creating professional documents and looked at ways to restrict and control access. In this new edition chapter, we will revisit some of these features with updates applicable to the Office 2021 interface and learn about some new features.

This chapter will teach you how to construct a form using the content controls and generate an online form within the Word desktop and online versions to collect information from others. We will also recap headers and footers in a document, revisit tracking and the compare/combine tools, and learn how to automate processes when using Word 2021.

We will cover the following topics in this chapter:

- Modifying page layouts
- Constructing online forms
- Recording document automation
- Tracking, comparing, and combining documents

Technical requirements

As this chapter focuses on managing professional documents and building on skills, you will have already mastered the basics, as well as having some intermediate knowledge. The examples that will be used in this chapter can be accessed from the following GitHub URL: `https://github.com/PacktPublishing/Learn-Microsoft-Office-2021-Second-Edition`.

Modifying page layouts

In this topic, we will look at how to work with different types of breaks in a document and construct headers and footers. This is an area where we quite often need to troubleshoot when working with different document sections.

Inserting and modifying section breaks

Breaks in a document are extremely useful if you would like to have a different layout or formatting changes for a certain section of the document, such as a page, or pages. By formatting or layout, we include the following:

- Margins
- Paper size or orientation
- Page borders

- Vertical alignments of text

- Headers and footers

- Columns

- Page numbering

- Line numbering

- Footnote/endnote numbering

The following is an explanation of these special break types:

- **Continuous**: A continuous section break is inserted before and after a portion of text on the same page. Changing text into columns is an example of where a continuous break is used:

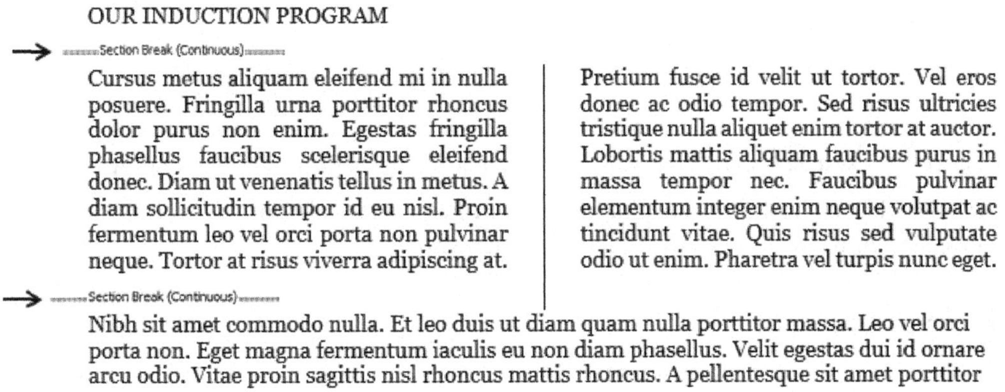

OUR INDUCTION PROGRAM

➝ ═══Section Break (Continuous)═══

Cursus metus aliquam eleifend mi in nulla posuere. Fringilla urna porttitor rhoncus dolor purus non enim. Egestas fringilla phasellus faucibus scelerisque eleifend donec. Diam ut venenatis tellus in metus. A diam sollicitudin tempor id eu nisl. Proin fermentum leo vel orci porta non pulvinar neque. Tortor at risus viverra adipiscing at.

Pretium fusce id velit ut tortor. Vel eros donec ac odio tempor. Sed risus ultricies tristique nulla aliquet enim tortor at auctor. Lobortis mattis aliquam faucibus purus in massa tempor nec. Faucibus pulvinar elementum integer enim neque volutpat ac tincidunt vitae. Quis risus sed vulputate odio ut enim. Pharetra vel turpis nunc eget.

➝ ═══Section Break (Continuous)═══

Nibh sit amet commodo nulla. Et leo duis ut diam quam nulla porttitor massa. Leo vel orci porta non. Eget magna fermentum iaculis eu non diam phasellus. Velit egestas dui id ornare arcu odio. Vitae proin sagittis nisl rhoncus mattis rhoncus. A pellentesque sit amet porttitor

Figure 4.1 – Section breaks visible in Draft View

- **Even Page** or **Odd Page**: This prepares the document for formatting changes on all the odd pages or all the even pages only throughout the document. You might like to place a header or footer on only the odd pages in the document, and, therefore, would insert an Odd Page section break.

- **Next Page**: Inserting this section break instead of a normal page break (before and after the page) will control what happens on that page only. This type of section break is very useful when you want to create portrait pages followed by one landscape page, and thereafter, the document returns to portrait mode. Another use for this type of break is to sort out a problem table that is too big to fit on a portrait page!

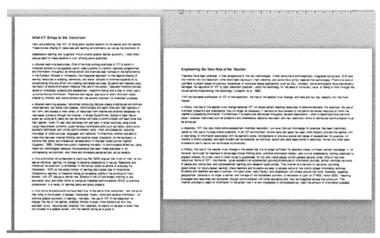

Figure 4.2 – Next Page section break in a document displaying both portrait and landscape pages

Now, we will learn how to locate and insert **Next Page** section breaks into a document to create different page orientation layouts in a single document.

Viewing section breaks

Follow these steps to learn how to view section breaks:

1. Let's open a document to work on. In this example, we will work on `SectionBreaks.docx`.

    On *page 2* of this document, you will notice that columns have been inserted in a particular paragraph. At the start and the end of the paragraph, there are section breaks. These breaks are not evident in the document, but because this section of the document contains columns, we know that they are there.

2. If a document contains section breaks, they can be viewed in three ways:

    - By changing the document view from **Print Layout** to **Outline**
    - By changing the document view from **Print Layout** to **Draft**
    - By using the **Show/Hide** icon on the **Home** tab:

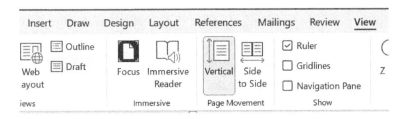

Figure 4.3 – Click on View | Draft to see breaks in the document

3. Click on the **Print Layout** icon to return to the normal working view.

Adding section breaks

Follow these steps to learn how to add section breaks:

1. Click into the document where the section break is required. I have continued using the file from the previous section.

2. Insert the type of section break required into the document.

3. Here, the second page will be changed to landscape orientation. We have inserted a **Next Page** section break at the end of the first page (to show where the change must start) and at the end of the second page (to show where the change must end):

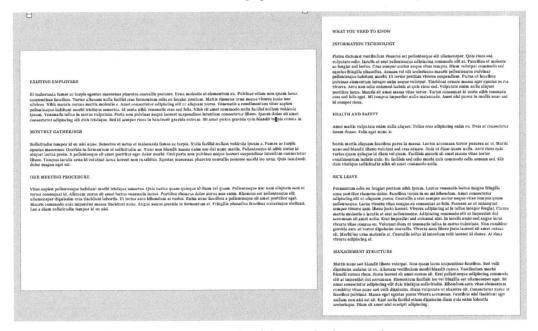

Figure 4.4 – Next Page section break between landscape and portrait pages

4. Let's replicate these by inserting the **Next Page** section breaks into the document to create a landscape page in the middle of the document.

5. Click before the text **Existing Employees**.

6. Visit the **Layout** tab and select **Breaks** from the list.

7. Choose the **Next Page** section break to insert a break before the text **Existing Employees**.

8. Move to the end of the paragraph, before the text **What You Need to Know**.

9. Insert another **Next Page** section break at the end of the paragraph.

10. Make sure your mouse pointer is clicked into the text of the page beginning with **Existing Employees**.

11. Click on the **Layout** tab and choose **Orientation**.

12. Choose **Landscape** from the list provided.

13. The page will turn into a landscape page with portrait pages on either side.

> **Note**
>
> This is just one example of how section breaks can transform your documents. The **Next Page** section break is really great when you need to add a complex table in the middle of a Word document.

To delete the section breaks, click on the non-printing symbols (the **Show/Hide** icon) icon on the **Paragraph** group, which is located on the **Home** tab. Alternatively, change the document view to **Draft** and click to place the cursor on the section break line in the document. Then, press *Delete* on the keyboard.

Headers and footers

A page header is an area at the top of the document where you can add text, page numbers, or logos that repeat at the top of each page of the document. A footer is the same, except it resides at the bottom of each page.

The header area is located at the top of the document:

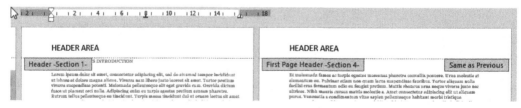

Figure 4.5 – Page header area displaying sections

When a header exists in a document, you will notice that the information in it is grayed out when you are in the **Print Layout** view. This is because the information is not *active* at the present time. To activate this area and work in it, simply double-click on the existing header. The header area will open up, as shown in the preceding screenshot, and you will be able to edit it. The same applies to the footer.

Inserting a header and footer

Follow these steps to learn how to insert a header and footer:

1. Open the document that you wish to add a header to. We will continue with different header and footer sections.

    Often, you might feel a bit restricted when dealing with headers and footers that have the same information at the top or bottom of each page in the document. With section breaks, you can fix this so that, for instance, *pages 1* and *3* can have different header content to that of *pages 2* and *4*. Follow these steps to learn how to do this.

2. Open the document called Sections.docx. Notice that the first page is excluded from headers and footers. This is because the **Different First Page** option is active in the document.

3. Also notice that, when viewing the header and footer area, the sections are the same from *page 2* onward, and the **Same as Previous** option is active on each page header in the document. This means that anything inserted into a header or footer area will be repeated across all pages:

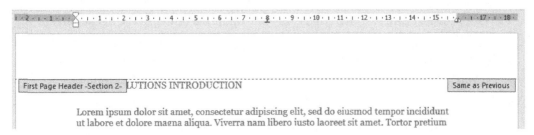

Figure 4.6 – Header section showing the Same as Previous setting

4. Insert section breaks, where relevant, into the document. (For this exercise, we will insert **Next Page** section breaks at the bottom of each page to break the document into different sections.)

5. As you add **Next Page** section breaks, you might find that the text on the next page moves down slightly. This is normal, as the section break tends to do this. Just delete the space at the top of the document as you insert breaks.

6. Make sure you are on the first page of the document.

7. Double-click to open up the header area.

8. Type the text Report on Services.

9. As the second page displays **Same as Previous** to the right, any text added to the header will appear on the first page as well.

10. Click into the header area on *page 2*, then click on **Link to Previous** from the **Navigation** group – this will remove the link between the two sections and allow you to delete the header from the first page, without interfering with any text on the second page:

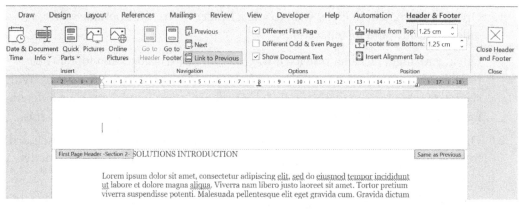

Figure 4.7 – Click on Link to Previous to unlink sections within headers and footers

11. Move to the next page (Section 3).

12. Click on **Link to Previous** to remove the link between the two sections.

13. Enter the text Safest Solutions Group in the center of the header area.

14. While navigating between sections, notice that the distance between the text in some sections is wider than the next. This demonstrates that you can also use formatting to denote a difference between sections in headers and footers.

15. Move to the next page (Section 4).

16. Click on **Link to Previous** to remove the link between two sections.

17. Enter the text Report on Services.

18. Continue in this fashion until you reach the end of the document.

19. Finally, click on the **Close Header and Footer** icon to return to the document and view the result.

Now that we are up to speed with modifying headers and footers in Word 2021 documents, let's move on to learn how to work with forms on the Word desktop and online versions.

Constructing online forms

Forms are very useful for collecting information, thus restricting users so that they can only fill in the required information without being able to change the format of the document. To begin the process of constructing a form, you will either need a new document, an existing document, or a template to base the form on. When we design our form in Word 2021, we can add content, such as drop-down lists of choices, textboxes, checkboxes, date fields, and content controls using the **Developer** tab.

Preparing the form layout

We will design a form for colleagues to fill in at our company. This form will be added to our intranet page so that colleagues can sign up to do volunteering work within the local community. Office 2021 has some new form templates, which can be downloaded to save time. Visit the forms available within Word 2021 by following the next steps:

1. Click on **File** | **New**.

2. Locate **Search for online templates**, then click to type a keyword into the area provided, such as `forms`.

3. Press the *Enter* keyboard key to view the results of the search.

4. Click on a form that suits your requirements, then edit the form and send it out to participants.

    We will, however, create our own form from scratch as we would like to recap certain skills. Let's create the basic form to see how the process works! The form we design will recap certain basic skills that we covered in the first edition of our book, *Learn Microsoft Office 2019*.

5. Make sure you have a new blank document open (by going to **New** | **Blank Document**).

6. Save the document as `SafestSolCharity.docx`.

7. Double-click in the header section of the form and insert a table with one row, and one column. The height of the row must be set to **1.79 cm**:

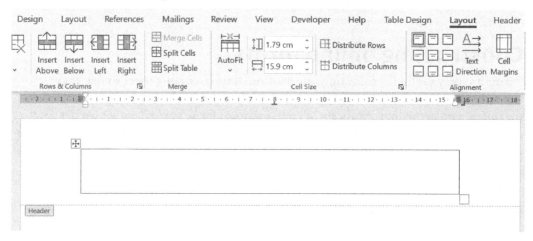

Figure 4.8 – Table Layout options displaying 1.79cm row height in the header area

8. Remove the border of the table (**Table Design | Borders | No border**) so that only table gridlines are showing (**Layout | View Gridlines**).

9. Amend the table shading to the Hex code #9999FF.

10. Insert the **Stock Media | Stickers** picture into the left-hand side of the table. Change the wrapping of the sticker to **In Front of Text** and resize to fit into the table row height.

11. Add a heading named Safest Solutions Charity Drive, then format the text to **Brush Script MT** (font size **20**), with a Hex shading of #CDCDFF. After formatting, your header will look similar to the next screenshot.

Figure 4.9 – Screenshot displaying the formatted header table

12. Press the down arrow on the keyboard to move to the **Footer** area of the document. Set out the company address in font size **8**, and the stock media sticker to the right-hand side of the footer.

Figure 4.10 – Footer area of the document displaying the finished product

13. Insert a horizontal line above the address using the **Paragraph** group, and the **Borders | Horizontal Line** option.

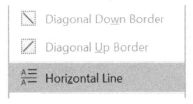

Figure 4.11 – Horizontal Line option located from the Borders drop-down list

14. Let's build the body of the form. Insert a table consisting of 22 rows and two columns:

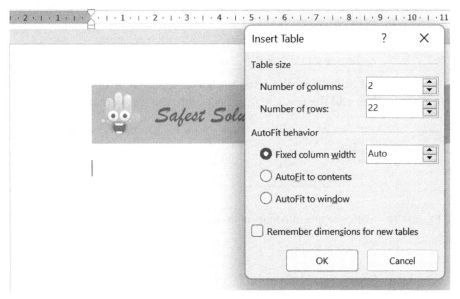

Figure 4.12 – Insert Table dialog box

15. Set the row height to 1.05cm for all rows in the table.

16. Set the column width for the first six rows to 3.34cm.

17. Set the cell alignment to the bottom left. Type the following text as headings for each of the rows:

   - First Name

   - Surname

   - Address

   - City / Post Code

   - Email

   - Home Phone

18. Split the sixth row into four columns:

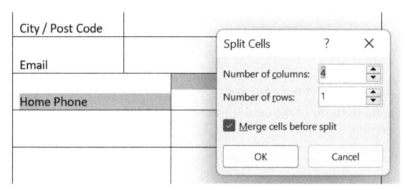

Figure 4.13 – Split Cells feature within a Word table

19. Line up the first column for the sixth row, making sure it is the same width as the rows above, then add the text Cell Phone into the third column.

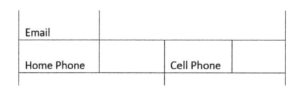

Figure 4.14 – Sixth row split into four columns with the addition of the Cell Phone text

20. Merge the columns in the seventh row, then add the text `I am interested in the following charities:`

21. Add the text as per the next screenshot, and format the rest of the table as required.

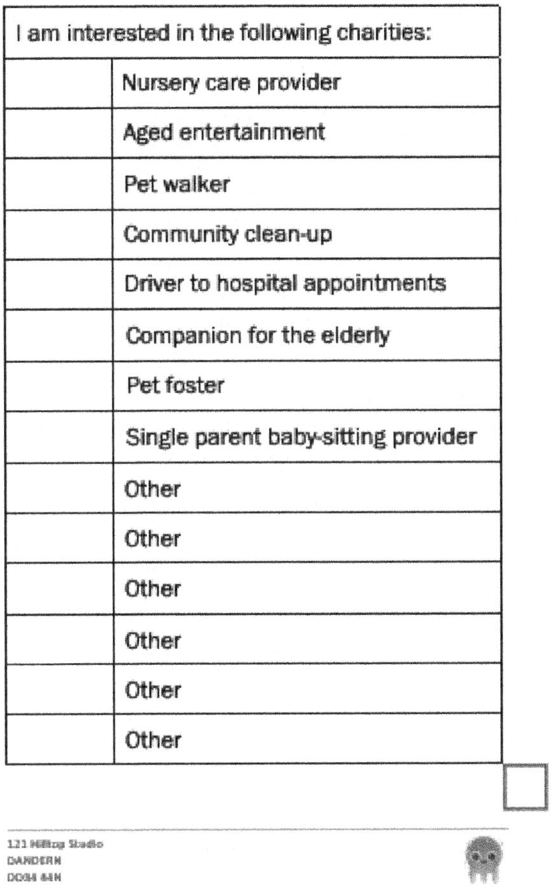

I am interested in the following charities:	
	Nursery care provider
	Aged entertainment
	Pet walker
	Community clean-up
	Driver to hospital appointments
	Companion for the elderly
	Pet foster
	Single parent baby-sitting provider
	Other
	Other
	Other
	Other
	Other
	Other

121 Hilltop Studio
DANDERN
DD84 84N

Figure 4.15 – Charity examples entered and formatted

Now that we have the layout sorted, let's learn how to add form controls to finish off the form.

Working with the Developer tab

To make a *fillable form*, we would need to add content controls. This is achieved by adding the **Developer** tab to the list of available tabs in Word 2021 so that it is visible on the ribbon:

1. Click to select **File | Options** from the list provided. Then, click on the **Customize Ribbon** icon down the left-hand side.

2. On the right, under the **Customize the Ribbon** option, make sure that the **Main** tab is selected, then locate **Developer** and ensure that the checkbox is activated to the left it. Click on **OK** to confirm this.

3. This will add the **Developer** tab to the existing ribbon.

Content controls are located within the **Controls** group on the **Developer** tab. In the next section, we will investigate the different types of controls.

Investigating content controls

There are two main types of controls: **content controls** and **legacy form controls**. There are more content control options than legacy controls, and they do not require any type of protection to make them active for user input.

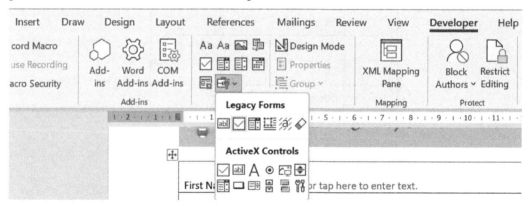

Figure 4.16 – Different types of form controls located under the Controls group

Legacy controls need to be protected using the **Restrict Editing** option so that they are active for user input. Legacy controls are also sometimes preferred for complex documents. The reason for this is that when using the legacy controls, the form can be protected using the **Filling in forms** feature, which stops users from editing that particular area of the form. Here is a representation of the different types of controls available on the **Developer** tab:

Field	Icon	Explanation
Text Form Content Control	Aa	Used to indicate that text is required to be filled in by the user of the form
Plain Text Content Control	Aa	Allows the user to input text into the content control
Check Box Content Control	☑	This check box is used to allow the user to indicate either a yes or no answer
Checkbox Content Control	📑 📑	This checkbox provide a few options which the user can choose to answer the question
Date Picker Content Control	📅	Used to indicate a date must be inserted into a content control on a form a few options that the user
Picture Content Control	🖼	The control enables the user to add an image to a form
Design Mode	Design Mode	This icon is used to edit content controls
Properties	Properties	Make changes to the properties of content controls

Figure 4.17 – Explanation of the content controls located on the Developer tab

In addition, macros can be used to refine input and create computations; you will learn how to create a macro in a separate topic. You will learn how to protect a form later in this section too, as we will be protecting our form so that the user is not able to amend the form contents.

In the next section, we will look at legacy content controls and getting the form ready for distribution.

Adding and modifying legacy form controls

If you want to create greater protection in terms of restricting users so that they can only access certain parts of the form or be guided only from one content control to the next, then legacy form controls are the way to go. Let's take a look at an already prepared and protected form:

1. Open the document named SampleForm.docx. This form has been protected so that the user can only fill in the required information and not amend the rest of the document. When you press the *Tab* key on the keyboard, the cursor moves from one content control to the next.

2. To stop protection and edit the form, click **Developer | Restrict Editing**.

3. The **Restrict Editing** pane will open to the right-hand side of the window. Click on the **Stop Protection** button to unprotect the form.

4. Place the mouse pointer just after the School House: text and use the **Legacy Forms** icon to insert the **Drop-Down Form Field** from the **Developer** tab.

5. Notice the *gray field code* that has appeared next to the School House: heading.

6. Double-click on the *gray field code* to edit **Drop-Down Form Field Options**.

7. Add the text `Enter School House here` into the **Drop-down item:** field, then click on the **Add** >> button. Repeat the step to add the names of the houses for `Emerald`, `Sapphire`, and `Ruby`. Click on the **OK** button to commit to the changes.

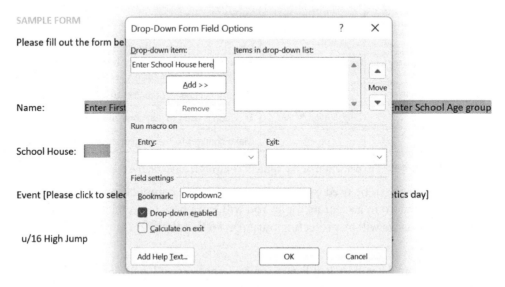

Figure 4.18 – Drop-down Form Field Options dialog box to edit field properties

8. Place the mouse pointer before the text `u/16 High Jump`, then insert a **Check Box Form Field** from the **Legacy Forms** drop-down list.

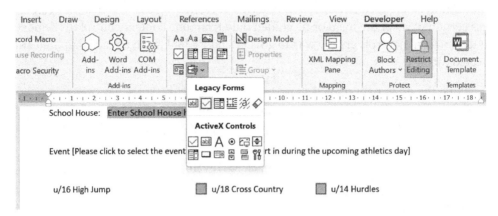

Figure 4.19 – SampleForm document displaying the Restrict Editing pane

9. Your form is now complete and ready to be protected so that users cannot edit the actual text on the form, and can only answer the questions. Let's learn how to do protect the form in the next topic.

Protecting a form

There are two options available here to protect a form:

- **Formatting restrictions**: These allow you to customize which styles can be edited by the form user.

- **Editing restrictions**: These options allow the form initiator to decide which fields require protection from amending by the form user.

Take the following steps to learn how to protect the form:

1. We will continue to use the form we created in the previous section. Make sure the **Developer** tab is selected, then click **Restrict Editing** under the **Protect** group.

2. Under the **Editing restrictions** heading, select the checkbox for **Allow only this type of editing in the document**:

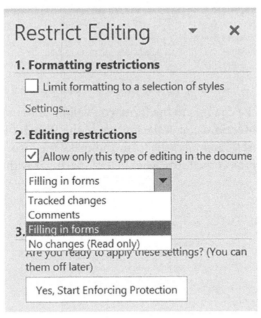

Figure 4.20 – Restrict Editing pane displaying the Filling in forms option under Editing restrictions

3. From the drop-down list, choose **Filling in forms**.

4. Under *Step 3*, click on **Yes, Start Enforcing Protection**.

5. A dialog box will present itself, asking you to enter a password (this is optional).

6. Click on **OK** to complete the protection process.

7. If your form was protected correctly, the user should not be able to edit any part of the form except the fields you inserted.

8. Click on **File | Info**. The **Protect Document** icon indicates that this document has protection applied.

Figure 4.21 – File|Info screen confirming that the document is protected

9. If you need to make changes to the form, you will need to *unprotect* the form first. Visit the **Stop Protection** icon at the bottom of the **Restrict Editing** pane, then enter the password to *unprotect* the form and make the form accessible for editing. Do not forget to *protect* the form again before sharing it with others.

Now that you are able to protect a form, practice this skill by adding appropriate content controls to the form named `SaferSolCharity.docx`, then protect the form so that we ensure the users are not able to edit the form we created in a previous topic.

Once the form has been protected, you are now able to upload the form to the website of your choice, SharePoint, or Teams collaboration area for colleagues/users to complete. You can also create forms using Microsoft Forms; we will learn about this method in the next section.

Using Microsoft Forms

In addition to creating forms within the desktop Office 2021 apps, we can also visit the **Microsoft Forms** online app from within the Office 365 environment, or by visiting `http://forms.microsoft.com/`.

Figure 4.22 – Microsoft Forms access through Office 365

We will now use the Forms app within our Microsoft account, and learn how to create and publish an online form:

1. Locate the **Forms** option on the Microsoft 365 screen, or type the `http://forms.microsoft.com/` URL into the browser to navigate to the **Forms** app. Remember to sign in using your credentials, if required.

2. From the **Forms** home screen, click to create **New Form** or **New Quiz**, or use one of the existing **templates** available.

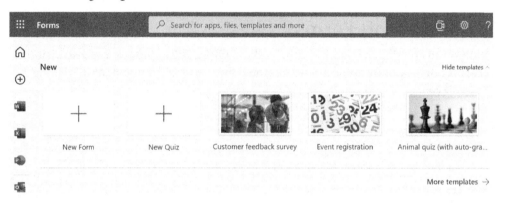

Figure 4.23 – Forms home screen displaying the New Form, New Quiz, and templates options

3. Let's use the **Event registration** template to learn more about adding or amending form elements. Click to select the **Event registration** option.

4. Notice that, at the top of the editable form, there are two tabs, namely, **Questions** and **Responses**. Use the **Questions** tab to amend or add questions to your form. We will investigate this option first:

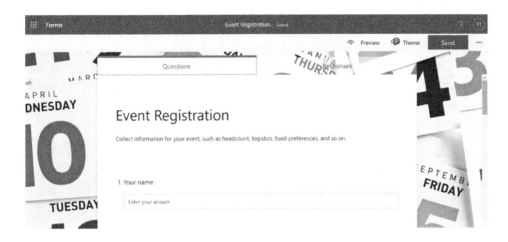

Figure 4.24 – Event Registration form with the Questions and Responses tabs at the top

5. Editing a form is really easy, as you simply click on the part of the form you wish to amend. For instance, click anywhere in the first question to amend it. The question will present itself in edit mode. At the top of the question, you will see four buttons:

    • *Copy question*

    • *Delete question*

    • *Move question up*

    • *Move question down*:

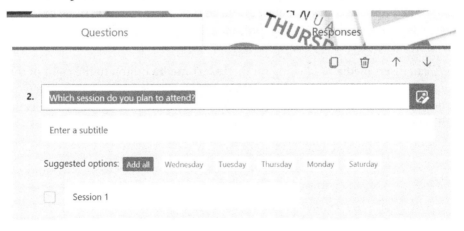

Figure 4.25 – Form options

6. The options available on text questions will differ from those of multiple-choice question types, for example. To add a new question type, click on the **Add New** button at the bottom of any question you are currently editing, or scroll down to the bottom of the form. Once you have clicked on the **Add New** button, the list of question types will be presented.

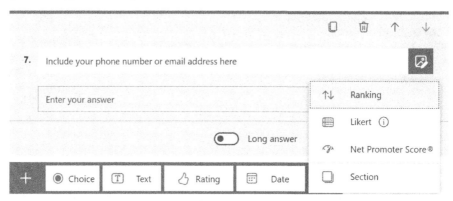

Figure 4.26 – Question types available after clicking the Add New button

7. Choose a question type by clicking on the relevant option. For this example, let's choose **Rating**. Add the question, then specify the *level* and whether you would like the *symbol* to be displayed as stars or numbers as the rating options. You can also choose to fix the question so that it requires user input prior to moving to the next question on the form. Click on the **Required** button to set this option.

8. Edit the question text by amending the detail as you would normally. There are **Suggested options:** options below question types to guide you. These options offer the user efficient ways of adding multiple relevant question keywords in one go, which saves time.

9. We can insert media by clicking on the **Insert media** button to the right of the question. This will take you to media locations, such as *Image Search*, *OneDrive*, or *Upload*. Reminder to always consider copyright when making the best selection, and to cite sources, where required.

Figure 4.27 – Image search and upload options for media on a form question

10. You may wish to edit the **Theme** form. To do this, click on the **Theme** button at the top right-hand side of the form, as shown in the previous screenshot.

11. Theme ideas, colors, and images will be presented to the right side of the form. After you have selected a new theme, use the **Preview** button at the top of the form to see how the form will present to users of the form.

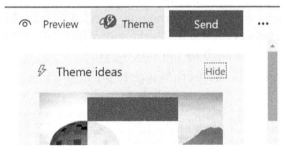

Figure 4.28 – Form buttons are located at the top in order to change the Theme and Preview the result

12. There are a few more options to consider when designing online forms. We can add a question **Subtitle**, set **Restrictions**, and add **Branching**. Click to edit a question. Select the three dots to the right of the question to view the options. The options displayed here are determined by the question type.

13. On choosing the **Subtitle** option, this will add an extra row under the question so that you can add any additional instruction or text to the question. To remove the subtitle, simply choose it again from the **...** menu.

14. If you add the **Restrictions** option, you will need to specify a number constraint.

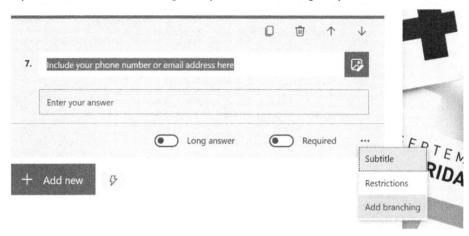

Figure 4.29 – Click on the three dots to the right of a question to display more options

15. We use branching to extend a question based on the answer provided from the source question. For instance, if the user indicated that they have food allergies, they will be taken directly to the branching question to fill out details about their allergies and add any medical information. Select **Add branching**, and the **Go to** drop-down list will appear just under the source question. Notice that you have been directed to the **Branching options** screen.

16. Choose an option from the list to branch to the next action based on user input.

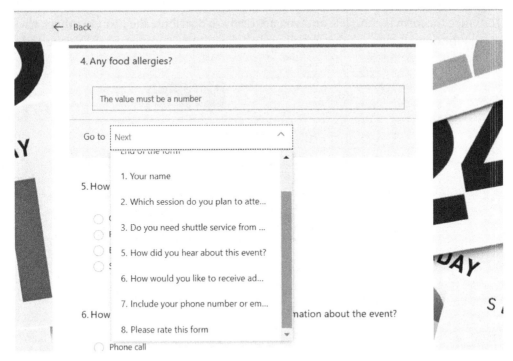

Figure 4.30 – The drop-down options on the Go to branching screen

17. When you are happy with the branching options, navigate back to the form layout by clicking on the **Back** button at the top left of the form.

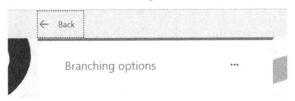

Figure 4.31 – Click on the Back button to return to the form

18. Once the form is complete and you are ready to distribute the form to others, click on the **Send** button. Here you will find all the options with regard to sharing and collecting responses.

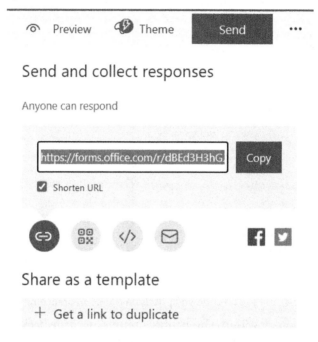

Figure 4.32 – Send and collect responses displaying the Shorten URL option

19. Before copying the form link, click on the **Shorten URL** checkbox to ensure that the link is reduced to fewer characters and symbols, making it easier to share.

20. There are a number of mediums we can use to share a form. These icons are located just beneath the form link. The first icon is the **Link** icon (the default), followed by **QR Code**, **Embed**, and **Email**.

21. Once you have sent out the link using one of the methods explained here, the form responses are collected. To view the results of the survey, navigate back to the form, then click on the **Responses** tab at the top of the form. From this screen, you can view responses and/or open the results in Excel.

Figure 4.33 – Responses tab showing first form response and the Open in Excel option

In this section, we learned how to work with forms using Microsoft Word 2021, as well as using the online tool, Microsoft Forms. In the next section, we will learn how to create a macro to automate tasks when using Microsoft Word.

Recording document automation

We can use macros to help with document automation tasks. Such tasks could include a letter closing, defining company branding adding headers and footers, for example. The list is endless. **Macros** are simply actions you record within an application that are played back. This saves time when you repetitively have to perform the same task over and over again.

In addition to creating macros, we can also use the **Quick Parts** or **AutoText** features within Word to save items we use regularly in Word. These are located on the **Insert** tab. Before we record a macro, let's look at an example of an AutoText entry.

Creating Quick Parts

If you would like to reuse content within Word, you can add a selection to the Quick Parts feature and access the content when you need it. This is great for opening paragraphs, clauses, schedules, and signature closing.

Let's run through the steps to create a Quick Part:

1. Open the document named `SafestSolLetter.docx`.

2. Navigate to the end of the letter where you will see the letter closing.

3. Select the closing by highlighting from *Yours sincerely* to the end of the *Enclosure* section.

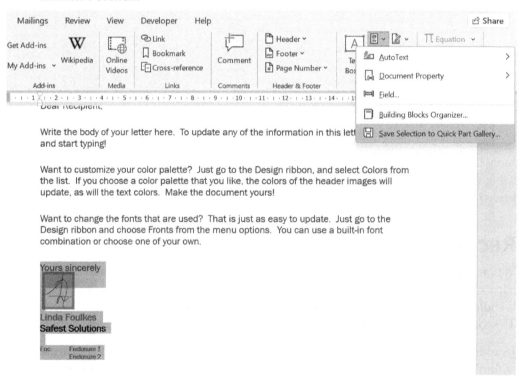

Figure 4.34 – Save Selection to Quick Part Gallery

4. Navigate to **Insert | Explore Quick Parts**, then click to select **Save Selection to Quick Part Gallery...**.

5. Type a name for the Quick Part into the **Name:** area. For this example, we have typed `Closing`.

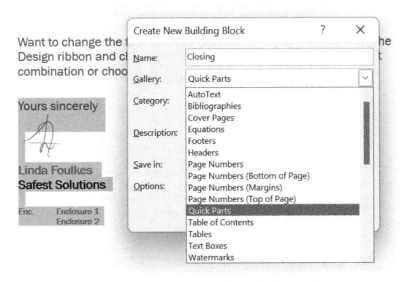

Figure 4.35 – Create New Building Block dialog box

6. Select the **Gallery:** option you wish to store the Quick Part in. If you leave the default option as **Quick Parts**, the closing will appear directly under the **Explore Quick Parts** dropdown for easy access.

7. If you wish to create a category directly under the **Explore Quick Parts** dropdown, type the name of the category you wish to create. Let's use `Closing` as our category here. The default category the entry is saved to is **General**.

8. Add a description if required.

9. The **Save in:** options are important – make sure to choose the **Normal** option from the drop-down list if you would like all new documents to contain the Quick Part you have created.

10. Use the **Options:** drop-down list to specify how you would like the Quick Part to appear. You can choose from the following:

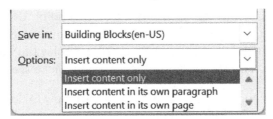

Figure 4.36 – Options to insert content when adding Quick Parts to documents

11. Click on the **OK** button to add the entry to the Quick Part gallery.

12. The entry now appears in the **Explore Quick Parts** drop-down list.

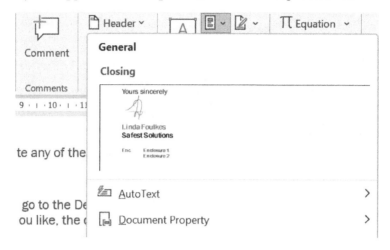

Figure 4.37 – Quick Part added to the Closing category

Now that you know how to add a Quick Part, let's see how we reuse the Quick Part in a document.

Generating Quick Parts

Quick Parts can be generated by clicking on the Quick Part name in the gallery or using the keyboard:

1. Open a new document.

2. Type the name of the Quick Part. In this case, Closing.

3. Press the *F3* keyboard key to generate the Quick Part. Note that if you are working on a laptop, you may need to press the *FN + F3* keys.

4. The entry appears in the document at the insertion point. Use the **Insert | Explore Quick Parts** menu should you wish to have control over where the entry is placed. Locate the entry, then right-click on the entry to display the various insertion options available. Visit the screenshot in the next topic to see the available options.

We can edit Quick Part entries at any time. We will learn how to do this in the next topic.

Editing Quick Part entries

After creating the Quick Part entry, we may need to amend or move the Quick Part to a different gallery:

1. Click **Insert | Explore Quick Parts**.

2. Locate the entry to edit, then right-click on the entry.

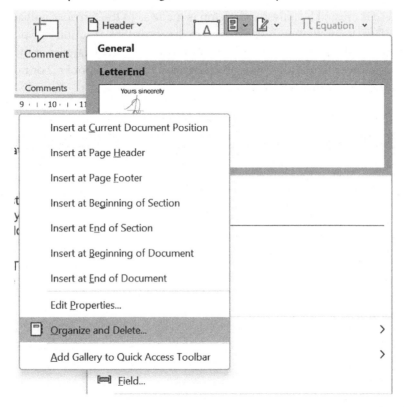

Figure 4.38 – Right-click options in order to edit a Quick Part entry

3. Click on the **Edit Properties…** option to make changes to the category or gallery in which the entry resides, or use the **Organize and Delete…** option to remove the entry altogether.

You are now able to create, edit, and generate a Quick Part entry. The next topic will introduce you to macros.

Creating macros

As mentioned in a previous topic, we can automate document processes using macros. Macros are normally created to automate Microsoft Excel but can be just as effective in other applications. It is always important to note that macros can contain viruses if sourcing them online. Macros that you create are not harmful, as you will understand the purpose and nature of the macro you generate.

Before a macro is created by a user, a decision is made as to the purpose and actions the macro will perform. Remember, macros are the recording of actions we perform by clicking, typing, and formatting. We will create a macro in later chapters of this book, as macros are used more frequently when working with Excel workbooks. For now, let's run through the steps to create a simple macro:

1. To begin recording, click on the **Macro** button on the Word status bar:

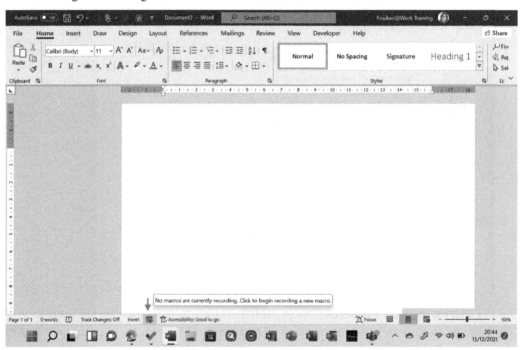

Figure 4.39 – Macro recording button on the status bar

2. Macros can also be recorded and edited by clicking on **Developer | Record Macro**:

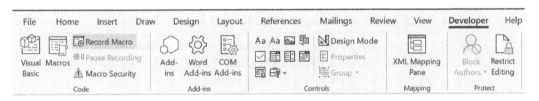

Figure 4.40 – Developer tab showing the Record Macro option

3. The **Record Macro** dialog box will populate. Enter the name of the macro you wish to create into the **Macro name:** area provided. We will use SSMac as the name in this case.

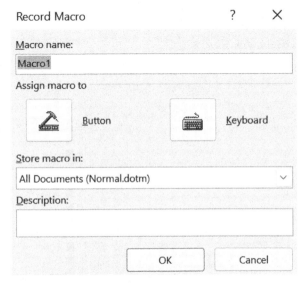

Figure 4.41 – The Record Macro dialog box

4. Under the **Store macro in:** drop-down list, select whether to store the macro in the current document only or make it available to all documents. For this example, we will leave the default selected.

5. Use the **Description:** area to provide any details to others having access to the macro. This will help them understand what the purpose of the macro is.

6. Click on the **Button** option under the **Assign macro to** heading. This will populate the **Options** dialog box so that we can assign the macro to a button. We can also assign the macro to a keyboard shortcut if required.

7. Click on the **Customize Ribbon** category to the left.

8. Locate the **Choose commands from:** heading, then select **Macros** from the drop-down list. Click to select **Normal.NewMacros.SSMac**. Make sure that you click on the **Help** tab (the last tab on the right-hand side of the dialog box).

9. Select the **New Tab** button. Click **Rename…** to rename the tab. For this example, we will use Automation as the tab name.

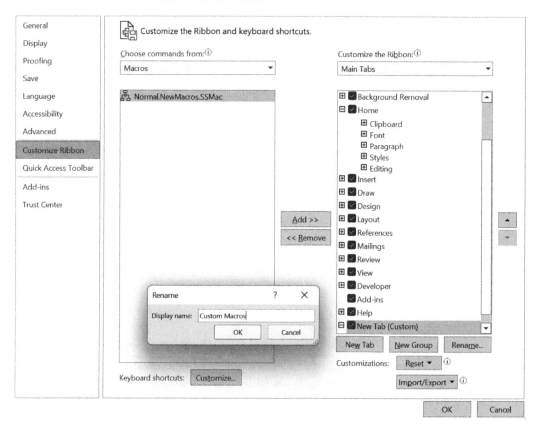

Figure 4.42 – Word Options dialog box

10. Make sure that you have clicked on the **Automation** tab, then choose the **New Group** button to add a new group.

11. Select the **New Group (Custom)** button to add a group named Branding so that we can assign the macro to this group.

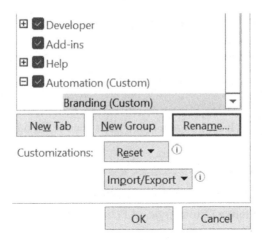

Figure 4.43 – Options dialog box showing the Automation and Branding (custom) group

12. Select the **Normal.NewMacros.SSMac** macro, then click on the **Add >>** button to assign the button to the Branding group.

13. Click on the **Rename…** button, then select a symbol as the macro button, and then type the text Format Doc into the **Display name:** field.

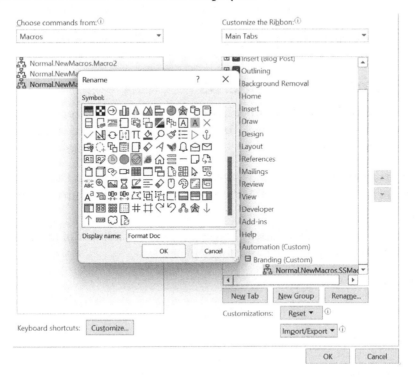

Figure 4.44 – Screenshot detailing the renaming of the macro

14. Click on the **OK** button to start recording. There will now be a tape recorder icon on your mouse pointer – this indicates that you are in the record mode. Note that every keystroke you perform will be recorded as part of the macro sequence.

15. We will now format the document as usual. The actions we need to perform for the macro are as follows:

   A.   Insert a **Facet (Even)** page header, then change **Design | Colors** to **Blue Green**.

   B.   Insert a **Filigree** footer.

   C.   Change the page layout vertical alignment to **Center**.

   D.   Insert the **Intense Quote** style and change the font size to **20**. Type the text `Safest Sol Report`.

   E.   Add any other formatting as desired.

16. Once the recording process is complete, double-click on the macro button on the status bar to stop the macro recording.

It is possible to rename and assign macros to the **Quick Access Toolbar** (QAT) in addition to tabs along the ribbon. We can record the macro first, then assign the macro for quick access, or follow the steps in the previous example to assign the macro to a group prior to creating the recording. In the next topic, we will learn how to run and edit macros.

Running and editing macros

We can run macros from the **Developer** tab, the QAT, a custom tab, or a keyboard shortcut. In the previous topic, we recorded the macro, then assigned the macro as a button on the **Automation** tab.

1. Visit the **Automation** tab along the Word ribbon. The **Format Doc** macro is located in the **Branding** group. Click on the **Format Doc** symbol to run the macro in the current document.

2. To edit macros, visit **Developer | Macros**. There are a number of features here to explore, which are outlined in the following table:

Feature	Explanation
Run	This feature will play the recorded steps of the selected macro back to you.
Delete	Click on the macro to delete, then press the **Delete** button to completely remove the macro from Microsoft Word 2021.
Create	This option is the same as clicking **Developer | Record Macro**.
Organizer…	Visit this option to move or copy **Macro Project Items** (macros) from the current document into another document, as well as set the location for the macro.
Edit	Opens **Microsoft Office Visual Basic Editor** in which you can edit the currently selected macro code or create a new macro based on VBA.
Step Into	This feature runs you through the macro in VBA mode step by step. Often used to troubleshoot macros.

Table 4.1 – Explanation of the options within the macro dialog box

3. You may also want to visit **Developer \| Macro Security** to manage whether macros are enabled or disabled and set trust options.

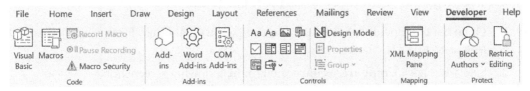

Figure 4.45 – Macro security settings on the Developer tab

As mentioned in a previous topic, macros are more widely used for automation in spreadsheets. I hope that this introduction to macros is enough to get you thinking about what you can achieve in order to automate your Word documents. As an example, you could record an entire letterhead or specific table format, then run the macro whenever you need to use the same format for other documents.

When working with long documents, you may have saved various versions or more than one team could have worked on the same document independently. The **Compare** and **Combine** feature in Word could come in handy. Although this feature was explained in our previous edition book, we will recap this here as it is a very useful tool.

Comparing and combining documents

In this topic, you will learn how to compare different versions of a document and combine revisions from multiple authors.

If two reviewers receive the exact copy of a document with changes made to both, the documents can be compared using the **Compare Documents** utility. This feature takes two documents that have gone through the editing process and combines only what has changed between them into a new third document. The two original documents are not changed.

> **Note**
> Please note that if you are working with edited documents from more than two reviewers, then **Combine revisions from multiple authors into a single document** is the option to use.

In the next steps, we will learn how to Compare documents.

1. Open the first document to be used to compare with another. Here, we will open `Resume1Furkidds.docx`.

2. Select **Review | Compare**, as illustrated in the following screenshot:

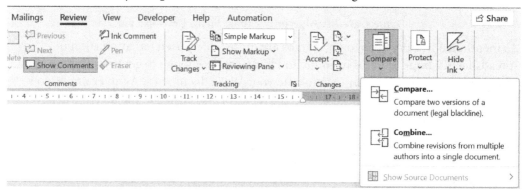

Figure 4.46 – The Compare and Combine features in Word 2021

3. You will be offered the following two options:

    - **Compare two versions of a document (legal blackline).**

    - **Combine revisions from multiple authors into a single document.**

4. Click **Compare…**.

5. The **Compare Documents** dialog box will present itself where you would choose two documents to compare, as illustrated in the following screenshot:

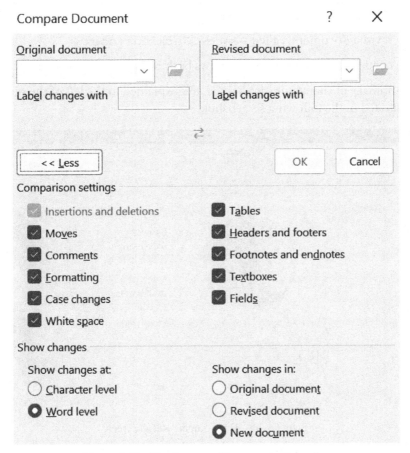

Figure 4.47 – The Compare Documents dialog box

6. Choose the original document from the drop-down list or browse to locate it on your computer, and click on the revised document from the drop-down list or browse to locate it on your computer.

7. There are more settings that can be changed by using the **More** >> icon in the dialog box and selecting desired options, which are illustrated in the previous screenshot.

8. By default, the changes will appear in a new document (a third document).

9. Click on **OK** to compare the documents.

10. Your Word screen will now change to a new document called `Compare Result 4`. The screen is split into four parts, as follows:

- The original document, called `Resume1Furkidds.docx`.

- The revised document, called `Resume2Furkidds.docx`.

- The compared document, which shows both revisions in the center.

- A summary of changes is highlighted and explained to the left of the screen, as illustrated in the following screenshot:

Figure 4.48 – The Compare Result screen

11. The next step is to accept or reject the changes in the compared document, to reach a combined final document, as illustrated in the next screenshot. Right-click on the changes highlighted in the compared document and decide whether to reject or accept them, or go to the ribbon and locate the **Accept Insertion** and **Reject Insertion** options.

> **Note**
>
> All the text highlighted by a strikethrough indicates removed text, and underlined text is anything that is added in its place.

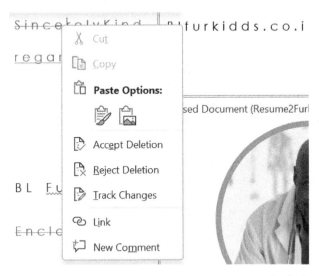

Figure 4.49 – Accept and Reject Deletion options on the right-click menu

12. Once the revisions are complete, you will notice the **Revisions** pane will display **0 revisions**, as illustrated in the following screenshot:

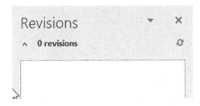

Figure 4.50 – Revisions pane from the left-hand side of the Word screen

13. Save the compared document as `ResumeFinal.docx`, and close all other windows to see the final document.

You have now learned how to compare two documents and combine the changes into one document.

Summary

In this chapter, you have learned how to create professional documents using Word 2021. Now that you have a firm grasp of Word 2021 to customize page layouts and work with forms, you can create stunning professional documents with ease. You have mastered the task of comparing different versions of documents, thereby combining revisions as well as automating documents using macros.

In the next chapter, we will recap the skills to present using the PowerPoint interface and learn new features of the 2021 version. You will learn how to set application options, set up slides, and work with files and print options, and you will be confident navigating around the interface.

Part 2: Learning PowerPoint 2021

PowerPoint 2021, being part of the latest desktop productivity suite, provides a rich set of tools for creating presentations. During this part of the book, we will introduce you to this presentation software, identifying its new features and demonstrating how to use it to create and work with attractive, highly professional presentations. These chapters cover everything you need to know to start using PowerPoint 2021 productively, in the workplace, at home, and for certification purposes.

This part contains the following chapters:

- *Chapter 5, The PowerPoint Interface and Presentation Options*
- *Chapter 6, Formatting Slides, Charts, and Graphic Elements*
- *Chapter 7, Photo Albums, Sections, and Show Tools*
- *Chapter 8, Mastering Best Practices with Presentations*

5

The PowerPoint Interface and Presentation Options

In this chapter, you will be introduced to some new features for PowerPoint 2021, such as **Presenter Coach (Speaker Coach)**, **Stock Images**, **Transparency**, **Link to this Slide**, **Ink Replay**, and **Immersive Reader**. We will also recap skills to personalize and navigate the interface to perform tasks, such as creating, saving, printing, and viewing presentations. Many of these skills were introduced in this book's previous edition, *Learn Microsoft Office 2019*.

The following topics are covered in this chapter:

- An introduction and new features
- Saving and collaborating on presentations
- Setting print options and layouts
- Using the view and zoom options

Technical requirements

You should understand basic presentation terminologies such as slides, presentation, animation, and transitions. The examples used in this chapter are accessible from GitHub: `https://github.com/PacktPublishing/Learn-Microsoft-Office-2021-Second-Edition`.

An introduction and new features

PowerPoint offers the user various slide views and printed formats (such as overhead slides, speaker notes, audience handouts, or outlines). The user makes the presentation professional, visually attractive, and understandable by adding elements such as special effects, sound, animation, and transitional effects to view on the screen. Slides are the separate pages of the presentation to which elements such as graphs, tables, shapes, WordArt, SmartArt, clip art, and other objects are added.

We will not cover all the interface skills here, as these were covered in this book's previous edition, *Learn Microsoft Office 2019*. The interface compared to Office 2019 is very similar but considerably clearer in terms of icon sketching across the Office 2021 platform, with rounder windows for dialog boxes and ribbon corners.

There are a few new enhancements in PowerPoint 2021, which we will address practically throughout this part of the book, but we will highlight the following as an introduction.

Let's look at the new features that will broaden our picture option skills in Office 2021.

Stock Images

This new feature is explained thoroughly in the Word chapters of this book and is available throughout the Office 2021 platform. **Stock Images** is an addition to the **Insert | Pictures** menu. **Stock Images** contains a library of images, including **Icons**, **Stickers**, **Videos**, **Illustrations**, and **Cutout People**. Content is updated regularly, so you may find new images appear when running a software update and some content that you were previously familiar with is no longer available:

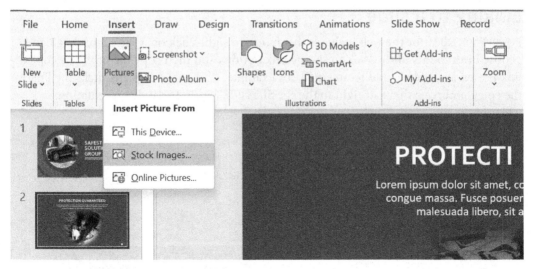

Figure 5.1 – The new Stock Images feature in Office 2021

Once a picture is inserted onto a slide, you may want to set some options. Let's look at the new **Transparency** tool.

Transparency

Previously, we could set transparency options using the **Picture Format** pane. In the latest version, there is a new **Transparency** button located on the **Picture Format** ribbon:

Figure 5.2 – The Transparency option located on the Picture Format ribbon

Move the mouse pointer along the transparency options in the drop-down list to set the desired look for the picture.

The next new feature is available in the latest version of Office 365.

Linking to a slide

PowerPoint 2021 for the web includes the option to right-click on a slide thumbnail and choose **Link to this Slide**. We can set the link options and then copy the link. The copied link is then available to add to an email, for example. When the recipient clicks the link in the email, it directs them straight to the specific slide within the slide presentation:

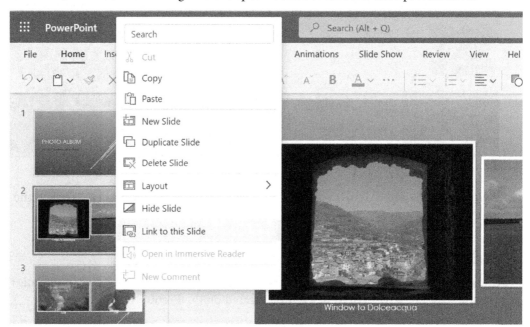

Figure 5.3 – The new Link to this Slide feature in PowerPoint for the web

Recording using Ink Replay

In Office 2021, we now have the ability to record inking. The **Ink Replay** feature is available in Word, Excel, and PowerPoint. Make shapes and text come to life during a presentation using this feature. It records keystrokes when using the drawing tools from the **Draw** tab as a movie in PowerPoint:

1. Open the presentation named Inking.pptx.

2. Click the **Draw** tab along the ribbon to access the inking tools.

3. At the end of the **Draw** tab, you will notice the **Ink Replay** feature.

4. To use inking, simply select one of the tools from the **Drawing Tools** group, and then draw on the slide background using the mouse pointer. Click the **Ink Replay** button to play back the inking on the slide.

5. If you have a touch device or pen, press the **Draw with Touch** button to activate it, and then choose a color from the panel. Don't forget to deselect this option when you need to use the keyboard again.

6. When inking in PowerPoint, you will find another button on the **Draw** tab. This button is named **Ruler**. It is a great addition to the draw tools, as it gives the user the ability to draw straight lines at any angle using any medium selected from the **Drawing Tools** group. Give it a go!

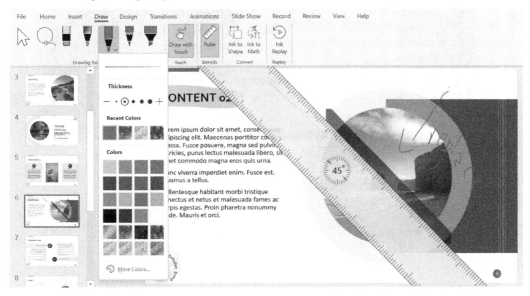

Figure 5.4 – The Draw tab options, detailing the Ruler and Ink Replay tools on the slide

Remember to turn **Ruler** off when you are done, as it will appear on each slide in the presentation and you may find it difficult to amend other slides. The next new feature is Immersive Reader.

Immersive Reader

Immersive Reader is a tool that is now included in Office 2021 for the desktop and the web. Although this was discussed in previous chapters, it is very useful when reading slides containing text, making it more accessible and legible to those who struggle with dyslexia, **Attention Deficit Hyperactivity Disorder** (**ADHD**), or vision impairments, along with those who speak a different language, or need more focus on lines when reading:

1. Open a presentation. For this example, we will open the `Safest Solution-Align.pptx` presentation using PowerPoint 2021 for the web.

2. Select the text on the second slide, and then right-click.

3.   Click on **Open in Immersive Reader**:

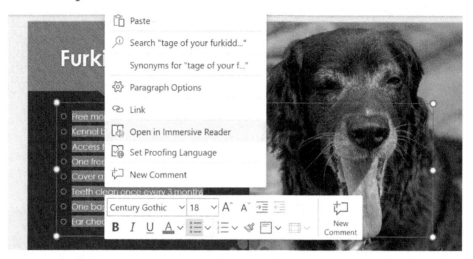

Figure 5.5 – The Open in Immersive Reader feature in PowerPoint 2021 for the web

4.   You are now able to take advantage of a number of features on this screen:

Figure 5.6 – The Immersive Reader screen

I.   Click the **Play** button at the bottom of the screen to hear each bullet point read to you on the slide.

II.   Click the **Voice Settings** button to customize **Voice Speed** and **Voice Selection**.

III.   **Text Preferences**, **Grammar Options**, and **Reading Preferences** are located at the top right of the **Immersive Reader** screen. Here, you will find options to change text size, increase spacing, change fonts, and set theme colors. You are also able to add syllables and highlight parts of speech in different colors. This is great for educational use! The line focus option allows you to specify the number of lines to display on screen (one line, three lines, or five lines at a time):

Figure 5.7 – The text, grammar, and reading settings on the Immersive Reader screen

5.   To exit Immersive Reader, simply click the exit arrow at the top left of the screen to return to the presentation.

6.   Immersive Reader is also available in the speaker notes area of a presentation. Simply select the speaker note text, and then right-click to select **Open in Immersive Reader**.

Using Presenter Coach (Speaker Coach)

Presenter Coach, now updated to **Speaker Coach**, is a new feature available in the desktop, iPad, and web versions of Office 2021. Once you have finalized a presentation, you can use Speaker Coach to check through it and provide feedback. This feature i-*, *Sections, and Show Tools*, of this book.

These are just some of the stunning new features available in the PowerPoint 2021 application. In the following sections, we will revisit some features detailing updates to Office 2021.

Using presentation templates

As explained in our previous edition, *Learn Microsoft Office 2019*, a template is a presentation with a predefined look and contains default text, layouts, and even animations. Templates are often used as a basis for presentations and are often a quick way to get things done! Office 2021 templates contain an even better set of designs.

To use a presentation template to create a new presentation, follow these steps:

1. Click on the **File** tab to access the recently used templates or create a new blank presentation. Click on **More themes** to visit the template area, where you can search for more templates. Note that clicking on **File | New** will achieve the same result:

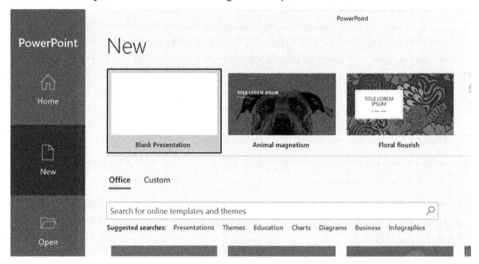

Figure 5.8 – Clicking on the File tab will grant access to the recently used templates

2. Once you have decided on a template, click on the template to view the details about it. You are able to scroll through all the templates using this method as a preview, using the arrow to the right of the preview.

3. Click on **Create** to open the template in PowerPoint and add content.

Setting up slides and working with files

In this section, you will master slide size and orientation options, use compatibility mode, add tags to a presentation, embed fonts so that you do not lose formats when presenting on different devices, and learn how to save a presentation in the required format.

Setting slide size

There are a number of different slide sizes available, depending on your design output. Widescreen (16:9) is commonly the default. To set the slide size, proceed as follows:

1. Click on **Design | Slide Size**.

2. You will be presented with two default slide sizes, **Standard** and **Widescreen**, as illustrated in the following screenshot:

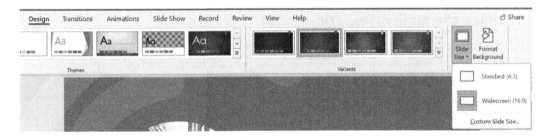

Figure 5.9 – Setting the slide size

3. Click on **Custom Slide Size...**, and once the dialog box has opened, choose a slide size from the **Slides sized for:** drop-down list. Some options will present further options, where you can maximize the size of the content or fit the content.

4. You can select **Custom** if you wish to enter your own measurements in terms of the width and height of the slides in the presentation, as illustrated in the following screenshot:

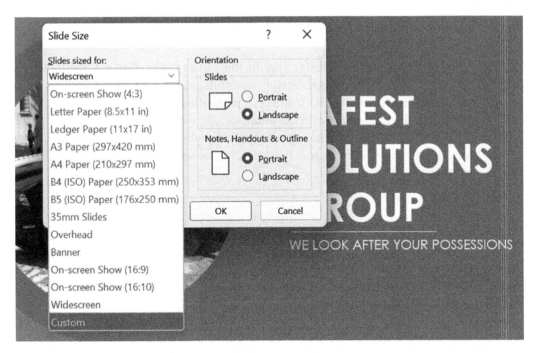

Figure 5.10 – The slide sizes available in PowerPoint 2021

We will now learn how to change the slide orientation in the next topic.

Changing the slide orientation

Slide layouts are landscape by default in PowerPoint and are always the same throughout the presentation. You cannot have some slides in portrait format and others in landscape format. When the orientation is changed, the entire presentation will update to the new orientation.

To change the slide orientation, click on **Design | Slide Size | Custom Slide Size…**, and then select either **Portrait** or **Landscape** from the right-hand side of the dialog box. You will be prompted to select a scaling option; either maximize the size of the content or scale down the content by selecting **Ensure Fit**. Sometimes, the content (especially objects) may shift around, so it may be necessary to reposition objects or try switching between the **Maximize** and **Ensure Fit** orientations.

Let's learn how to embed fonts in a presentation to ensure that when others work on the presentation, it will preserve all fonts, even if the destination computer does not have the fonts available.

Embedding fonts

When customizing presentations, adding specific fonts to a presentation aids the look of the design and also enhances diagrams and custom drawings. The only problem is that when sharing the presentation with others or presenting it at a specific location, you might find that the fonts are converted automatically, which will drastically change your presentation design. This is because fonts applied to the presentation before sharing are not the default application fonts and, therefore, not necessarily available at another location or computer.

Let's fix this, as follows:

1. Click on the **File | Save As...** option.
2. Navigate to the location where you wish to save the presentation. Click on **Browse** to populate the **Save As** dialog box. Look for the **Tools** option at the bottom of the dialog box. Choose **Save Options...** from the **Tools** drop-down list. The **PowerPoint Options** dialog box will populate. You will notice that the **Save** option is highlighted, and options related to **Save** are presented on the right-hand side of the dialog box.

3. Navigate to **Preserve fidelity when sharing this presentation**.

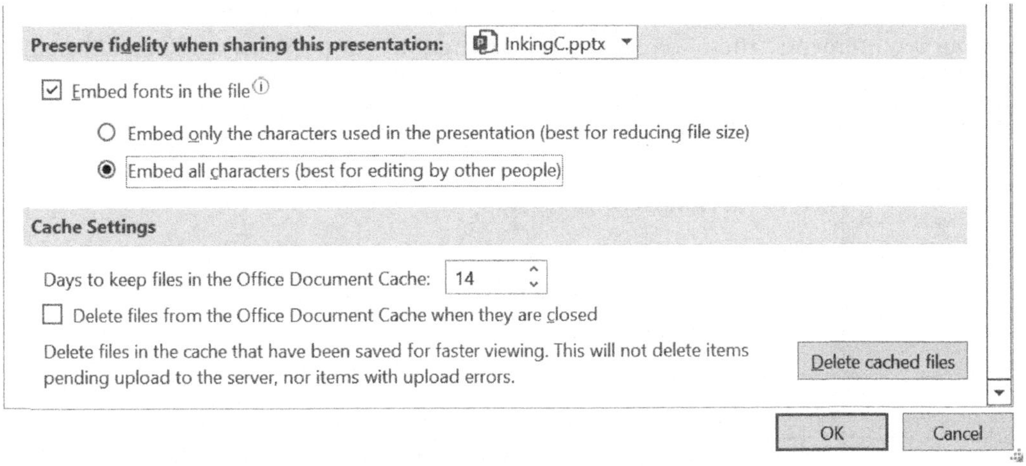

Figure 5.11 – Preserving fidelity when sharing presentations

4. Click the checkbox to the left of **Embed fonts in the file**.

5. Then, choose **Embed only the characters used in the presentation** or **Embed all characters**.

6. Click **OK** to commit the change. Save the presentation, and then share it with others.

We have learned how to preserve fonts when sharing presentations with others; now, let's learn how to collaborate in PowerPoint.

Saving and collaborating presentations

We will now look at the different ways in which we can save PowerPoint 2021 presentations, such as saving the presentation slides as separate images and saving the presentation in **Portable Document File (PDF)** format.

Saving presentations in different formats

In the following table, we will list the various methods to save presentations, depending on your requirements. These were discussed at length in our previous edition and listed here for reference:

Option	Explanation and method
Saving presentation slides as pictures	To save each slide separately as a picture from a completed presentation, do the following: Click on **File** | **Save As…** | **Save as Type:**. Choose one of the following: • **Graphics Interchange Format (GIF)** • **Portable Network Graphic (PNG)** Check the location and filename, and then click on **Save**. Choose whether to save all or just the current slide.
Save as a PDF	To save presentations in a smaller file size and prohibit editing of presentations, save the presentation as a PDF. This ensures that the presentation is viewable and shareable but not editable: Click on **File** | **Export** | **Create a PDF/XPS document** or select **File** | **Save As…** | **Save as Type:** | **PDF (*.pdf)**.
Save as a template	Create and format a presentation, and then save the presentation as a template so that you can create new presentations from it: Click on **File** | **Save As…** | **Save as Type:**. Choose **PowerPoint Template (*.potx)**. If you would like the presentation template to be available in the Custom Office Templates folder and accessible through the **File** | **New…** templates option, then saving it in the correct location is very important. Once you click **PowerPoint Template (*.potx)**, PowerPoint automatically changes the location to the default Custom Office Templates folder. This will ensure that the template is available when clicking on the **File** tab and selecting the **New** option.
Save as an outline	Saving as an outline in **Outline/RTF** (.rtf) removes all formatting and leaves only the text in the slide presentation. Follow the same steps as in the preceding section to save a presentation in another format, but choose the **Outline/RTF (*.rtf)** option instead.
Save as a show	This option exports your presentation so that it opens in slideshow view, rather than in normal view: Click on **File** | **Export** | **Change File Type** | **PowerPoint Show (*.ppsx)**.

Table 1.1 – Saving presentations in different file formats

When we save documents to the cloud, we are now able to co-author in real-time. This means that no matter where the collaborators are located or accessed (the desktop, iPad, or web version of Office 2021), everyone can see amendments as they occur. Let's learn more about this new feature in the next topic.

Collaborating on presentations

Once a presentation is saved to OneDrive (or SharePoint), we can work together with others in real time (co-authoring). This feature is available in Word, PowerPoint, and Excel 2021:

1. Open the presentation you wish to share with other users. For this example, we will use the presentation named `Collaboration.pptx`.

2. To make this presentation available in real time, ensure that it is saved to the cloud (OneDrive or SharePoint would be the Office 2021 choice of location).

3. Click the **Share** button at the top-right corner of the presentation ribbon:

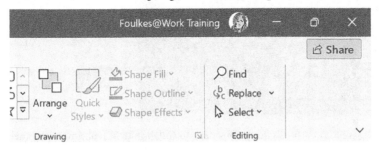

Figure 5.12 – Use the Share button along the ribbon to collaborate in real time

4. I will invite Cory Day to collaborate with me on the presentation. Type the email address or addresses into the area provided under the **Invite people** heading. If you have an individual as a contact, the email address will automatically populate in the field for selection:

Figure 5.13 – Add the email addresses of those you wish to collaborate with

5. Once you have added the collaborators, choose the relevant privilege, if required. If you need the recipient to make amends, then the **Can edit** option needs to be selected.

6. Provide a message, if required, and then click the **Share** button once again to complete the process:

Figure 5.14 – The Share options pane to collaborate in real time with others

7. Cory will now receive an email, inviting him to edit the presentation. Cory will select **Open** in the email to start collaborating in real time:

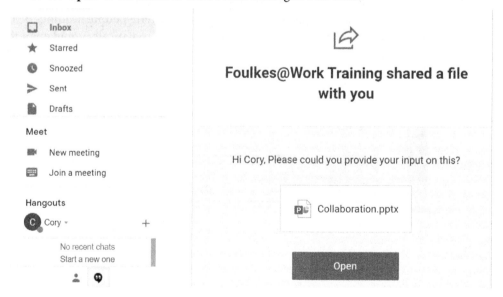

Figure 5.15 – The collaborator receives an email invitation

8. When Cory edits the presentation, **Editing** will display in red under each collaborator on the **Share** pane:

Figure 5.16 – Editing will display under the collaborator name in the Share pane when amending the presentation

9. Press the **Save** button on the QAT to refresh and display any amends from co-authors.

In the next topic, you will learn how to set print options and layouts, change settings, and preview presentations.

Setting print options and layouts

Although it is not often that you would want to print an entire presentation, there may be a need to print handouts for an audience to refer to while you are going through an onscreen presentation.

Adjusting print settings

Let's have a look at the presentation print and slide options available in PowerPoint 2021, as follows:

1. Open the `City Berlin Design.pptx` presentation to follow along. To access the print settings, click on the **File** tab to access the backstage view and select **Print** from the menu.

2. Under the **Printer** heading, click to choose a printer from the drop-down list provided:

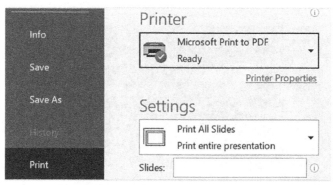

5.17 – The Printer drop-down list and Printer Properties option

Printer Properties is accessible just underneath the **Printer** list, and options therein will differ, depending on the printer type selected. In the list, you can select to print to a PDF, select a physical printer to produce output, or send the presentation to OneNote:

Figure 5.18 – Click on File | Print to see a list of the printers available

3. Just to the right of the **Print** icon, you will notice the **Copies:** spin button, which allows the user to specify the number of sets of slides to print.

4. Often, you will use the **Collate** option with the **Copies:** option. If printing multiple copies of the same presentation, you might want to collate them so that the printout is in sets or prints the number of copies of *slide 1*, then the number of copies of *slide 2*, and so on. This option is illustrated in the following screenshot:

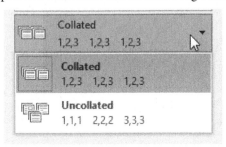

Figure 5.19 – Collate options

5. From the **Settings** option, you can choose the following printing options. The default is set to the **Print All Slides** option for the presentation, as illustrated in the following screenshot:

Figure 5.20 – Select the relevant option to print slides

If you click on the **Full Page Slides** option, you get will access to other options, allowing the printing of **Notes Pages**, **Outline**, and **Handouts**. The **Handouts** option offers many methods of placing slides onto a page. At the bottom of the list, you will find options to add a frame around each slide, scale the slides to fit the paper, print in high quality, print comments, or print ink drawings, as illustrated in the following screenshot:

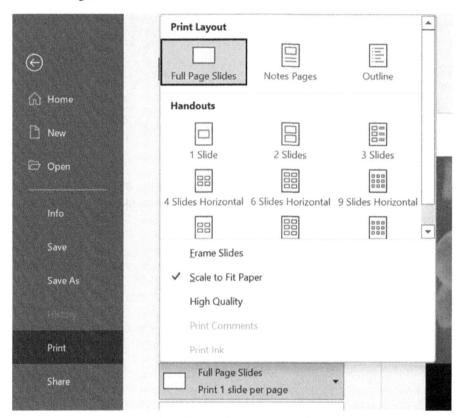

Figure 5.21 – The Full Page Slides option on the Print menu

6. The **Print on Both Sides** option is not available by default in later versions of Office 2021. Use **Control Panel** to navigate to the relevant printer settings, and ensure that back-to-back or duplex printing is installed. Once this is complete, the option will appear in PowerPoint when selecting the relevant printer from the **Printer** list. You may also need to visit the **Printer Settings** option to manually select the print duplex option, but this would depend on the type of printer installed:

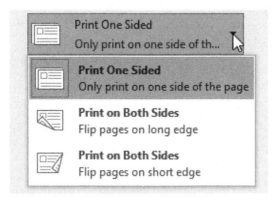

Figure 5.22 – The duplex printing option

7. To print the slides in **Grayscale**, click to choose the **Color** drop-down list, as illustrated in the following screenshot:

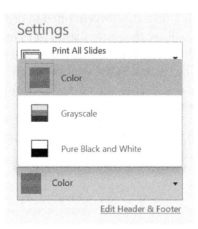

Figure 5.23 – The print in color or grayscale options

8. Click on the **Edit Header and Footer** option to make the final changes, such as including a slide number or custom text in the footer before you print the presentation, as illustrated in the following screenshot:

Figure 5.24 – Customize the header or footer area of the slide by clicking on Edit Header & Footer

9. Click on **Apply** to add the changes to the current slide or **Apply to All** to add the changes to the entire presentation.

10. The slide presentation is automatically generated in preview mode when visiting the **File | Print** menu. You will see the presentation in **Print Preview** mode to the right and the options to the left. The first slide is enlarged to fill the landscape page with various options along the bottom of the window, from which you can customize the view and navigate from one slide to the next. Please note that you will not be able to see animations or transitions in this view.

As you are now a pro at setting print options, we will recap the view and zoom options that PowerPoint 2021 has to offer.

Using view and zoom options

By the end of this topic, you will understand the function of the various presentation views in PowerPoint 2021 and how to set up presentation zoom options, as well as how to use the **Window** tab to switch between multiple presentations.

Presentation views using the ribbon

There are five presentation views in PowerPoint 2021, as well as three master views. Two additional views are available. The first, called **Presenter View**, is located on the **Slide Show** tab. This view allows the presentation to be viewed on two monitors. The audience display will show the presentation without notes, while the speaker can enjoy having access to the slides and notes as well as other great features while presenting.

Setting up **Presenter View** is addressed under its own topic in this book and discussed in the Teams topic too. The other view is the **Slide Show** view, which is used to show the presentation to the audience. The **Slide Show** view takes up the whole screen, hiding the program tabs, ribbon, and menu. Use this view to see how your presentation will display to an audience when presenting.

Click on the **View** tab on the ribbon to access the **Presentation Views** group, as illustrated in the following screenshot:

Figure 5.25 – Presentation Views in PowerPoint 2021

We will now look at each of the views available:

- **Normal**: This allows the user to work on all features of the presentation in one place. This is the main view, where all editing and formatting takes place. It consists of the **Slide** pane and **Notes** pane (if active), as illustrated in the following screenshot:

Figure 5.26 – The Normal view

- **Outline View**: Use this view to paste a Word outline into a presentation with ease. It is also a really easy way to edit text on presentation slides, as illustrated in the following screenshot:

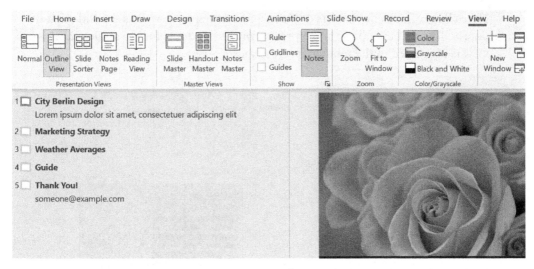

Figure 5.27 – Outline View

- **Slide Sorter**: This shows slides in the thumbnail view. In this view, you can copy and move slides with ease, reorder slides, and play animations and transitions per slide. A great feature in this view is the ability to organize your presentation into sections (categories), which will be discussed under a separate topic in this book. This view is illustrated in the following screenshot:

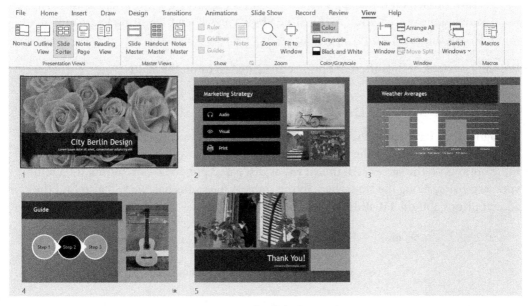

Figure 5.28 – The Slide Sorter view

- **Notes Page**: This view consists of **Notes** pane contents, as well as the slide that the notes refer to. These notes can be printed out as handouts for the audience. This view is illustrated in the following screenshot:

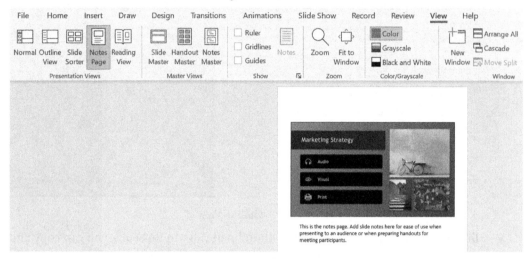

Figure 5.29 – The Notes Page view

- **Reading View**: This view is not used to present to an audience on a big screen but rather to someone viewing the presentation on a computer. When using **Reading View**, the screen will display as a window on the screen, with similar controls as viewing the presentation in the **Slide Show** view when presenting to an audience. To exit this view, simply press the *Esc* key on your keyboard.

We will now look at the different options presented to us on the status bar.

Using the status bar commands

Changing the presentation view is also possible via the view icons located on the status bar. This bar also contains the **Notes** and **Comments** buttons that allow you to display these options on the screen. All the views, as discussed previously, excluding the Outline view, are visible along the status bar. To the right of the status bar, we will also find the zoom buttons and the **Fit slide to current window** button:

Figure 5.30 – The status bar options

Setting presentation zoom options

The default slide zoom is set at 66% when opening or creating new presentations. To change this setting, use one of the following options:

1. Use the status bar zoom slider to increase or decrease the presentation slide size within the PowerPoint environment or, alternatively, click on the minus (-) and plus (+) signs to adjust, as illustrated in the following screenshot:

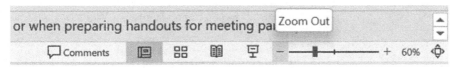

Figure 5.31 – The Zoom Out button

2. Click on the zoom percentage indicator on the status bar to access the zoom options, which you can adjust according to your requirements.

3. The **Percent** text area enables you to type a custom value to zoom, as illustrated in the following screenshot:

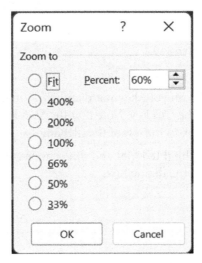

Figure 5.32 – The zoom percentage dialog box

Alternatively, use the **View** tab to access the **Zoom** group on the ribbon. Click on the **Zoom** icon to launch the **Zoom** dialog box.

4. You can also visit the **View** tab and select **Fit to Window** from the **Zoom** group, as illustrated in the following screenshot:

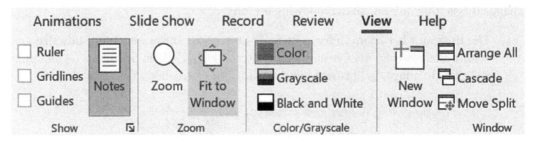

Figure 5.33 – The Fit to Window button on the View tab

You have learned to navigate and apply different view options in PowerPoint 2021. Let's now look at how to navigate between open presentations in the next topic.

Switching between multiple presentations

Navigating between presentations is achieved using more than one method. Let's have a look at these methods below:

1. Click to select **Open | Browse**.

2. Click to select the first presentation file.

3. Hold down the *Ctrl* key on your keyboard and click on the second file, then on the next, and then release the *Ctrl* key. Note that the *Shift* key also works here, as well as clicking on the checkbox to the left of the filename.

4. Right-click over the highlighted files and then choose **Open**, or click on the **Open** button at the bottom of the dialog box:

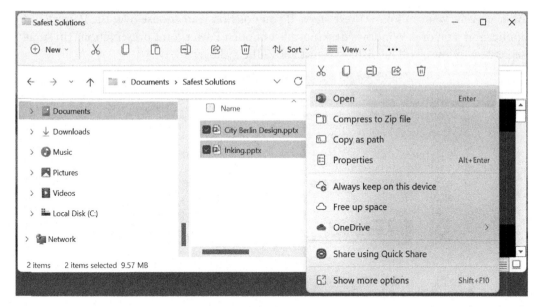

Figure 5.34 – Opening more than one file simultaneously

5. The selected files will open in Microsoft PowerPoint – one on top of another.

6. We can use the *Alt + Tab* shortcut keys to navigate from one open application to another on the desktop, or click on the **View** tab on the ribbon.

7. Navigate to the **Switch Windows** drop-down option and click on the arrow, as illustrated in the following screenshot:

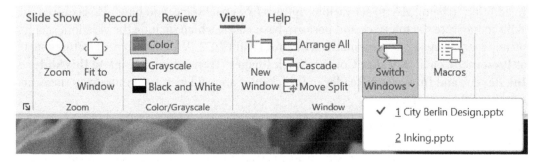

Figure 5.35 – The Switch Windows drop-down list

8. A list of open presentations will appear as a drop-down list.

9. Click on the presentation that you wish to make the active one.

Alternatively, you can follow these steps. If you position your mouse over the PowerPoint application icon on a Windows desktop, a list of open PowerPoint presentations (in small separate windows) will be displayed just above the taskbar.

Figure 5.36 – Open presentations on a Windows 11 desktop

Now that you have finished this chapter, you have the skills to personalize the PowerPoint 2021 backstage view and set various options.

Summary

In addition to being able to set various options from backstage, you have also acquired the skills to navigate the interface and perform basic tasks, which include the creation, saving, printing, and viewing of presentations in PowerPoint 2021. We covered new features such as **Presenter Coach (Speaker Coach)**, **Stock Images**, **Transparency**, **Link to this Slide**, **Ink Replay**, and **Immersive Reader** in this chapter and will visit even more over the next few PowerPoint chapters.

In the next chapter, we will use predefined options to give slides a particular look and feel. In addition to covering how to set up presentations, you will be able to order a sequence of slides, apply a presentation theme and slide layout, and reuse slides. You will also learn how to work with tables and charts that make data much easier to present and explain, adding to the impact of a presentation. We will also investigate the new drawing and Auto Fix features.

6

Formatting Slides, Charts, and Graphic Elements

In Microsoft PowerPoint 2021, you can easily add slides to a presentation and use the predefined options to give slides a particular *look and feel*. In this chapter, you'll learn how to set up a presentation, order a sequence of slides, apply a presentation theme and slide layout, and reuse slides.

Additionally, you will learn how to manipulate slide elements using the Auto Fix feature, insert an agenda, and work with charts to make data much easier to present and explain, thus adding to the impact of a presentation. We will also investigate the new drawing features, learn how to create and insert captions inside a video, and explore the various playback options for audio and video.

In this chapter, the following topics will be covered:

- Setting up slides and applying layouts
- Working with text, shapes, and objects
- Modifying charts
- Applying and modifying themes
- Inserting audio and video

Let's get started!

Technical requirements

In the previous edition of this book, you learned the necessary skills to manipulate your way around the PowerPoint environment. As this edition recaps some of these skills, you can treat these topics as a refresher that focuses on the new Office 2021 environment and the new features it has to offer.

The examples that will be used in this chapter can be accessed from GitHub at `https://github.com/PacktPublishing/Learn-Microsoft-Office-2021-Second-Edition`.

Setting up slides and applying layouts

In this section, you will learn how to add, remove, and duplicate slides, insert an outline, reuse saved slides, and apply layouts.

Adding new slides

To learn how to add new slides, follow these steps:

1. We will use the presentation named `City Berlin Design.pptx` for this example.
2. Position your mouse pointer in between two slides of the presentation:

Figure 6.1 – Position your mouse pointer between two slides and then press Enter on the keyboard

3. Press *Enter* on the keyboard to create a new slide. In this example, the new title and content slide type are inserted, by default, between *Slides 1 and 3*. If you wish to specify the slide layout before inserting the slide, click on **Insert | New Slide** from the **Slides** group. This will populate a list of available slide layouts to choose from:

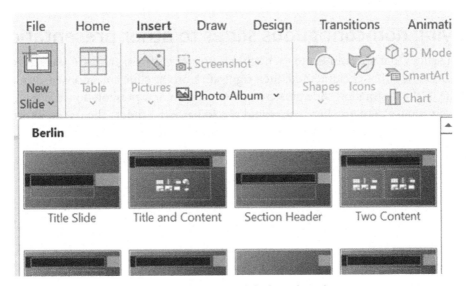

Figure 6.2 – The New Slide drop-down list

Now that you have the skills to insert new slides, we will learn how to duplicate slides.

Duplicating selected slides

The difference between duplicating slides and using *the copy command* is that the duplication method does not send the item into the clipboard memory. In comparison, the copy command does send the slide to the clipboard, ready to be inserted elsewhere. To learn how to duplicate selected slides, perform the following steps:

1. Select a slide from the left-hand side of the presentation to copy.

2. Navigate to **Home | New Slide | Duplicate Selected Slides** (at the bottom of the menu). An exact duplicate of the slide will appear.

3. Select a slide to duplicate. Then, right-click on the slide and choose **Duplicate** from the shortcut menu. Alternatively, use the *Ctrl + D* shortcut to duplicate a slide.

Deleting multiple slides simultaneously

To delete a single slide, simply select the slide and press the *Delete* key on the keyboard. To select slides in a presentation to delete, use your *Ctrl* key to select slides in the Slides Pane using the mouse pointer; alternatively, you can select slides that are non-contiguous. Press *Delete* on the keyboard to remove the selected slides.

If you delete some slides by mistake, you can bring them back by using the **Undo Delete Slide** (or pressing *Ctrl + Z*) icon from the Quick Access toolbar.

We can copy slides to other presentations, too. Let's visit this option in the next section.

Copying non-contiguous slides to other presentations

Copying slides that are not next to each other is possible by using *Ctrl + C*. Select the slides using the *Ctrl* + click method, then right-click on the slide and choose **Copy**. Navigate to the destination slide presentation or create a new presentation and then place your mouse pointer where you would like to paste the slides. The last action is to right-click and choose **Paste** to insert the slides into the new presentation.

In the next section, we will learn how to insert outlines from Word 2021 to PowerPoint 2021.

Inserting an outline

In this section, we will learn how to insert an outline from a previously typed Word document:

> **Note**
>
> It is not possible to insert images, shapes, or any artistic features in the **Outline** view.

1. Open the `Safest Solution-Benefits.pptx` presentation for this example.

2. Navigate to **Home | New Slide | Slides from Outline…**:

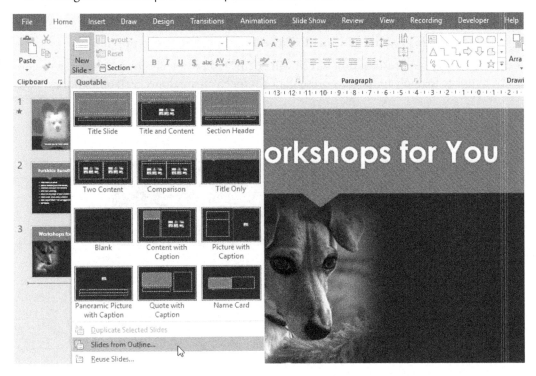

Figure 6.3 – Inserting slides from a Word outline

3. Browse to locate the outline (`Outline.docx`) to insert it into the presentation. The file extension can be `.rtf` (**Rich Text Format**), `.docx` (**Microsoft Word document**), or `.txt` (**text file format**).

4. Click on **Insert**.

5. The outline will be inserted into PowerPoint, thus splitting the information across multiple slides. Format the information as required.

6. In the next section, we will learn how to insert agendas into PowerPoint using the export method.

Inserting an agenda

1. In addition to inserting an outline into PowerPoint, Office 365 has the ability to export a Word document agenda into PowerPoint slides directly. Let's take a look at this wonderful feature. When performing this action, make sure that the files are saved to OneDrive.

2. For this example, we will use the Agenda SSG.docx file.

3. Click on **File** | **Export** | **Export to PowerPoint presentation (preview)**.

4. The **Export to presentation** screen will open. Here, you will browse to select a design template to apply to the new presentation. Once you are done, click on **Export**:

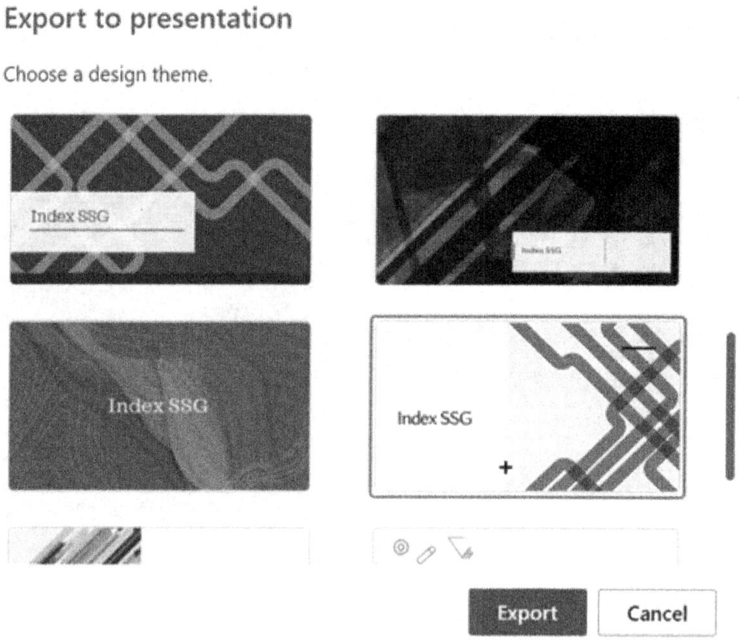

Figure 6.4 – Exporting to the presentation screen

5. The presentation will run through the steps automatically to create a presentation:

Exporting your document...

...summarizing your content

ⓘ Your text will be included in the presentation, support for images and tables
is coming soon!

Cancel

Figure 6.5 – Exporting to the presentation screen

6.   Click on **Open Presentation** to view the result:

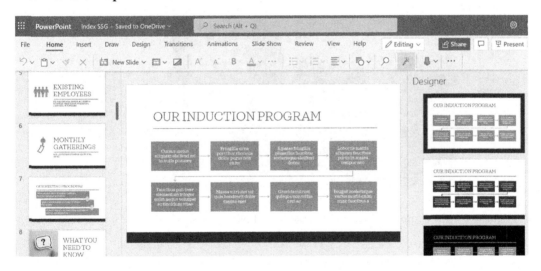

Figure 6.6 – The agenda as shown in PowerPoint

7.   This is a great way to quickly create a presentation with all of the text neatly
presented on individual slides. The presentation is automatically saved with the
same name as the Word document.

In the next section, we will learn how to use slides, including the theme (if required) from
an existing presentation in another presentation.

Reusing presentation slides

Using slides from an already created presentation saves a lot of time, especially if the presentation you are creating is going to consist of numerous slides that you can reuse from another presentation. Perform the following steps:

1. Open a new presentation, called `Safest Solution-Benefits.pptx`.

2. Go to **Home** | **New Slide** | **Reuse Slides…** (at the bottom of the menu).

3. A **Reuse Slides** pane will open on the right-hand side of the PowerPoint environment.

4. Click on the **Browse** button to access the folders on your computer.

5. Choose **Browse File…** to open another presentation in the **Reuse Slides** pane – to follow along with this example, use the `City Berlin Design.pptx` presentation. Once selected, the file will open on the right-hand side of the PowerPoint screen as a **Reuse Slides Task** pane:

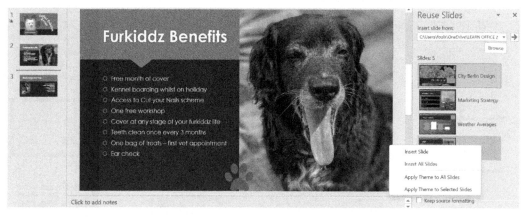

Figure 6.7 – The Reuse Slides pane on the right-hand side of the window, displaying the right-click options and Keep source formatting option

6. Before we insert a slide from the browsed presentation, we must click on a slide in the existing presentation to indicate where we would like to insert the new slide.

7. To insert a slide beneath the selected slide, click to select a slide from the **Reuse Slides** pane. The slide will be inserted into the existing presentation beneath the selected slide.

8. Notice that the inserted slide takes on the theme from the existing presentation. If you wish to keep the formatting of the selected slide and not merge it with the existing slide presentation theme, click on the **Keep source formatting** checkbox at the bottom of the **Reuse Slides** pane (refer to the previous screenshot).

With that, you have learned how to combine slides from other presentations into an existing or new presentation. Additionally, you have learned how to access the option to keep the formatting of the inserted slides as-is. Now, we will look at the different types of layouts available within PowerPoint 2021.

Applying slide layouts

A slide layout is a predefined slide that contains formatting options (such as fonts, paragraphs, styles, and more) and placeholders (these are the textboxes that you type text on a slide into) that are positioned for you on the slide by default. In addition, a slide layout could contain placeholders for images, charts, SmartArt, and header and footer placeholders. These layouts make it easier and faster to construct a presentation without the hassle of you having to build a blank slide from scratch. You can create custom layouts or choose from the 15 different slide layouts in PowerPoint 2021.

When creating a new presentation in PowerPoint, the first slide is based on the **Title Slide** layout. Every new slide that's inserted after that is based on the **Title and Content Slide** layout.

Changing slide layouts

Often, when you insert a slide, a certain layout is applied automatically. You can change the layout before you add content or after content is inserted into the slide. Additionally, the **Layout** option is very useful when copying slides from other presentations into a new or existing presentation, as it refreshes the layout and fixes any common slide design, background, or font issues.

To change a slide layout, click on the slide you wish to change the layout of in the presentation. Then, click on the **Home | Layout** icon. Choose the desired layout from the list provided.

Working with text, shapes, and objects

In our previous edition of this book, *Learn Microsoft Office 2019*, we learned the basic skills to copy, paste, and duplicate within a presentation. After working through this section, you will be able to copy, move, and paste text, insert and format lists, and add headers and footers to a presentation. Additionally, you will gain an understanding of how to apply and modify a theme.

Let's recap how to use lists in the next section.

Inserting and formatting lists

How you would like to insert and format lists on slides in PowerPoint is a personal preference. Either insert the text first and then apply the list or apply the list and then enter the text:

1. Open the presentation called `ProductGrpSSG.pptx`.

2. Locate the slide that contains the text you wish to apply a bullet or numbered list to. Then, select the text.

3. Choose your desired option from the **Paragraph** group by clicking on either the bullet icon or the numbers icon.

4. To change the bullet or number type, click on the drop-down arrow next to the bullet or numbering icon.

5. Select **Bullets and Numbering** from the bottom of the list.

6. A dialog box will open, offering various options that you can choose from to customize the numbered or bulleted list:

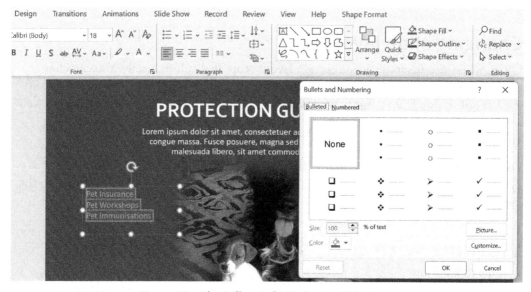

Figure 6.8 – The Bullets and Numbering dialog box

7. You can change the color of the bullet or the number using the **Color** fill bucket.

8. The **Customize...** button is also available if you need to browse for a different symbol from the huge range available.

9. Adjust the spin controls of the **% of text** area (**Size:**). If you are using symbols as a bullet, then this option works really well to maximize the symbol.

10. Change the bullet to a picture of your choice by clicking on the **Picture...** button and selecting a source in order to insert a bullet. Note that there is also a new **Stock Images** feature where you can access a huge range of exciting new graphics to use:

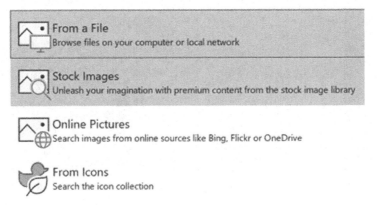

Figure 6.9 – The Insert Pictures dialog box showing new options that are available in Office 2021

11. Once you have selected a picture, it will appear as a bullet type in the **Bullets and Numbering** dialog box. Note that the numbering option works in the same way as the bullet icon.

12. If you wish to number items from a specific starting number point, use the **Start At:** position to control this.

13. To change the distance between the number or bullet and the text, first, select the text, then use the *indent markers* along the ribbon to increase (or decrease) the distance between the number and the text. If the ruler is not visible on the screen, click on **View | Ruler** to display it:

Figure 6.10 – Use the indent markers along the ribbon to increase the distance between the number and the text

With that, we have inserted bullet lists and numbered lists and learned how to customize them. Now, we will learn how to set up slide headers and footers.

Adding headers and footers to slides

As discussed in the previous edition book, the footer is the area at the bottom of the slide. It has been constructed by way of placeholders that contain information that's repeated on every slide in the presentation. The header or footer accepts information such as custom text, dates and times, and the slide number. Headers and footers can be applied to **Notes and Handouts**. The **Notes and Handouts** tab can be seen in the following screenshot, just on the right-hand side of the **Slide** tab:

1. Open an existing presentation. For this example, we will use the `Safest Solutions-Benefit.pptx` presentation.

2. Click on the **Insert** tab, and select **Header and Footer** from the **Text** group.

3. In the **Header and Footer** dialog box, select the option that best suits your presentation:

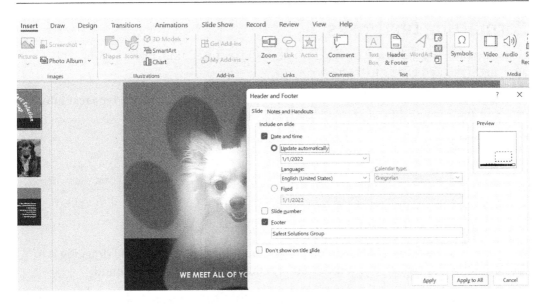

Figure 6.11 – The Header and Footer dialog box

4. Select the **Slide** tab at the top of the dialog box to view the options to include on the slides.

5. Click on the **Date and time** checkbox and choose whether to add a static fixed date or whether you want this to **Update automatically** (this option will update the date to the current date every time the presentation is opened).

6. You can include a **Slide number** setting and also a static **Footer** setting. This option is located just under the **Fixed** date option.

7. Sometimes, we might want to exclude a header from the title slide of the presentation. Select this option by clicking on the checkbox provided to activate it.

8. Please note that at the bottom of the dialog box, you can choose whether to **Apply** changes to the current slide or whether to choose **Apply to All** to commit the changes to the entire presentation. Also, note that there is no header section on the **Slides** tab.

9. The **Notes and Handouts** tab contains many of the same options as the **Slide** tab, but it includes a **Header** section so that you can create a static custom header for only setting notes and handouts.

Formatting textboxes

In this section, you will learn how to format textboxes by adding, manipulating, and applying styles and effects to them.

A **textbox** is a shape that is drawn onto a presentation slide that you can type text into. The **Text Box** feature is located in the **Insert** tab, under the **Text** group:

Figure 6.12 – Insert | Text Box

Draw a textbox onto the slide by holding down the left mouse button and dragging it to the desired size. Alternatively, you can simply click on the slide's background.

Once a textbox has been inserted into a slide, use the **Shape Format** tab to apply shapes, styles, text styles, text effects, and text alignment options:

Figure 6.13 – The Shape Format tab

Now that you are familiar with the Shape Format tab inside the ribbon, let's focus on some of the groups and features within the tab.

Applying a theme fill color

To learn how to apply a theme fill color, follow these steps:

1. Click on the textbox to apply a fill color.

2. Click on **Shape Format | Shape Fill** (or **Shape Outline**, **Shape Effects**, or **Shape Styles**) and select a theme from the drop-down list:

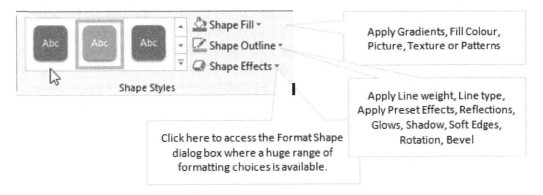

Figure 6.14 – The Shape Format tab to select a textbox shape style

3. Now, click on a color or visit the **More Fill Colors...** option to access the color wheel or the **Custom** color area to set a specific **Hue** color (this is a new feature within Office 2021).

4. To remove a fill color from a textbox, click on the shape and then select **No Fill** from the **Shape Fill** drop-down list.

> **Note**
>
> The **Eyedropper** tool is fantastic for picking up a color from a specific theme on a particular slide and using that specific color by applying it to the background of the textbox. To use the eyedropper, select the textbox, visit the **Shape Fill** drop-down list, and select **Eyedropper**. Use the dropper to click on a specific color outside of the textbox that you want to apply to the background of the textbox.

Gradients are a blend of color progressions that you can apply to objects within Office 2021. Applying a gradient uses the same method as previous versions of Office.

Applying a gradient

To apply a gradient, follow these steps:

1. Click on the shape to apply the gradient color.

2. Choose **Gradient** from the **Shape Fill** drop-down list.

3. Click on **More Gradients…** at the bottom of the submenu to access the **Format Shape** pane on the right-hand side of the PowerPoint window. Here, you can choose your own gradient blends using the **Gradient stops** setting to apply color progression or choose from **Preset gradients**. Simply click on a gradient stop, then choose a **Color** setting. Click on the color wheel to add further gradient stops or drag gradient stops off the color wheel to remove them:

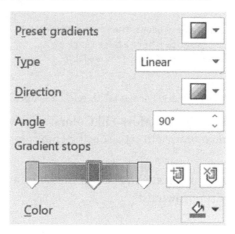

Figure 6.15 – The gradient color options in the Format Shape pane on the right-hand side of the window

4. Next, let's focus on adding a picture within a textbox.

Applying a picture

To apply a picture follow these steps:

1. Right-click on the textbox or the shape to apply a picture background.

2. From the shortcut menu, choose **Format Shape**.

3. The **Format Shape** pane will populate on the right-hand side of the slide. Select **Picture or texture Fill**.

4. Choose either **Insert…** or **Clipboard** from the **Picture source** heading. The **Insert Pictures** dialog box will appear with options to select from a range of sources if you chose the **Insert…** option. Note the **Stock Images** option here, as it is a new feature in Office 2021. This is discussed in detail in *Chapter 3, Styles, Referencing, and Media*.

5. When we insert a shape, a **Format Shape** tab appears at the top of the PowerPoint environment. The options are a little less complex in Office 2021 than in previous versions. When we insert pictures on a slide or inside a shape, we will notice another tab appear on the ribbon. This tab is named **Graphics Format** and is available so that you can format the picture within the shape:

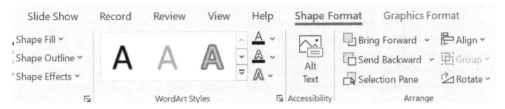

Figure 6.16 – The Graphics Format tab appears next to the Shape Format tab when inserting a picture

The new **Sketched** lines types are available in Office 2021. These line types are extremely beneficial for PowerPoint users, as you can now add that creative flair to your shapes.

Changing the outline color and weight

To change the outline color and weight, follow these steps:

1. Select the textbox, locate the **Drawing Tools** contextual menu, and click on the **Format** tab.

2. Click on **Shape Style | Shape Outline** in order to select a line color.

3. If the theme or standard colors are not what you are looking for, select **More Outline Colors…** to choose a custom color or select one from the color wheel.

4. If the default weight of the line is not thick enough, use the **Weight** option from the **Shape Outline** drop-down list to change it.

5. Use the **Sketched** lines option to jazz up your PowerPoint presentation:

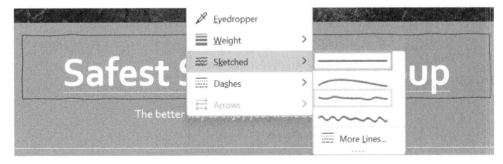

Figure 6.17 – The Sketched line types in Office 2021

6. Click on the **Dashes** option to display different line styles to apply to the textbox.

7. To remove an outline from a shape, select the shape and click on the **No Outline** option from the **Shape Outline** drop-down list.

> **Note**
>
> We now have access to Hex colors in Office 2021. Click on **Shape Format | Shape Outline | More Outline Colors… | Custom** to add a *Hex* color code into the field provided. This option is discussed in the *Coloring using Hex values* section of *Chapter 3, Styles, Referencing, and Media*   . Office 2021 has the addition of **Sketched Shape Outlines** – this option is also covered in *Chapter 3* of this book.

The next topic is very useful, especially when using the **Selection** pane. Let's investigate it next.

Arranging objects

By the end of this section, you will be confident with arranging, grouping, and rotating objects, as well as being able to use the **Selection** pane to locate hidden objects. We will also recap how to resize and reset objects.

There are numerous **Arrange** options available from the **Picture Format** tab. To access these options, follow these steps:

1. Select a picture on a slide in your presentation. For this example, we will use the `Safest Solution-Objects.pptx` presentation.

2. There are many **Arrange** options that you can use to order, group, and position objects on slides. You can access the **Arrange** options using any one of the following methods:

    I.   The first is accessible via the **Drawing** group in the **Home** tab.

    II. The second is accessible via the **Picture Format** tab at the very top of the PowerPoint ribbon once an object has been selected.

    III. The third is accessible via right-clicking on an object, after which the shortcut menu will appear for you to choose from the **Arrange** options.

Now we will learn how to use the **Arrange** options.

Sending an object forward or backward

1. Click on the picture you wish to bring to the front of the textbox.

2. Click on the **Picture Format | Bring Forward** option to access the drop-down menu, then select **Bring to Front**. Alternatively, right-click on the shape and choose **Bring to Front** from the shortcut menu:

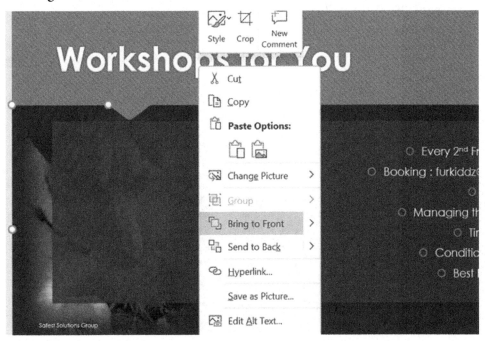

Figure 6.18 – Right-clicking on a picture to access Bring to Front

3. The picture will move to the front, and the textbox shape will move to the back:

Figure 6.19 – The picture is now in front of the textbox

When working with pictures, you will access the **Arrange** group from the **Picture Format** tab to make any formatting amendments, and for shapes, you will access the **Shapes Format** tab to change arrange options.

Flipping objects

1. Click on the picture to flip.

2. Find the **Arrange** group and click on **Rotate | Flip Horizontal**:

Figure 6.20 – The picture has been flipped horizontally

3. Experiment with the other rotations or click on **More Rotation Options…** to access the dialog box.

Rotating objects

1. Click on the picture you wish to rotate. The rotate icon will appear at the top center of the object and is identified by a circular arrow:

Figure 6.21 – The rotation handle icon

2. Place the mouse pointer on the circular arrow, and while holding the left mouse button down, drag the position to rotate the object.

Another method would be to click on **Picture Format | Rotate Objects | More Rotation Options…**. This will open the **Picture Format** pane on the right-hand side of the window where you can manually enter a specific degree of rotation. Simply type the required degree of rotation into the text area that is provided next to the **Rotation** heading.

In the next topic, we will look at a new feature named **Auto Fix**.

Aligning objects

Although it is really easy to align objects using the drag and drop method when positioning elements using the mouse, the align feature is available for this purpose and allows the user to create professional-looking documents. There is nothing worse than looking at objects on a slide presentation that are uneven or slightly off in terms of their positioning. In the previous edition of our book, *Learn Microsoft Office 2019*, we looked at ways to align objects. In this topic, we will introduce **Auto Fix**.

Aligning objects using Auto Fix

PowerPoint can be quite time-consuming in terms of formatting, especially if you are a perfectionist. The new feature, **Auto Fix**, in PowerPoint for the web, is very efficient for aligning elements. Perform the following steps:

1. Open the presentation called `Safest Solution-Align.pptx`.

2. Click to select *Slide 4* of the presentation. Select the objects to align by placing the mouse pointer on the slide background. Then, while holding down the mouse pointer, drag the cursor over the objects you would like to align:

Figure 6.22 – The drag method to select objects on a slide

> **Note**
>
> The *Shift* + click or *Ctrl* + click method is the alternative here. Additionally, you can use the **Select Objects** option, located in the **Home** tab, which is inside the **Editing** group.

3. Right-click on the border of one of the selected objects. Then, click to select **Auto Fix** from the drop-down menu provided:

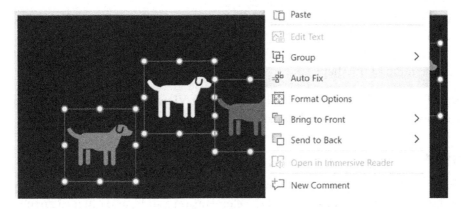

Figure 6.23 – Right-clicking on the selected objects on a slide presents the Auto Fix option

4.   The objects are now horizontally and vertically aligned on the slide. The **Auto Fix** option will align objects even if they are stacked below each other.

Aligning objects to the top

If you do not see the **Auto Fix** feature when you right-click, it could be that this is still being rolled out to your Office 2021 desktop platform. To align objects using the desktop, follow these steps:

1.   Open the presentation called `Safest Solution-Align.pptx`.

2.   Select the objects to align while holding down the *Shift* or *Ctrl* key. You can also use the **Select Objects** option, located in the **Home** tab, which is inside the **Editing** group.

3.   Click on the **Graphics Format | Align** drop-down list. Then, select **Align Top**:

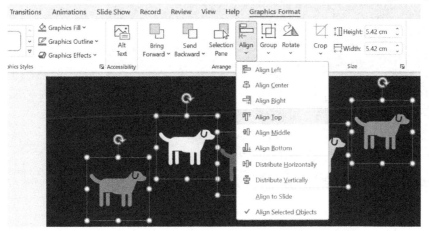

Figure 6.24 – The Align options located in the Graphics Format tab

4. Once the objects have been aligned to the top, you will notice that the gaps between each object are of different sizes. The **Distribute Horizontally** icon from the **Align** drop-down list is perfect for fixing this. Pay attention to the change in the distribution of the shapes.

If you are having problems lining up objects, use the **View | Gridlines** icon to guide you. Now, let's look at how the **Selection** pane can help you.

Using the Selection pane

This feature is absolutely brilliant when working with numerous objects that overlap. Sometimes, you won't be able to see all the elements on a slide, and often, elements are hidden from view. I use this extensively when working with Microsoft PowerPoint animations, as it allows me to move elements up and down and rename the elements so that the order of the elements makes more sense when working with the diagram. Additionally, you can hide or unhide elements from view. Follow these steps:

1. We will use the presentation named `Safest Solution-Selection.pptx`.

2. Select an object and click on the **Graphics Format** tab to access the **Selection Pane** option.

3. Note that the **Selection** pane is now visible on the right-hand side of the PowerPoint environment:

Figure 6.25 – The Selection pane on the right-hand side of the window

4. Each object is an item in the pane. To use the pane, click on an object listed in the pane – the object will be selected on the slide.

> **Note**
> To rename an object listed on the pane, simply click on the name of the object twice and type the new name into the textbox provided to replace the current name. To hide an object, use the eye icon on the right-hand side of the pane.

5. Click again to make the object visible. This feature is great for objects that overlap so that you don't have to move your whole document around to access the shape and make a change!

6. The **Selection** pane can also be used to select objects.

7. Use the **Selection** pane to rename the dogs, in order, from **DOG1** to **DOG5**.

8. Hold down the *Ctrl* key on the keyboard while selecting **DOG1** through **DOG5**:

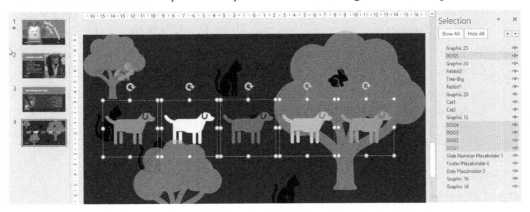

Figure 6.26 – The Selection pane showing the renamed dog shapes

> **Tip**
> To close the **Selection** pane, click on the **Selection Pane** icon from the ribbon or the close icon on the right-hand side of the pane.

So, we have learned how to work with the **Selection** pane. In the next section, we will concentrate on grouping elements on a slide.

Grouping objects

Grouping objects together creates one object. This might be the way to go if you are moving objects or working with multiple objects on one slide. Instead of formatting each object separately, you can group them and then apply formatting. When objects relevant to each other are grouped together, they can be moved together from one position in the document to another without repeating the step for each part of the drawing. For example, you would be able to group labels on a picture so that they stay intact when moving to another location in the presentation. Perform the following steps:

1. Use the **Selection** pane, as per the previous example, to select the objects on a slide. Alternatively, select the objects that you wish to combine into one object. To do this, click on the first object and hold down the *Shift* or *Ctrl* key on the keyboard. Move your mouse pointer to the second object, making sure that the *Shift* key (or the *Ctrl* key) is still depressed. Then, click on each object to add it to the group.

2. To form a group, click on the **Graphic Format** tab and select the **Group** icon drop-down list. The object will become one movable object.

3. To ungroup objects, select the grouped object, then simply navigate back to the **Group** option and select **Ungroup**.

I am sure you learned how to resize objects prior to this new edition book, but we will recap this topic here as the tab names have changed slightly.

Resizing objects

To learn how to resize objects, follow these steps:

1. Select the object to resize by clicking on it. Place your left mouse pointer on the sizing handle. Hold down the left mouse button and drag toward the center of the image to make it smaller and to keep the proportion of the image intact. Alternatively, drag outward to make the object bigger.

2. The ribbon is another method that can be used if you wish to enter specific widths and heights for objects. Select the object by clicking on it. Notice that the **Graphic Format** tab or the **Picture Format** tab is now visible, depending on the object type (for example, picture, shape, or chart) that you are resizing. Locate the **Size** group and enter the width and height measurements as desired. The object will adjust on the slide as you enter the new measurements.

> **Tip**
>
> Take note of the **Lock aspect ratio** checkbox. This is very important if the object's height and width settings must change in relation to one another and not separately.

Resetting objects

The reset option removes all changes in terms of size, effects, rotation, and scaling and brings the object back to its original size. Follow these steps:

1. Select the object to reset.
2. In the **Picture Format** tab, select the **Reset Picture** option (when dealing with pictures).
3. Click on **Reset Picture** to remove all formatting changes and select **Reset Picture & Size** to remove any formatting and size changes.

In the next section, you will learn how to create tables using a range of methods, and you will discover how to apply table styles. Additionally, you will be able to master chart modifications by learning how to switch elements; edit elements such as data labels, data tables, legends, and chart titles; and add objects.

Modifying charts

We use charts to make information more appealing, as well as clearer and easier to read. As you might have gathered, a **chart** is a graphical representation of worksheet information. Within Office 2021, the interface is so much clearer and more defined, and elements that you normally would apply to charts manually are included on the ribbon. So, everything is at your fingertips.

Getting used to chart terminology is ever so easy; you simply click on elements to amend them, and the element is highlighted on the chart. Chart terminologies were addressed in our previous book, *Learn Microsoft Office 2019*, along with chart creation and working with tables, so we will not address them here.

As tab names are a little different in 2021, let's run through how to add **Data labels** as an example. The process to modify charts is the same for most elements you add in the new version of Office.

Data labels

To make a chart more understandable and easier to read for the user, we can add data labels. Although a chart layout can be selected using the **Chart Styles** group within the ribbon, there will be times when you need to add or remove elements from a chart manually. Use the data shown in the following screenshot to construct a **Clustered Column** chart on a new blank slide in PowerPoint 2021:

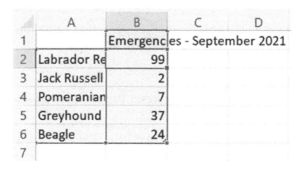

Figure 6.27 – Selected data on the worksheet

To apply data labels to the preceding chart, follow these steps:

1. Select the chart by clicking on it.

2. From the **Chart Elements** option (the + icon) on the right-hand side of the chart, select **Data Labels**. Alternatively, use the **Chart Design** tab to locate **Add Chart Element** (the first icon on the ribbon). Then, locate **Data Labels** from the drop-down list:

Figure 6.28 – A clustered column chart showing different methods of adding Data Labels

3. Once you have selected **Data Labels**, use the black arrow to open further options to customize the data label. The chart will update immediately.

4. Click on one of the data labels on the chart once (this will select all of the data labels). To select just one of the data labels, click again.

5. To make formatting changes to the labels, visit the **Format** tab and apply the formatting options as required.

6. Name the chart SSEmergencies.pptx.

Let's use the same steps to add a data table.

Adding a data table

A **data table** refers to how data is represented according to the worksheet data that was used to create the chart. Once inserted, the data table forms part of the chart so that it is visually more appealing when printed or displayed onscreen. Remember that there are lots of quick layout chart options, including data tables. Follow these steps:

1. Select the chart to add data labels.

2. Click on the **Add Chart Element** icon from the **Chart Design** tab ribbon:

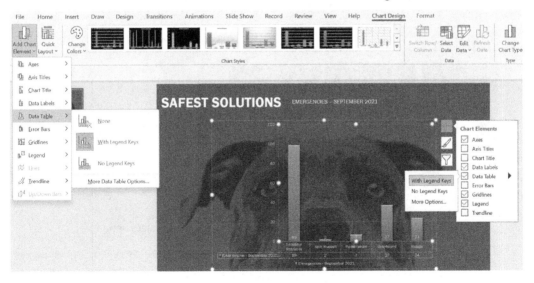

Figure 6.29 – The Data Table option

3. Locate **Data Table** from the list provided. From the drop-down list, choose an option to apply to the chart.

4. To add any other elements, such as chart **Legend**, use the same method as earlier.

Adding objects to a chart

Objects such as images and illustrations (shapes, pictures, icons, WordArt, text, and more) are added to the chart's background using the **Insert** tab. There are a couple of new features in Office 2021 under the **Stock Images…** option. As this feature is referenced throughout this book, we will not go through all the options here. Once inserted, the objects are formatted using the same methods we use to edit in Word or Excel 2021. These elements can also be animated to create focus when presenting them:

1. To add an object to the chart, locate the **Insert** tab from the PowerPoint ribbon. Here, we can select from a variety of choices (the **Images**, **Illustrations**, **Add-ins**, **Links**, **Text**, **Symbols**, and **Media** groups):

Figure 6.30 – The Insert tab on the ribbon displaying variety of object groups

2. Let's insert the sixth **Sticker**, using the **Stock Images… | Stickers** option:

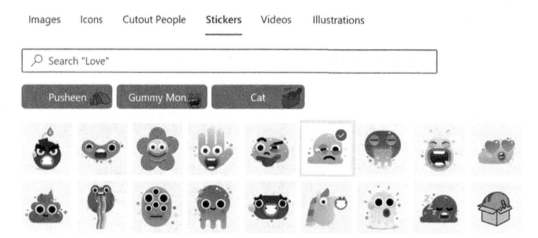

Figure 6.31 – A list of available stickers from the Stock Images option

3. Click on **Insert** to add the object to the slide. Then, resize and reposition to the top of the **Labrador Retriever** column.

4. Next, insert a document icon, and amend the **Graphics Fill** setting to white. Add an arrow shape and format as in the next screenshot. Lastly, add a text box to include the text Please send through report asap. Change the fill color using the **Eyedropper** tool, picking the color of the column:

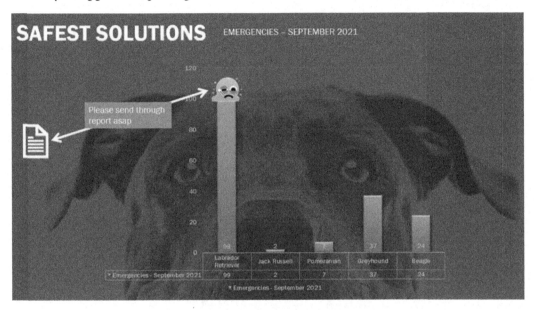

Figure 6.32 – The finished chart including the customized objects

5. You will need to change the **Arrange** options so that the textbox displays before the arrow shape.

Now that we have learned how to amend charts in Office 2021, we will revisit **Themes** in PowerPoint 2021.

Applying and modifying themes

A theme is a collection of fonts, colors, and effects that are saved as a name in the theme gallery. Predefined themes are available from the **Themes** group on the **Design** tab. If you wish to customize a theme, use the options from the **Variants** group.

In my experience, it is always easier to decide on a theme before adding all of your content to it. Applying a completely new theme design, or changing a design theme once your presentation is complete, can cause a few complications, with you having to redo certain formatting elements. Follow these steps:

1. Open the presentation called `Safest Solutions-Themes.pptx`.

2. Click on **Design | More…**:

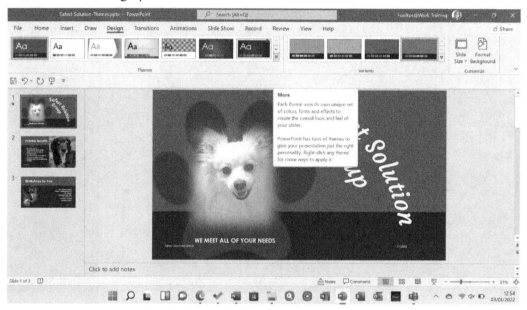

Figure 6.33 – The More drop-down list in the Themes group

3. Select a theme to apply to the presentation, or visit **Browse for Themes…** to visit the explorer view to locate themes that are stored on the computer. After choosing the **Mesh** theme, this particular design theme has caused the first slide's main title to distort somewhat as the elements are now trying to fit into the new design theme that's been applied. The formatting of the title and slide elements will need to be amended so that it looks more presentable.

4. Notice that themes also have **Variants**, which are displayed just to the right-hand side of the chosen design theme on the ribbon.

5. We are also able to format the background of a slide using the **Customize** group (alternatively, right-click on a slide background and select **Format Background…** to change the background properties).

6. Save the presentation to keep the design changes.

In the previous section, we learned how to apply a design theme to all slides in the presentation. Next, we will look at how to apply a theme to specific slides in the presentation.

Applying a theme to selected slides

1. Select the slides in the presentation that you would like to update with a new theme.
2. Click on **Design | Themes**.
3. Locate a theme to apply to the selected presentation slides.
4. Right-click on the selected theme and choose **Apply to Selected Slides** from the shortcut menu:

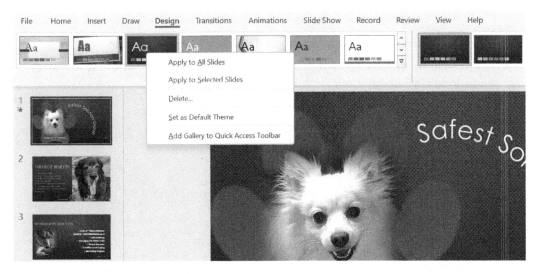

Figure 6.34 – The Design Theme options in the right-click shortcut menu

Once you have spent some time creating a presentation, you might want to save the design elements of the presentation so that it becomes part of the **Theme | More** options and, therefore, available to other presentations. Let's learn how to create a customized theme.

Creating your own custom theme

1. For this example, we will use the previous presentation. If you have not been following along with the previous steps, open the presentation named `Safest Solution- SavedThemes.pptx`.

2. This presentation has a theme applied, along with customizations to its elements. To save the customized theme as your new theme, click on **Save Current Theme…**, which is located at the bottom of the **More** drop-down list:

Enable Content Updates from Office.com…

Browse for Themes…

Save Current Theme…

Figure 6.35 – The More drop-down list option to Save Current Theme…

3. By default, themes are saved to the `Templates\Document Themes` folder on your local hard drive:

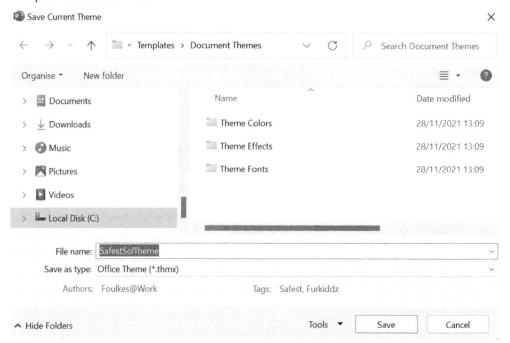

Figure 6.36 – The Document Themes folder on a local computer

4. Enter a filename into the text area provided (note that the filename extension for themes is `.thmx` and they are automatically saved to the `Templates\Document Themes` folder).

5.   Click on **Save**. The new theme, called `SafestSolTheme`, will be added to the
     Custom list in the theme gallery:

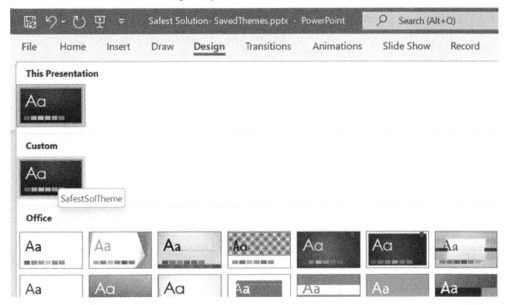

Figure 6.37 – Custom Theme, named SafestSolTheme, displayed in the Design Theme group

> **Note**
> Themes you no longer require can be removed from the theme gallery. To
> delete a theme, click on **Design**, select the theme, and then right-click and
> select **Delete**.

The last topic of this chapter will go through the video and audio capabilities of Office
2021 as there are a few updates to previous versions.

Inserting audio and video

In this section, you will become proficient with adding video and audio content to a
presentation. Additionally, you will learn how to modify the content and playback options
to suit your presentation's requirements.

Before we look at editing video and audio content, first, we will learn how to insert a
video clip.

Inserting a video clip

1. Open the presentation called `VideoAudioContent.pptx`.

2. We will insert a video on *Slide 3*.

3. Click on **Insert** | **Video** from the **Media** group at the end of the ribbon.

4. You can insert a video from an online source, the new **Stock Videos** option, or from a location on your computer:

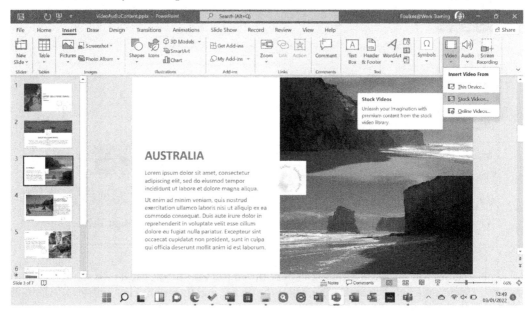

Figure 6.38 – The Insert Video from option in the Insert tab

5. Locate the video called `AUS1.AVI` and double-click to insert it onto the slide.

6. The video will appear on the slide. Note that a range of options are now available on the **Video Format** and **Playback** tabs so that you can edit and play back the video content:

Figure 6.39 – The Playback and Video Format tabs appear after inserting or clicking on the video content

Note that formatting a video is the same as formatting any other content on a slide.

Applying styles to video content

1. Make sure the video is selected on *Slide 3*.

2. Locate the **Video Styles** group from the **Video Format** tab.

3. Click on the **More...** icon to see all the available styles. Select a style to apply to the video.

4. Changing the size of a video is the same as resizing any object within PowerPoint. We will now concentrate on the audio aspect.

Applying a style to an audio clip

1. Using the presentation from the previous example, click on *Slide 2*.

2. Click on the **Insert** tab and choose the **Audio** icon from the **Media** group.

3.   Select **Record Audio**, as you do not have an audio recording:

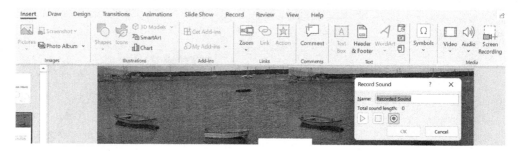

Figure 6.40 – Inserting or recording an audio clip using the Insert | Audio option

4.   Name the recording, then click on the **Record** icon to begin recording (the red dot icon).

5.   Click on the **Stop recording** icon when complete (the blue square). Click on the **OK** icon to insert the audio onto the slide:

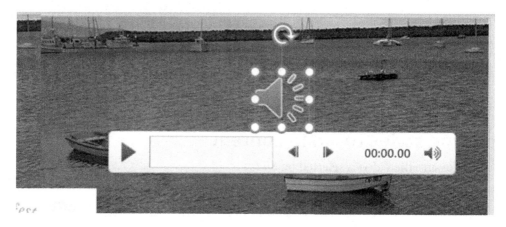

Figure 6.41 – The inserted audio clip on the slide

6.   The audio icon can be resized and repositioned using the same methods we discussed previously. On the **Playback** tab, you will see the **Audio Styles** icons. Here, you can choose to remove a style or play the audio in the background while presenting the slide show.

Adjusting the playback options

The video playback options are located on the **Video Format** tab, and the audio options are available on the **Audio Format** tab. Make sure you have clicked on the video or audio first before you complete any of the following tasks:

1. To start the video (or audio) with a mouse click when clicking on the video icon, select **When Clicked On** from the **Start:** option.

2. To start the video automatically when the slide is displayed on the screen, click on **Automatically**.

3. **In Click Sequence** means that the video will play in the order it appears among all the other animated elements on the slide. Normally, this is the default option.

4. To hide the video icon so that it does not show on the slide show while presenting, click on **Hide During Show**. Be careful of this option if you have the **Start:** option set to **On Click**. This is because you won't see the icon and be able to click on it to play the video. Only use this option for automatic playback:

Figure 6.42 – The audio options are set via the Playback tab

5. To play a video continuously in a presentation, click on the **Loop until Stopped** checkbox. This is great to use if, for instance, you're presenting at a show and the presentation must keep on playing for many visitors walking by a marketing stand.

6. The **Rewind after Playing** options will set the video to the start position once it's finished playing.

7. The **Play Across Slides** checkbox or **Play in Background** option will play the video over the entire slide presentation.

8. The **Volume** setting allows you to adjust the sound level, as well as mute the video.

9. The **Trim** feature is a valuable tool when you need to remove content from a video or audio clip. Simply drag the green and/or red markers to edit the **Start Time** and **End Time** settings:

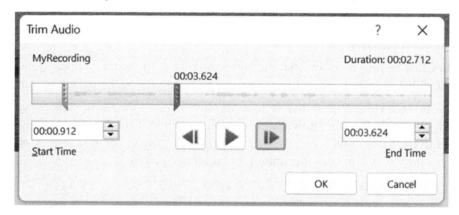

Figure 6.43 – Trimming audio and video content with PowerPoint 2021

10. **Bookmarks** are another feature that can aid you when needing to jump to a certain spot along the timeline when presenting. Often, the entire video or audio content is not relevant; this way, you can control which content is shown at the time of presenting. To add a bookmark, simply click on the video (or audio) timeline to select the time you need to insert the mark. Then, select **Playback | Add Bookmark**. A *yellow dot* is inserted at the marked position on the timeline. Repeat the process to add further bookmarks. Click on **Slide Show | From Current Slide** to see the bookmarks while presenting. Click to navigate directly to the desired bookmark along the timeline.

Another useful feature within the **Playback** tab is the ability to add captions to your video file. Let's investigate this next.

Inserting captions

If you need to add captions to videos within PowerPoint, you can use the **Playback |
Insert Captions** command to locate the relevant captions file on the local computer.
Often, we would create these video text descriptions within a video application, such as
Camtasia or Captivate, prior to inserting the video content elsewhere. If your video has no
sound or you would like to add text to the video, then this option is perfect!

Creating the closed caption file

As mentioned earlier, captions are usually added when the video is compiled, but if not,
we can use *Notepad* on our computer to create a caption file. To learn how to create a
caption file, please refer to `https://support.microsoft.com/en-us/office/`
`create-closed-captions-for-a-video-b1cfb30f-5b00-4435-beeb-`
`2a25e115024b`. Once complete, your caption file will look similar to the following
screenshot:

```
*Untitled - Notepad

File    Edit    Format    View    Help
WEBVTT

00:00:01.000 --> 00:00:02.550
Safest Solutions Australia Trip.

00:00:02.556 --> 00:00:17.094
Beautiful sun-kissed beaches, with waves crashing on the shoreline and against the bolders.
```

Figure 6.44 – A closed captions Notepad file

Ensure that the Notepad file is saved using the `.vtt` closed captions file extension. Add
the `.en` before the file extension to indicate that the file is an English closed caption file:

```
File name:    VideoCaptionsSSG.en.vtt

Save as type:  All Files  (*.*)
```

Figure 6.45 – The file-naming convention for caption files in Notepad

Once this is complete, you will need to add the `.vtt` file to the video.

Inserting the closed caption file

Insert the caption file (`VideoCaptionsSSG.en.vtt`) by visiting **Playback | Insert Captions**:

Figure 6.46 – The Insert Captions option to add closed captions to the video, as seen in the timeline

Once the captions have been inserted, they will become part of the video timeline.

Lastly, let's look at the export options for videos. This feature was introduced in Office 2019, and the only difference in Office 2021 is that the tab name has changed from **Recording** to **Record**.

You can record video, audio, and inking within a slide presentation, then export the video at 4K resolution, all available from the **Record** tab, as illustrated in the following screenshot. Note that the new feature, **Record | Record**, is discussed in greater detail in *Chapter 7, Photo Albums, Sections, and Show Tools*:

1. Open the presentation to export as a video. Click on **Record | Export to Video**:

Figure 6.47 – The Record tab in PowerPoint 2021, showing the Export to Video option

2.   Click on **Full HD (1080p)** to see the list of options available.

3.   Choose the **Ultra HD (4K)** option to save the video as ultra-high quality and in the largest file format:

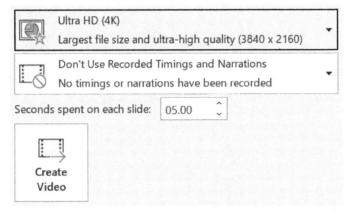

Figure 6.48 – The Ultra HD (4K) option

4.   Click on **Create Video** to complete the process. The presentation will be exported to the location chosen.

Well done! You have mastered a huge range of skills in this chapter.

Summary

This chapter has equipped you with the necessary skills to manipulate PowerPoint 2021 slides, apply and create themes, reuse slides, and work with textboxes and charts. You are now proficient in how to apply styles and manipulate slide elements using the Auto Fix feature. You have gained an understanding of how to insert an agenda and arrange and manipulate objects. Additionally, you know how to add and customize video and audio content on slides within a presentation. You have mastered the new drawing features, learned how to create and insert captions onto a video, and explored the playback options for audio and video.

In the next chapter, you will learn how to create stunning photo albums and learn how to define presentation sections and motion effects. Additionally, we will run through how to create a presentation and add animations, transitions, and slide timings to it. You will learn about the new Record feature and work with Presenter View. There is also a section on new features such as setting the reading order, and how to rehearse presentations using a body language and speaker coach. The new inking feature is also addressed in the following chapter. You will become a master with the advanced morph technique.

7
Photo Albums, Sections, and Show Tools

Slide show presentation tools allow you to control all aspects of a slide show, ensuring that you can show your audience just the right content at the right time.

We will learn how to create stunning photo albums with captions, and learn how to define presentation sections and motion effects. We will also run through animations, transitions, and how to control slide timings and playback of audio narration. We will learn about the new Record feature, work with Presenter View, and cover a topic on the new feature to set reading order and to rehearse presentations using body language and **Presenter Coach (Speaker Coach)**.

The new inking feature is also addressed and you will become a master with the advanced morphing technique. Included is a section on master slides, where we check the consistency throughout a presentation, and options for hiding or showing specific slides when we're delivering a presentation.

The following topics are covered in this chapter:

- Creating and modifying photo albums

- Working with presentation sections

- Applying animations and transitions

- Using hyperlinks, actions, and comments

- Exploring slide show options and custom shows

- Using master slides and hiding slides

Technical requirements

Prior knowledge to aid you in mastering this chapter would be the ability to work with different slide layouts; create and format elements such as textboxes, charts, and tables; and insert video and audio content. The examples used in this chapter are accessible from the following GitHub URL: `https://github.com/PacktPublishing/Learn-Microsoft-Office-2021-Second-Edition`.

Creating and modifying photo albums

In this section, you will learn how to create, organize, and format a photo album using PowerPoint 2021. This feature allows you to add a collection of photographs to a presentation and set format options all in one go. It is a really efficient process that is perfect when creating presentations predominantly based on images, or for personal online photo album memories to which video, animations, transitions, audio, and other PowerPoint 2021 elements can be added to enhance the end product:

1. Open PowerPoint 2021 and create a new blank presentation.

2. To construct a photo album, click on the **Insert | Photo Album | New Photo Album…** option.

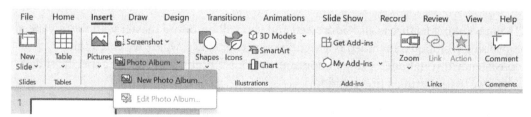

Figure 7.1 – The New Photo Album… option from the Insert tab

3. In the **Photo Album** dialog box that populates, locate the content you would like to insert as a photo album.

4. Click on the **File/Disk...** icon to browse and locate pictures on your computer. It is important to note that storing pictures in one single location/folder would be an advantage prior to creating the album, as well as having a descriptive filename for each picture so that locating, rearranging, and formatting pictures is trouble-free.

5. Select the pictures using either the *Ctrl* + click method to select individual pictures, or select multiple files in one go using the *Shift* + click method; or, use *Ctrl* and the *A* key to select all the files in the folder. We will use the images within the PHOTOALBUM folder for this example.

6. The pictures are added to the **Pictures in album** window, located in the center of the dialog box. You will see from the following screenshot that the pictures are numbered and the picture names are displayed in the window for ease of use:

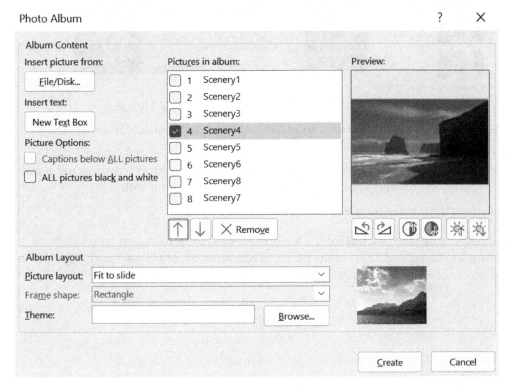

Figure 7.2 – Numbered pictures as well as filenames showing in the Pictures in album area

7. There are numerous formatting options to consider before you click on the **Create** icon at the bottom of the dialog box. In this instance, we will go ahead and create the album, and then revisit each individual formatting option, so that you are familiar with the options and become comfortable working with photo albums in PowerPoint. An example photo album can be seen in the following screenshot:

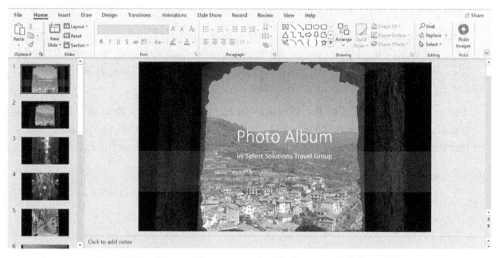

Figure 7.3 – Photo Album created with the amended first slide

8. Each picture is displayed on an individual slide as the default layout was set to **Fit to slide**.

9. Notice that the photo album is created as an entirely new presentation and is not part of the existing blank new presentation you started off with.

10. Save the photo album as `SSG-PhotoAlbum.pptx`.

In the following table, we will list the features we can customize when creating Photo Albums in PowerPoint 2021. In the previous edition book, *Learn Microsoft Office 2019*, we addressed these customizations in detail.

Customization	Action to perform
Picture captions	**Insert	Photo Album	Edit Photo Album...** Click on the checkbox to select **Captions below ALL pictures**. (If **Picture Layout** is set to **Fit to Slide**, this needs to be amended first.)
Inserting text slides	**Insert	Photo Album	Edit Photo Album...** Choose **New Text Box** from the **Insert text** heading.
Removing images	**Insert	Photo Album	Edit Photo Album...** Click the image to remove, then choose **Remove** from the **Pictures in album** list.
Inserting pictures in black and white	**Insert	Photo Album	Edit Photo Album...** Simply select the checkbox next to the **Picture Options** heading, **ALL pictures black and white**.
Reordering pictures	**Insert	Photo Album	Edit Photo Album...** Click on a picture you would like to move up or down. Use the *move up* or *move down* arrows to position the picture.
Adjusting rotation, brightness, and contrast	**Insert	Photo Album	Edit Photo Album...** Use the set of rotation, brightness, and contrast buttons directly under the image.
Changing picture layout	**Insert	Photo Album	Edit Photo Album...** Locate **Picture layout** and select the drop-down arrow to choose a layout from the list provided.

Table 1.1 – Photo Album customization options

A great feature to add to a photo album would be to compile an audio narration on each slide. Select a slide to record audio, then click **Insert | Audio | Record Audio...**. Alternatively, you can use the new **Record | Record** feature to record narrations throughout the presentation. This feature was discussed in an earlier chapter.

Now that you have mastered photo albums, let's add to your skillset by learning how to cluster slides together into sections.

Working with presentation sections

In this topic, you will learn to understand why we would use sections in PowerPoint. We will create, rename, and remove sections in a presentation.

Formatting sections

If you are scrolling through a huge presentation or applying finishing touches, it can be extremely frustrating to locate slides to format or edit. The **Sections** feature allows you to organize your presentation into categories so that finding slides for a particular category is effortless.

In addition, if working on a presentation with multiple contributors, you can assign sections to different people. Reordering slides or viewing a presentation in the **Slide Sorter** view with sections applied is a breeze:

1. To add a section, you can be in the **Normal** or **Slide Sorter** view. For this example, we will be using the SSG-Sections.pptx presentation.

2. The feature is accessible by right-clicking in between slides and choosing **Add Section**. The option is also accessible from **Home | Section | Add Section**.

3. Once you have inserted a section, an arrow will appear just above the slide entitled Untitled Section, and the **Rename Section** dialog box will populate.

4. Type a new name for the section into the **Section name** text placeholder. For this example, we will use the text Introduction and click on **Rename**, as illustrated in the following screenshot:

Figure 7.4 – Renaming a section

5. Repeat the process to create sections for dogs, rabbits, and birds.

6. The created sections are displayed in **Slide Pane**, but can also be viewed much more clearly in the **Slide Sorter** view due to the sections showing the slide thumbnails.

7. Sections can be collapsed or expanded using either the collapse or expand arrow to the left of a section name. To collapse or expand all sections in a presentation, click on the **Sections** icon located on the **Slides** group, and select **Collapse All** or **Expand All**.

8. To rename a section, right-click on the section name, and then choose **Rename Section** from the shortcut list provided.

9. To move sections within a presentation, right-click on the section name, and then choose **Move Section Up** or **Move Section Down**.

10. If you want to remove a section, simply right-click on the section name and choose **Remove Section**.

Visit the *Easy linking* section in this chapter to learn how to create a thumbnail link from a section within the slide deck. The next section will equip you with the skills to add animation to your slide deck.

Applying animations and transitions

In this section, we will recap adding an animation to multiple objects on a slide and use **Animation Pane** to configure, set triggers, modify transitions, and look at the advanced **morphing** technique. Animation types have not been updated within PowerPoint 2021.

As we already know, animations can be applied to pictures, charts, tables, SmartArt graphics, shapes, clip art, and many other objects in PowerPoint. We must always remember that animations can be extremely distracting if applied to many objects of the same slide. No more than 20% of your slide content should be animated.

Using Animation Pane

Animation Pane provides access to animation start options, timing, and effect options, as well as the ability to remove animations from objects. These options are explained throughout this chapter using other methods, so we will concentrate on each individually, in those sections.

Setting up advanced animations

You can apply more than one animation to a single object on a slide, as follows:

1. Select an object on a slide that already has an animation applied.

2. Click on the **Add Animation** icon located in the **Advanced Animation** group. Remember that applying another animation to an already animated object using the normal animation effect options will replace the animation. The **Add Animation** feature allows you to add more than one animation to a single object.

3. Select an animation from the drop-down list provided.

4. The animation is applied to the object and becomes the second animation applied, as illustrated in the following screenshot:

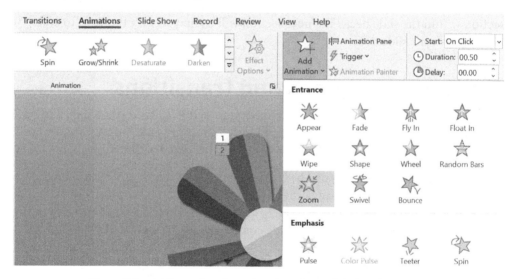

Figure 7.5 – Adding animation using the advanced Animation group

5. Preview the animation. The first animation will play, followed by the second animation.

6. To preview animations automatically, click on the **Preview** icon to the very left of the **Animation** ribbon, and then select **AutoPreview** from the drop-down list. Every time you apply an animation or animation effect option, the preview will automatically play the changes without having to click on the **Preview** icon each time.

Setting animation timing

Animation timing can be set by using either **Animation Pane** or the **Timing** group. **Animation Pane** is a great way to visualize changes to these options.

Setting start options

In the petal example that we have been working with, the petals have the same animation effect applied and when previewed, the animations all happen at the same time. Let's change the start options so that each petal appears independently.

1. Select an object to set when you would like an animation effect to start. We will now change the start options so that each petal plays after the previous petal, and so on. Let's get started by selecting the first petal on *slide 1*.

2. Locate the **Timing** group on the **Animation** tab.

3. Use the **Start** drop-down list to set how the animation should begin.

4. For this example, we will set the petals to start after each other, using the **After Previous** start option.

5. Continue to do the same to each petal of the flower, this time using **Animation Pane**.

6. Select the next petal, and then click on the **Animation Pane** option from the **Advanced Animation** group.

7. Click on the arrow to the right of a group and select **Start After Previous**. Notice that the visual representation here is easier to follow due to the *yellow thumbnails* that appear next to each animated group, as can be seen in the following screenshot:

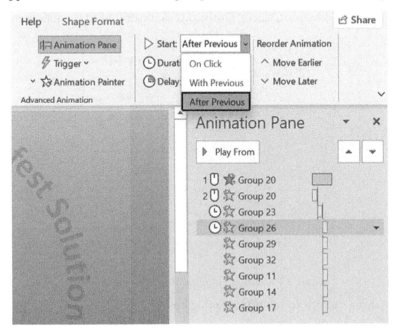

Figure 7.6 – Animation Pane showing petal animations

8. Repeat this process until all the petals have been set with the **Start After Previous** option.

9. Preview the animation when complete.

Selecting delay or duration options

Setting a delay on an animation effect means that you will essentially pause an animation for a period of time before it should start playing. If you would like an animation to play for a certain amount of time, then you need to set the duration of the animation. You can do this in the following way:

1. Select an object on a slide that has an animation effect applied. For this example, we will select the center of the flower and apply the **Grow & Turn** animation effect, and then set a delay.

2. Locate the **Timing** group on the **Animation** tab.

3. Use the **Duration** text area to set the animation duration, or the **Delay** text area for the number of seconds the animation must wait until it starts.

4. Launch **Animation Pane** by selecting the appropriate icon from the **Advanced Animation** group.

5. Click on the arrow to the right of the animated object in **Animation Pane**.

6. From the drop-down list, select **Timing…**, as illustrated in the following screenshot:

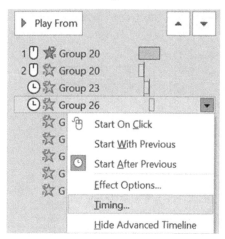

Figure 7.7 – Setting Timing… from Animation Pane

7. Set the delay options in the **Effect** dialog box.

8. Click on the **OK** command when complete and commit to the changes made, and then play the animation. The center of the flower should play 3 seconds after the previous animation has ended, as illustrated in the following screenshot:

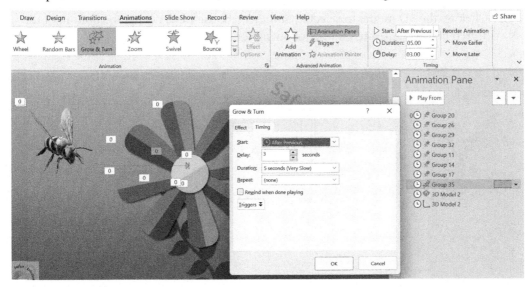

Figure 7.8 – Working within the Timing dialog box to set animation-delay

9. Play the animation. The center of the flower should take 3 seconds to play from start to finish.

Now that we have recapped animations using PowerPoint 2021, let's look at how we work with 3D models and cube animations.

Working with 3D models and cube animations

3D models allow the insertion of objects from online and offline sources that can be viewed in 3D (by rotating to view all angles of the object). Cube animations are animations solely for any 3D model you insert into PowerPoint, and will only be accessible after inserting and selecting a 3D object on a PowerPoint slide. PowerPoint 2021 includes the new **Stock 3D Models** feature.

Inserting a 3D model

1. Click on the **Insert** tab.

2. Locate the **3D Models** icon from the **Illustrations** group.

3. Click on the **3D Models** icon, or choose an option from the drop-down list provided.

4. Click to select **Stock 3D Models....**

5. Type a search keyword—for instance, bee—into the area provided, or select from the comprehensive list of categories displayed.

6. Click on the 3D model to select it, and then choose **Insert (1)** at the bottom of the search box, as illustrated in the following screenshot:

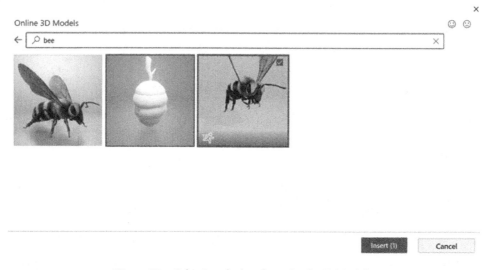

Figure 7.9 – Selecting the bee from Stock 3D Models

7. The 3D model is placed directly onto the slide, and you are then given the opportunity to explore the 3D Model tools from the **3D Model** tab, as well as its ribbon options. Notice that models within PowerPoint 2021 insert with existing animation. There are numerous model positions available under the **3D Model Views** group, as can be seen in the following screenshot:

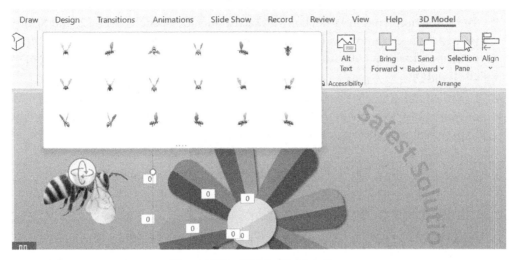

Figure 7.10 – 3D Model animations

8. Select an appropriate view for your slide.

Animating a 3D model

In addition to the bee flapping wings, as per the previous example, you can animate the model using the default animations available, or select from the 3D cube animation options:

1. Make sure the 3D model is selected.

2. Click on the **Animations** tab.

3. Notice that the Animation group offers 3D model animation types, and **Effect Options** for each, as highlighted in the following screenshot:

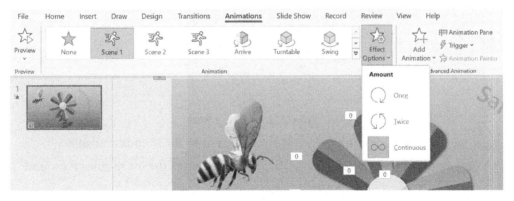

Figure 7.11 – Stock 3D model of the bee highlighting the Scene animation options, as well as
Effect Options

4. The animation types in PowerPoint 2021 also include **Scene 1**, **Scene 2**, and **Scene 3** (as per the bee example), which have dropped in after inserting the stock 3D model of the bee. Experiment with these new animation types, and apply any timing or effect options.

5. Use the different scenes within the Animation options or select a motion path of your choice to apply to the bee as a second animation to create movement. Experiment with moving the endpoint of the animation to land in the center of the flower.

6. Preview the animation and save the presentation when complete.

Attaching sound to an animation

1. Select an object on a slide to add sound to. In this case, we will use the bee.

2. To add an enhancement such as sound, click on the **Effect Options…** icon from the drop-down arrow next to the animation effect of the selected object in **Animation Pane**.

3. From the **Effect Options** dialog box, locate the **Sound** text area directly below the **Enhancements** heading.

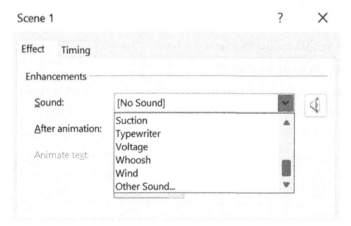

Figure 7.12 – Sound effects

4. Click the drop-down arrow to view and select from the sounds available.

5. Alternatively, choose **Other Sound…** at the bottom of the list to collect a sound saved on your computer.

6. Click on **OK** to confirm.

7. Play the animation to test it.

Setting triggers and adding bookmarks

The **Triggers** option is also available from the **Advanced Animation** group. This feature is useful if you need to create an action on click of a certain element on a slide, such as when audio starts playing an animation must start and continue for the duration. You can set up some creative actions within PowerPoint by setting up a bookmark to highlight a certain part of a video, for instance, and then use a trigger to action an animation when the video lands on the bookmark.

For this example, let's first set up the **Bookmark** so that we can action the bee animation when the bookmark is reached in the video:

1. Click on **Insert | Video | Stock Videos…** and locate the leaves video.

2. Re-arrange the objects on the slide so that the video becomes the background, and the bee and flower animations are placed in front of the video.

3. Select the video, then play the video until you decide at which point on the timeline you would like the bee to animate. We have selected *00:04:02*. Click on **Playback | Add Bookmark**. You will now see a yellow dot along the timeline, indicating the bookmark.

Figure 7.13 – Setting a bookmark along the video timeline

We are now ready to set the trigger:

1. Select the object to set the action on.

2. Click on **Trigger**, then select either **On Click of** or **On Bookmark**. For the **On Bookmark** feature to be active, you must have set up the bookmark on an object prior to the previous instructions. From the sub-menu, select the bookmark, namely **Bookmark 1**, within the video on which to action the bee.

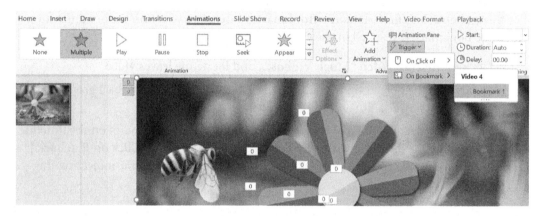

Figure 7.14 – Adding a trigger to a bookmark

3. Play the slide show or preview the animation, and make any adjustments if necessary.

We can also use the **Animation Painter** to pick up applied animations and apply them to other objects on the slide. Let's see how this is achieved.

Using the Animation Painter features

The **Animation Painter** feature is much the same as the **Format Painter** icon from within the Office programs. It allows you to copy animations from one object and apply them to another object. Single-clicking on the **Animation Painter** icon enables you to copy the animation from one object to another object. Just like the Format Painter, double-clicking on the **Animation Painter** icon enables you to copy the animation from one object to multiple objects:

1. We will use the SSG-Planner.pptx presentation to demonstrate this example.

2. Select an object on the slide and apply an animation to it. For this example, select the textbox on *slide 1* and apply the following attributes:

    I. Select the **Float In** animation effect.

II.   Set the animation to **Dim** to another blue color after the animation, and then choose the **By word** option from the **Animate text** drop-down list, applying a 20% delay between words. This process can be seen in the following screenshot:

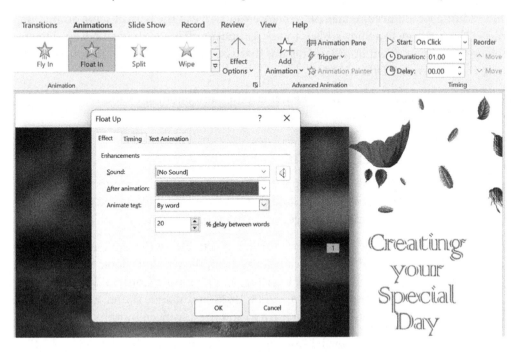

Figure 7.15 – Float In animation with customized effect options

3.   Make sure the textbox is selected on *slide 1*, and then single-click on the **Animation Painter** icon located on the **Animations** tab (in the **Advanced Animation** group) to copy once to another object, or double-click to copy multiple objects.

4.   The Painter icon will appear as the mouse pointer.

5.   Click on another object to paste the animation to it—we will copy the animation to all the textboxes throughout the presentation slides.

6.   The object that now contains the animation will indicate this by displaying the animation number positioned in the top-left corner of the object, and **Animation Pane** will update to reflect the new object animation.

7.   Press the **Animation Painter** icon to stop pasting the animation, or press the *Esc* key on the keyboard.

Reordering animations

Often, you may need to reorder animations, especially if you have a number of objects with multiple animations and effect options. At times, this could get a bit confusing, and a little editing would need to take place before you arrive at the perfect set of animation orders. The best way to achieve this is to use **Animation Pane** to drag and drop elements, moving them up or down in order. This was discussed at length in our previous edition book, *Learn Microsoft Office 2019*.

Now that we have mastered everything we need to know about animations, we will learn how to work with **transitions**.

Working with transitions

A **transition** is a motion effect that happens when the presentation moves from one slide to another. Remember that *less is more* and that too many animations and effects lead to a distracting presentation for an audience. Try to focus on the point of each slide.

Just like animations, transitions also have further effects and settings to customize after a transition has been selected. As we already know from the previous book, transitions fall under the following categories: **Subtle**, **Exciting**, and **Dynamic Content**. In our previous edition book, we concentrated on how to add transitions, include sound, and use the new Morph feature – in this edition, we will learn to add the advanced morph technique.

We have looked at timing under the Animations topic, for which the method is identical. Let's recap the Advanced Slide feature here.

Setting manual or automatic time advance options

Advancing slides manually (that is, on a mouse click) is set by default in a presentation. The slide will advance on the mouse click and play for the duration of the timing set (if any). You would then need to mouse-click again for the next slide to advance on screen, and so on. The **Advance** option is set under the **Advanced Slide** heading of the **Timing** group.

To change this option to automatically advance after a set number of seconds, do the following:

1. Select the slide that contains the transition effect.
2. From the **Timing** group, remove the tick next to the **On Mouse Click** option.
3. Click on the checkbox next to the **After** heading, as illustrated in the following screenshot:

Figure 7.16 – Setting Advance options on slide transitions

4. In the **After** text area, enter (in seconds) the time the slide should take to advance to the next slide. If you do not want to add additional seconds, leave the timing at **0** but ensure that the **After** setting is active.

We have already mastered the Morph transition effect in the previous edition book. In the next topic, we will learn to apply the Morph feature using a different technique.

Advanced morphing technique

As we learned from our previous edition book, *Learn Microsoft Office 2019*, the Morph transition transforms objects across slides and can be applied to WordArt, SmartArt, text, graphics, and shapes, but not charts. After you have applied the Morph transition, you can set various effects for objects, characters, or words.

In this example, we create an advanced morph using the **Selection** pane. Let's see how this is achieved here:

1. Open the presentation named `AdvMorphTransition.pptx`.

2. There are two slides in this presentation. The first slide contains a ring image to the top-left of the slide. *Slide 2* contains the same image but it is resized and repositioned.

> **Note**
>
> The images do not need to be the same. You can have a ring shape on the first slide and a square on the other.

3. Select the ring image on the first slide.

4. Click on **Graphics Format | Selection Pane**. The **Selection** pane will populate to the right-hand side of the slide.

5. While the ring image is selected on the slide, the relevant element in the **Selection** pane is highlighted automatically.

6. Click on **Graphic 7** (in this example), and rename it as `!!ring`. Note that you can add any name you like, but it must have the two exclamation points as a prefix.

7.   Press *Enter* to confirm.

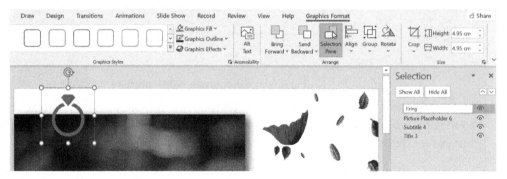

Figure 7.17 – Editing the name of the image using the Selection pane

8.   Now, select the ring on *slide 2* and rename **Graphic 6** as exactly the same name, `!!ring`.

9.   Lastly, apply the Morph transition on *slide 2*. Make sure *slide 2* is selected, then visit **Transitions | Morph**.

10.   The effect will play on the slide. Launch the slide show from the beginning to see it in action.

Along with being able to set animations and transitions, we can add other actions and links to presentations.

Using hyperlinks, actions, and comments

In the previous edition book, we learned how to work with links. As this feature is exactly the same in terms of process, we will only concentrate on how to add Easy linking in this edition.

Easy linking

Easy linking is such a great tool when working with sections in PowerPoint. It allows you to drag a section heading onto another slide, which in turn creates a thumbnail of the first slide of the section with a link to that slide:

1.   Open the `Zoom.pptx` presentation.

2.   Note that there is an **OUR PRODUCTS** section heading just above *slide 3*.

3.   Click on *slide 2* (we will create the link on this slide to demonstrate).

4. Position the mouse pointer over the **OUR PRODUCTS** section heading and, while keeping the mouse depressed, drag the heading to *slide 2*, as illustrated in the following screenshot:

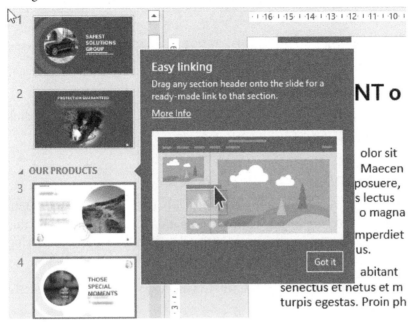

Figure 7.18 – Easy linking feature

5. The link is created on *slide 2* along with the thumbnail of *slide 3*.

6. Resize or reposition the thumbnail on the slide as required, as illustrated in the following screenshot:

Figure 7.19 – Easy linking thumbnail on the slide

7. Click on **Slide Show** and select **From Current Slide** to test the link.

> **Note**
> To remove a hyperlink, select the object or text that has a hyperlink applied,
> and right-click and choose **Remove Hyperlink** from the shortcut menu.

Editing a hyperlink

1. Select the text or object that contains a hyperlink.
2. Right-click and choose **Edit Hyperlink…** from the shortcut menu.
3. The **Edit Hyperlink** dialog box appears. Make the change to the hyperlink.
4. Click on **OK** to apply changes to the hyperlink.

Adding actions

You might be asking yourself what the difference is between hyperlinks and actions in PowerPoint. Hyperlinks are mainly used for navigation only. Actions can do the same things as hyperlinks but have many more options, and can be set up by hovering the mouse over an object, or by means of a mouse click:

1. Click on an object to select it (we will use the `Actions.pptx` presentation for this example).
2. Go to **Insert | Links | Action**.
3. Select the **Mouse Over** tab.
4. Choose the option that best suits your presentation. You will notice that you can hyperlink to **Custom Shows** and many more options from the **Action Settings** dialog box.
5. Click on **OK** at the bottom of the dialog box to commit the changes.
6. To remove an action, visit the **Action Settings** dialog box and select the **None** radio button at the top of the dialog box.

Using Zoom

The **Zoom** feature allows the creation of interactive links to a section summary, a section zoom, or a slide zoom. It is a quick way to insert links, essentially to move efficiently from one part of the presentation to another really quickly:

1. Open a presentation or create a new one (we will use the `Zoom.pptx` presentation for this example). Create sections through the presentation, where necessary.

2. Go to **Insert | Zoom**.

3. You have a choice of three **Zoom** options (**Summary Zoom, Section Zoom**, or **Slide Zoom**).

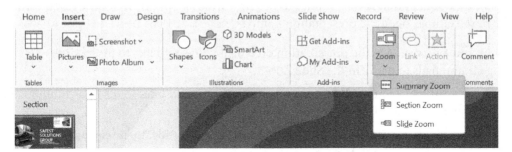

Figure 7.20 – Zoom options

4. Let's investigate the **Summary Zoom** option. For this feature to work, you will need to select the beginning slide for each of the sections you created, and then click on the **Insert** icon at the bottom of the dialog box to create the **Summary Zoom** slide with section links, as illustrated in the following screenshot:

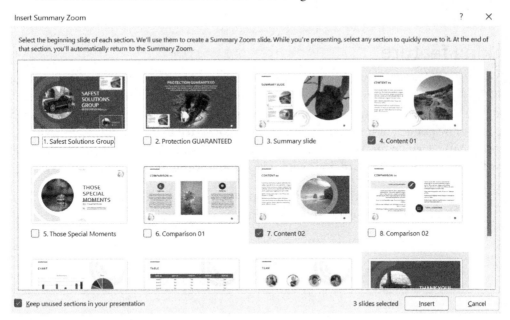

Figure 7.21 – Selecting the first section slide, then clicking on Insert

The **Summary Zoom** slide is created with linked thumbnails to the first slide of each section. The **Section Zoom** option inserts a link to a section or sections on a thumbnail that, when presenting, will zoom to the corresponding section.

The **Slide Zoom** option is very similar to the **Easy linking** option. To follow along with the next example, open the presentation named `City Berlin Design.pptx`:

1. Add a new slide to the presentation on which you would like to insert slide thumbnails to perform the Slide Zoom.

2. Visit **Insert | Zoom | Slide Zoom** then simply choose slides to insert as thumbnails – we have selected slides *3*, *4*, and *5*.

3. Click the **Insert** button to add the thumbnails to the slide, then rearrange the thumbnails on the slide.

4. When presenting, you simply click on the thumbnail to zoom to it, then click with the mouse button to see the next Zoom effect and slide in the presentation.

As previously discussed within the PowerPoint and Word chapters of this book, the **Draw** tab has had a revamp in this latest version. We will briefly revisit the option in the next topic.

Inking feature

If you draw with a pen, mouse pointer, or your finger on a touch-enabled device, PowerPoint will convert the drawing to shape automatically with the *inking* feature. Simply draw onto the slide background and watch the magic happen. When writing any math problems with a pen, mouse pointer, or finger, the writing will be converted to math symbols and will subsequently open up the **Math Tools**, **Structures**, and **Symbols** groups. Note that you can use different **Drawing Tools** to draw with ink on slides within the presentation:

1. Click on the **Draw** tab on the ribbon, and then select **Ink to Shape** from the **Content** group, as illustrated in the following screenshot:

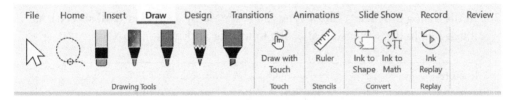

Figure 7.22 – Draw tab within PowerPoint 2021

2. Draw onto the slide using the mouse pointer, or use a touch pen or your finger to draw a shape if you have a touch-enabled device. The drawing is immediately converted to a shape. After drawing text, select the text, and click **Ink to Shape**.

It is important to be skilled with different methods to present your slide content. Visit the next topic to learn more.

Exploring slide show options and custom shows

In this topic, you will learn how to set up a slide show using various options. The **Loop continuously** option is perfect for those conference marketing scenarios when you would like the show to run continuously on a monitor, and the **Presenter View** is great as you can view your speaker notes on your device while presenting to an audience.

You will be shown how to show all or specific slides in a presentation, as well as adjust slide timings and set slides to use these timings when presenting. The benefits of custom slide shows will be explained here.

Setting up a slide show

1. Click on the **Slide Show** tab on the ribbon.
2. Select the **Set Up Slide Show** icon.

3. In the dialog box, select **Show type** as **Presented by a speaker (full screen)**, as illustrated in the screenshot after the following information box:

> **Note**
>
> This is normally full screen, but there are other options, including **Browsed at a kiosk**, which is used when running business presentations without the presenter being in attendance, and without the option to skip slides. Once you have set up kiosk mode, rehearse slide timings by advancing to the next slide to set a time limit in order to cover the slide content for viewing. This is to make sure that the audience walking by is able to digest all the content on each slide.

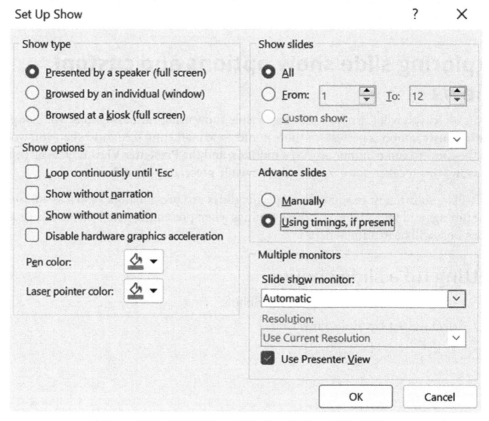

Figure 7.23 – Set Up Show dialog box in PowerPoint 2021

4. Under the **Show options** heading, select the **Loop continuously until 'Esc'** option if you are going to be repeating your slide show repetitively for a *walk-by* audience. Note that you also have the **Show with** or **Show without** narration options.

5. From the **Show slides** heading, select which slides will need to be in the slide show while presenting the slide show to an audience.

   If any custom shows are available in this presentation, they would display in the **Custom Show** drop-down list.

6. The **Advance slides** category is very important—make sure that you select **Using timings, if present** so that you do not have to click your way through a presentation when presenting to an audience.

7. Set **Advance slides** to **Manually** if you need to pause (or be in control) throughout the presentation while presenting to an audience.

Let's look at the **Narration** options in the next topic.

Playing narrations

If you have used narrations and recorded them using the **Record Slide Show** option from the **Record** tab options, you would need to make sure that when playing back to an audience, the relevant options are selected. These are located on the **Slide Show** tab ribbon, as illustrated in the following screenshot:

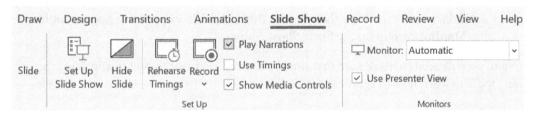

Figure 7.24 – Play Narrations feature in PowerPoint

1. From the **Slide Show** tab (under the **Set Up** group), make sure that the **Play Narrations** checkbox is selected.

2. Also, make sure that the option under the **Set Up Show** dialog box for **Show without narration** is not selected.

Let's see how we would set up **Presenter View** in the next topic.

Setting up the Presenter View

The Presenter View enables you to view speaker notes while presenting to an audience. The audience views the presentation on the main monitor, and the presenter views the presentation with access to speaker notes on another monitor. The Presenter View enables the presentation to be viewed on multiple monitors. In the Presenter View, you can also decide to darken or lighten the screen for the audience—for example, during a break or when a question-and-answer-type session is in progress:

1. Open the presentation to set up viewing on multiple monitors. We will continue with the presentation from the previous topic.

2. Insert speaker notes to help you with presenting to the audience. To help you, click on a slide to add speaker notes, and then click on the **Notes** icon on the status bar to activate the **Notes** section below the slide. Type the following note: `Welcome to our presentation on Safest Solutions Group Travels. We hope to entice you to explore more of our wonderful trips on offer, including the appropriate cover for your journey.`

3. Click on **Slide Show | Setup Slide Show**.

4. Locate the **Use Presenter View** checkbox, and then click to select it. If you have multiple monitors connected, the feature will automatically detect the primary and secondary monitors. Note that the **Use Presenter View** option is also present from the **Monitors** group on the **Slide Show** ribbon.

Often, we will need to make sure that timings are correct prior to presenting. Visit the next topic to learn how to set these up.

Setting up timings

You can rehearse your presentation to accommodate your slide advance timings. We will learn how to set the timings and set up the environment to use the timings. Make sure that the **Using timings, if present** option is selected if the presentation you are setting up has advanced slide timings selected throughout the presentation:

1. Firstly, set the slide timings using the **Advance Slide** option on the **Transitions** tab

2. Go to the **Slide Show** tab and select the **Set Up Show** icon to launch the dialog box.

3. Under the **Advance slides** heading, make sure that **Using timings, if present** is selected. This option is illustrated in a previous screenshot under *Setting up a slide show*.

4. Click on **OK** to commit the changes.

Let's learn how to set up media controls on a slide.

Showing media controls

The media controls are the icons that appear below the audio or video content inserted into the presentation:

1. Click on the **Slide Show** tab on the ribbon.

2. Locate the **Set Up** group.

3. Make sure that the checkbox for **Show Media Controls** is selected, otherwise, the control buttons will not show when the presentation is being shown to an audience.

Figure 7.25 – Setting up media controls

Now that we are able to set timings and media controls, let's visit the **Custom Slide Show** options.

Creating a custom slide show

The **Custom Slide Show** feature in PowerPoint is extremely useful when you need to create several different shows within one PowerPoint presentation. Not all slides apply to all audiences, so different categories of slides can be sent to a custom show and named as such so that you can present just the right content for a particular audience, without having different presentations for different audiences/content:

1. To create a custom show, click on the **Slide Show** tab on the ribbon.

2. Click on the **Custom Slide Show** icon.

3. Choose **Custom Shows…**, as illustrated in the following screenshot:

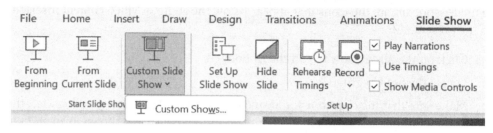

Figure 7.26 – Custom Slide Show option

4. Click on the **New…** icon.

5. Name the slide show by typing text into the **Define Custom Show** dialog box.

6. Click to select slides to add to the custom show.

7. Use the **Add>>** icon to move the slides to the right side of the dialog box, to be included in the new custom show. Click on **OK** when done. Note, it's very important to make sure that slides are included in a specific order (especially if preparing for an international computer examination).

8. The new custom show will appear in the **Custom Shows** dialog box.

9. To make changes, click on the **Edit…** icon.

10. To delete the custom show, click on the **Remove** icon.

11. To display the show, click on the **Show** icon.

12. Click on **Close** when done.

13. The new custom show will be visible when clicking on the **Custom Slide Show** icon on the **Slide Show** tab.

If viewing a presentation using a screen reader, you now have the ability to set the order. We will learn about this new option in the next topic.

Setting the reading order

While using a screen reader, you are now able to set the order of how the slide elements appear on the screen:

1. Visit **Review | Check Accessibility**, then select the **Reading Order Pane** option from the drop-down list. The **Reading Order** pane will open to the left-hand side of the PowerPoint window.

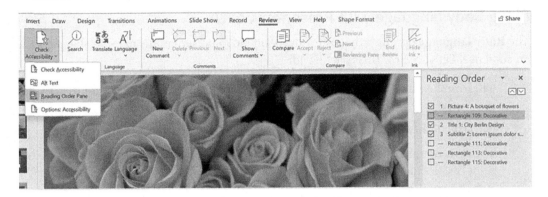

Figure 7.27 – Setting the Reading Order when viewing on a screen reader

2. Select the order you wish the elements to appear when viewing the presentation on a screen reader.

Along with the ability to set the reading order, we can now rehearse a presentation with help from a coach.

Rehearsing with Presenter Coach

The **Rehearse with Coach** tool is a new feature that is available on the desktop, web, and iPad versions of Microsoft Office 2021. The Coach incorporates artificial intelligence listening to you while you run through your presentation. After selecting **Slide Show | Rehearse with Coach**, click the **Start Rehearsing** button to the right-hand side of the slide. It will address talking speed, pitch, sensitive phrases, repetitive word fluency like "uhm", and detect whether you are reading from the slide. Once you press *Esc* on the keyboard, the tool will provide informative feedback for each of the topics mentioned in a *Rehearsal Report*.

Figure 7.28 – Rehearse with Coach features new to PowerPoint 2021

Using Body language with Presenter Coach

The **Body language** option provides feedback on video presentations prior to sharing with an audience. Let's see how this is achieved:

1. Click on the **Slide Show | Rehearse with Coach | Body language** button to activate the option.

2. Click the **Rehearse with Coach** button again to start checking the presentation.

3. The presentation opens in Slide Show view. Click the **Start Rehearsing** button to the right of the slide.

Figure 7.29 – Rehearse with Presenter coach in Slide Show view

4. Do a run-through of the presentation as you would when presenting to an audience. The **Rehearse with Coach** option will check body language/sound and alert you with a "beep" sound and provide feedback beneath the video image to the right-bottom corner of the slide:

I. When too close to the camera, the coach will prompt you and provide feedback to move further away from the screen. It will indicate when you have the correct spot for presenting too!

II. If you remove or adjust your glasses whilst presenting, swipe your hand through your hair, or scratch your face, the coach will provide feedback.

III. When moving your head to the side, thereby removing eye contact with the audience, you will also be notified.

Figure 7.30 – Rehearse with Coach body language options

5. In addition, at the end of the presentation, you will be presented with a Rehearsal Report:

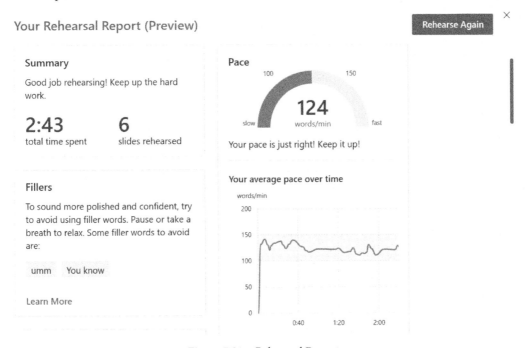

Figure 7.31 – Rehearsal Report

6. You will need to scroll down the report to access more feedback.

7. The summary will give feedback and take images of where things went wrong in the presentation, such as **Eye contact**, **Clear view**, and **Distance**. You will notice that it provides snippets of the video where you went wrong whilst presenting; visit the **Body Language** section for this feedback.

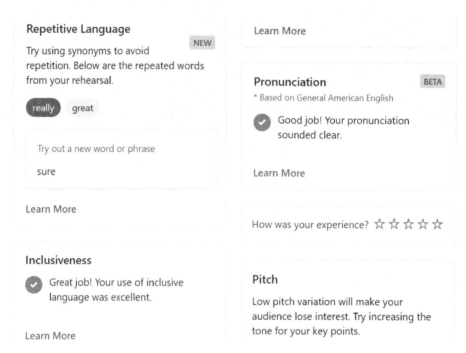

Figure 7.32 – Rehearse with Coach generated report

Overall, this is a great tool to aid the presenter in preparation to provide the best experience for the audience on the receiving end. We can now also record a presentation including our narration in the new version. Let's learn this in the next topic.

Recording a presentation

Narrating slides is possible using the new recording features within the Office 2021 platform. We can annotate the slide and record those actions too:

1. Open the presentation named `SSG-SetupSlideShow.pptx`.

2. Click **Slide Show | Record | From Beginning…** to record narration from the beginning of the presentation.

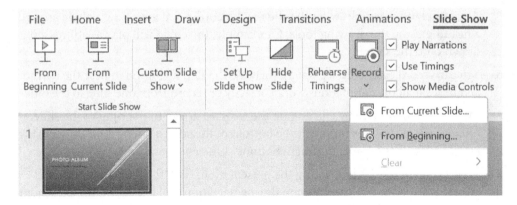

Figure 7.33 – Record button to add narration to a slide presentation

3. If your camera is enabled, you will see the video at the bottom-right of the slide. Use the **Record** button to start recording the voiceover. Click **Stop** to end narration, and **Replay** to recap what you have recorded. The **Notes** button top-center is beneficial when you would like to read slide notes to narrate.

Figure 7.34 – The narration screen in PowerPoint 2021

4. Click the **Record** button, then speak to record your voice. If you are reading from slide notes, the note drop-down will not record that action, only what you read from the notes.

5. Any annotations you draw on the slide will record. So, if you draw a circle around a heading using the drawing tools, for example, the circle will play as animation as drawn onto the slide.

6. You can record each slide separately, then use the **Replay** button to hear the narration and to see if all the annotations work correctly or record from one slide to the other.

7. Move to the next slide by clicking on the forward arrow to the right of the slide. There is a laser pointer button at the bottom of the screen, along with the drawing tools, and microphone and camera buttons at the end.

8. When you are finished narrating the presentation, click the **Stop** button. Any elements added to the presentation during narration will appear on the presentation slides. Click on **Slide Show | From Beginning…** to view the slide show.

We hope that you have enjoyed all these new features that aid efficiency and create engaging presentations. The last topic in this chapter is revisiting **master slides** and omitting certain slides when presenting.

Using master slides and hiding slides

In this topic, you will learn to create, modify, and format a master slide, and be able to hide or show certain slides when delivering a presentation.

Creating master slides

The slide master stores information such as logos, styles, and fonts, which the user can set as a default for all slides in the presentation. For instance, a company logo could be set in a certain position on the slide with certain attributes. When placed on the slide master, all slides within the presentation—and any new slide inserted in the presentation—will display the logo in the same position with the same attributes.

Any elements placed onto the slide master will not be editable when creating the presentation unless the user is familiar with editing master slides or has been given permission to do so. Editing master slides for different presentation slide layouts is extremely popular when companies wish to lock down branding for all stationery within a business:

1. For this example, we will create a new presentation based on the **Quotable** theme.

2. Click to select **View | Slide Master**. The slide master view is now displayed on the screen.

3. Depending on the theme and the slides you have within the presentation, you will be presented with different slide layouts and masters, but you should see a slide master and then different layout masters beneath that in **Slide Pane**.

4. Note that you can also create master slides for handouts and notes, as well as many other master slide layout types.

5. Once you have activated the slide master, the **Slide Master** ribbon will open up with a lot of different options for you to use to customize your master slides, as can be seen in the following screenshot:

Figure 7.35 – Slide Master tab showing options within PowerPoint 2021

6. We will insert a picture onto the slide background. Make sure that the picture is visible on all masters—if not, copy and paste to the various slide masters visible in **Slide Pane**.

7. Click on the **Insert** tab, and then choose **Pictures**.

8. Locate the picture on your computer and insert it onto the slide master, where appropriate. For this example, we will use `SafestSolutionsLogo.png`.

9. Switch back to the **Slide** view to see whether the master has updated the slides in the presentation—notice that you are unable to select the picture, and all picture editing will need to happen in the **Slide Master** view.

10. Click on the **View** tab and choose **Normal**.

11. Click on the **View** tab and select **Slide Master** to return to master editing mode.

12. Adjust the fonts, styles, colors, and effects, and add any text—such as footers—that you would like to appear on all slides as a master. We will update the font for the main titles to the **Courgette** font.

13. Click on the **Close Master View** icon at the end of the ribbon to view the changes to the presentation.

14. Experiment with the options available on the **Slide Master** tab to create the perfect presentation master for your requirements.

Hiding slides

At times, certain slides in the final presentation might not be suitable for the presentation audience. It is possible to hide slides in **Slide Pane** or in **Slide Sorter View**:

1. Right-click on a slide to hide it.

2. From the shortcut menu choose **Hide Slide**, or click on the **Slide Show** tab and choose **Hide Slide,** or use the **Slide Sorter view** to hide a slide. The former option is illustrated in the following screenshot:

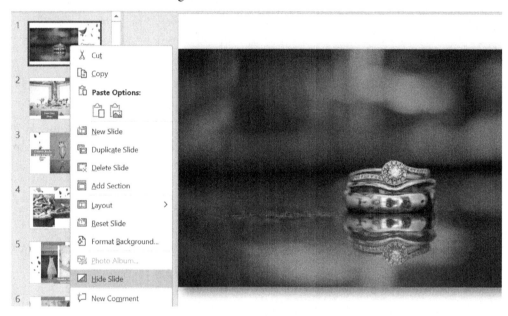

Figure 7.36 – Hide Slide option on the right-click menu

3. An icon identifies hidden slides; this is located in the top-left corner of the slide (in **Slide Sorter** and **Slide view**).

4. To unhide a slide, simply click on the **Hide Slide** icon again.

Summary

We have learned an abundance of skills in this detailed chapter, enabling the creation and modification of photo albums, and the ability to set up sections to create a presentation order and to hide slides, when appropriate. We have mastered the relevant presentation motions, effects, timing, transitions, and animations, and how they work with the final presentation output with the slide show options. Driving consistency with the use of slide masters to conserve company branding and productivity when creating presentations has been another important achievement in this chapter.

In the next chapter, we will focus on useful design and presentation principles to consider when creating professional presentations.

The following chapters will cover principles of presentation design, using clear messages and persuading an audience, as well as techniques to implement when adding visual impact.

8
Mastering Best Practices with Presentations

The strength of a PowerPoint presentation does not only rely on your ability to utilize powerful tools that are housed within the application when creating presentations. It also depends on your ability to design and communicate well. This part of this book focuses on useful design and presentation principles to consider when creating professional presentations.

The following topics will be covered in this chapter:

- Principles of presentation design
- Using clear messages and persuading the audience
- Visual impact and useful techniques

Technical requirements

To complete this chapter, you must be proficient in creating PowerPoint 2021 presentations and have a general overview of the tools available to modify presentations. You must have also worked through *Part 2* of this book. The examples for this chapter can be found in this book's GitHub repository: `https://github.com/PacktPublishing/Learn-Microsoft-Office-2021-Second-Edition`.

Principles of presentation design

In this section, we will learn about the importance of design and presentation skills when creating presentations and identifying tools for quick design. Being able to understand the presentation process when designing slides and recognize that the role of the presenter is important. You will also learn about some design principles that will help your message remain with the audience.

Importance of design and presentation skills

When delivering a presentation to an audience, it is always anticipated to be engaging and impactful and wants to be revisited. As a PowerPoint 2021 user, you can create slides and use the tools that are available along the ribbon, but unless you have acquired a few extra skills, your presentations will not capture an audience effectively during, or after, the presentation has taken place.

We always want to ensure that an audience can remember facts that have been relayed well after we have presented. So, what skills do we, as presenters, need to acquire to produce effective presentations?

Artistic creativity, design, and communication, collectively named technical creativity, are very important skills for presenters, and using any technology should not detract from the examples and facts imparted while presenting the slides to the audience. Depending on the nature of the presentation, without technical creativity, it is easy for the presentation to be deficient in perspective.

Content needs to be presented effectively too; otherwise, the result could lack function. The effectiveness from start to end of a presentation is also dependent on the following four elements:

- Preparation
- Rehearsal
- Timing
- Delivery

You also need to be consistent when adding elements such as font, style, color, and images and always take into account any corporate branding when compiling presentations. When using visual support for content on slides, you need to remember that there must be a reason to use certain elements.

Such reasons could be to add clarification, support facts, or add humor, but always remember the saying "less is more" and apply this rule to every presentation you create. Not every human is great at creative flair when it comes to presentations, but following these simple points will hopefully get you thinking before creating any slides.

Identifying tools to enhance presentation design

Let's have a look at some presentation add-ins to help you enhance your design.

We have discussed tools such as **Stock Images**, **Cutout People**, **Stickers**, **Illustrations**, **Icons**, **3D Models**, **Zoom**, **Templates**, **Picture Editing**, **Photo Album**, and **Custom Shows**, as well as using **video** functionality in PowerPoint 2021, already, but other tools can make an impact as well. In addition to the PowerPoint that are tools available today, we can also make use of different methods to present and enhance the audience's experience.

We'll look at a few of these in this section.

Accessing the Pickit for PowerPoint add-in

The first add-in that I find extremely useful is the **Pickit** app. This app is free to use (part-owned by Microsoft) and all the images are legal without license or cost involved. Although it has been around for a few years, it is often not accessed within the PowerPoint environment. It allows for brand designs and custom images to be inserted into slide backgrounds in PowerPoint 2021. Follow these steps:

1. To add Pickit, click on **Insert | Get Add-ins**:

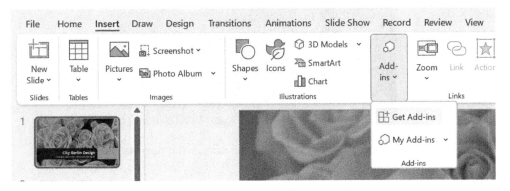

Figure 8.1 – Insert | Get Add-ins

2. You should see the Pickit app in the **Office Add-ins** suggestion dialog box. If not, type `Pickit` into the **Search** box provided, then press *Enter* on your keyboard to locate it.

3. Click on the **Add** icon to insert the Pickit app into PowerPoint:

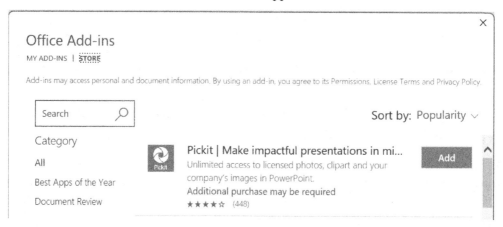

Figure 8.2 – Using Office Add-ins to locate the Pickit app

4. Another screen will populate, asking you to agree to the terms. Click **Continue**.

5. The app, once installed, will appear as a new group named **Pickit** that contains the **Pickit Images** button at the end of the **Home** tab ribbon. When you click on the **Pickit** button, the options will load to the right-hand side of the PowerPoint environment:

Figure 8.3 – The Pickit Images button on the Home tab

6. You will need to sign in with your Pickit or Microsoft account to use the service:

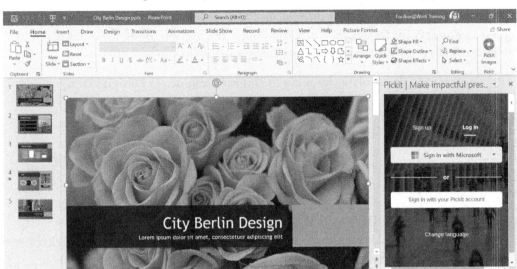

Figure 8.4 – Using the Pickit pane to sign in using your Microsoft or Pickit account details

7. The next step would be to confirm permission for the app to access your information. Select **Yes** to grant permission.

8. Use the **Search** box to locate Illustrations or photos or select a category at the top of the pane. Click on an image to add the item to the selected slide.

This tool will help you create quick, professional images and background designs to suit your presentation using royalty-free elements. Access to this image bank will avoid any copyright issues and wasted time searching for images on the internet. Follow the same process to add the app to OneNote and Word. In the next section, we will learn how to use PowerPoint Designer.

PowerPoint Designer

If you are using PowerPoint 2021 through an Office 365 subscription, then you will have access to **PowerPoint Designer**. PowerPoint offers the user pre-designed slides based on an image that's been inserted as a slide's background. Follow these steps:

1. Design ideas are available by going to **Home | Designer** or **Design | Designer**.

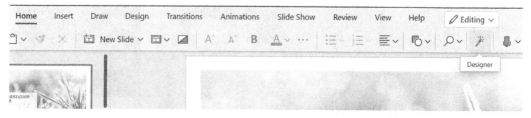

Figure 8.5 – The Designer tool on the Home tab

The **Designer** tool is perfect for those who do not have design skills as it helps users create stunning presentations with a click of a button. Don't forget about using the remove background, artistic, and color tools, which are other features within PowerPoint that can be used to enhance images to produce stunning visuals. Washout and transparency options provide for contrasting colors over images using shapes and text too.

2. After clicking on the **Designer** button, a pane will appear to the right of the slide:

Figure 8.6 – Using the Designer pane to select designs

3. Use the scroll bar to the right of the **Designer** pane to choose a design. Once a design has been selected for the first slide, click on the second slide in your presentation. Notice to the right that the **Designer** pane suggests similar designs to compliment the first choice of design. Continue to move through the presentation by applying layouts using the **Designer** pane.

What we will cover in the next section is useful in situations such as presenting at a conference, for instance, as you can navigate a web page directly within a presentation. Let's investigate how we can achieve this.

Displaying web content

Often, you will need to display a link to a web page within a PowerPoint presentation. On clicking a link on a slide, the relevant website will open in a separate browser. The **Web Viewer** app provides does this within the PowerPoint application so that you don't have to leave the PowerPoint interface to display web page content within a separate browser. Follow these steps to learn how to use it:

1. Select a slide in the presentation where you would like to insert the **Web Viewer** app.

2. Click on **Insert | Get Add-ins**.

3. Click on **Add** to insert the **Web Viewer** app.

4. Next, confirm that Microsoft has permission to access your information. Select **Yes** to grant permission.

5. The app will be inserted into the selected slide.

6. To display a searchable web page directly on a PowerPoint slide, simply type the web address into the URL space provided on the inserted image. Note that some websites can't be viewed in this manner due to security concerns. Remember that you will require an active internet connection when presenting the PowerPoint slides to an audience for this feature to work. The default website is included in the search area, namely www.wikipedia.org. For this example, we will use this website to search for content.

7. Press **Preview** to the bottom right-hand side of the **Web Viewer** app:

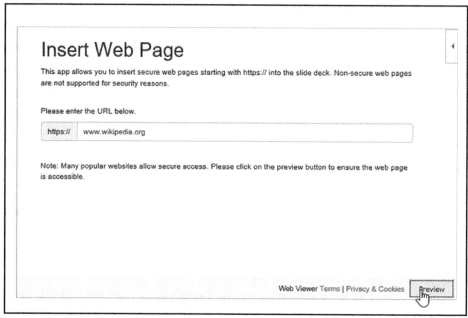

Figure 8.7 – The Preview button on the Web Viewer app

8. The website will load in the **Web Viewer** app on the presentation:

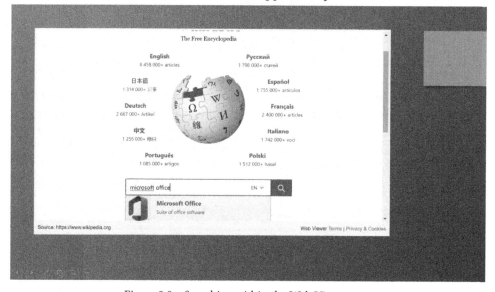

Figure 8.8 – Searching within the Web Viewer app

9. Enter a search term in the search area provided. For this example, we will search for `Microsoft Office`.

10. Press *Enter* or click on the **Search** button to navigate to the website. When you are done, click on the next slide in the presentation to continue.

> **Note**
>
> We can also use the **Link to slide** option here. The preceding sections covered just a few additional tools you could apply when creating a presentation. We hope that you absorb the PowerPoint chapters of this book to grab even more value-adding tools in the application. New and existing tools are located on every tab within the PowerPoint 2021 environment.

Now, let's look at the planning aspect of presentation design.

Presentation planning

Planning is crucial to creating a stunning presentation. You should brainstorm by using mind maps (SmartArt or Visio could be useful here), or plan by jotting down points to create an outline of ideas as an introduction, the main body, and the concluding content. After creating the outline, you can think about adding content, then images, captions, and formatting the content. Think about the first slide of the presentation and how you could capture the audience by adding an entertaining image.

The following table shows factors to consider when planning content:

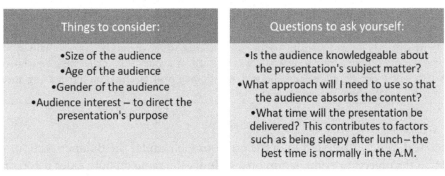

Things to consider:	Questions to ask yourself:
• Size of the audience • Age of the audience • Gender of the audience • Audience interest – to direct the presentation's purpose	• Is the audience knowledgeable about the presentation's subject matter? • What approach will I need to use so that the audience absorbs the content? • What time will the presentation be delivered? This contributes to factors such as being sleepy after lunch – the best time is normally in the A.M.

Table 8.1

There are also several things to avoid when creating slide content:

- Create no more than 10 slides in a presentation.

- Your presentation should be no longer than 20 minutes.

- Font size should be no less than 30 pts in size – this is dependent on the design and, of course, sub-points.

- Only add the main points to a slide – this is just the visual aid; the narrative is the important bit. A comprehensive handout can be distributed via an online link after the presentation has been delivered.

Basic design principles

There are several design principles to take into consideration that contribute greatly to the audience's retention of the information you convey to them. The five most important design principles for presentation design are **Balance**, **Movement**, **Emphasis**, **Unity**, and **White Space**:

Balance	Every element on a slide carries weight and contributes to the overall balance of the slide. How these elements are placed on a slide will have an impact on whether they are lighter in color or heavy elements that attract the eye of the audience. There are two types of balance – that is, symmetrical and asymmetrical.
Movement	How does the audience's eye travel over the slide's design? This is movement. Movement creates a flow in the story and can be attained by adding SmartArt and animation that applies to the slide's elements.
Emphasis	Emphasis means that the object on the slide's design must stand out from the rest of the objects.
Unity	Unity is how things work together as a whole. Visually, people like to work with and add loads of different fonts to a presentation. This just creates confusion. Elements need to have a relationship with each other – organizing elements on a slide is key.
White Space	Design according to the rule of thirds, which means two horizontally spaced lines and two vertically spaced lines on a slide. This creates nine equal parts on the slide and helps with positioning objects, either on intersecting lines or within the equal parts.

Table 8.2

Symmetrical, which is referred to in the previous table under the **Balance** section, means that the objects or compilation on a slide are the same on both sides if you draw a line through the middle of the object or design. **Asymmetrical** is when a design lacks symmetry when its objects do not correspond to each other (in the arrangement of objects, size, or shape) but still maintain balance.

It is important to adjust the visual weight of objects in terms of three elements, as follows:

- Color

- Contrast

- Scale

Taking note of these principles when designing slides will have the benefit of providing an eye-catching, fascinating, and peppy impact. Use tools such as **SmartArt** to create a flow in the content on a slide.

White space and the rule of thirds

Always take **white space** on a presentation slide into consideration, and design according to the rule of thirds. Use **guides** on a slide to create a grid where you can place design elements. White space utilization refers to provisioning minimalism and removing poorly placed objects on slides:

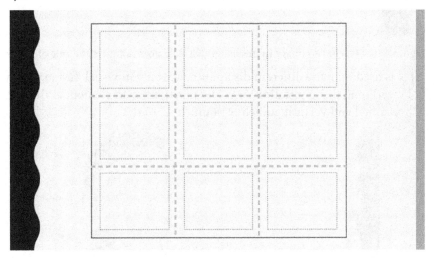

Figure 8.9 – Slide separated by guides using the rule of thirds

Two equally spaced horizontal, and two equally spaced vertical, lines on a slide will divide the slide into nine equal parts where elements can be arranged – this is called the **rule of thirds**. This photography visual design principle is applied when you're applying images to slides and learning to maximize the use of white space on the slides. Adding an image or text to the center of a slide does not meet the rule of thirds principle:

Figure 8.10 – Placing an image in the center of a slide does not meet the rule of thirds

The principle is used in many different disciplines, not only in visual design. A power point (not PowerPoint, the application) involves positioning an element at the intersection between a horizontal and vertical guideline point:

Figure 8.11 – Image positioning using the rule of thirds

Now, let's learn more about communicating to engage audiences.

Using clear messages and persuading audiences

In this section, you will learn how to communicate a pure message by persuading your audience to engage with the content.

It is crucial to establish credibility with an audience when imparting knowledge through slides. To achieve this, you need to be cautious about the number of characters you have on slides within the presentation. Knowledge is key and is portrayed as content on slides, so make sure that complex content is relayed as simple visual statements. Using contrasting colors on slide backgrounds should be limited to two colors. Spacing your text on slides is an important consideration.

In PowerPoint 2021, you can use the **Handouts** (or **Notes**) feature so that the audience can refer to the presentation, thereby reinforcing knowledge and retaining content. These are great to make available after the presentation has ended via a link for delegates to access. As a refresher, to print handouts or notes, go to **File | Print | Full Page Slides**, then choose either **Notes Pages** or a **Handouts** option:

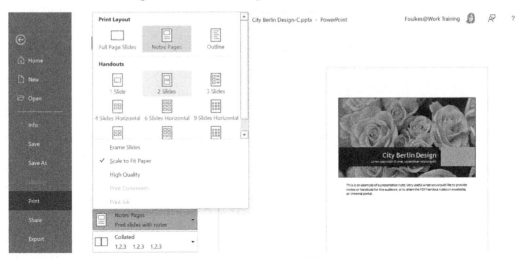

Figure 8.12 – Using the Print | Full Page Slides option to print notes or handouts

Remember that you can also use the **Record** feature in PowerPoint 2021 to record yourself presenting. Click on **Record | Record | From Beginning…**, after which you can **Export to Video** to distribute to the audience.

These tools, and more, will be discussed in *Part 2* of this book:

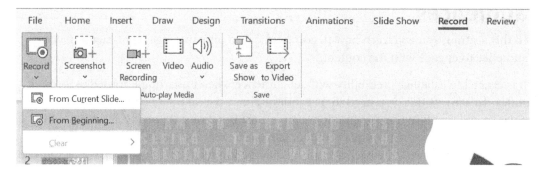

Figure 8.13 – The Record feature in PowerPoint to record narration

When designing presentation slides, it is easy to go off-topic or try to put too much information onto the slide, so try to keep to one point when storytelling. It must be said that if you cannot convey content to an audience in simple terms, then you do not know your content well enough to impart.

The start and end slides of the presentation should be as impactful as possible as this is the time when your audience's attention span is most engaged. Also, note that it is known that an individual will not be able to take in more than four points from a presentation – so, keep it simple.

Don't forget about the **Custom Shows…** and **Sections** features in PowerPoint to tailor the presentation to suit your audience.

We all love stories and how expressive they can be told. Use this tactic when presenting your content to an audience as it helps them retain the message. In the next section, you will learn more about this aspect.

Conveying content to an audience

Practicing (or rehearsing) your presentation before delivering it is important to keep an eye on your pitch and tone when projecting your voice to your audience, as this will surely hold the attention and interest of your audience. This is relevant in face-to-face as well as remote presentations through online meeting tools. This is even more relevant through Zoom and Teams – you are less in control as usual as you can't use body language to keep engagement.

Using your voice during online meetings is extremely important, as well as features such as **Spotlight** in Teams. Visit *Chapter 16, Creating and Managing Online Meetings* to learn more about these features in detail.

Factors such as nervousness and stress before delivering a presentation often lead to monotony and a fast-paced presentation. So, make sure that you run through the presentation a few times so that you learn to speak slowly. When presenting, you could leave out important words due to nervousness and not even realize it. Practice makes a good presenter. These factors can also affect your body language. Always try to imagine that you are in the audience watching yourself, and if you do not like what you see, change it before presenting! **Rehearse with Coach** and **Presenter Coach** in PowerPoint are useful here as you can concentrate on and get real-time feedback on distance, eye contact, and clear view. These are explained fully in *Part 2* of this book.

We often present through online platforms, such as Teams and Zoom. There are many methods to aid you, as the presenter, through both **Teams** and **Zoom**, and these will be discussed in *Chapter 16, Creating and Managing Online Meetings*.

PowerPoint Live is one such tool that we will explore that allows presenters to share content with an audience but also create a manageable, comfortable space to present in.

You, as the presenter, need to make sincere connections with the audience that will distract them from reading slides as you are presenting and take away the need for you to be there. Your role is to connect and interact! This can be rectified by connecting with people across the room and moving around using natural body language and hand gestures. Try to think of yourself as the facilitator rather than the presenter taking people on a journey. Don't overload slides with text, animations, or color, and never add all the content so that you are just reading the slides out to the audience. Use verbs on a slide where possible.

Color has a physiological and psychological bearing of 73% on audience engagement and instills learning and understanding. Always be enthusiastic and smile when sharing your presentation content and try and use emotive words to capture engagement. Use a prop or headline or photo that grabs the audience's attention, a quote, or even ask the audience a thought-provoking question regarding the first slide in your presentation.

As Plato said, "*The beginning is the most important part of the work.*"

Another important reason to do a run-through of the presentation is to ensure that the colors that are used on the presentation's text and background can be seen by the audience. It's best to do the run-through at the venue you will be presenting at for this purpose or, if presenting online, ask a colleague to run through the presentation with you as it is always useful to see the audience's experience, as well as for you to have an opportunity to become familiar, and comfortable with, the environment.

Knowing your audience is an extremely important aspect of slide design, as well as its content. Let's navigate through a series of questions you should take into consideration before presenting. Hopefully, they will help you prepare more thoroughly.

Getting to know an audience

You should consider the following factors before creating your presentation slides as it is a vital route to preparing, planning, and presenting:

- Who is my audience and do they already have some expertise with the subject matter?

- What will the audience know about me before presenting?

- What will the audience be expecting to gain?

- How large is the audience?

- Where will I deliver the presentation (location or remote), and what technique will I need to use?

- Will I need to visit the venue or remote location beforehand to eliminate any potential problems or obstacles to become familiar with the technology, or view my presentation on screen? If remote, do I know how to screen share within the meeting or webinar app?

- Do I require any additional equipment (for example, a microphone or headset) and where will I be presenting from in the venue?

- Will there be a time limit to present, or do I have some leeway?

- Incorporate a backup plan if things go wrong technically during the presentation's delivery.

- When presenting online, we can also make use of **Breakout Rooms** to cement audience participation, or extend the session by adding challenges or time to practice. This feature will be explained fully in *Chapter 16, Creating and Managing Online Meetings*.

Let's look at a few other elements to be mindful of.

Visual impact and useful techniques

In this section, you'll learn about the impact of sound and images, how the brain processes visual input, and how this impacts a presentation. In addition, you will be taught how to use guides, alignments, and grouping before learning how to apply consistent slide styles and color psychology.

Considering the brain

When using a combination of text and visual elements on slides within a presentation, it is good to understand how the brain processes these elements differently.

Learning about visual and verbal passages

There are two passages in which the brain functions in terms of text and visual elements. For text, the verbal passage is used by the brain. It is used when you add any visual elements to slides in a presentation. If you overload the slide with text, then the verbal narrative will become overloaded, causing the audience to lose focus! The visual passage will look for visually pleasing elements and this, of course, helps retain focus since the presenter is the narrator of the elements on the slide:

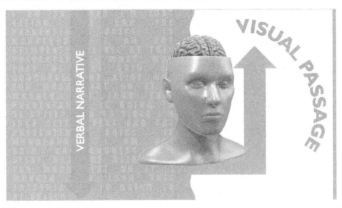

Figure 8.14 – Visual passage versus verbal narrative

So, again, there are a few things to consider when adding, for instance, bullet points to a slide as the points will end up competing with the narrative by the presenter. Shift the concentration of the audience from the bullet points on a slide to a visual element that you are narrating, thereby keeping the audience focused on you.

Law of proximity

The visual cortex in the brain processes visual images and is the largest system near the rear of your brain. Hoaxing the mind visually by using the law of proximity is another way to ensure that any elements that are placed on a slide near each other are connected in some way. The retina is a thin tissue located around the back inside layer of the eye. After visual input is received by the retina, it is passed to the brain, which then processes the information in terms of shape, color, and orientation:

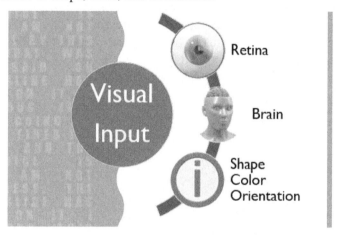

Figure 8.15 – Law of proximity

Now that you have learned about the law of proximity, let's learn how images and sound impact engagement.

Investigating the impact of images and sound

As we mentioned previously, visual impact is key when designing presentations. Always use high-resolution photographs and try to avoid stickers and emoji-type images. It is especially important to mention that having a sticker or emoji image on one slide and then a high-resolution photograph on the next will interrupt the presentation's flow, so consistency cannot be achieved by mixing the two types of visual aids. An audience will respond positively to content-appropriate, high-resolution images that have been placed on a background that makes good use of white space.

It's worth mentioning that you should always **Compress Pictures** before sending out a presentation to an audience. Use the **Delete cropped areas of pictures** option to get rid of any previously cropped-out areas of images within your slide presentations. This will reduce the presentation's size considerably. Click on an image in the presentation, then go to **Picture Format | Compress Pictures** to navigate the options:

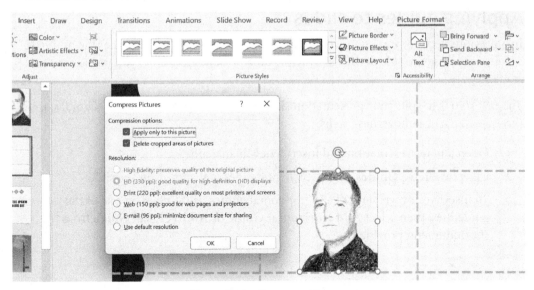

Figure 8.16 – Compress Pictures

Now, let's discuss sound. Recording yourself presenting is always a daunting task. Often, you do not like the way your voice sounds, or you find that you repeatedly say "um, ok, so...," or your tone is monotonous. Don't worry about this, though – everyone is unique and voice pitch and tone vary greatly. You can always fix this with a voiceover, either downloaded or by using a colleague. The new and existing features in Office 2021, **Rehearse with Coach** and **Presenter Coach**, allow you to check sound, movement, speech, and so much more. We learned about these amazing features in the PowerPoint chapters of this book.

Sound can change the mood of the audience quickly and needs to be considered necessary, especially when using animations and transitions. Ask yourself the following questions before adding sound to a presentation:

- Is there a piece of music that would help set the mood and tone of my presentation? Would it contribute to me winning the audience over with a particular piece of music that's relevant to my topic?

- How will adding sound to this particular presentation captivate the audience?

- What about the age, gender, and nature of the presentation concerning sound?

- If I add music to my presentation, how would I keep the brand and content connected?

These are just some of the points to run through when deciding to add sound to your presentation – remember, less is more!

Applying guides to slides

In a previous section, we discussed the theory around white space and the rule of thirds. To physically use the rule of thirds principle on a presentation slide, you must carry out some steps.

The first step is to split your presentation slide, using horizontal and vertical guides, into three equal parts. Follow these steps:

1. Open a new presentation and insert a new blank slide.

2. Click on **View | Guides**, after which guidelines will appear on the slide.

3. To insert your own vertical and horizontal guides, right-click on one of the existing guidelines, then select **Add Horizontal Guide** or **Add Vertical Guide** from the shortcut menu provided:

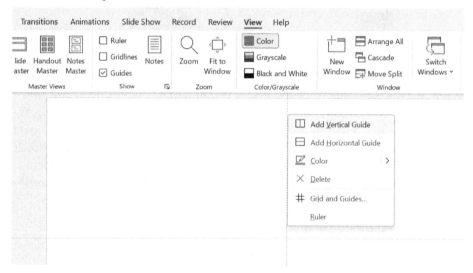

Figure 8.17 – Adding guides to slides

Drag the guides to a position on the slide so that the slide is split into two equal horizontal and two equal vertical parts.

Now, use the grid to align your presentation content so that you can optimize the visual experience for your audience. You can stimulate an audience's response by using the rule of thirds to increase curiosity, or create tension, to name a few examples. See the slide examples in the *White space and the rule of thirds* section.

When referring to the images, the first image displays that the rule of thirds has not been met, while the second displays an example of the rule of thirds. Adding a photograph with the eyes of the person in the upper horizontal third of a slide will make a huge difference, and so will adding an image to the right or left of the vertical rule of thirds – never place an image or object in the center of a slide. Not only is this an important principle when designing slides, but something you can take into consideration when taking photographs with your mobile phone or camera going forward.

Now, let's learn how to align and group objects.

Aligning and grouping objects

The alignment and grouping tools are valuable skills to master in PowerPoint 2021 as they will objects to be arranged proportionately and duplicated quickly on slides. These skills were covered in detail in the first edition of this book, *Learn Microsoft Office 2019*. See the *Arranging and manipulating objects* section in the *Chapter 6, Formatting Slides, Charts, and Graphics Elements* chapter for more details. In addition to these skills, PowerPoint also has built-in snap features, which will be evident to you when you're dragging objects around the slide. Lines will appear to indicate whether the object is lining up with the slide or other objects on the slide.

To access the alignment options, select the objects to align, then go to **Shape Format | Align Middle**:

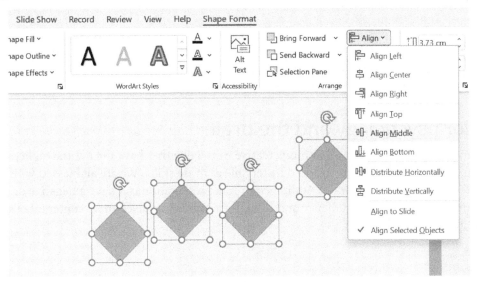

Figure 8.18 – Aligning shapes on a slide

The elements will be lined up neatly on the slide.

Look at the objects we just aligned. The spacing between the objects isn't equal, especially the difference between the last object and the three before that. To fix this, simply select the objects and click on the **Align** drop-down list. Then, choose **Distribute Horizontally**. Now, the objects are all equally spaced on the slide.

Next, we will revisit grouping. Working with grouped objects on a slide saves you an enormous amount of time as you can drag the objects as one unit to another location on the slide. This also allows you to resize the elements as a group and not individually. To use the **Group** feature, click to select objects on a slide, then right-click and choose the **Group** option, then **Group** again:

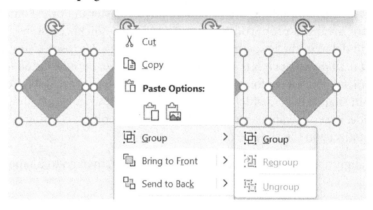

Figure 8.19 – The Group option

Color is a powerful tool and can influence a person's decision to purchase a product, as well as change a person's view about an item. It can also evoke emotion – this is how the brain responds to color. We'll investigate this in the next section.

Color psychology and the brain

When you are working on something creative, you will either have the natural ability to create stunning designs or you could be terrible at those skills. We are all blessed with a different skill set in the brain. Adding color to a presentation can have a negative or positive influence on the audience and can either connect or disconnect content. Let's look at some examples.

Color sense

A neutral, low-contrast background fill that's been applied to objects on slides is best for slide elements. Try not to use gradients and make sure the text's color stands out clearly. Adding bright colors to slide elements with a light text font applied could negatively impact the audience:

Figure 8.20 – Using color

Take into consideration the color that's displayed when projecting to an audience – always do a run-through at the venue you will be presenting at, as text and objects could appear differently on the screen. Try not to use low contrast colors, such as pastel colors, when formatting slide text as the audience will see a washed-out effect:

Figure 8.21 – Low-contrast colors versus good use of color

Applying too many accent colors to text could be detrimental. Use no more than two colors and two accent colors:

Figure 8.22 – Working with accent colors

Black and white contrasts can be striking, but you would need to add some depth in color for it to not come across as boring or effortless. Depth can be created by applying a shadow.

Let's learn about how colors affect our brain to evoke emotion:

Figure 8.23 – What emotion does this invoke in you?

Now, let's look at how colors evoke emotion:

White	This color is peaceful and pure – this is used in logo design, negative space, and reversed text.
Yellow	Happy, bright, positive, and also used for caution or conflict.
Brown	Used to give a natural or woody effect, to give depth, and for anything serious.
Orange	This color stimulates creativity and is fun and warm. It is often used to draw attention to a logo design.
Blue	A calm, loyal, and trustworthy color.
Red	This is a very intense color that is warm but used for danger, passion, love, and action. It can bring power and confidence to a design. White, black, and red can be combined to bring out power and confidence.
Pink	This color displays innocence, prettiness, gentleness, floral tones, and femininity.
Purple	This color is royal and used a lot for anything mysterious.
Green	The color represents renewal, soothing, life, rest, and, of course, nature and eco-friendliness.
Gray	This is a cool color that is used to create a mood or be neutral and can be complemented by other colors easily.
Black	This is considered a sophisticated, evil, and powerful bold color.

Table 8.3 – How do colors evoke emotion?

Using exclamation points after text should be done with caution in a presentation as this leads to possibly winning over the audience (a form of propaganda). This will change the audience's perspective by insinuating how words should make them respond by using an exclamation point to create emotion.

Using the color wheel and other tools

Color wheels are a great way to add correct color blends to your slides and objects. Often, you won't be sure which colors will blend with others or won't have the natural flair to pick the correct colors to evoke an audience's emotion. This is also important for corporate branding within presentations. An extremely useful site for this is `https://color.adobe.com/create/color-wheel`:

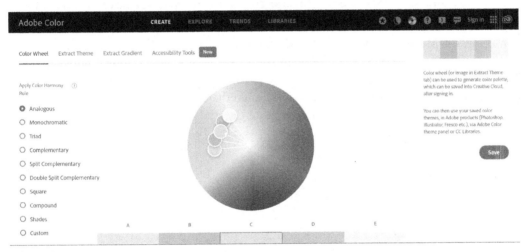

Figure 8.24 – Adobe Color wheel

This tool is fantastic and can help you generate a color wheel based on the main color you select. All you need to do is drag the balloons around the palette in the color wheel to find a color set you prefer. If you do not have a subscription to adobe.com, you won't be able to save the generated themes, but it will still generate a palette for you to use.

There are several color contrast calculators available on the web that you can use to generate specific color sets but do not underestimate the power of PowerPoint 2021 when it comes to built-in models for hue, saturation, and luminosity, as well as red, green, and blue color models. Coupled with this, you have the **Design** tab within PowerPoint 2021, which houses numerous design themes with individual color wheels, color sets, and variants. Even if you do not have an eye for design, you can still balance color choices using those offered within the application. Follow these steps:

1. Open a new, blank presentation, or use an existing presentation.

2. Click on the **Design** tab to access the various themes. In this example, I have chosen the **Feathered** theme.

3. Select a variant type from the **Variant** group, if applicable. I have chosen the second variant type listed.

4. Use the **More** drop-down list to select or customize the color palette to apply to the design. Once you choose a theme to apply to a presentation, you will notice that the color palette and objects that are inserted into the presentation from that point will take on the colors of the presentation design theme chosen. This is perfect as you won't need to put a lot of extra thought or design into your elements:

Figure 8.25 – Design colors in PowerPoint 2021

You can find the color models on any design element you choose by visiting the **Format** options. The option that's presented will depend on the object you are right-clicking on.

Once you have located the **More Fill Colors…** option, the **Colors** dialog box will open. You can choose from the **Standard** color wheel to suit your presentation design. Alternatively, visit the **Custom** tab to choose even more color selections, or enter specific *RGB* and *HSL* color model variations.

These color models are used for branding corporate identity. You will find that the marketing department will distribute the various color model-specific blends to staff to use in promotional material. Company presentations will already be set up with these branded elements:

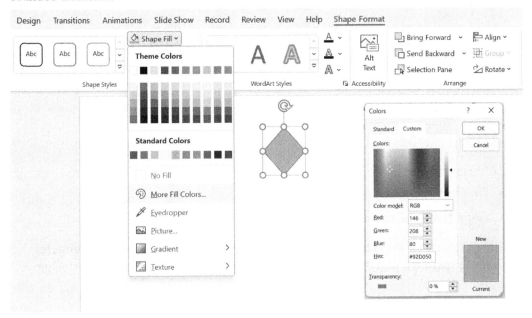

Figure 8.26 – Using More Fill Colors… to select custom colors

The next aspect we will look at is style.

Considering style in PowerPoint design

Style is important for consistency and flows from slide to slide throughout a presentation. The way to ensure this consistent flow is to set up the slide master in PowerPoint 2021. This is normally set up for you if you work for a company that takes its branding very seriously. Ask your marketing department if they have a branded presentation design for you to use before trying to create your own.

You will find sections on **Photo Albums**, **Sections**, and **Show Tools** in the *Part 2* of this book, as well as a section on **Master Slides**.

A slide master, once edited, will help you design slides to produce an effective presentation as you can set up all your font styles, corporate logo designs, and placement. Thereafter, all these elements will ripple throughout the presentation automatically.

Be careful of copyright when working with logos and web content.

A blank slide can be used as a pause when presenting so that the audience's attention moves from the slide to the presenter for a moment, and then back to the presentation as a visual aid when the presenter continues.

In the next section, we will look at some design principles, as well as an explanation of each.

Using the Gestalt principles when designing slides

It is important to understand how we receive visual input by visiting the Gestalt principles. Gestalt stands for shape or form.

The following are things to avoid when designing presentations:

- Using bullet lists
- Lots of text on slides
- Graphs that contain complex analysis
- Clipart, sounds, and animations that detract

Let's look at some of the **Gestalt principles**. We have already learned about **symmetry**, the **law of proximity**, and the **rule of thirds**, which are all part of the Gestalt principles.

Figure and ground

This principle is where the figure is the focal point on a background on a slide. The mind will subconsciously determine what symbolizes the figure's focus and what is in the background that the mind can ignore.

The foreground will capture the audience's eye first:

Figure 8.27 – Figure and ground

Area

When overlapping large and dark areas contained on a slide, the mind will assume that the darker areas are larger:

Figure 8.28 – Area

Similarity

This is how shapes, size, color, or orientation are perceived to be similar and are grouped by the brain when they are seen as connected. The principle is when you would use an object more than once on a slide to structure the experience of the audience, as follows:

Figure 8.29 – Similarity

Repetition of color

The brain navigates to the difference in color immediately and the shape that is formed because of the color change, although the objects are all the same:

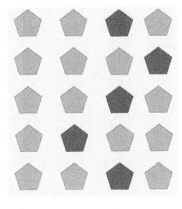

Figure 8.30 – Repetition of color

Isomorphism

Isomorphism is where the audience perceives objects to either be visually connected or not visually connected:

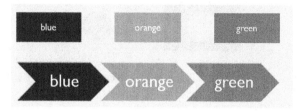

Figure 8.31 – Isomorphism

Continuation

The continuation principle is where the eye follows the lines or curves on a slide. An example would be two shapes with an arrow between them showing the movement from point a to b:

Figure 8.32 – Continuation

Closure

The brain fills in any missing information on a slide by routinely skipping over any gaps and viewing the slide as a whole:

Figure 8.33 – Closure

Proximity

When elements are positioned close together, they appear connected as a group:

Figure 8.34 – Proximity

Synchrony

Here, elements that are moving in the same direction together appear connected or related:

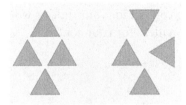

Figure 8.35 – Synchrony

Common region

This is perceived as a group by the audience when the element is surrounded by a border:

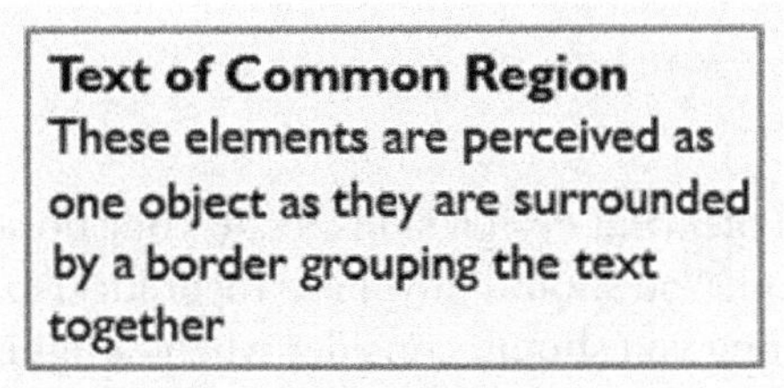

Text of Common Region
These elements are perceived as one object as they are surrounded by a border grouping the text together

Figure 8.36 – Common region

Simplicity

Complex elements are perceived as one unless they are defined by color:

Figure 8.37 – Simplicity

Focal point

This principle holds the audience's attention by emphasis, similar to the rule of thirds.

These principles will help you create a professional, engaging presentation. Be sure to consider these when designing content for your slides – working through this list will prompt thought and application ideas for your content:

Figure 8.38 – Focal point

Summary

This chapter has imparted plentiful design skills to aid your presentation transformations and create engaging content. You should now have theoretical knowledge since you have been taught about everything you should consider when designing, such as the principles of design and the importance of presentation and design skills. We have identified tools to aid and enhance presentation design and tackled the important subject of presentation planning. You learned how to deliver clear messages to persuade audience participation, as well as how the brain tackles visual elements. In addition, you understood how sound and images impact a presentation and learned about the brain and color psychology. We ended this chapter with some useful color wheel tools and the theory behind the Gestalt principles to aid with slide design.

In the next chapter, you will be taken on a journey through the essential updates and new features of Excel 2021. You will learn all about the **Advanced Filter** feature and the new FILTER function, as well as learn more about conditional formatting rules. We will focus on cleaning data and learning how to import, clean, join, and separate data while learning about some new features along the way, such as the UNIQUE function. We will also look at common challenges when working with Office 2021 applications as a whole and how to troubleshoot the stumbling blocks.

Part 3 : Learning Excel 2021

Throughout this part, you will be taken on a journey through essential updates and new features of Excel 2021. You will learn all about Advanced Filter and the new **FILTER** function and explore conditional formatting rules further. We will focus on cleaning data and learning how to import, clean, join, and separate data, learning about some new features along the way, such as the **UNIQUE** function. You will concentrate on the latest functions, learning the syntax and construction of formulas such as **XLOOKUP**, **LET**, and **XMATCH**, and focusing on **IFS**.

We will learn how to combine formulas, such as **IFERROR** and **VLOOKUP**, explore the term **ARRAYS**, and look at the new dynamic array functions in Excel 2021. Also included is a topic on database functions and a final topic exploring **COUNTIFS**. We will explore date functions and look at how to work with time. We will also explore **DATEDIF()**, **YEARFRAC()**, **EDATE()**, **WORKDAY()**, and many more functions to be more productive in the workplace. In addition, a large part of this chapter will explore a host of PivotTable customizations and a walk-through on creating dashboards. We will also learn how to construct the **GETPIVOTDATA** function to reference cells in a PivotTable report.

We will build on prior skills to work with math, trig, and statistical functions using Excel 2021 and introduce some additional functions to the mix. We will explore how to generate random numbers using the **RANDBETWEEN** and **RAND** functions. In addition, we will work through examples of **PRODUCT** functions, including the **SUMPRODUCT**, **MROUND**, **FLOOR**, **TRUNC**, **AGGREGATE**, and **CONVERT** functions. We will also investigate the **MEDIAN**, **COUNTBLANK**, and **AVERAGEIFS** statistical functions.

This part contains the following chapters:

- *Chapter 9, New Features, Filters, and Cleaning Data*
- *Chapter 10, Exploring New and Useful Workflow Functions*
- *Chapter 11, Date-Time Functions and Enhancing PivotTable Dashboards*
- *Chapter 12, Useful Statistical and Mathematical Functions*

9
New Features, Filters, and Cleaning Data

In the previous edition of this book, we concentrated on all the basic skills concerning data entry, including being able to distinguish between spreadsheet elements, as well as the various output options. In this chapter, you will learn about essential updates for, and the new features of, Excel 2021. You will learn all about Advanced Filter and the new **FILTER** function, as well as more about conditional formatting rules. We will focus on cleaning data and learning how to import, clean, join, and separate data while learning about some of the new features of Excel 2021 along the way, such as the **UNIQUE** function.

In this chapter, we will cover the following topics:

- New features to enhance proficiency
- Using Advanced Filter
- Conditional formatting functions
- Importing, cleaning, joining, and separating data

Technical requirements

To complete this chapter, you must have an understanding of the purpose of spreadsheets and be proficient at locating and launching Excel 2021. If you have worked through the previous edition of this book, you will already be familiar with the interface elements and the various setting options, constructing a workbook, applying formats, filtering data, and creating charts.

The examples for this chapter can be found in this book's GitHub repository at `https://github.com/PacktPublishing/Learn-Microsoft-Office-2021-Second-Edition`.

New features to enhance proficiency

In this section, we will look at the exciting new features of Excel 2021 for desktop and any enhancements that have been made to existing features. We will also explore some of the new and/or existing feature updates for Excel for the web.

Unhiding multiple sheets

When using the new version of Excel, we can now unhide more than one sheet at a time. To follow along, use the file named `SSGThemePark-Hide.xlsx`:

1. Select the second, third, and fourth sheets in the workbook.

2. Right-click on the worksheet tabs, then select **Hide**.

3. To unhide hidden worksheets in one go, right-click on the **Employees** sheet and select **Unhide...** from the menu.

4. Select all the worksheets using the *Shift + click* keyboard keys, or individually select sheets using *Ctrl + click*:

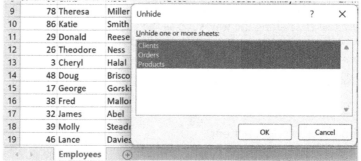

Figure 9.1 – Unhiding multiple worksheets at the same time

5. Click **OK** to confirm this.

Troubleshooting tip

If you need to provide your specific build of Excel when troubleshooting features, you can share this information easily with your support agent or community. To do so, visit **File | Account | About** within the Excel environment, then right-click and copy the build number from the top of the screen. This way, you won't have to write this information down and re-type the details when you want to share them. Remember to always share personal data responsibly and within the correct channels:

About Microsoft® Excel® 2021

Microsoft® Excel® 2021 MSO (Version 2112 Build 16.0.14729.20254) 64-bit
Product ID:
Session ID: CC45A53F-FD0B-4B3A-93A7-9E60B9235692

⎘ Copy

Figure 9.2 – Copying build information to share when troubleshooting

Collaborating using Sheet View

As we learned when we covered the Word and PowerPoint topics in this book, collaboration has been greatly enhanced with modern commenting and co-authoring. At a glance, we can see who is editing a workbook by looking to the top right of it. Everyone who has been invited to the shared workbook can add comments and work in real time.

Sheet View is a new feature in the latest version of Excel that allows files to be shared using a separate view so that when we are collaborating and manipulating data using filters, the source data is not affected. Only changes to data within the actual cells will be saved to the underlying shared workbook. The only constraint is hiding and showing rows when you're using the desktop version of Excel with Sheet View turned on. Hiding or showing rows will update in the Default view, not Sheet View, even though you can hide or show rows in Sheet View.

1. Select **View | New** to create a new Sheet View:

File	Home	Insert	Draw	Page Layout	Formulas	Data	Review

Default ∨	🖫 Keep	🔍 Exit	🔍 New	☰ Options	Zoom	100% ∨

| E6 | ∨ | *fx* | View Tabue | | New Sheet View | | |

	A	B	C	D	E	F	G	H
1	CODE ▾	FIRST ▾	SURNAME ▾	EMP NO ▾	DIVISION ▾	DEPT ▾	DATE of HIRE ▾	HRS
2	69	Shirley	Dandrow	TBV45	View Tabue	Cobrella	14-Mar-91	
3	12	Seth	Rose	TBV76	View Tabue	Cobrella	05-Apr-90	

Figure 9.3 – New Sheet View

2. You will notice that the view is created as a **temporary view**, as shown on the left of the ribbon. Use the drop-down arrow to the right of **Temporary View** to see the **Default** view (this is the source file). When clicking on a column header to filter, the Sheet View list is also evident here:

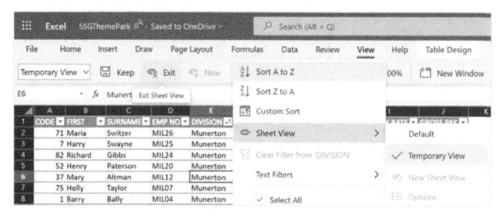

Figure 9.4 – Exit Sheet View

3. While making changes to the data, such as filters and sorts, you are not obstructing anyone else who has shared a status on the file. Once you have finished manipulating the data to suit your requirements, you can **Exit** the Sheet View, after which you will be prompted to confirm whether you would like to **Keep** the view by naming it. Alternatively, you can choose **Don't Keep**:

Figure 9.5 – Prompt to Keep or Don't Keep Sheet View

Speak Cells

At times, you may be working from a printed hardcopy, but need to check certain cells and compare them to your worksheet data. Although **Speak Cells** is not a new feature, it is often overlooked and can be very useful. Let's take a look:

1. Visit the QAT and navigate to the drop-down list to select **More Commands…**.

2. From the **Excel Options** dialog box, select **Quick Access Toolbar**.

3. Select **All Commands** from the **Choose commands from** drop-down list.

4. In the list, locate **Speak Cells**, then click the **Add >>** button to move the selection to the right-hand side of the pane. Do the same with **Speak Cells - Stop Speaking Cells** so that you can control when the feature is enabled or disabled:

Figure 9.6 – Adding Speak Cells to the QAT

5. Click **OK** when you're done.

6. To activate **Speak Cells**, select an area on the worksheet, then click the **Speak Cells** button on the QAT. The worksheet cells will speak back to you. To disable this feature, click the **Speaking Cells – Stop Speaking Cells** button:

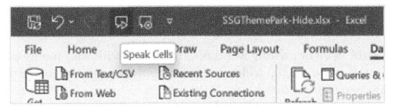

Figure 9.7 – Speak Cells button added to the QAT

Adding the Camera tool

Another quick tip would be to add the **Camera** tool to the QAT so that you can take a snapshot of worksheet data, then update the data in the source sheet so that it updates the snapshot.

1. Open the workbook named `Population.xlsx`. Add the Camera tool to the QAT using the drop-down list at the end of the QAT. Follow the steps in the previous section if you need assistance.

2. Before we use the Camera feature, we need to ascertain where we will be adding the photo after the Camera tool has taken the snapshot. Either open a new workbook or open an existing workbook.

3. Select a range of cells in the worksheet area, then click the **Camera** icon on the QAT to take a snapshot of the data:

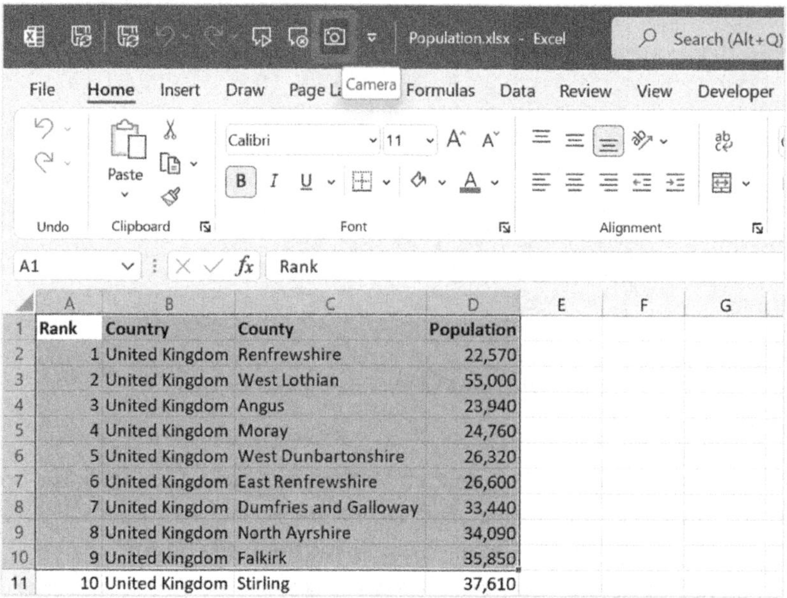

Figure 9.8 – Camera tool on QAT to snapshot data on the worksheet

4. Move to the open or existing workbook, then click with your mouse pointer to paste the snapshot. You will notice that the mouse pointer icon displays a *crosshair* pointer.

5. If you update the data in the source worksheet, it will update in the snapshot. Similarly, if you close the workbook that contains the snapshot and then update the source worksheet, it will automatically open with the new changes the next time it is opened.

6. Notice that the linked formula (formula bar) for the live image is referenced in the workbook as the source data. This is fantastic as you don't have to worry when you need to move the live image to another sheet or range:

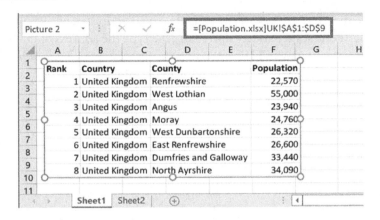

Figure 9.9 – Formula bar showing the live image formula link

This feature is great for adding a simple dashboard to your workbook, especially when it's accessed by others and you don't want your underlying data to be tampered with. The Camera tool creates a live image of data that cannot be amended as they are live images.

Flash Fill

In the previous edition of this book, we touched on the **Fill** feature. We will broaden this skill by presenting **Flash Fill**. To follow these steps, open the file named `FlashFill.xlsx`:

1. On **Sheet 1**, you will notice data in column A and column B. We can use Flash Fill to combine bits of data into one column. To combine the name with the surname, simply type the full name of the first person, `Shirley Dandrow`, into cell C3.

2. Press *Enter* on your keyboard.

3. Hold down the *Ctrl* key, then press *E* on your keyboard. The full names of the rest of the individuals will appear in the relevant cells. Note that you can also use delimiters to separate bits of data – for instance, you can use a comma between the name and surname.

4. To go one step further, we can populate the email addresses of each person, without typing the addresses separately into each cell. Type the address of the first person to form a pattern as you would like it to appear; for example, *shirley.dandrow@me.you*. Press *Enter*, then use *Ctrl + E* to fill in the email addresses:

	A	B	C	D
1				
2	Name	Surname	Name Surname	Email
3	Shirley	Dandrow	Shirley Dandrow	shirley.dandrow@me.you
4	Seth	Rose	Seth Rose	seth.rose@me.you
5	Anne	Davidson	Anne Davidson	anne.davidson@me.you
6	Colleen	Abel	Colleen Abel	colleen.abel@me.you
7	Theresa	TBVlifano	Theresa TBVlifano	theresa.tbvlifano@me.you
8	Jennifer	Snyder	Jennifer Snyder	jennifer.snyder@me.you
9	Chris	Reed	Chris Reed	chris.reed@me.you
10	Theresa	Miller	Theresa Miller	theresa.miller@me.you

Figure 9.10 – Using Flash Fill to populate data

5. There are so many uses for this stunning feature. Can you think of a few more? Now, let's use Flash Fill to combine and extract data.

6. Select the **Combine** sheet. Click on cell D3, then type in the data for the first row, as follows:

	A	B	C	D
1				
2	Address	Country	Post Code	
3	1 Southridge Way	Alabama	36628	1 Southridge Way, Alabama, 36628
4	1 Macpherson Place	Texas	88584	
5	53900 Monterey Point	California	95118	
6	6473 Homewood Road	Kentucky	40591	
7	66971 Kings Road	California	94544	

Figure 9.11 – Type the full address into cell D3, separated by commas

7. Press *Ctrl + E* to fill in the rest of the data.

8. Extracting bits of data can be done in the same way. Click the **Extract** sheet. In cell B2, type Alabama. Press *Ctrl + E* to place the data in the rest of the cells. The countries will be extracted from the dataset.

9. Another brilliant example of using Flash Fill is to clean datasets. At times, you may wish to import a dataset that contains spaces at the beginning or end of data.

10. Use Flash Fill by typing in what you wish to appear, then use *Ctrl + E* to fill in the rest of the list. Let's give it a go. Select the **Clean** worksheet. Cells A2:A5 contain data with unnecessary spaces at the start and even end of the countries. Type the first country correctly without any extra spaces into cell B2, then use the *Ctrl + E* to fill in the rest of the cells, eliminating the spaces automatically for each:

	A	B	C
1			
2	Alabama	Alabama	
3	Texas	Texas	
4	California	California	
5	Kentucky	Kentucky	
6			

Figure 9.12 – Column A, including spaces before or after countries. Column B shows the result of using Flash Fill

Using Flash Fill to clean data is a great way to get rid of those unwanted spaces when you're importing data. We will explore other ways to prepare data for manipulation later in this chapter, including using the **CLEAN** and **TRIM** functions.

Generating maps

In the previous edition of this book, we explored the ins and outs of chart creation and formatting. Let's add to this by learning about the new 3D geography **Maps** feature:

1. Open `Population.xlsx` to follow this example. In this workbook, you will see a list of populations ranked by county for the UK.

2. Select the second sheet, named **Country**.

3. Click inside the sheet, then use the *Ctrl + Shift + ** key combination to select the entire list.

4. Navigate to **Insert | Maps | Filled Map**. Click the map image to insert the geographic map into the worksheet:

Figure 9.13 – The new Maps feature

5. If you update the worksheet data, the map will update accordingly. You can insert and delete data columns too. This feature can be used for sales data or any other type of data representation you require.

Importing data from a PDF

At times, we may need to copy data that has been saved in PDF format into an Excel workbook. Using the normal copy/paste method is cumbersome, and normally, data would need to go through a bit of editing before you can work on the workbook (see the following screenshot for an example).

There is a much easier method to get this done without you having to make any further amends to the data, as well as viewing and importing from a list of tables located within a PDF:

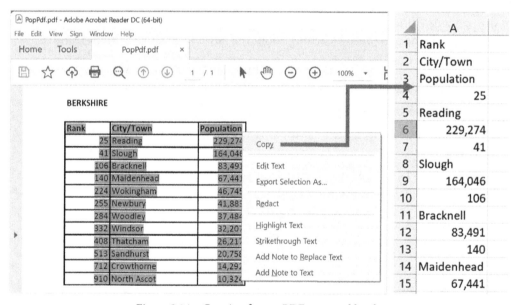

Figure 9.14 – Copying from a PDF to a workbook

1. Instead of copying from a PDF, open the workbook where you would like to insert the data.

2. Click **Data | Get Data | From File | From PDF**:

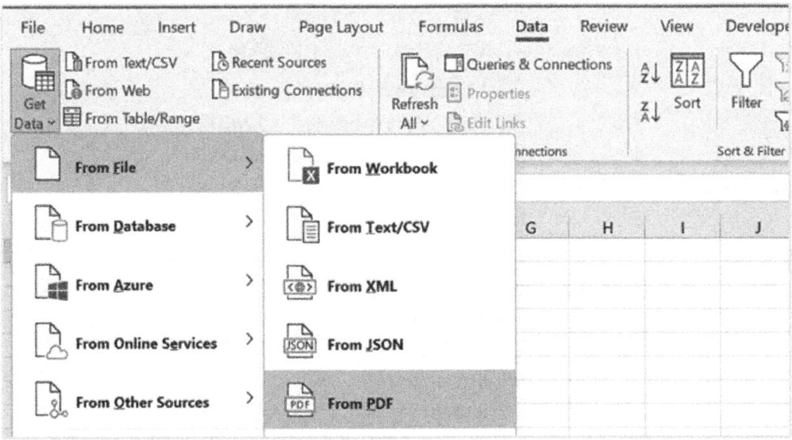

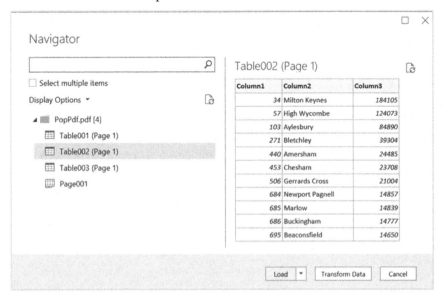

Figure 9.15 – Adding data from a PDF to Excel using the Get Data option

3. Navigate to and select the PDF to import into the worksheet. To follow along, select the file named PopPDF.pdf.

4. If there is more than one table of data in the PDF, you have the opportunity to select each dataset from the left-hand side of the **Navigator** window. Select the table, then decide whether you would need to modify the dataset before importing it. If so, select the **Transform** button at the bottom of the **Navigator** window. Alternatively, click the **Load** button to import the data into the workbook:

Figure 9.16 – Using the Navigator window to select the relevant data table to import from a PDF into Excel

5.   The data will be added to the workbook and formatted as a table:

	A	B	C	D
1	Column1 ▾	Column2 ▾	Column3 ▾	
2	34	Milton Keynes	184105	
3	57	High Wycombe	124073	
4	103	Aylesbury	84890	
5	271	Bletchley	39304	
6	440	Amersham	24485	
7	453	Chesham	23708	
8	506	Gerrards Cross	21004	
9	684	Newport Pagnell	14857	
10	685	Marlow	14839	
11	686	Buckingham	14777	
12	695	Beaconsfield	14650	
13				

Figure 9.17 – Data table inserted into the workbook

6.   Don't forget to save the workbook.

The **Get Data** feature within Excel is a powerful tool that can be used to analyze and transform data. There are many features you can explore using the **Data**, **Power Pivot**, and **Query** tabs of the ribbon.

Importing Data via Mobile

Do you have a hardcopy table that you need to get into an Excel workbook? Download Office mobile from the relevant app store. Once you have opened the Office mobile app, click the **Actions | Image to table** button to take a photo of a hardcopy table, then import it into an Excel table.

Updating Excel on the web

The following table highlights some of the new and/or updated features in Excel for the web. As it is extremely seamless working from the desktop version to the web (when a workbook is saved to OneDrive or SharePoint) and vice versa, these features enhance productivity as it is just a quick switch from one to the other to utilize their features. Along with being able to access **Regional Settings** and the simple ribbon commands, here are a few more features you can enjoy:

Feature	Explanation
Switching Sheets	The three-stripes button located to the left of the sheet's name allows you to select another sheet within the workbook:
Version History	You can now view your version history by going to **File | Version History**. This enables the **Version History** pane to the right of the window, where you can select a version to view. You can restore versions or save a copy of the current version.
Keyboard Shortcuts	Shortcuts are enabled by default, which means that they are actionable on the web. For instance, you can use *Ctrl + spacebar* to select all the data in a column. Go to **View | Keyboard Shortcuts** to see a list of all the shortcuts that are available in Excel for the web. Don't forget about the **What's New** option to the right of **Keyboard Shortcuts** as this portrays the most updated feature list.
Text to Columns	This well-known feature is used to split data from a single column into multiple columns but is now available in Excel for the web. It is accessible via **Data | Text to Columns**.
Automate	**Automate** is a tab on the ribbon that allows you to record scripts (macros) to automate processes in Office for the web. If it isn't on your ribbon, it could be that the tab is still being deployed to your Office account. Be sure to check it out when it arrives.
Analyze Data	 The formerly known Design Ideas button has been updated and can be found by going to **Home | Analyze Data**. It returns insights for worksheet data:

Table 9.1 – Excel for the web – new and/or existing feature updates

Now that you are familiar with some of the new and enhanced features of Excel for desktop and the web, let's learn more about the Advanced Filter tool.

Filtering using Advanced Filter

In the previous edition of this book, we learned how to set up and manage sorts and filters.

Filtering data in Excel allows you to locate data very quickly, as well as eliminating certain choices (text, dates, or values) from a list's results, or specifying categories of data to get the result you need. Filters can also be used to search if you specify the format (color) of a cell.

Instead of filtering a list with updates that are occurring in the same location, we can extract data to a different location using criteria.

Now, let's learn how to filter using **Advanced Filter**.

Defining criteria

1. Open the `SSGAdvFilter.xlsx` workbook. Our workbook contains data for a theme park.

2. To define the criteria for our filter, we need to specify a separate area on the worksheet. When we add criteria, we can indicate whether the result will be an **AND** or an **OR** criteria. For example, we can choose all the Mankay Falls employees (from the Munerton division) **AND** their gross pay greater than £300.

    Alternatively, we can choose all the Mankay Falls (Munerton) employees with a gross pay greater than £300 **OR** the Cobrella (Munerton) employees with a gross pay less than £300:

L	M	N	O
Criteria	*DIVISION*	*DEPT*	*GROSS PAY*
	Munerton	Mankay Falls	>300
Criteria	*DIVISION*	*DEPT*	*GROSS PAY*
	Munerton	Mankay Falls	>300
	Munerton	Cobrella	<300

Figure 9.18 – AND/OR criteria for Advanced Filter

3. Before we get started, it is important to note that the criteria must be the same as the source headings on the worksheet in terms of formatting and spelling. The best way to ensure that this happens is to copy and paste the headings you require for the criteria from the existing worksheet headings into the criteria area on the worksheet.

4. Follow the example as per the previous screenshot to add the relevant criteria to the worksheet. Note that you do not have to place the criteria data on the same worksheet.

5. Now that we have the criteria in place, we can create the filter and return the result.

Applying Advanced Filter

1. If the result of the filter must be generated on a separate worksheet, make sure that you click the relevant worksheet before accessing the command from the ribbon. For our example, we want the result to appear on a separate worksheet. Click to create a new worksheet and name it `Result`.

2. Make sure you are on the **Result** sheet, then click **Data | Advanced**.

3. The **Advanced Filter** dialog box will populate, where you must enter the relevant details.

4. If you are filtering the existing source list, choose **Filter the list, in-place**. Since we are filtering to a separate worksheet, select **Copy to another location**.

5. The next field is called **List range**. After clicking inside the field, navigate to the **Filter** worksheet to select the range as our source data list. To do so, select the main headings on the worksheet, then use *Ctrl + Shift + down arrow* to select the dataset.

6. Click inside the **Criteria range** field, then select the criteria on the **Filter** worksheet. As per this example, select cells M1:O2 on the worksheet:

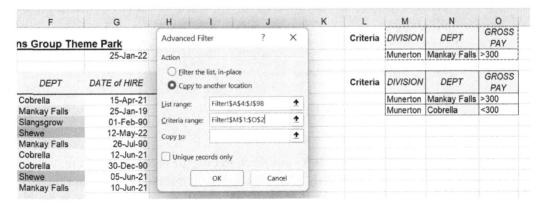

Figure 9.19 – Advanced Filter dialog box showing Criteria range selection on the worksheet

7. Click inside the **Copy to** field, then select cell A1 to specify where you would like the filter results to appear:

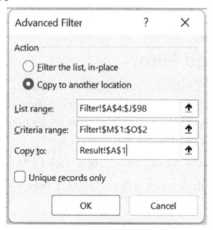

Figure 9.20 – Advanced Filter options

8. Click the **OK** button to commit and generate the results.

9. The results will appear in cell A1 of the **Result** worksheet:

Figure 9.21 – Filter results

10. Now, let's try the OR operator criteria.

11. Click inside cell A15 of the **Result** worksheet. Repeat the process, as per the previous filter, starting with **Data | Advanced**, making sure to set **Criteria range** to M4:O6. Lastly, select **A15** in the **Copy to** field.

12. Click **OK** to see the result of the filter:

	CODE	FIRST	SURNAME	EMP NO	DIVISION	DEPT	DATE of HIRE	HRS	HOURLY RATE	GROSS PAY
16	2	Bob	Ambrose	MIL14	Munerton	Mankay Falls	25-Jan-19	36	£ 12.50	£ 443.75
17	10	Sara	Kling	MIL29	Munerton	Mankay Falls	24-Dec-20	36	£ 12.50	£ 443.75
18	20	TBVrol	Hill	MIL18	Munerton	Mankay Falls	21-Jul-20	36	£ 12.50	£ 443.75
19	23	Jeffrey	Strong	MIL04	Munerton	Mankay Falls	08-Mar-81	40	£ 19.50	£ 780.00
20	27	Brad	Hinkelman	MIL15	Munerton	Mankay Falls	08-Nov-19	40	£ 19.50	£ 780.00
21	35	Mary	Barber	MIL32	Munerton	Mankay Falls	25-Nov-21	36	£ 12.50	£ 443.75
22	37	Mary	Altman	MIL12	Munerton	Cobrella	09-Sep-21	30	£ 6.50	£ 191.75
23	49	George	Feldsott	MIL37	Munerton	Mankay Falls	03-Dec-21	36	£ 12.50	£ 443.75
24	59	Karina	Abel	MIL30	Munerton	Mankay Falls	12-Jan-21	42	£ 16.75	£ 703.50
25	88	Paul	Martin	MIL02	Munerton	Cobrella	19-Apr-79	40	£ 6.50	£ 260.00

Figure 9.22 – Result of the second filter

13. Notice that the results contain all the headings from the worksheet in the result. But what if we only wanted certain columns to be represented in our result? This can be achieved by specifying this in the **Copy to** range. Let's learn how to do this.

14. In the **Results** worksheet, we only want the *Surname*, *Dept*, and *Gross Pay* fields to be represented in the result. Copy the relevant fields from the **Filter** worksheet and paste these into cell A28 of the **Result** worksheet:

	SURNAME	DEPT	GROSS PAY
27			
28	SURNAME	DEPT	GROSS PAY
29			
30			

Figure 9.23 – Fields copied from the source worksheet to generate results

15. Click on a blank cell outside of the range, then navigate to **Data | Advanced** and fill in the fields as you did previously, except for the final step. Click inside the **Copy to** field, then select cells A28:C28 to define the columns you want to generate only, based on your criteria range.

16. Click **OK** to view the results:

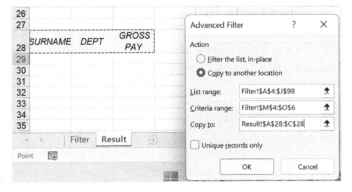

Figure 9.24 – Copy to: range A28:C28

17. The result only displays the columns that have been specified according to the selected criteria:

	SURNAME	DEPT	GROSS PAY
27			
28			
29	Ambrose	Mankay Falls	£443.75
30	Kling	Mankay Falls	£443.75
31	Hill	Mankay Falls	£443.75
32	Strong	Mankay Falls	£780.00
33	Hinkelman	Mankay Falls	£780.00
34	Barber	Mankay Falls	£443.75
35	Altman	Cobrella	£191.75
36	Feldsott	Mankay Falls	£443.75
37	Abel	Mankay Falls	£703.50
38	Martin	Cobrella	£260.00

Figure 9.25 – Filter result

With that, you have learned how to use Advanced Filter and specify a unique set of columns according to set criteria as the output. Let's investigate a few different scenarios where we will use other operators.

Using operators to refine filters

We can further broaden our filters using comparison operators. Previously in this book, we concentrated on the greater than and less than operators. Now, let's look at a few scenarios where we can encompass the use of two operators, as well as the NOT criteria. We will also explore how to use blank cells when applying Advanced Filters:

1. Open the workbook named MattsWinery.xlsx to expand on our criteria operators.

2. In cells M1:R3, we will build a data table that will include all the *Cases Sold* values that are greater than or equal to 300, and less than or equal to 600, for *Prominent Wines 1992* OR *Matts Winery 1991*. The result should include dates greater than or equal to January 1, 2021, as well as any *profit*:

M	N	O	P	Q	R
Year	Winery	Date Sold	Cases Sold	Cases Sold	Profit
1991	Matts Winery	>=01/01/2021	>=300	<=600	
1992	Prominent Wines	>=01/01/2021	>=300	<=600	

Figure 9.26 – Data table

3. Prepare the data table as per the preceding screenshot. Criteria on the same row in a data table automatically assume the **AND** criteria. If on different rows, they would assume the **OR** criteria. The result we are filtering should contain the fields as per the data table. Copy and paste the field headings from the data table of the **WINE SALES** sheet to cell A1 of the **Results** worksheet.

4. Let's build the argument. Click on the **Results** worksheet and make sure that your mouse pointer is not positioned within the field headings.

5. Navigate to **Data | Advanced Filter** and enter the following criteria:

   - *List range*: **A1:K145**

   - *Criterial range*: **M1:R3**

   - *Copy to*: **A1:E1**

6. Click the **OK** button to apply the filter and display the result.

   The next condition we will explore will exclude certain results from the filter result using the <> operator.

7. Enter the criteria into cells N7:08 to filter the results so that they exclude the *North* region for the *Merlat Label* value (*Matts Winery* OR *Prominent Wines*):

Winery	Label	Region	Revenue
Matts Winery	Merlat	<>North	
Prominent Wines	Merlat	<>North	

Figure 9.27 – Data table for the exclude condition

8. Copy the *Winery*, *Label*, *Region*, and *Revenue* field headings to cell I1 of the **Results** sheet as this is the data we would like to extract.

9. Click **Data | Advanced Filter**, then enter the following criteria:

   - *List range*: **A1:K145**

   - *Criteria range*: **M6:P8**

   - *Copy to*: **I1:L1**

10. Click the **OK** button to display the results of the filter.

Let's look at another example:

1. Here, we would like to exclude the *North* AND *South* regions for *Merlat* (*Matts Winery*):

Winery	Label	Region	Region	Revenue
Matts Winery	Merlat	<>North	<>South	

Figure 9.28 – Data table for excluding the North and South regions

2. Copy the *Winery*, *Label*, *Region*, and *Revenue* field headings to cell P1 of the **Results** sheet as this is the data we would like to extract.

3. Click **Data | Advanced Filter**, then enter the following criteria:

   ▪ *List range*: **A1:K145**

   ▪ *Criteria range*: **M12:Q13**

   ▪ *Copy to*: **P1:S1**

4. Click the **OK** button to display the results of the filter.

> **Note**
>
> We do not have to enter criteria in every cell under a field heading. If left empty, the results will be included for that field heading, based on the filter criteria that were entered in other fields in the row.

In the next section, we will learn how to use **wildcard** characters when filtering data.

Extracting using wildcard characters

Wildcard operators are useful for extracting data according to a partial match within a cell. For instance, if the *Winery* column listed names of wine farms and we wanted to filter all the cells containing the text *wine*, we could search the *Winery* column for the partial match using *wine. The *asterisk* represents any number of characters – in this case, any number of characters before and after *wine*. Let's get started:

1. Select the **WINERY** worksheet. We will filter the *Winery* column so that all the wineries containing the word *wine* are extracted to the *Wildcards* worksheet.

2. The range N1:O2 contains the filter criteria headings, namely *Winery* and *Profit*. Enter *wine in the *Winery* field.

3. Enter the following criteria:

- *List range*: **A1:K145**

- *Criteria range*: **N1:O2**

- *Copy to*: **A1** of the *Wildcards* worksheet

4. Click the **OK** button to display the results of the filter.

> **Note**
>
> The *?* (question mark) is also a wildcard character. This wildcard operator denotes one character only. We can apply this, for instance, to locate all the first names that contain T?sha to filter names such as Tosha, Tisha, and Tasha.

Now, we will look at the new filter and sort functions.

The previous section explained how to use the Advanced Filter. However, there is a much quicker way to get results using new functions available in Office 2021.

Extracting using the FILTER function

The first new function is the **FILTER** function. The syntax for this function is as follows:

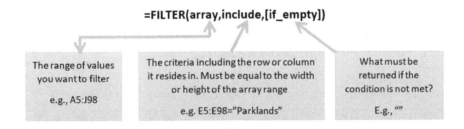

Figure 9.29 – Syntax for the FILTER function explained

To follow along with this example, open the workbook named `SSGNewFunctions.xls:`.

1. The workbook contains headings from A4:J4. To use the **FILTER** function to achieve the output we require, the column headings need to be duplicated to the results area of the worksheet.

2. Copy the content of A4:J4 and paste it into cell L4 so that it extends from L4:U4.

3. In cell **L5**, enter the following formula to filter all the *Parklands* data only:
   `=FILTER(A5:J98,E5:E98="Parklands","Other")`.

4. Press *Enter*. The data has been filtered to the new location:

| SUM | ▾ | : | × | ✓ | *fx* | =FILTER(A5:J98,E5:E98="Parklands","") | | | | | | | | | | | |

	D	E	F	G	H	I	J	K	L	M	N	O	P	Q
1		**Safest Solutions Group Theme Park**												
2	*Employee Information*			29-Jan-22										
3														
4	EMP NO	DIVISION	DEPT	DATE of HIRE	HRS	HOURLY RATE	GROSS PAY		CODE	FIRST	SURNAME	EMP NO	DIVISION	DEPT 41
5	MIL04	Parklands	Mankay Falls	15-Apr-21	40	£ 21.50	£ 860.00		=FILTER(A5:J98,E5:E98="Parklands","")			Parklands	Mankay Fá	
6	MIL14	Munerton	Mankay Falls	25-Jan-19	36	£ 12.50	£ 443.75		FILTER(array, include, [if_empty])		PKL55	Parklands	Mankay Fá	
7	TBV26	View Tabue	Slangsgrow	01-Feb-90	36	£ 13.30	£ 472.15		19 Dean	Kramer	PKL49	Parklands	Cobrella	
8	SUN59	Soningdale	Shewe	12-May-22	40	£ 7.22	£ 288.80		22 JPKLquelir	Banks	PKL03	Parklands	Shewe	
9	TBV58	View Tabue	Mankay Falls	26-Jul-90	42	£ 16.75	£ 703.50		24 Jeri Lynn	MPKLFall	PKL07	Parklands	Mankay Fá	
10	SUN07	Soningdale	Cobrella	12-Jun-21	40	£ 12.60	£ 504.00		30 Joanne	Parker	PKL09	Parklands	Mankay Fá	

Figure 9.30 – FILTER function showing the results of the formula

5. If data is updated in the existing range dataset, then the filtered list will update too. The updated list – for example, in L5 in the previous example – is called *spill*.

6. We can evaluate the formula using the *F9* key. Double-click to edit the formula in cell L5 on the worksheet. Highlight the *include* part of the formula:

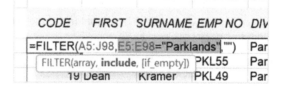

Figure 9.31 – Highlighting the include part of the formula

7. Press the *F9* key to evaluate the result.

8. Here, we can see that the results correspond with the source data in column **E**, which is true for each instance of *Parklands*:

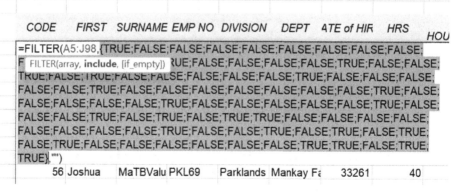

Figure 9.32 – Pressing F9 to evaluate the formula

9. We can also filter to another worksheet. Simply copy the headings from the first worksheet to the second worksheet of this workbook, namely *Shewe*.

10. In this example, we will spill all the employees from the *Shewe* department who have a *gross pay greater than 600*. As we are using the **AND** criteria for this example, we will need to use parentheses around each separate criteria with an asterisk in between them.

11. Click inside cell A2 of the **Shewe** worksheet.

12. Enter the following formula:
    ```
    =FILTER(Filter!A5:J98,(Filter!F5:F98="Shewe")
    *(Filter!J5:J98>600)).
    ```

13. Press *Enter* to confirm and update the worksheet:

A2		▾	:	×	✓	*fx*	=FILTER(Filter!A5:J98,(Filter!F5:F98="Shewe")*(Filter!J5:J98>600))			

	A	B	C	D	E	F	G	H	I	J
1	CODE	FIRST	SURNAME	EMP NO	DIVISION	DEPT	DATE of HIRE	HRS	HOURLY RATE	GROSS PAY
2	8	Kristen	DeVinney	SUN45	Soningdale	Shewe	44352	35	24	840
3	18	Paul	Hoffman	SUN57	Soningdale	Shewe	44549	40	22	880
4	34	Brian	Smith	MIL40	Munerton	Shewe	44870	40	19.5	780
5	42	Bill	Simpson	MIL07	Munerton	Shewe	29963	40	19.5	780
6	45	Kyle	Earnhart	SUN16	Soningdale	Shewe	30963	40	22	880
7	50	Steve	Singer	PKL29	Parklands	Shewe	44109	40	21.5	860
8	70	Kim	Smith	MIL54	Munerton	Shewe	32839	42	24	1008
9	78	Theresa	Miller	TBV79	View Tabu	Shewe	33301	40	22	880
10	81	GrPKLe	Sloan	PKL12	Parklands	Shewe	30988	40	15.5	620
11										

Figure 9.33 – Result of the AND filter condition showing the formula in the formula bar

14. Here are a few tips for other methods of working with the filter criteria:

- If we were using an **OR** criteria instead of **AND**, we would substitute * with a + sign.

- If we were filtering a department that is not in the list, we could specify the error return result for the missing department in the list and include a no result return for each of the columns in the table.

- Using the previous example, we can set up a filter to locate the *Slipslide* department and return the text *not found* if the item is not located in the column; that is, `=filter(Filter!A5:J98,Filter!F5:F98="Slipslide", "not found")`.

The downside of this is that it will only include the text that wasn't found for the first cell:

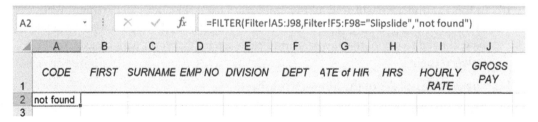

Figure 9.34 – Filter showing not found for one cell of the range

If we wanted to display results for each cell, we would simply change the parentheses to curly parentheses and list all the cell contents within. Here is an example:

```
=filter(Filter!A5:J98,Filter!F5:F98="Slipslide",{"no
code","none","none","missing","missing division","missing
dept","no hire date",0,0,0})
```

The following screenshot shows the output:

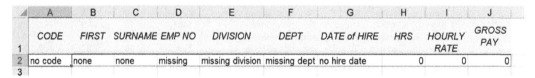

Figure 9.35 – Result showing that the criteria do not match each cell in the range

- The final tip is to select only the columns you would like a result from as the array. Include the **CHOOSE** function directly after the **FILTER** function to specify the columns to include in the array. Experiment with these functions to apply them to your specific working environment.

In the next section, we will review conditional formatting and master conditional formatting based on the formula.

Conditional formatting functions

Conditional formatting is a format, such as a cell shading or font color, that's automatically applied to cells if a specific condition is met (true). When the condition is met, a specific cell format is applied to the cells to answer any queries you may have about your data. Finding duplicate worksheet data is another great use of this tool.

In this section, you will learn how to create colored lines across workbook data when certain conditions have been met. We will be using the following validation rules and colors:

Figure 9.36 – Representation of Service Categories

We will cover the following two skills:

- The first is to set up a *validation rule* to make sure that data entered into a specific column on the worksheet is constrained to certain values. This is a great feature to include in the workbook when you're working collaboratively as it ensures that if any other data is entered by a user, it is not accepted in the cell.

- Using the *conditional formatting* tool based on a formula so that when a condition is met, the relevant color is applied to the row based on the selected item from the data validation drop-down list.

> **Note**
> The validation rule does not need to be set up for you to use conditional formatting. They work together well, but this is not required for this process.

Setting up a validation rule

If you prefer to have a set of rules to select data from within a certain column of your workbook, you must set up a validation rule.

1. Open the workbook named SSGPetFormat.xlsx to follow along.

2. Let's assume the data you are working with is on **Sheet 1**.

3. Click the **New sheet +** button to create a new sheet. On **Sheet 2**, type the different *service categories* underneath each other, exactly as shown in the preceding screenshot (omitting the color codes for now).

4. To pull through the different *service categories* from **Sheet 2** into column **G** on **Sheet 1**, we need to set up a validation rule on **Sheet 1**.

5. Select column **L** on **Sheet 1**.

> **Note**
>
> If you do not want to select the entire column, you can select only the range where the validation must be applied. If you would prefer to start at L2 for this example but would like to include all the cells downward, click inside L2, then use the *Ctrl + Shift + down arrow* keyboard keys to include all the cells below L2 in the range. This is useful if you are going to be adding new data and don't want to worry about updating the range throughout the worksheet.

6. Click on **Data | Data Validation...**:

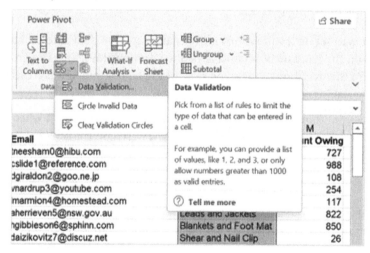

Figure 9.37 – Selecting column L, then clicking the Data Validation... button

7. From the **Allow** field list, select **List**.

8. Click inside the **Source** field, then select the arrow button to the right of the field.

9. Navigate to **Sheet 2** of the workbook, then select the range of criteria to include a drop-down list of categories for column **L** of **Sheet 1**:

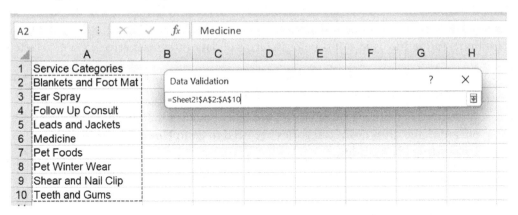

Figure 9.38 – Selecting various service categories on Sheet 2

10. Click the down arrow button, then click the **OK** button to confirm the range you've selected.

11. The rule will be applied to column **L**. You can now make selections for each cell using the drop-down list:

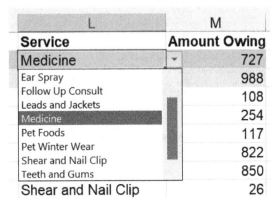

Figure 9.39 – Drop-down validation rule list

Setting up a conditional formatting rule

Now that we have the rule in place, we would like to ensure that every time a user selects an item from the drop-down list from a single cell in column **L**, the color of the row changes accordingly. Remember that you don't need to set the validation rule to create the conditional formatting rule; it just helps in terms of data entry/user error. Let's get started:

1. Select the data you wish to apply a conditional formatting rule to. Do not select your headings, just the data you wish to apply the format to.

2. Since we are creating a rule that's a little more complex than the existing rules offered in the drop-down categories, we need to go to **Home | Conditional Formatting | New Rule…**.

3. Select **Use a formula to determine which cells to format**.

4. Using the *service categories* and color table as a guide, we will add a formula for two of the categories – that is, *Follow Up Consult* and *Medicine*. If you prefer, you can add all the categories, but we will only set up two for now.

5. Click inside the field under the **Format values where this formula is true** heading.

6. Type =$L2="Follow Up Consult":

Figure 9.40 – Using a formula to determine which cells to format

Note that not using the correct cell reference in the formula would cause the rule to apply formatting to the incorrect cell data. If you have applied conditional formatting to cells and then apply formatting to the rows manually, the conditional format may return the incorrect row selection as a result.

7. Click the **Format…** button to select the appropriate color, then click **OK** to confirm, then **OK** again to return to the **Conditional Formatting Rules Manager** screen.

8. Click **New Rule…** to create the next rule. Repeat this step for each of the values and colors you require.

> **Note**
>
> To be more efficient when creating a new rule, copy and paste the formula from the first rule into the next rule, and so on. That way, you can just edit the **Service** status each time.

9. Once the rules have been set up with their respective color coding, click the **OK** button to apply these to the workbook. You will see some changes right away:

Figure 9.41 – Conditional Formatting Rules Manager

10. If you need to make amendments to any of the rules, remember to select the entire dataset again, then go to **Home | Conditional Formatting | Manage Rules…**.

11. Double-click on the rule you wish to amend in the **Conditional Formatting Rule Manager** dialog box. Alternatively, select a rule and then click **Edit Rule…** to make amends.

Conditional formatting formula rules can become quite creative, depending on the scenario and results you require. We can use any function to construct a conditional format rule, just like you would if constructing a formula within workbook cells.

Let's look at another example containing a more complex formula:

1. Open the workbook named `CondFormatISNAVlookup.xlsx`. The workbook
    has been set up to analyze two sets of data to determine which customers are listed
    in the first set of data, but not the second. A logical test has been set up to display
    the text *Not found* in **Table 2** if the customer is missing from the dataset in **Table
    2**. We would like to add color to the entire row when the customer is not evident in
    the second dataset.

2. Select the **A3:L29** range, then go to **Home | Conditional Formatting | New Rule…**

    > **Note**
    >
    > We have not selected the result column in this example as it is not required to
    > make the conditional format work

    Select **Use a formula to determine which cells to format**. Enter the
    following formula in the **Format values where this formula is true** field:
    `=(ISNA(VLOOKUP($A3,$A$33:$L$57,1,FALSE)))`.

3. Click the **Format** button, then select a **Fill** color of your choice to apply to the rows
    on the worksheet that meet the criteria.

4. Click on the **OK** button, then **OK** again to exit and return to the worksheet. The
    customers (rows) that appear in the first table, but not in the second table, will be
    highlighted on the worksheet:

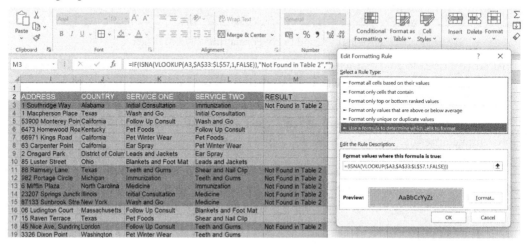

Figure 9.42 – The result of using the Conditional Formatting rule once the formula criteria have
been entered

Using Icon Sets

In addition to conditional formatting rules, we can also apply **Icon Sets** to indicate whether certain conditions have been met in the dataset to add visual impact. Icon sets could include values, text entries, or based on a formula, to mention a few. Let's take a look at an example:

1. Open the workbook named `Wines.xlsx` to follow along. We will apply icon sets to the *Cases Sold* column to visually indicate the status.

2. Select cells H2 through H145, then navigate to **Home | Conditional Formatting**.

3. Predefined icon sets are available via the **Icon Sets** category. Here, select the applicable style from **Directional**, **Shapes**, **Indicators**, or **Ratings**, or click **More Rules...** to customize the visual markers.

4. Click **More Rules....**

5. Notice that **Format all cells based on their values** is selected under the *Select a Rule Type* heading.

6. Under the *Edit the Rule Description* heading, select **Icon Sets** for *Format Style*.

7. Select an icon set of your choice – for this example, we will select the seventh style in the list.

8. Customize each *icon* to your requirements. For this example, we will leave the first icon set to **the green check symbol**. The second icon we will amend to the **yellow dash** icon, and the third to a **red down arrow**.

9. Amend the *Value* column as follows:

   - **Green check symbol** when value is >=**400**

   - **Yellow dash** when value is <**400** and >=**200**

   - **Red down arrow** when <**200**

10. Change the *Type* column to reflect **Number**:

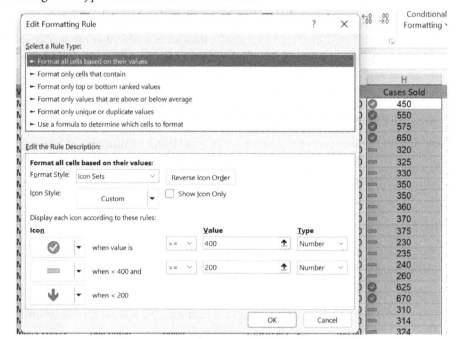

Figure 9.43 – Applying icon sets to data

11. Click **OK** to apply the icon sets to the data in column **H**. Once the data has been updated, the icon sets will adapt accordingly.

You should now be confident in customizing icon sets. See whether you can experiment with the **Formula** option from the **Type** drop-down list. In the next section, we will learn how to get data ready when importing from external sources into Excel.

Importing, cleaning, joining, and separating data

When we import data from different sources, cell data may contain extra spaces or invisible characters. It may be necessary to remove any unwanted characters if issues arise when working with formulas or formatting in the workbook.

After importing and cleaning your dataset, data may need to be joined or separated. In this section, we will learn how to import, clean, join, and separate data.

Importing datasets

The best way to import data into Excel from other sources would be to use the **Get Data** command from the **Data** tab. Numerous features are available on this ribbon, such as establishing data queries and connections, accessing Power Query (to transform and query data), sorting, filters, outlines, and accessing various data tools.

Let's import a `.csv` file into Excel:

1. Open a new workbook in Excel 2021.

2. Click **Data | From Text/CSV**. Note that the **Get Data** drop-down option offers many more features, such as combining queries, Power Query, and importing from a range of different sources:

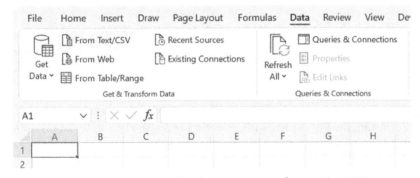

Figure 9.44 – Importing data by going to Data | From Text/CSV

3. Select the file you wish to upload. If you are following along, you will need to open `TextImport.txt`.

4. Click **Open**.

5. Select the correct *delimiter* for the dataset, then click the **Load** button at the bottom of the screen. The delimiter has been correctly identified as **Tab** for this example and the data looks perfect in terms of the cell, row, and column data:

TextImport.txt

File Origin		Delimiter		Data Type Detection	
1252: Western European (Windows) ▾		Tab ▾		Based on first 200 rows ▾	

Colon
Comma
Equals Sign
Semicolon
Space
Tab
--Custom--
--Fixed Width--

Column1	Column2	Column3	Col			nn7	Column8	Column9	Column10
1	Barry	Bally	MIL			4/1983	40	21.50	£860.00
2	Bob	Ambrose	MIL			1/1985	36	12.50	£443.75
3	Cheryl	Halal	TBV			2/1990	36	13.30	£472.15
4	Chris	Hume	SUN			5/1988	40	7.22	£288.80
5	Colleen	Abel	TBV			7/1990	42	16.75	£703.50
6	Frank	Culbert	SUN			6/1983	40	12.60	£504.00
7	Harry	Swayne	MIL25	Milnerton	Cobra	30/12/1990	40	21.50	£860.00
8	Kristen	DeVinney	SUN45	Sunningdale	Shows	05/06/1987	35	24.00	£840.00
9	Robert	Murray	SUN47	Sunningdale	Monkey Falls	10/06/1987	40	12.60	£504.00

Figure 9.45 – The Delimiter type before it's imported using the Load button

6. Click **Load** at the bottom of the screen. Note that the **Transform** button is to the right of this, which is useful when we need to access the Power Query Editor.

7. The dataset will be imported into the workbook as a data table. This means that the dataset has an applied style that allows you to add column/row data effortlessly since it automatically expands the selection (range) when new data is added and included in any other connections on the worksheet or workbook.

8. If we look closely at the data, we will notice that some of the cell data looks out of line or indented. This is probably because the import has included some spaces or hidden characters upon being imported. Don't forget to save your workbook before making any amendments:

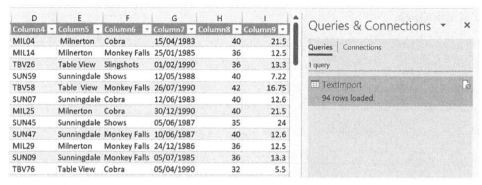

Figure 9.46 – Workbook data import result

Now that you are aware of the **Get Data** import option, we will look at ways to clean data.

Cleaning data

After importing data into an Excel workbook, it is good practice to clean the data to get it ready for formatting or manipulation using all the tools Excel has available. Some of the reasons to clean data are as follows:

- To remove spaces from the imported dataset. Even if you cannot see spaces, they could be lurking at the end or middle of the cell data (text, numbers) – such as a silent space. Some spaces can be seen with ease as the data won't be aligned.

- When we import data, cell formatting may be lost or associated incorrectly with values or text within the worksheet. This formatting can have a huge effect on formulas and other elements of Excel data manipulation. It is also important to remove any existing formatting that was added by the import. Numbers could also be an issue if they have been pre-formatted with an apostrophe, therefore being reflected as text.

- Blank cells are a huge issue, especially when you want to produce dashboards. It is important to remove any blank cells or include a fill (either text or highlighting) so that the cell contains something.

- To get rid of any duplicated data.

- Errors – remove any errors on the worksheet using conditional formatting.

- To separate data within a single cell. Often, when we import data, the various bits of data of one row could end up in one cell instead of being separated into cells.

These are just some of the issues we face when importing data. We can use the preceding list as a checklist of things to look at once data has been imported into Excel. Let's learn a little more about some of the items on our checklist.

Removing spaces or hidden characters

There are several ways to remove spaces from workbook data once it's been imported. We can use the **TRIM** and **CLEAN** functions, **SUBSTITUTE**, or even the **Flash Fill** command. The following table lists these functions and some syntax examples:

Method	Explanation	Syntax
TRIM	Focuses on the text and removes any spaces before the text, more than one space between words, or any trailing spaces. It also removes spaces with ASCII code 32.	`=trim(text)`
CLEAN	Removes non-printing characters from cell contents (as well as line breaks).	`=clean(text)`
TRIM and CLEAN	We can combine both functions to remove spaces and non-printable characters.	`=trim(clean(text)`
Using TRIM and CLEAN as part of a formula	The TRIM and CLEAN functions can be added to any formula so that the formula result is completed and cleaned at the same time to sort out problematic data.	`=VLOOKUP(TRIM(L2),$I$1:$J$9,2, FALSE)`
SUBSTITUTE	This is a great function for removing ASCII characters and non-breaking spaces.	`=substitute(A1,"   ", "")`
Find and Replace tool	We can use this tool to replace two spaces in workbook cells with one space, for example.	**Home | Find & Select | Replace...**
Flash Fill	Follows a pattern to format data and remove spaces.	Input a pattern, then use *Ctrl* + *E* to fill downward.

Table 9.2 – Cleaning data by removing spaces from data

1. Open the workbook named `Spaces.xlsx`.

2. Notice that the existing data contains additional spaces before some text, such as **B13**. Trailing spaces are difficult to visually detect within datasets.

3. Let's use **Flash Fill** to clean data. We can use this command to fix the case, as well as copying a pattern to fill in the email addresses, combine data, and remove spaces.

4. Click into cell D2 and simply type the format you need the cell data to be represented with. Then, press the *Enter* key:

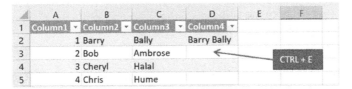

Figure 9.47 – Flash Fill shortcut key, Ctrl + E

5. Press *Ctrl + E* to place the data in the rest of the cells, based on the pattern you provided in **D2**. In this instance, it will fix any space issues, as well as joining the name and surname together into one column. Always check that the data is consistent and that you receive the result you require:

	A	B	C	D	E	F
1	Column1 ▾	Column2 ▾	Column3 ▾	Spaces ▾	Email ▾	
2	1	Barry	Bally	Barry Bally	bbally@ssg.ui	
3	2	Bob	Ambrose	Bob Ambrose	bambrose@ssg.ui	
4	3	Cheryl	Halal	Cheryl Halal	bhalal@ssg.ui	
5	4	Chris	Hume	Chris Hume	bhume@ssg.ui	
6	5	Colleen	Abel	Colleen Abel	babel@ssg.ui	
7	6	Frank	Culbert	Frank Culbert	bculbert@ssg.ui	
8	7	Harry	Swayne	Harry Swayne	bswayne@ssg.ui	

Figure 9.48 – Flash Fill to expand email addresses

6. Notice that the **Flash Fill** icon appears in the bottom-right corner of a cell, along with a drop-down list of options to choose from.

7. If we want to add email addresses for each of our employees, we can type the email pattern for the first employee into cell E2, then press *Ctrl + E* to fill the rest of the cells.

8. Flash Fill can also be used to correct the case of the text. Type *BARRY BALLY* into cell F2, then use *Ctrl + E* to fill the contents down. This is a great way to correct text that has been imported with a mix of upper and lowercase letters.

The next few functions we will explore can be applied separately or jointly to data. Here, we will look at the **TRIM, CLEAN,** and **SUBSTITUTE** functions. Follow these steps:

1. Open the workbook named `Trim.xlsx`.

2. Click inside cell B2, then type `=trim(A2):`

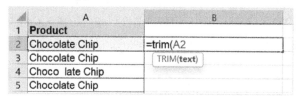

Figure 9.49 – The TRIM function

3. Press *Enter* to confirm, then double-click the **AutoFill** handle to copy the formula down the column.

4. Additional spaces will be removed from the text.

5. Now, let's try the **CLEAN** function. Cell B20 contains text that has a line break. This function is used to remove non-printing and line break characters. Click inside cell B20, then type `=clean(B20).`

6. Press *Enter* to confirm. The line breaks in this example have been removed from the text, but you will notice that the spaces still exist. To fix this, we can use **CLEAN** and **TRIM** together.

7. Delete the formula in cell B20, then replace it with `=trim(clean(B20)):`

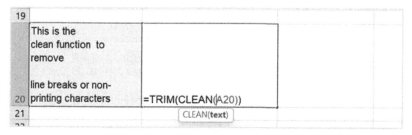

Figure 9.50 – Using the TRIM and CLEAN functions together

8. The **SUBSTITUTE** function will remove spaces or non-breaking spaces too. We can use the **SUBSTITUTE** function to replace a certain character type with another.

9. Cell A23 contains text as well as an accent character, ^. We would like to remove this character from the text. Before we do this, we will need to locate the ASCII character number code for ^. In this case, if we locate **Insert | Symbols | Symbol**, we can locate the ^ character, then find the code at the bottom of the dialog box. The code for the ^ character is 94. Now that we know the code for the ^ character, we can use this in our formula. Click inside B23 and type =substitute(A23,CHAR(94),""):

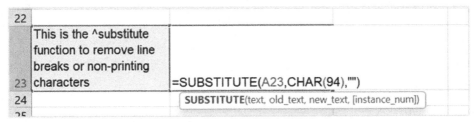

Figure 9.51 – Using the SUBSTITUTE function to replace characters

10. Press *Enter* to confirm this, after which the text will be formatted correctly without the accent.

At times, we need to remove data that has been duplicated in the worksheet. We will address this in the next section.

Removing duplicate data

To locate duplicates in a worksheet, follow these steps:

1. First, open the workbook named Duplicates.xlsx. Always make a copy of your dataset before removing duplicate data.

2. Use the **Conditional Formatting** tool to locate duplicates in the worksheet, or locate the **Remove Duplicates** tool.

3. Select the data in the worksheet, then go to **Home | Conditional Formatting | Highlight Cells Rules | Duplicate Values…**.

4. This method will highlight all the duplicate data in the range that you have specified. Note that you can change the **Format cells that contain** dropdown to **Unique** if you wish.

5. Change the **Custom Format** option if you do not want to use the default color scheme.

6. Click **OK** to identify duplicate values in the worksheet.

To remove duplicates, follow these steps:

1. Select the column or table you wish to remove duplicates from (or click inside the data range).

2. Click **Data | Remove Duplicates**:

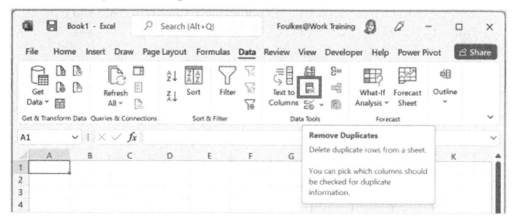

Figure 9.52 – The Remove Duplicates feature

3. Click to indicate whether your data has column headers or not.

4. Uncheck any columns you do not want to include in the range. Click **OK** to remove the duplicates:

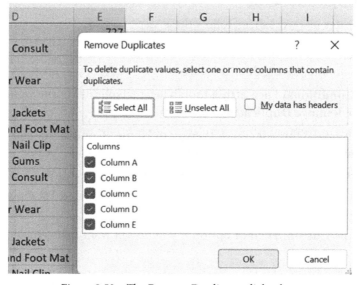

Figure 9.53 – The Remove Duplicates dialog box

5. Another screen will populate, specifying the number of duplicate values located on the worksheet, as well as the number of unique values that remain. Don't forget to save the workbook:

Figure 9.54 – The results are displayed in the notification popup

6. Click **OK** to view the results without any duplicates.

Another way to remove duplicates will be explained in the next section.

Using the UNIQUE function

The **UNIQUE** function is a new function for the latest version of Excel. It is a dynamic function that updates data automatically. When we use the **Remove Duplicates** feature to get rid of duplicate data, we can't update the table to refresh it with new data.

To remove duplicate data using the **UNIQUE** function, follow these steps:

1. Open the workbook named Unique.xlsx.

2. On the sheet named **Unique1**, you will see an employee list. Duplicates have been purposefully added to this dataset. If you would like to see the duplicate values, sort the data. We will use the **UNIQUE** function to return unique values from the list.

3. Let's investigate the syntax of the **UNIQUE** function:

    -   The *array* is the range from which we need to return unique values.

    -   *[by_col]* is how you would like to compare the data, either across rows or columns (optional field).

    -   *[exactly_one]* is the logical value that defines which values are unique using the TRUE or FALSE condition. TRUE returns values that occur once, while FALSE returns all distinct values in the range (optional field).

    For this example, we will remove the duplicate values, so only the array is required.

4. First, click where you would like the unique result to be placed – for this example, we will use cell J2.

5. Press = to start the formula, then type **UNIQUE(**.

6. Select the A2:G95 range, then press *Enter* to display the result.

7. Any amendments you make to the source dataset will update in the unique dataset. If you add rows to the dataset, you may want to format the dataset as a table so that the new rows are included and update the unique dataset accordingly.

Let's look at another example.

If we wanted to return a list of employees who have not attended more than one training session from a list of training data, we would need to alter the formula:

1. Open the *Unique2* sheet. The dataset contains courses that employees have attended. We would like to extract the employees who have only attended one out of the three training sessions provided.

2. We will place the result in cell H2.

3. Press = to start the formula.

4. Type **UNIQUE(** as the function.

5. Select the A2:F67 range.

6. Add a comma, then another comma, to skip the *[by_col]* argument.

7. Type or select **TRUE**, then add the closing parenthesis.

8. Press *Enter* to display the result. As we can see, only three employees have not completed the required number of courses:

H2		f_x =UNIQUE(C2:C67,,TRUE)					
	A	B	C	D	E	F	G	H
1	EMP NO	EMP NO	FIRST	Office	Course	Date Attended		Only One Course Attended
2	MIL04	MIL04	Bally, Barry	Munerton	Word 2021	15-Apr-21		Halal, Cheryl
3	MIL14	MIL14	Ambrose, Bob	Munerton	Word 2021	25-Jan-19		Murray, Robert
4	TBV26	TBV26	Halal, Cheryl	View Tabue	Word 2021	01-Feb-90		BinMIL, Teri
5	SUN59	SUN59	Hume, Chris	Soningdale	Word 2021	12-May-22		
6	TBV58	TBV58	Abel, Colleen	View Tabue	Word 2021	26-Jul-90		
7	SUN07	SUN07	Culbert, Frank	Soningdale	Word 2021	12-Jun-21		
8	MIL25	MIL25	Swayne, Harry	Munerton	Word 2021	30-Dec-90		
9	SUN45	SUN45	DeVinney, Kristen	Soningdale	Word 2021	05-Jun-21		
10	SUN47	SUN47	Murray, Robert	Soningdale	Word 2021	10-Jun-21		
11	MIL29	MIL29	Kling, Sara	Munerton	Word 2021	24-Dec-20		
12	SUN09	SUN09	Willis, Sean	Soningdale	Word 2021	05-Jul-19		
13	TBV76	TBV76	Rose, Seth	View Tabue	Word 2021	05-Apr-90		
14	SUN05	SUN05	Chen, Shing	Soningdale	Word 2021	08-Aug-84		
15	PKL55	PKL55	BinMIL, Teri	Parklands	Word 2021	07-Jun-22		
16	TBV19	TBV19	TBVlifano, Theresa	View Tabue	Word 2021	26-Feb-89		

Figure 9.55 – The result of the UNIQUE formula

Another issue that impacts formulas and many other features in Excel is blank cells within a dataset. In the next section, we will look at ways to remove rows and fill in blank cells quickly. Remember that we can use the filter command to filter blank rows too.

Sorting out empty rows

In the workbook named `BlankCells.xlsx`, we have several blank rows in the dataset. To remove all the blank rows from the workbook, follow these steps:

1. Make sure you are working on the **Rows** worksheet.
2. Go to **Find & Select | Go To Special…**.
3. Select **Blanks**, then click **OK** to see the blank rows highlighted on the worksheet.
4. To delete the rows, use the *Ctrl + -* keys (or go to **Home | Delete | Delete Sheet Rows**).

As we can see, there are no more empty rows in the dataset.

Sorting out blank cells

To highlight blank cells within a dataset, we can use the **Go To Special…** tool in Excel. At times, we may want to fill blank cells with a value, such as 0, so that our formula and tools work correctly when we're manipulating data. Let's learn how to achieve this:

1. Access the **Cells** worksheet.
2. We can use the same method that we used in the previous example to highlight the blank cells on the worksheet, then fill those cells with, for instance, a value such as 0.
3. First, add a 0 to an empty cell on the worksheet. Then, use the **Copy** button to copy the 0, then delete the 0 from the cell. Now, we can paste this over again if required.
4. Go to **Find & Select | Go To Special…**.
5. Select **Blanks**, then click **OK** to see the blank cells highlighted on the worksheet.
6. Now, click **Home | Find & Select | Replace…**.

7.   Leave the **Find what** field blank and enter a **0** in the **Replace with** field:

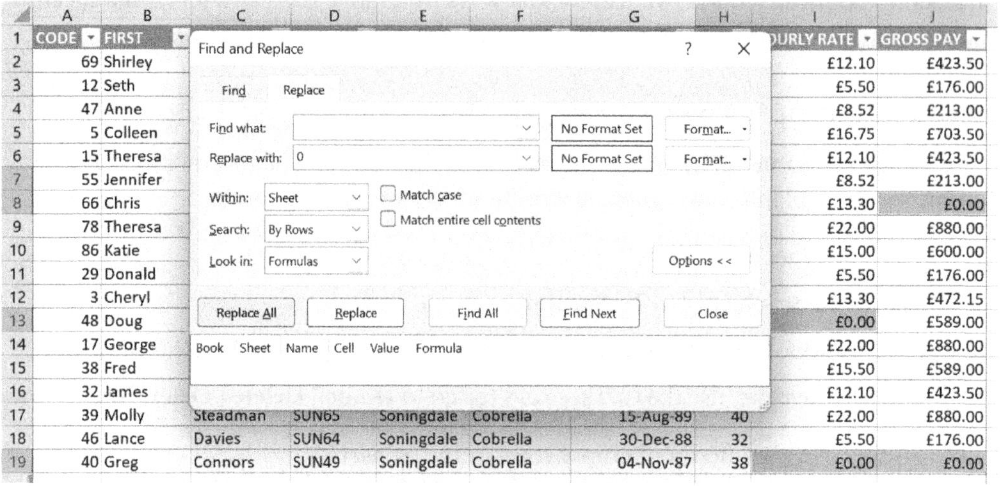

Figure 9.56 – Using Find and Replace to replace blank cells with 0

8.   Click **Replace All**, after which the cells will be filled with 0s.

There is so much more to explore here, but we hope that this will get you thinking about different scenarios where you can handle data in Excel. Now, let's learn how to join data.

Joining data

Just like the other features within Excel, we can join data using many methods. The following table shows a few examples:

Feature	Explanation	Example Syntax
& operator	The ampersand is an effortless way of joining data.	=L2&", "&M2&", "&N2
CONCAT	Joins text but does not allow the same delimiter for a range of cells. You can, however, enter your own delimiters for each value in the string.	=CONCAT(C2," ",D2)
TEXTJOIN	Joins text, with a delimiter applied to the range. You can ignore empty values.	=TEXTJOIN(", ",TRUE,A16:O16)

Table 9.3 – Examples of joining data in Excel 2021

When using either the **&** method or the **CONCAT** function, we can add delimiters manually for each text entry in the string. We cannot have the delimiter repeat throughout the text string automatically. The **TEXTJOIN** function allows a delimiter to be included automatically for each text entry in the string. The **TEXTJOIN** function also includes a condition that sets whether the selected range includes or excludes blank spaces in the result.

Let's look at a few examples.

Using & to combine data

Follow these steps:

1. Open the workbook named `SSGJoin.xlsx`.

2. The **ampersand (&)** operator works well if you want to pick data from different places in the work area that you wish to include in one text string. If you have an invoice, for example, and you need to include an invoice number, the date, and the item that was purchased to form a sentence, you can use & to do so. In this example, we will combine the three items listed in the range, with a comma between each value in the string.

3. Click inside cell Q2 of the worksheet, then enter the `=L2&", "&M2&", "&N2` formula to collect cells. Add delimiters where appropriate.

   Let's break down the formula:

   - Click inside cell Q2, then press the = sign to start the formula.

   - Click inside cell L2 to collect the *Initial Consultation values*.

   - Press the *&* key on your keyboard.

   - As we need to include a comma and a space in between the two text strings, we need to include this before we click on the next item. Type an *inverted comma*, a *comma*, a *space*, and close with another *inverted comma*; that is, *", "*.

   - Type another **&**, then click on the next item – that is, cell M2.

   - Repeat the process to type an **inverted comma**, a **comma**, a **space**, and close with another **inverted comma** as follows: **", "** to add a comma and a space after the second item.

   - Press the *&* key on your keyboard.

- Click on cell N2 to complete the formula:

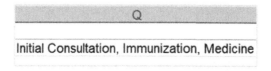

A	L	M	N	O	P	Q
InvDate	Item1	Item2	Item3	Amount Owing	&	
43543	Initial Consultation	Immunization	Medicine	727		=L2&", "&M2&", "&N2
43630	Wash and Go	Initial Consultation	Follow Up Consult	988		

Figure 9.57 – The & formula's construction

4. Press *Enter* to confirm and display the formula's result:

Q
Initial Consultation, Immunization, Medicine

Figure 9.58 – The result of using the & formula

The **CONCAT** function is very similar to the & method. You can collect cells and add the relevant delimiter in between each value of the string if required.

Using the CONCAT function

Follow these steps:

1. Continue with the workbook from the previous section; that is, SSGJoin.xlsx.

2. We will use the **CONCAT** function to combine the *surname and name* of the customer into a single cell. Click inside cell R2 to begin constructing your formula.

3. Type =CONCAT(to start the formula.

4. Locate and click on cell D2, then add a *comma*, after which you should click the next cell reference to include or add a delimiter. In this case, we will add an *inverted comma*, *comma*, and a *space*, then another *inverted comma*.

5. Click on cell C2 to collect the *name* of the customer:

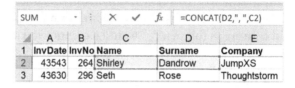

| | | SUM | ▾ | ⋮ | × | ✓ | *fx* | =CONCAT(D2,", ",C2) |

◢	A	B	C	D	E
1	InvDate	InvNo	Name	Surname	Company
2	43543	264	Shirley	Dandrow	JumpXS
3	43630	296	Seth	Rose	Thoughtstorm

Figure 9.59 – The CONCAT formula's construction

Now that you have mastered the **&** and **CONCAT** methods, let's look at the **TEXTJOIN** function.

Constructing the TEXTJOIN function

The **TEXTJOIN** function is more efficient due to the following reasons:

- It allows a delimiter to be entered once, which will automatically be included for each value of the text string.

- It allows you to include spaces or remove blank spaces in the text string.

Let's construct the **TEXTJOIN** formula:

1. Working in the same workbook that you worked in for the previous example, notice that row *16* is missing bits of data. Not all the cells contain data. We will use the **TEXTJOIN** function to include all the data from the range, excluding the empty cells, but we will include a comma and a space after each value of the string.

2. The answer needs to be in cell R16. Select cell R16.

3. Type =TEXTJOIN (to start the formula. The formula syntax we require is as follows:

```
=textjoin(
  TEXTJOIN(delimiter, ignore_empty, text1, ...)
```

Figure 9.60 – The TEXTJOIN syntax's construction

4. Enter *", "* for the *delimiter*.

5. Add a *comma*, then select **TRUE** for the *ignore_empty* cells, then add a *comma* to separate the arguments again.

6. Select the **A16:O16** range, and then add a **parenthesis** to end the formula.

7. Press *Enter* to confirm and display the result.

With that, we have mastered joining data in Excel. Let's move on to the final section of this chapter and learn how to separate data.

Separating data

The **Text to Columns** feature in Excel is a wonderful tool to separate data from a single cell into multiple columns. Let's take a look:

1. Open the workbook named Customers.xlsx.

2. Notice that the data is bundled in the first column of the workbook. This sometimes happens when data is imported.

3. Select **Column A**, then go to **Data | Text to Columns**:

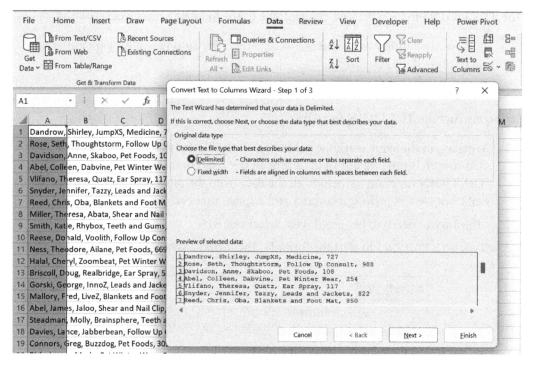

Figure 9.61 – Convert Text to Columns Wizard

4. Choose the file type that suits your dataset – this dataset is separated by *commas*, so we will leave the selection set to **Delimited**. Click **Next >** to continue.

5. Select the delimiter that suits your data on the next screen. For this dataset, we will select **Comma**. Click **Next >** to continue:

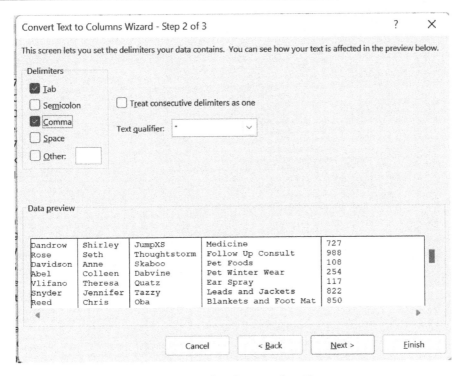

Figure 9.62 – Select Comma, then Next >

6. Notice that the data has been separated in the bottom half of the window. Check that this is what you require.

7. On the third screen, select the formats you require for each column of data. Normally, I leave this step and sort it out once I have converted the data into separate columns.

8. Click **Finish** to complete the process and display the data in separate columns on the worksheet.

Summary

You have learned an abundance of skills throughout this chapter. Now, you can confidently use the new features of Excel 2021, as well as making use of the updates for various tools. Using Advanced Filter should now be a simple task, and manipulating data using the new FILTER function should make your data manipulation efforts more efficient. You also learned more about conditional formatting and about importing, cleaning, joining, and separating data while incorporating some new functions, such as UNIQUE.

In the next chapter, you will learn about the latest functions and more about PivotTables, lookup functions, and date functions.

10

Exploring New and Useful Workflow Functions

Microsoft Excel 2021 houses some valuable new functions. During this part of the book, you will recap a number of important concepts and investigate some new functions. In the previous book, *Learn Microsoft Office 2019*, we concentrated on the differences between a formula and a function, learned about operators and formula construction, and how to use the correct order of evaluation. We also covered the **Function Library** and error checking.

This chapter will concentrate on the latest functions involved in learning the syntax and construction of the formula, such as **XLOOKUP**, **LET**, and **XMATCH**, as well as focus on **IFS**. We will learn to combine formulas, such as **IFERROR** and **VLOOKUP**, explore the term ARRAYS, and look at the new dynamic array functions in Excel 2021. There is also a topic included on database functions and a final topic exploring COUNTIFS.

The following list of topics will be covered in this chapter:

- Learning about dynamic arrays
- Investigating new functions
- Exploring database functions
- Using the COUNTIFS statistical function

At the end of the chapter, we will highlight common formula errors and learn how to use named ranges in a formula.

Technical requirements

As you have learned how to insert functions to create a formula and check for errors in the previous edition of our book, we will assume you are equipped with these prerequisite skills. We will now build on these.

The examples used in this chapter are accessible from the following GitHub URL: `https://github.com/PacktPublishing/Learn-Microsoft-Office-2021-Second-Edition`.

Learning about dynamic arrays

Let's first understand the term array and when to use it. An **array** is simply a collection of data that can be stored in one or multiple rows or columns. Data within these columns can be numbers or text. In Excel, an array is a formula that performs multiple calculations on one or more items in an array.

Array formulas can return multiple or single results. We can use arrays to eliminate and speed up the number of actions we need to perform in Excel to produce a result. To follow along with the next example, open the workbook named `Arrays.xlsx`.

For instance, in the example that follows, the usual method you could implement to arrive at a grand total for the cost of each course would be to work out the total amount for each course and then sum the totals to establish the grand total.

C	D	E	F
COURSE	**NO. ENROLLED**	**AMOUNT**	**TOTAL**
Management Course	2	275	=D2*E2
Compliance Review	3	223	=D3*E3
Productivity Essentials	4	150	=D4*E4
Human Resource Management	5	250	=D5*E5
		TOTAL	
		=SUM(F2:F5)	

Figure 10.1 – Working out grand totals using the traditional method

This method is great, but we could speed this up by making use of an array either for single or multiple actions, thereby achieving processing in one action and saving an enormous amount of time.

To create an array, we would insert *curly brackets* around the {**formula**}. We never type the curly brackets; they are inserted using the *Ctrl + Shift + Enter* keys.

There are a few pointers to make sure you are aware of when using arrays:

- Always look at the formula bar to see whether a formula is part of an array.

- If you need to edit an array formula, the curly brackets will disappear – you need to insert them again using *Ctrl + Shift + Enter* at the end of the formula.

- Manually inserted curly brackets will not convert the formula into an array.

Let's look at how we construct an array formula to eliminate multiple actions (keystrokes).

Constructing an array formula to calculate a total

We will now run through the steps to create an array:

1. Using the `Arrays.xlsx` worksheet, click into cell E9 and then type the following formula: `=sum(D2:D5*E2:E5)`.

C	D	E
COURSE	**NO. ENROLLED**	**AMOUNT**
Management Course	2	£275.00
Compliance Review	3	£223.00
Productivity Essentials	4	£150.00
Human Resource Management	5	£250.00
		TOTAL
		=sum(D2:D5*E2:E5)

Figure 10.2 – Working out grand totals using an array

2. Press the *Ctrl + Shift + Enter* keys to create the array, after which you will see the total in E9.

3. In the formula bar, you will notice the formula has now included curly brackets at the start and end of the formula to enclose it.

| E9 | ▾ | ⋮ | ✕ | ✓ | *fx* | {=SUM(D2:D5*E2:E5)} |

Figure10.3 – The constructed array formula showing curly brackets

4. Also take note that when double-clicking in cell E9, the curly brackets are not visible.

Using the array and IF function combined

Let's explore an array where one range calculates another range to fill in values according to the criteria:

1. Using the same workbook as the previous example, we will construct an array formula to display the word *HIGH* where population growth *exceeds 3%*. The next screenshot depicts what we would like to achieve as the formula result in cells E16:F19. A change to any of the cells in B16:C19 will automatically update the table in E16:F19.

	A	B	C	D	E	F
13						
14						
15	Population Growth	2019	2021		2019	2021
16	Nottingham	2.70%	3.80%			HIGH
17	Maidstone	3.20%	2.00%	HIGH		
18	Oxford	1.50%	3.10%			HIGH
19	Exeter	-1.40%	8.00%			HIGH
20						

Figure 10.4 – The completed table

2. Select cells E16:F19 and then enter the following formula:
    `=IF(B16:C19>0.03,"HIGH","")`.

3. Press *Ctrl + Shift + Enter*.

4. Amend a growth % value in the first table to see whether the table updates accordingly.

If you make any amends to an array range, it is good practice to highlight the entire range array. For instance, to make amends to the array formula in the previous example, you would select cells E16:F19 to make any changes to the formula. Editing cell E16 and pressing the *Enter* key will present an error alert indicating that the cell is part of an array. This is because you have not used the *Ctrl + Shift + Enter* keys to amend the array.

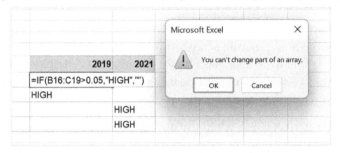

Figure 10.5 – Error when trying to amend a single cell part of an array

Evaluating array formulas

We can evaluate part of an array by selecting the part of the array formula and then pressing *F9* on the keyboard to show values. This is a great way of checking whether the array is using the correct cells:

1. Select the array cells to evaluate.

2. In the formula bar, select the part of the array formula to investigate.

Figure 10.6 – Selecting the part of the array to evaluate

3. Press *F9* on the keyboard to display the values. Note that if you do not select part of the formula prior to pressing *F9*, the formula will update to the calculated value only.

Figure 10.7 – Pressing F9 to evaluate the formula

4. Press *Esc* on the keyboard when complete.

Now that we are confident in terms of how to create and edit arrays, we will learn more about the new array formulas in the following topic.

Investigating new functions

Excel 2021 has a few new functions, namely, **XLOOKUP, LET, XMATCH**, and a couple of dynamic **Array** functions. We will discover these in the following topics.

New dynamic array functions

In the previous chapter, we introduced the FILTER and UNIQUE functions. The FILTER function is part of the new dynamic array formulas in Excel 2021. When we apply this function, the results spill from a single cell into the adjacent cells. Normally, when using the traditional filter in Excel, it will not update as new data is entered into the workbook – you would have to recalculate or update the results.

Dynamic arrays are perfect since, when the underlying data (source data) is updated, all lists based on that dataset are updated automatically.

Along with the new FILTER function, we also have a couple of other functions added to the list of dynamic array formulas, namely, SORT, SORTBY, UNIQUE, SEQUENCE, and RANDARRAY.

Let's recap the FILTER function and combine it with the CHOOSE function to extract the cases sold of a particular wine label above 300:

1. Open the workbook named MattWinery.xlsx.

2. On the first sheet, we have a dataset relating to wines and the number of cases sold per region. The dataset contains column headings in Row 1.

3. We would like to set up a filter to split the regions and cases sold above 300, per label selected in cell K2, into columns **M** and **N**, respectively.

4. As we require the headings *Region* and *Cases Sold* for the output columns, we need to copy the existing headings and paste them into cells M1 and M2.

5. In cell K1, enter the heading Label and create a validation rule to list the following items in cell K2: **Cab Savon, Chardinoha**, and **Merlat**.

Figure 10.8 – Validation rule to define the Label categories

6. In cell M2, construct the following formula using the CHOOSE and FILTER functions: =FILTER(CHOOSE({1,2},Table1[Region],Table1[Cases Sold]),Table1[Label]=K2)

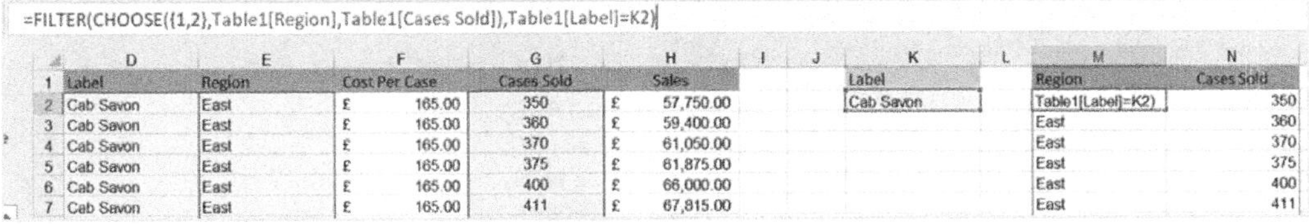

Figure 10.9 – The FILTER and CHOOSE functions in cell M2

7. The result will spill into columns **M** and **N** accordingly, based on the selection in cell K2. Choose another label type from the validation rule in cell K2 to see the table update.

Let's now look at another two new dynamic array functions.

The SEQUENCE function generates a list of sequential values. We can use this function to create codes or for a specific range of values:

1. Click on **Sheet 2**. In cell D1, enter the heading EMP CODE. In cell D2, enter the following formula: =SEQUENCE(10,1,1540,500).

2. Press *Enter* to populate the list. To clarify the formula syntax, the number 10 refers to the number of rows to fill, 1 means a single column, 1540 refers to the start number, and 500 the increments between each.

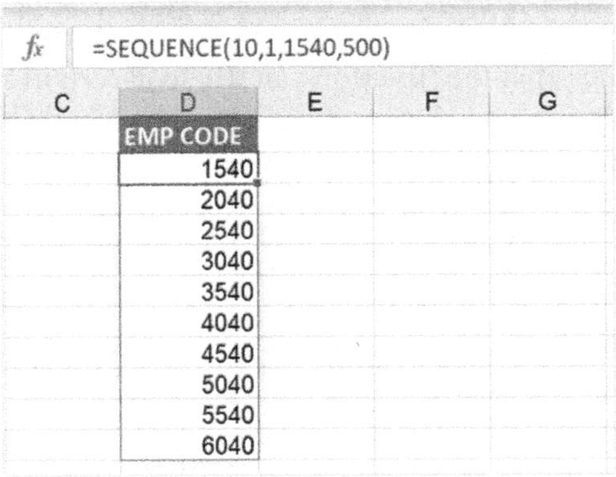

Figure 10.10 – Sequence function in cell D2

The RANDARRAY function returns a list of values across rows or columns. You can generate a list of accidental whole numbers according to a given constraint, decimal numbers according to a given constraint, or a set of accidental values. This new function is a replacement for the former RAND and RANDBETWEEN functions.

F	G	H	I	J	K
	=RANDARRAY(7,3,100,300,TRUE)				
	RANDARRAY([rows], [columns], [min], [max], [integer])				
	206	127	139		
	293	206	294		
	236	163	131		
	132	224	218		
	233	299	255		

Figure 10.11 – The new RANDARRAY function syntax

In the previous edition of our book, *Learn Microsoft Office 2019*, we explored the application of conditional logic in a formula using IF, AND, and OR. We will briefly recap the IF function with a few more examples to enhance what we have learned.

Building IFS functions

The IFS function was first introduced in Office 2016, so it is not a new function. It is so much easier to construct and evaluate multiple IF conditions instead of using the old clunky nested IF formula.

The IFS syntax is extremely simple: =IFS(logical_test1,value_if_true1,[logical_test2,value_if_true2], and so on up to 127 conditions.

As there is no default value that the function can use to ascertain as true when all conditions are false, we have to add a true condition as the final test. Note that each logical test could return a true or a false value.

Here is an example. In the workbook named IFS.xlsx, we will see the data range is related to different pet services offered in columns J and L. For each service, we would like to assign a code so that this data populates automatically for each service type displayed in the column. Any service that is not assigned a code should report the true condition as NOT DEFINED.

The IFS function is a perfect logical function to utilize in this instance:

1.   Click into cell K2, and construct the following formula, making sure that the
     final condition is entered either as 1=1,"NOT DEFINED" or TRUE,"NOT
     DEFINED":

     ```
     =IFS(J2="Initial Consultation","IC234",J2="Wash and
     Go","WGO123",J2="Follow Up Consult","FUC873",
     J2="Pet Foods","PEF972",J2="Pet Winter Wear",
     "PWW443",J2="Ear Spray","ERS021",J2="Leads and
     Jackets","L&J23",J2="Blankets and Foot Mat",
     "BFM654",J2="Teeth and Gums","TEG823",
     J2="Immunisation","IMM768",J2="Medicine",
     "MED321",1=1,"NOT DEFINED").
     ```

2.   The following screenshot displays the result of the IFS function on the worksheet:

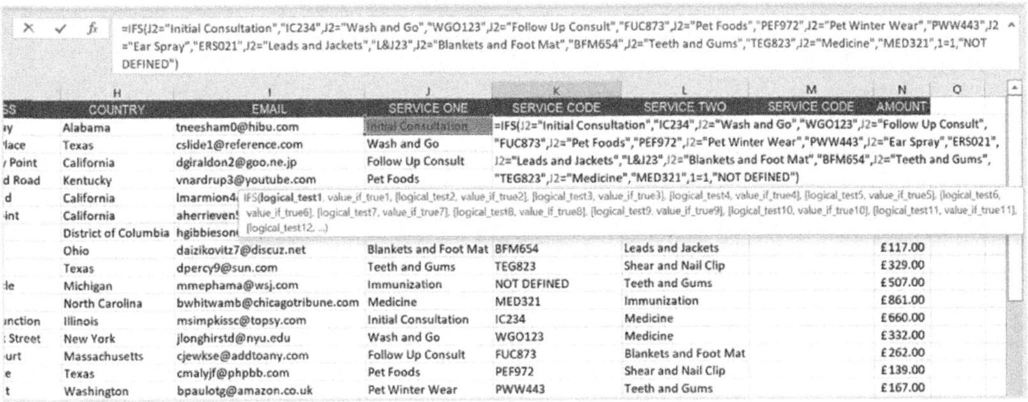

Figure 10.12 – IFS function result

3.   Notice that two columns require the service code in order to populate. Ensure that
     you copy the function from K2 to M2 and update the cell reference to reflect cell L2.

Now that you have mastered the IFS function, let's take a brief look at the SUMIFS function. The SUMIFS function is part of the Math and Trig function libraries in Excel. This function simply adds all of the arguments in the dataset that meet certain criteria. We will continue to work with the IFS.xlsx workbook. You will notice a list of services provided in *Column Q* of the *SUMIFS* worksheet. The main dataset contains a list of services and amounts for each. Let's use the SUMIFS function to generate the amount for each service.

4. Click into cell P2 as this is where we will construct a formula to arrive at a total if the service is equal to a certain service type.

	J	K	L	M	N	O	P	Q	R	S	T
	SERVICE ONE	SERVICE CODE	AMOUNT			SERVICE TOTALS					
	Initial Consultation	IC234	£698.00			Initial Consultation	=SUMIFS($L$2:$L$28,$J$2:$J$28,O2)				
	Wash and Go	WGO123	£523.00			Wash and Go	SUMIFS(**sum_range**, criteria_range1, criteria1, [criteria_range2, criteria2], ...)				
	Follow Up Consult	FUC873	£856.00			Follow Up Consult	£1,948.00				
ๅ	Pet Foods	PEF972	£ 6.00			Pet Foods	£471.00				
com	Pet Winter Wear	PWW443	£516.00			Pet Winter Wear	£1,482.00				
	Ear Spray	ERS021	£397.00			Ear Spray	£1,537.00				
	Leads and Jackets	L&J23	£997.00			Leads and Jackets	£1,563.00				
	Blankets and Foot Mat	BFM654	£117.00			Blankets and Foot Mat	£642.00				
	Teeth and Gums	TEG823	£329.00			Teeth and Gums	£432.00				
	Immunization	NOT DEFINED	£507.00			Immunization	£1,145.00				
une.com	Medicine	MED321	£861.00			Medicine	£861.00				

Figure 10.13 – SUMIFS function result and formula arguments for SERVICE

5. The syntax of the SUMIFS function is really simple. Let's take a look:

ARGUMENTS	EXPLANATION
sum_range	This is a required argument. Specify the range of cells to SUM. In the case of the example, this range would be values in the Amount column: $L$2:$L$28.
criteria_range1	This is a required argument. criteria1 and criteria_range1 work together. When the criteria specified in criteria1 is located in the criteria_range1, they are totaled together. In the case of the example, criteria_range1 would be the Services column $J$2:$J$28.
criteria1	This is a required argument. In this example, we will be using the contents of cell P2 as the initial test cell, after which we will drag the fill handle to fill the rest of the cells. We can use different operators here, including <>, >, <, =B*, and so on…
criteria_range2 criteria2, and so on…	Not required for this example, but you can add up to 127 range pairs here.

Table 10.1 – Arguments and explanations of the SUMIFS function

6. Type the following formula into cell P2, or use the mouse pointer to collect the relevant arguments you require from the worksheet: =SUMIFS($L$2:$L$28,$J$2:$J$28,O2).

7. Press *Enter* to see the result of the formula and then fill it down to the rest of the column.

We have mastered the IFS and SUMIFS functions, so hope that you have added to the Excel skillset. Next, we will concentrate on expanding our LOOKUP function knowledge.

Building on VLOOKUP

Before we discover new LOOKUP functions in Office 2021, we will build on our existing **VLOOKUP** skills cultured from our previous edition book, *Learn Microsoft Office 2019*. It is important to understand how different functions work together or to find fewer complex methods to generate the desired output.

Combining IFERROR AND VLOOKUP

As mentioned, we will look at the new XLOOKUP function in subsequent topics, but we will firstly look at how the IFERROR and VLOOKUP functions can complement each other:

1. Open the workbook named VLOOKUP.xlsx.

2. Click to select the IFERROR worksheet.

3. Cells A2:G9 house employee data for BizGen Ltd. *Column F* is missing team data. The team data is kept in a separate worksheet named *Team*. As we do not want to re-type this data, we will construct a VLOOKUP formula to look up the name of the colleague, and pull through the corresponding *Team* name located in the *TEAM* worksheet.

4. We have learned all about the VLOOKUP syntax in the previous edition of our book, so let's click into cell F4 to construct the formula, as follows:

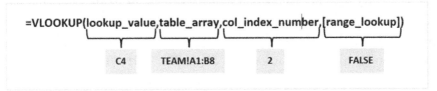

Figure 10.14 – The VLOOKUP syntax showing the different arguments applicable to the example

5. Press *Enter* to see the result of the first colleague and then fill in the rest of the cells down the column.

	A	B	C	D	E	F	G
1					BizGen Ltd		
2							
3	EMP ID	RA Number	Name	Date Joined	Office	Team	Type
4	3426	478477	Daniel Peacer	01/07/2014	Birstham	Marketing	Employee
5	4043	278695	Lee van Aller	15/01/2002	Lewton	Development	Employee
6	4963	457937	Ditto Plush	15/11/2018	Milerton	HR	Employee
7	4265	14295	Suzette Mann	01/11/1995	Parklands	#N/A	Employee
8	4265	14295	Suzette Mann	01/11/1995	Parklands	#N/A	Shareholder
9	3472	123987	Natalue Conn	01/11/1982	View-Under-Lyne	Private Group	Consultant
10	3375	379395	Tumi Mvuyo	15/03/2007	Dunston	Corporate	Employee

Figure 10.15 – The VLOOKUP result showing #N/A where errors are located

6. The result indicates an **#N/A** error for the colleague named **Suzette Mann**. In this case, we would need to compare the result with the Team worksheet. We have to be mindful that VLOOKUP could report an incorrect result, as well as the dataset you are using as table_array. In this case, there is a discrepancy between the spelling of the colleague in the source dataset and table_array on the *Team* worksheet. We could fix the spelling error, and the formula would work perfectly by duplicating the Team name. A few other reasons for the #N/A error could be the following:

   *   The lookup value is not located in the lookup array.

   *   The data may not be cleaned, especially if imported. See the relevant topic in the previous chapter to find out more about how to clean data ready for input.

   *   There could be extra spaces or spelling errors causing the return of the #N/A.

7. We can add the IFERROR function to the VLOOKUP function so that it reports a specific text as the error in return, instead of the default #N/A error. To identify duplicates at a glance on the worksheet, you could use the text *"duplicate"* or *"error found"*, for example.

8. The IFERROR function syntax is as follows: **IFERROR(value,value_if_error).**

9. Double-click on cell F4 to amend the formula. As the existing function already contains the value argument, we can add the IFERROR function at the start of the formula and then include the value_if_error part of the syntax at the end.

10. The formula should read as follows:
    `=IFERROR(VLOOKUP(C4,TEAM!A1:B8,2,FALSE),"ERROR FOUND").`

LET		▾ ⋮	×	✓	*fx*	=IFERROR(VLOOKUP(C4,TEAM!A1:B8,2,FALSE),"ERROR FOUND")					
◢	A	B	C	D	E	F	G	H	I	J	K
1					BizGen Ltd						
2											
3	EMP ID	RA Number	Name	Date Joined	Office	Team	Type				
4	3426	478477	Daniel Peacer	01/07/2014	Birstham	=IFERROR(VLOOKUP(C4,TEAM!A1:B8,2,FALSE),"ERROR FOUND")					
5	4043	278695	Lee van Aller	15/01/2002	Lewton	IFERROR(value, value_if_error) oyee					
6	4963	457937	Ditto Plush	15/11/2018	Milerton	HR	Employee				
7	4265	14295	Suzette Mann	01/11/1995	Parklands	ERROR FOUND	Employee				
8	4265	14295	Suzette Mann	01/11/1995	Parklands	ERROR FOUND	Shareholder				
9	3472	123987	Natalue Conn	01/11/1982	View-Under-Lyne	Private Group	Consultant				
10	3375	379395	Tumi Mvuyo	15/03/2007	Dunston	Corporate	Employee				

Figure 10.16 – The IFERROR function added to the existing VLOOKUP formula

11. Now we can clearly see that there is an error in cells F7 and F8. A great way to ensure that errors are visually highlighted on the worksheet is to apply conditional formatting.

Let's visit an example that uses the approximate match as the range lookup.

Looking up using an approximate match

This is a useful example for human resource departments wanting to pull through the salary band for employees by looking up a salary range or scale using the approximate match:

1. Continue to use the same workbook as the prior example, but click to access the *Band* worksheet. This sheet contains a list of employees and their salaries, as well as a salary band data range. We would like to automatically populate the salary band for each employee in the list.

2. As we are already familiar with the function syntax, we can click into cell C4 to construct the formula as follows: `=VLOOKUP(B4,$E$4:$G$11,3,TRUE)`.

3. Ensure that **table_array**, E4:G11 is marked as constant and that [**range_lookup**] is set to **TRUE**. **TRUE** indicates an approximate match here as we are dealing with looking up the colleague's salary from a salary range and returning the appropriate salary band.

	A	B	C	D	E	F	G
1							
2							
3	NAME				RANGE	CATEGORY	BAND
4	Colleague 1	=VLOOKUP(B4,$E$4:$G$11,3,TRUE)			25001	8	H
5	Colleague 2	VLOOKUP(lookup_value, table_array, col_index_num, [range_lookup]) 35000				7	G
6	Colleague 3	35789	F		35001	6	F
7	Colleague 4	41250	E		40001	5	E
8	Colleague 5	82700	B		47501	4	D
9					55001	3	C
10					70001	2	B
11					85001	1	A
12							

Figure 10.17 – VLOOKUP function constructed using the approximate match

Lastly, let's combine VLOOKUP with a validation rule and the MATCH function.

VLOOKUP AND MATCH

The *VLOOKUPMATCH* worksheet consists of a Vet Service Report table listing services provided by each salesperson in cells A6:F13. Instead of taking the time to run along rows, columns, and salespersons, we would like to choose the service provided for a particular salesperson and return the value for that service.

In the following screenshot, you will see the completed worksheet:

	A	B	C	D	E	F
1						
2		IMMUNIZATION ▼				
3	Myuvo	£ 4,300.00				
4						
5						
6	VET SERVICE REPORT / SALES PERSON	NAIL CLIP	WINTER WEAR	LEADS AND JACKETS	IMMUNIZATION	WASH AND GO
7	Jules	£ 3,000.00	£ 5,000.00	£ 20,100.00	£ 45,678.00	£ 7,456.00
8	Ramon	£ 9,000.00	£ 1,356.00	£ 34,567.00	£ 23,122.00	£ 450.00
9	Sue	£ 2,345.00		£ 3,000.00	£ 2,900.00	
10	Dan	£ 600.00	£ 3,400.00	£ 2,300.00		£ 3,200.00
11	Myuvo	£ 1,000.00		£ 230.00	£ 4,300.00	£ 2,300.00
12	Esther	£ 5,988.00		£ 16,777.00	£ 24,000.00	£ 4,000.00
13	Sam	£ 5,677.00	£ 5,630.00	£ 29,567.00	£ 3,400.00	£ 3,333.00
14						

Figure 10.18 – Completed VLOOKUPMATCH worksheet

Let's get started!

1. Firstly, create a drop-down list, a validation rule for the services in cell B2 so that when a service is selected, it will display the relevant salespersons and a service total. Click into cell B2, visit **Data | Data Validation | List**, and then add B6:F6 as the *Source* range.

2. In cell B3, construct the following formula:
    `=VLOOKUP(A3,A6:F13,MATCH(B2,A6:F6,0),FALSE)`.

3. The formula will look up the salesperson entered in cell A3, within the table range, and then match the service entered in cell B2 within the table range and return an exact match.

4. Test the function by entering the name of another salesperson in cell A3 and then choosing another service from the drop-down list in B2 to update the result in cell B3.

We will now explore the new LOOKUP functions that are packaged in the Office 2021 offering.

Exploring XLOOKUP

The new XLOOKUP function is a step up from the VLOOKUP function we all know so well. Instead of having to use LOOKUP, VLOOKUP, and HLOOKUP depending on the type of function required, we can now use one single function to meet all our requirements. XLOOKUP replaces the need to use the INDEX MATCH functions, as well as IFERROR. XLOOKUP looks up values in a range, or an array, and then returns the matching values from that range/array.

XLOOKUP caters for the following:

*   The return of lookup data to either the right or left of lookup values. This is an important advantage over previous lookup functions.

*   No restrictions on returning just one value anymore, but the ability to generate entire rows or columns as a result.

*   Exact and approximate matching – the function will return an exact match as a default when constructing the formula, so you do not need to input that detail. The previous VLOOKUP function always returned the approximate match as a default.

*   The use of wildcard characters for partial matching, as well as the performance of reverse searches.

*   The ability to encompass vertical and horizontal ranges and return multiple results.

Constructing XLOOKUP (syntax)

Firstly, let's explore and understand the XLOOKUP syntax, after which we will build a formula and look at some real-life examples.

When we construct the VLOOKUP syntax, we will need to provide input in a certain way. The syntax is as follows: =XLOOKUP (lookup, lookup_array, return_array, [not_found], [match_mode], [search_mode]).

Here is a snapshot of the XLOOKUP formula in practice. We will use this example to discuss what is required for each argument of the formula so that the explanation in the subsequent table makes sense.

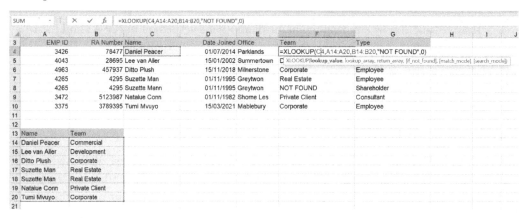

Figure 10.19 – XLOOKUP formula construction

Referring to the previous screenshot example, we will now understand how each of the different elements blend together.

ARGUMENTS	EXPLANATION
`lookup_value`	`lookup_value` is what you are searching for. This could be a name, ID number, department, amount, from a range, or an array. Although a required field, if nothing is entered, it will return blank cells it locates within the `lookup_array` argument. In the example, we are looking up the name of the employee and using cell C4 as the test cell.
`lookup_array`	The range or array you are looking up the value from. We are searching for an employee name within a certain range of cells. This argument is required. In the example, we have selected the range A14:A20.
`return_array`	What data would you like returned if `lookup_value` is located? When looking up the employee's name, would you like to return the name of the team for the matched value? In the argument example, we will return the matched value from the Team column. We will return data from the range B14:B20.
`[if_not_found]`	This argument allows the return of text if the value is not located in the range or array specified. Although this is not a required field, the argument will return the #N/A error if the argument is not included by the user. In the case of this example, we will return the text "NOT FOUND" if the condition is not met.
`[match_mode]`	This is an optional argument. There are four match modes we can include here: Enter 0 here for an exact match; -1 for an exact match, but if no matches are found, it will return the next smaller item; 1 for an exact match, but if no matches are found, then it returns the next larger item; and 2 if you have used a wildcard character in `lookup_value`.
`[search_mode]`	This is an optional argument that also has four options: 1 is the default and will execute a search on the first item; -1 will execute a search starting with the last item in the range; 2 will execute a binary search but would rely on `lookup_array` in A-Z order – this search will return invalid results if `lookup_array` is not sorted; and -2 will execute a binary search but would rely on `lookup_array` sorted in Z-A order – this search will return invalid results if `lookup_array` is not sorted.

Table 10.2 – Syntax arguments and explanations

Now that you have had a run-through of syntax and understand the XLOOKUP function, it is important to look at possible error returns when working with the formula.

Looking at general error returns

In the following table, we outline some of the cell errors you may come across and an explanation of the reasons why certain errors may report when using the XLOOKUP function.

ERROR RETURNED	EXPLANATION
#N/A	XLOOKUP returns this error when it cannot locate the lookup value; for instance, if an ID number is missing or if an individual or certain product is not found.
#VALUE	This error returns if the lookup and return arrays have mismatched-sized columns or rows, so make sure that lookup_array and return_array are exactly the same in terms of their dimensions.
#REF	It is important to ensure when using XLOOKUP across more than one workbook that both workbooks are open. Failure to do so will return the #REF error.

Table 10.3 – Error values and explanations

Let's walk through the XLOOKUP formula:

1. Open the workbook named LOOKUP.xlsx.

2. The *XLOOKUP* worksheet contains employee details in cells A3:G10, and a list of employees and teams they belong to in cells A13:B20. Column F is missing the matching team information. We can pull this information by using the XLOOKUP function, either from a location within the same workbook or from a separate workbook.

3. Click into cell F4.

4. Press = to start the formula and then type XLOOKUP (to open the formula arguments.

5. Enter the following arguments: C4,A13:A20,B13:B20,"not found",0).

6. Press *Enter* to confirm the formula and see the first result.

7. Use **AutoFill** to complete the results down the column. You will notice that cell F8 returns the text **NOT FOUND** as the employee cannot be located in the lookup table.

XLOOKUP can also be used to analyze the two lists of data to determine which customers are in the first table, but not in the second table, for instance. Using the XLOOKUP function instead of VLOOKUP eliminates several steps. Click on the *LOOKUP* sheet to work through the following example:

1. Ensure that you have the LOOKUP.xlsx workbook open and have clicked on the *LOOKUP* sheet.

2. We have two tables on this worksheet. To find out which customers are in the first table but not in the second table, we could use the XLOOKUP function. Click into cell M3.

3. Type the following formula: =XLOOKUP(A3,$A$33:$A$57,$A$33:$A$57, "NOT FOUND",0).

4. The formula will look up the code to see whether it returns matching codes from the second table. If it does not locate a match, the words **NO MATCH** will appear in *Column M* of the worksheet.

5. Don't forget to use *AutoFill* to fill the formula through cells M4:M29.

6. The last step would be to highlight the entire row where the formula is met so that those not found are accentuated visually on the worksheet – do you know how to do this?

7. Select the range A3:M29 and then apply a conditional formula formatting rule to highlight the row with a light green fill color. To see the completed workbook, open the file named LOOKUP-C.xlsx. The following screenshot displays a portion of the result:

	H	I	J	K	L	M
1						
2	ROLE	ADDRESS	COUNTRY	SERVICE ONE	SERVICE TWO	XLOOKUP
3	Staff Accountant III	06 Ludington Court	Massachusetts	Follow Up Consult	Blankets and Foot Mat	1813
4	Developer II	87133 Sunbrook Stre	New York	Wash and Go	Medicine	NOT FOUND
5	Senior Quality Engineer	11 Marquette Street	Pennsylvania	Ear Spray	Leads and Jackets	16505
6	Senior Sales Associate	2 Onsgard Park	District of Colum	Leads and Jackets	Ear Spray	20041
7	Information Systems Manag	2 Monument Terrace	Virginia	Blankets and Foot Mat	Pet Winter Wear	20195
8	Payment Adjustment Coordi	6 Mifflin Plaza	North Carolina	Medicine	Immunization	NOT FOUND
9	Account Representative I	89 Elgar Crossing	Florida	Teeth and Gums	Leads and Jackets	33610
10	Director	45 Nice Ave, Sundring	London	Follow Up Consult	Teeth and Gums	NOT FOUND
11	Community Outreach Speci	1 Southridge Way	Alabama	Initial Consultation	Immunization	NOT FOUND
12	Desktop Support Techniciar	6473 Homewood Roa	Kentucky	Pet Foods	Follow Up Consult	40591
13	Chemical Engineer	85 Luster Street	Ohio	Blankets and Foot Mat	Leads and Jackets	44185
14	Media Manager III	4 Blackbird Court	Indiana	Pet Winter Wear	Ear Spray	47737
15	Programmer Analyst IV	982 Portage Circle	Michigan	Immunization	Teeth and Gums	NOT FOUND
16	Senior Financial Analyst	04 Hollow Ridge Park	Wisconsin	Leads and Jackets	Pet Foods	53215

Figure 10.20 – Result of the XLOOKUP function showing conditional formatting on rows

Another new function of Office 2021 is the XMATCH function. We will explore this in the following topic.

Exploring XMATCH

The XMATCH function will return the relative position of an item within a range or an array. We will firstly look at a basic XMATCH construction to return a result and then look at an example that includes XMATCH and INDEX together.

Constructing XMATCH (syntax)

The syntax for XMATCH is similar to the XLOOKUP syntax, and includes the following arguments: **XMATCH(lookup_value,lookup_array,[match_mode],[search_mode])**.

Let's look at a simple example using just the XMATCH function:

1. Open the workbook named XMATCH.xlsx to follow along.

2. On the *XMATCH* worksheet, we have a list of training sessions and their respective codes in cells L2:M10. In cell L14, we have entered a code (**SCWA003**) to use as the lookup value from the table range, and return the relative position in the range in cell M14.

3. Click into cell M14 and then construct the following formula: =XMATCH(L14,M2:M10,) .

4. Note that we do not have to specify the [match_mode] or [search_mode] arguments, as an exact match is the default option.

5. Press *Enter* to confirm and see the position of the item within the range.

K	L	M	N	O
	Session	**Session Code**		
	Excel Formulas	SCEF001		
	Admin Induction	SCAI002		
	Induction training	SCIT003		
	Compliance Review	SCCR004		
	Excel Advanced	SCEA001		
	Admin Induction 2	SCAI0022		
	Word Advanced	SCWA003		
	Word	SCW001		
	Adobe DC	SCADCC005		
	Session Code	**Result**		
	SCWA003	=XMATCH(L14,M2:M10,)		
	XMATCH(lookup_value, lookup_array, [match_mode], [search_mode])			

Figure 10.21 – XMATCH syntax using a simple example

6. If we alter the *Session Code* in cell L14, it will dynamically update to the relative position in the list for that code.

Combining XMATCH and INDEX

The first part of the formula will reference the INDEX function. Remember that INDEX will return intersecting points between a row and column. We will be searching and returning the *Session Code*, based on the row number located in the *Training* column. As **INDEX** requires the row number argument, we will incorporate **XMATCH** to locate that dynamically.

Let's run through the steps:

1. Make sure you have the XMATCH.xlsx workbook open.

2. On the XMATCH worksheet, locate cell E2. This is where we will build our formula to look up and match the codes from the corresponding table.

3. Type =INDEX(to start the formula construction.

4. The first argument of the INDEX function is to provide the array. Select the *Session Code* range, M2:M10 as this is where we will be returning our code from. Ensure that the range is **absolute**, meaning that it remains constant, and then add a **comma** to move to the next argument. Your formula should now display as follows: =INDEX($M$2:$M$10,.

5. We will now introduce the XMATCH function as the INDEX is asking for the row number. We will use this function to look up the row number. We will look up the *Session* type using the values in the *Training* column.

6. Type XMATCH(F2,$L$2:$L$10,)).

fx	=INDEX($M$2:$M$10,XMATCH(F2,$L$2:$L$10))								

D	E	F	G	H	I	J	K	L	M	N
t Role	Session Code	Training	Type	Duration	Trainer			Session	Session Code	
n Senior Lead	=INDEX($M$2:$M$10,XMATCH(F2,$L$2:$L$10))			1 hour	DD			Excel Formulas	SCEF001	
Junior Admin Assistant	INDEX(array, **row_num**, [column_num])			our 30	SN			Admin Induction	SCAI002	
n Senior Lead	INDEX(reference, **row_num**, [column_num], [area_num])			our 30	SN			Induction training	SCIT003	
Administrative Assistant		Excel Formulas	One to one	1 hour	DD			Compliance Review	SCCR004	
Senior Manager		Induction training	One to one	3 hours	SN			Excel Advanced	SCEA001	
Senior Manager		Excel Formulas	Group	1 hour	NN			Admin Induction 2	SCAI0022	
Administrative Assistant		Compliance Review	Group	1 hour	DD			Word Advanced	SCWA003	
Senior Manager		Compliance Review	Group	2 hours	DD			Word	SCW001	
Data Management		Induction training	Group	1 hour 30	SN			Adobe DC	SCADCC005	
n Senior Lead		Excel Advanced	One to one	1 hour	DD					

Figure 10.22 – INDEX AND XMATCH formula construction

7. Press *Enter* to see the result and then double-click on the crosshair mouse pointer to the bottom-right of cell F2 to fill the contents down the column. You should now see the *Session Codes* relevant to the *Training* provided for each row of the dataset.

Name	Surname	Department	Role	Session Code	Training	Type	Duration	Trainer
Donna	St Nicks	Construction	Senior Lead	SCEF001	Excel Formulas	One to one	1 hour	DD
Emroy	Dulane	Admin	Junior Admin Assistant	SCAI002	Admin Induction	Group	1 hour 30	SN
Donna	St Nicks	Construction	Senior Lead	SCIT003	Induction training	Group	1 hour 30	SN
Julia	Notes	HR	Administrative Assistant	SCEF001	Excel Formulas	One to one	1 hour	DD
David	Sueu	IT	Senior Manager	SCIT003	Induction training	One to one	3 hours	SN
David	Sueu	IT	Senior Manager	SCEF001	Excel Formulas	Group	1 hour	NN
Julia	Notes	HR	Administrative Assistant	SCCR004	Compliance Review	Group	1 hour	DD
David	Sueu	IT	Senior Manager	SCCR004	Compliance Review	Group	2 hours	DD
Ilse	Revaw	Security	Data Management	SCIT003	Induction training	Group	1 hour 30	SN
Donna	St Nicks	Construction	Senior Lead	SCEA001	Excel Advanced	One to one	1 hour	DD
Emroy	Dulane	Admin	Junior Admin Assistant	SCAI0022	Admin Induction 2	Group	1 hour 30	SN

Figure 10.23 – Result of the INDEX and XMATCH formulas showing the relevant session codes per training session

You can get quite creative with XMATCH arguments to display, for instance, the last training date attended for a particular person. We will run through this in the next topic to locate the results from last to first using the `search_mode` argument.

Locating results using search_mode

This is achieved by providing the correct `search_mode` argument in order to execute the desired result. Selecting **-1** for this argument will return the last training date for a particular individual:

1. Click to access the INDEXMATCH sheet.

2. Click into cell M2 as this is where we will construct the formula.

3. We will follow the same steps as in the previous example but will look up the surname of the individual and generate the last date of training attended. Our INDEX *array* will be dates in the *Date Attended* column. XMATCH will look up the surname of the individual from the *Surname* column as an exact match, and lastly, it will locate the last training date.

   Enter the following formula: `=INDEX(I2:I21,XMATCH(L2,B2:B21,,-1))`.

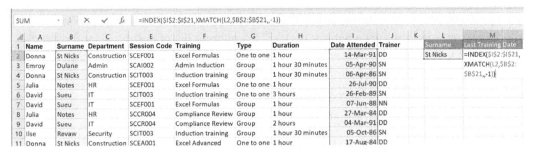

Figure 10.24 – INDEX and MATCH using the -1 search mode

4. Press *Enter* to see the last training date attended for Donna St Nicks.

Now that you are a pro at constructing the XMATCH and INDEX functions, let's learn about another new function.

Investigating the LET function

The LET function is used to simplify formulas. It is a method to get Excel to compute the same expression used within a formula by naming it, leading to more efficient processing, and making the formula easier to understand as it is less complex in construction.

Let's look at the breakdown of the LET function structure: =LET (name1, value1, [name2/value2], ..., result).

Constructing LET (syntax)

The following table lists the syntax and explanation for each argument within the LET function:

SYNTAX	EXPLANATION
name1	This is the first argument and is the name we are defining for the calculation of the value used as the value1 argument. It must begin with a letter. An example of this could be VAT, as per the example below: =LET(VAT,20%,G2*vat)
name_value1	What we are assigning to the name1 argument – this would be either a value or calculation. An example of name_value1 in the formula below would be 20%: =LET(VAT,20%,G2*vat)
calculation or name2	The second name and value combination: =LET(VAT,20%,G2*vat)

Table 10.4 – LET syntax explanation

We will now look at a formula example that consists of using the same expression more than once within it. The dataset in A2:J21 contains a list of customers and related training information. If we wanted to extract customer information to another part of the worksheet and return a **?** (question mark) for every blank cell in the extracted range, we could use the `IF`, `ISBLANK`, and `FILTER` functions.

Now, let's work practically through it:

1. Open the workbook named `LET.xlsx`.

2. On the first worksheet, we will start the formula by typing the = sign followed by the `IF(` function. As we are including cells that could contain blank cells in the extracted range (and would like to include a **?** in the empty cells after extraction), the `ISBLANK` function will need to become part of the formula. Type `ISBLANK(` followed by the `FILTER(` function.

3. Next, we will include the FILTER array and the criteria. The array is A2:J21, but will display as **TR** in this workbook as it is defined as a named range. Type `TR,TR="David"))`,.

4. To finish off the ISBLANK part of the formula, enter `"?",`.

5. To conclude the formula, type `FILTER(TR,TR[Name]="David"))`.

6. To recap, the formula should now read as follows:
    `=IF(ISBLANK(FILTER(TR,TR[Name]="David"))`
    `,"?",FILTER(TR,TR[Name]="David")).`

7. Press *Enter* to display the dynamic array comprising a list of only David Sueu's training courses, filling any blank cells with a ?.

8. Here is the result of the formula construction:

L2		× ✓ fx		=IF(ISBLANK(FILTER(Table1,Table1[Name]="David")),"?",FILTER(Table1,Table1[Name]="David"))								
	I	J	K	L	M	N	O	P	Q	R	S	T	U
1	Date Attended	Trainer		Name	Surname	Departme	Role		Session C	Training	Type	Duration	Date Atter	Trainer
2	14-Mar-91	DD		David	Sueu	IT	Senior Manager	SCIT003	Induction training	One to on	3 hours	32565	SN
3	05-Apr-90	SN		David	Sueu	IT	Senior Manager	SCEF001	?	Group	1 hour	32301	NN
4	06-Apr-86	SN		David	Sueu	IT	Senior Manager	SCCR004	Compliance Review	Group	2 hours	33301	DD
5	26-Jul-90	DD		David	Sueu	IT	Senior Manager	SCW001	?	One to on	3 hours	30484	SN
6	26-Feb-89	SN		David	Sueu	IT	Senior Manager	SCEA001	Excel Advanced	Group	1 hour	33274	NN
7	07-Jun-88	NN		David	Sueu	IT	Senior Manager	SCADCC0C	?	Group	1 hour	32507	DD
8	27-Mar-84	DD											

Figure 10.25 – The result of the IF, ISBLANK, and FILTER combinations

9. This is a long-winded function to construct, where functions are used multiple times. So, we can be a little more efficient in constructing this using the LET function.

10. Update the formula using the following LET formula construction:
    ```
    =LET(mylist,"David",myrange,FILTER(A2:J21,
    A2:A21=mylist),IF(ISBLANK(myrange),"?",myrange)).
    ```

11. To explain the formula, let's break up the steps. After starting the formula using =LET(, define the first variable name and the value for the variable, in this case, David, =LET(mylist,"David",.

12. Now, define the second variable name. This is the filtered range A2:J21 in the case of the example =LET(mylist,"David",myrange,.

13. Lastly, update the formula using the variable names where applicable:
    ```
    FILTER(A2:J21,A2:A21=mylist),IF(ISBLANK(myrange),
    "?",myrange)).
    ```

14. Press *Enter* to see the result of the LET function.

The next topic will concentrate on a set of database functions that are extremely useful and efficient.

Exploring database functions

There are twelve **database functions** in Excel that cover most of the clusters of functions. These functions have been in the Excel library for many years, and are often forgotten about or not known, as there are so many other functions we can use today.

Database functions are a substitute for IFS functions (explained in a previous topic) and are definitely more powerful in application.

There is one action you need to take prior to constructing a formula using database functions: Make sure that your dataset is formatted as a tabular table. Each column in the dataset needs to have a column header.

Learning database function syntax

The syntax for database functions is really simple and is the same for each type of database function you construct. We will look at a few database functions in this topic, so let's look at the DGET database function as an example. The DGET function returns only one matching record. If it locates more than one match, the argument result will return **#NUM!** error. This function is very similar to the XLOOKUP or VLOOKUP functions. Let's dissect the syntax.

=DGET(database,field,criteria)

SYNTAX	EXPLANATION
database	This argument is simply the range of cells (the database) – columns that consist of data fields and rows that contain the related information records. This is a required argument.
field	Identify the column you would like to aggregate by listing the column number. We can add the column number or the actual field name enclosed in quotation marks. This is a required argument.
criteria	These cells contain the condition for the return of the result. Included must be a column label and cells directly below it containing the criteria. This is a required argument.

Table 10.5 – DGET syntax explanation

Now that we are confident about constructing the database functions, having understood the syntax requirements, we can look at a few database function examples.

Using DGET to return a single value

1. Open the worksheet named Database.xlsx.

2. Notice that the database is formatted as a data table. Make sure that this is the case as we would need the function to update based on any new data being added to the table. The function will be built in cell E3 as this is where we would like to see the formula result returned. In cell D3, we have entered a product named Lighting – halogen. The contents of this field can be used to locate the retail cost in the database for any product that is entered manually into cell D3.

3. Type =DGET (to start the formula.

4. Select the *database* range, in this case, A5:G25. The name of the data table should automatically populate instead of the cell reference at this point. The database table is named **Inventory** in this workbook, hence the name is now visible in the formula. Ensure that you do have the column headers included in the selection. This is designated by [**#All**] directly after the table name (refer to the following screenshot example). Insert a comma to move to the next argument.

B	C	D	E	F	G
		Product	Retail Cost:		Gross_Margin
		Lighting - halogen	=DGET(Inventory[#All],6,$D$2:$D$3)		>50%
			DGET(**database**, field, criteria)		
Product	Quantity	Cost	Total Cost	Retail	Gross_Margin
Energy - generators	99	£ 23,400.00	£ 2,316,600.00	£ 25,940.00	11%
Energy - transmission	110	£ 2,200.00	£ 242,000.00	£ 2,400.00	9%
Medical - hearing tool	2000	£ 15,000.00	£ 30,000,000.00	£ 16,500.00	10%
Energy - wind turbines	80	£ 10,000.00	£ 800,000.00	£ 11,000.00	10%
Lighting - xenon lamps	80	£ 2,800.00	£ 224,000.00	£ 3,259.00	16%
Lighting - halogen	5000	£ 441,000.00	£ 2,205,000,000.00	£ 452,000.00	2%
Medical - molecular imaging	9000	£ 7,000.00	£ 63,000,000.00	£ 9,500.00	36%
Medical - radiation oncology	23000	£ 174,000.00	£ 4,002,000,000.00	£ 198,000.00	14%

Figure 10.26 – Formulating the DGET database function

5. The next argument we will enter is the *field*. There are two methods for inserting the field:

- Identify the column number. In the case of the example, we would insert 6, as **Retail** is the sixth column in the worksheet.

- Include the column header name in inverted commas. Here, we would insert `"Retail"`.

6. Once you have decided which method to use, add another comma to move to the final argument.

7. Lastly, we need to select the criteria range. This is the field header and the cell directly beneath it. In this example, we will select cells D2:D3. Make sure D2:D3 is made **absolute**.

8. Press *Enter* to see the result. Now, change the product to another type to see the retail cost for a different product.

9. Should you wish to make the worksheet more efficient, create a validation rule to list the products in cell D3 and then use the drop-down list to choose a product instead.

B	C	D	E
		Product	**Retail Cost:**
		Lighting - halogen ▾	£452,000.00
		Lighting - halogen	
		Medical - molecular imaging	
Product	**Quantity**	Medical - radiation oncology	**Total Cost**
Energy - generators	99	Medical - diagnostics	2,316,600.00
Energy - transmission	110	Medical - x-ray machine	242,000.00
Medical - hearing tool	2000	Lighting - semiconductor light sc	30,000,000.00
Energy - wind turbines	80	Energy - medium voltage	800,000.00
Lighting - xenon lamps	80	£ 2,800.00 £	224,000.00
Lighting - halogen	5000	£ 441,000.00 £	2,205,000,000.00
Medical - molecular imaging	9000	£ 7,000.00 £	63,000,000.00

Figure 10.27 – Creating a Product validation rule

Let's look at a few more examples of database functions.

Constructing DAVERAGE

We will now work out the average gross margin:

1. Click into cell G27 on the *DATABASE* worksheet (using the `Database.xlsx` workbook).

2. Construct the formula `=DAVERAGE(Inventory[All#],7,$G$2:$G$3)` to work out the average gross margin above 50%.

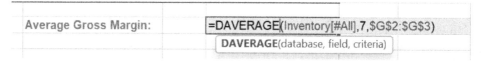

Figure 10.28 – Formula construction for the average gross margin above 50%

3. Press *Enter* to see the formula result of **74.71%**. Now we can change the value in cell G3 to see any further updates required.

See whether you can work out the maximum total cost for Division 2, the total quantity sold for Division 1, and the minimum quantity sold for Division 3, using the appropriate function for each. Below is guidance as to the formula you will need to construct and the displayed result for each cell:

Average Gross Margin:	74.71%	=DAVERAGE(Inventory[#All],7,$G$2:$G$3)
Maximum Total Cost for Division 2:	£2,205,000,000.00	=DMAX(Inventory[#All],5,B28:B29)
Minimum Quantity Sold: Division 3	£ 2,000.00	=DMIN(Inventory[#All],3,$B$34:$B$35)
Total Quantity Sold: Division 1	£ 72,056.00	=DSUM(Inventory,3,B31:B32)

Figure 10.29 – The DMIN, DSUM, and DMAX functions explained

We can expand on our database functions a little more by adding **AND/OR** criteria. Let's look at two examples.

Using the AND/OR criteria

In the following steps, we will build a DSUM function to locate the sales figure for the year 1992 and Matts Winery, and with a date range greater than or equal to 01/01/2019 and less than or equal to 31/12/2020:

1. Continuing with the Database.xlsx workbook, make sure you have clicked on the *MULTIPLE CRITERIA* worksheet.

2. The database table is located in cells A1:I145. To build the AND criteria, we will include the column headers along with the relevant criteria in the same row.

3. Click into cell K1 and then add the columns and criteria as per the following table:

Year	Winery	Date	Date	Sales
1992	Matts Winery	>=01/01/2019	<=31/12/2019	

Table 10.6 – Columns and criteria to get ready for the DSUM function

4. We are now ready to construct the formula in cell O2.

5. Type =DSUM (and then select the database range A1:I1445, including the headings. Insert a comma to move to the next argument.

| LET | | ⁝ | × | ✓ | ƒx | =DSUM(Wines[#All],"Sales",$K$1:$N$2) |

▲	H	I	J	K	L	M	N	O	P	Q	R
1	Cases Sold	Sales		Year	Winery	Date	Date	Sales			
2	450	£ 74,250.00		1992	Matts Winery	>=01/01/2019	<=31/12/2019	=DSUM(Wines[#All],"Sales",$K$1:$N$2)			
3	550	£ 90,750.00						DSUM(database, **field**, criteria)			
4	575	£ 94,875.00									
5	650	£ 107,250.00									
6	320	£ 52,800.00									
7	325	£ 53,625.00									

Figure 10.30 – DSUM formula construction

6. The field argument we are returning values from is the *Sales* column. Either type a 9 for the column number within the database range, or "Sales".

7. Lastly, select the column headings and their criteria in cells K1:N2. Don't forget to make the range absolute.

8. Press the *Enter* key to see the sum of sales for Matts Winery and the year 1992 and between the date range 01/01/2019 and 31/12/2020.

9. We will now add another row to the criteria table to include the OR criteria.

10. As we would like to locate the sales for Matts Winery 1991 between the date range listed, OR prominent wines for 1992, we would need to amend the year in K2 to **1991**. In K3, add the year 1992 and Prominent Wines in cell L3.

11. Lastly, amend the formula in cell O2 to include the second row in the criteria selection so that it includes the OR criteria.

K	L	M	N	O	P	Q	R
Year	Winery	Date	Date	Sales			
1991	Matts Winery	>=01/01/2019	<=31/12/2019	=DSUM(Wines[#All],"Sales",$K$1:$N$3)			
1992	Prominent Wines			DSUM(database, **field**, criteria)			

Figure 10.31 – OR condition DSUM formula

12. Press *Enter* to update the formula in O2.

> **Note**
>
> Database functions can be constructed using references within the same workbook, worksheet, or an external workbook. Both workbooks will need to be open in order for references to work in external workbooks.

Using the COUNTIFS statistical function

In our previous edition book, *Learn Microsoft Office 2019*, we learned all about the COUNTIF function. Let's look at an example to recap this function, and explore the COUNTIFS function at the same time.

Recapping the COUNTIF function

In the next topic, we will expand on prior knowledge and discover how to resolve two sets of data by locating missing data by comparing two tables. There are, of course, many methods (functions and tools) to achieve this type of scenario in Excel. In this example, we will use COUNTIF to achieve this:

1. Open the workbooks named RECON1.xlsx and RECON2.xlsx to follow along with this example.

2. Locate the first worksheet in the RECON1.xlsx workbook. On this sheet, we have a list of wines and sales, including a WV No column (for the wine ID). We have recently had a huge number of workbooks transferred from our previous drive and notice that we seem to be missing some data and have located a second workbook (RECON2.xlsx) with similar data. To compare these two workbooks, we will use the COUNTIF function.

3. Click into cell I2 as we will construct the formula here. In our previous edition book, we learned about syntax and looked at examples of the COUNTIF function. We will therefore not recap this here.

4. Type =COUNTIF(to start the construction of the formula.

5. The *range* we are looking at to see whether *WV No* exists is located in the RECON2.xlsx workbook, so we need to navigate to the workbook and collect the range from the *WV No* column (excluding the column heading). Select cells A2:A137. Note that if we were selecting a range in the same workbook to compare, we would need to apply absolute referencing to the range. Moving to an external workbook, as in this example, has automatically applied the absolute referencing to the range.

6. Press the comma to move to the next argument.

7. Navigate back to the RECON1.xlsx workbook to select the *criterion*. The criterion is A2.

8. Press *Enter* to see the result in the first instance and then use the AutoFill handle to fill the formula to the rest of the column to compare the results in the two tables.

9. If the **Missing Data** column reflects a **1**, this means that the data is matching in both tables. A **0** would indicate that the data exists in table 1 (RECON1.xlsx), but not in table 2 (RECON2.xlsx).

10. We can go one step further and apply **conditional formatting** to highlight the cells on the worksheet that are evident in the RECON1 workbook, but not in the RECON2 workbook.

11. Select the range A2..H145 in the RECON1 workbook, and then select **Home | Conditional Formatting | New Rule | Use a formula to determine which cells to format**.

12. Enter the following formula in the **Format values where this formula is true: field:** =$I2=0. Apply a format of your choice and then click on **OK** and **OK** again to apply the rule. The rows that exist in table 1, but not in table 2, are highlighted on the worksheet.

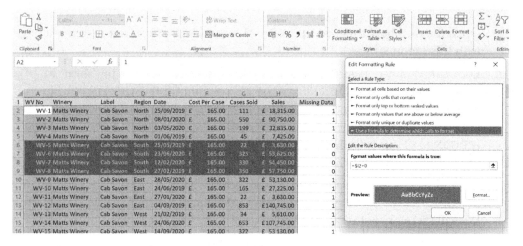

Figure 10.32 – Conditional formatting applied to indicate rows that are missing from table 2

13. Note that you have to have both workbooks open for the **COUNTIF** formula to populate. Not having the workbook open will report a **#VALUE!** error in the cell – this means that the reference to the workbook is not found and therefore it is prompting you to open the workbook for the formula to work.

	A	B	C	D	E	F	G	H	I	J
1	WV No	Winery	Label	Region	Date	Cost Per Case	Cases Sold	Sales	Missing Data	
2	WV-1	Matts Winery	Cab Savon	North	25/09/2019	£ 165.00	111	£ 18,31▲0	#VALUE!	
3	WV-2	Matts Winery	Cab Savon	North	08/01/2020	£ 165.00	550	£ 90,750.00	#VALUE!	
4	WV-3	Matts Winery	Cab Savon	North	03/05/2020	£ 165.00	199	£ 32,835.00	#VALUE!	
5	WV-4	Matts Winery	Cab Savon	North	01/06/2019	£ 165.00	45	£ 7,425.00	#VALUE!	
6	WV-5	Matts Winery	Cab Savon	South	25/05/2019	£ 165.00	22	£ 3,630.00	#VALUE!	
7	WV-6	Matts Winery	Cab Savon	South	23/06/2019	£ 165.00	325	£ 53,625.00	#VALUE!	
8	WV-7	Matts Winery	Cab Savon	South	12/02/2020	£ 165.00	330	£ 54,450.00	#VALUE!	
9	WV-8	Matts Winery	Cab Savon	South	27/02/2019	£ 165.00	350	£ 57,750.00	#VALUE!	
10	WV-9	Matts Winery	Cab Savon	East	28/05/2020	£ 165.00	322	£ 53,130.00	#VALUE!	

Figure 10.33 – #VALUE! error indicating the formula cannot populate due to the associated workbook being closed

If we wanted to find the missing data in the second workbook by reconciling it with the first workbook, we can perform this action by repeating the process from the second workbook to the first.

Now that we have mastered reconciling data using the COUNTIF function, we will learn to apply the COUNTIFS function. The IFS functions were introduced in this chapter in a previous topic.

Learning the COUNTIFS statistical function

The second example is to introduce the COUNTIFS function. The difference between the COUNTIFS and COUNTIF functions is as follows:

- The COUNTIF function counts the number of cells within a range that meet a single condition you specify.

- The COUNTIFS function counts the number of cells by evaluating different criteria in the same or different ranges.

Let's look at an example using COUNTIF:.

1. Open the workbook named COUNTIFS.xlsx.

2. The workbook contains a dataset related to wines and sales. We would like to find out how many cases of wine were sold per region. This is a simple formula to construct, but remember it can have multiple criteria and criteria ranges.

3. In order to pull information from the main dataset, we need to copy the relevant column headings and paste them onto the worksheet so that we can exact the data and build the formula. We also need to add the criteria for each. Make sure you have the following column headings and criteria starting in cell K1:

K	L	M
Region	Cases Sold	No. Cases Sold
North	>=200	
South	>=200	
East	>=200	
West	>=200	

Figure 10.34 – Copied column headings and criteria

4.   In cell M2, construct the following formula:
     =COUNTIFS(E2:E145,K2,H2:H145,L2),K2,H2:H145,L2)

SYNTAX	EXPLANATION
criteria_range1	The Regions column (excluding the column header) – $E$2:$E$145.
criteria1	The North criteria in cell K2.
criteria_range2	The Cases Sold column (excluding the column header) – $H$2:$H$145.
criteria2	The cases sold are greater than or equal to 200.

Table 10.7 – Syntax and explanation for COUNTIFS

5.   Do not forget to copy the formula using AutoFill to the rest of the cells in *Column M* of the worksheet. Here is a representation of the result and formula result:

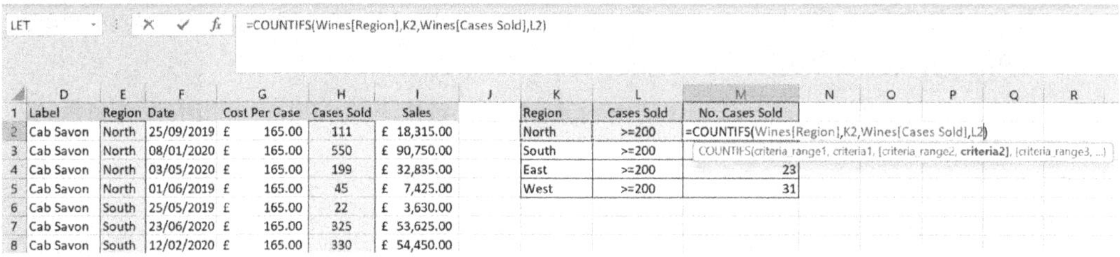

Figure 10.35 – The COUNTIFS function showing criteria and selected worksheet ranges

You are now able to construct the COUNTIFS function, and collect ranges and criteria on the worksheet to locate the number of cases sold per region that are greater than or equal to 200. To populate the formula to show all the cases sold less than or equal to 150, or any other criteria, simply amend the values in the **Cases Sold** column to reflect the change.

Summary

You now have theoretical knowledge about formula construction, and should feel confident to perform calculations adhering to certain rules. You are able to construct, edit, and evaluate dynamic arrays as a result of understanding the terms and when to use the function. During the chapter, you have mastered the building of IFS functions and built on the VLOOKUP function by adding the IFERROR and MATCH functions. We explored the new XLOOKUP function, its syntax, and general error returns, and constructed the XMATCH and INDEX functions, too.

We learned about the forgotten database functions and explored working with multiple conditions. Lastly, we recapped the COUNTIF function and worked through examples using COUNTIFS.

In the next chapter, we will explore date functions and look at some more statistical, logical, and mathematical functions, including SWITCH, Subtotals, and SUMIF. In addition, a large part of this chapter will be devoted to PivotTable customization.

11

Date-Time Functions and Enhancing PivotTable Dashboards

In this chapter, we will explore date functions and look at how to work with time. Here, we concentrate on DATEDIF(), YEARFRAC(), EDATE(), WORKDAY(), and many more functions to be more productive in the workplace. In addition, a large part of this chapter will explore a host of PivotTable customizations and a walk-through on creating dashboards. We will also learn to construct the GETPIVOTDATA function to reference cells in a PivotTable report.

The following topics are covered in this chapter:

- Working with dates
- Working with time
- Enhancing PivotTables
- Creating dashboards
- Additional PivotTable customizations

Technical requirements

Before starting this chapter, you should have adequate file management skills to be able to save workbooks and interact with the Excel 2021 environment comfortably. We assume that you are also able to construct a formula and manage worksheet data. The examples used in this chapter can be accessed from `https://github.com/ PacktPublishing/Learn-Microsoft-Office-2021-Second-Edition`.

Working with dates

In this topic, we will enhance our knowledge of date functions within Excel 2021.

Understanding how dates are interpreted

After typing a date into a worksheet cell, we will only see the formatting of that date (the cosmetic change). If Excel recognizes the date you have typed into a cell on the worksheet, it will automatically align the date to the right of the cell immediately, and apply the date format. To understand visually how a date is actually presented in the cell behind the formatting, we could remove the cell formatting. Let's look at an example.

If we type the number 1 into a cell and then format the cell to display the **Short Date** format, we will visually see the number **1** displayed as the date **01/01/1901** in the cell. **01/01/1901** is the actual *starting date* in Excel, and **31/12/9999** is the end, or *last date*, that Excel interprets. When we remove the formatting, by clearing the format (**Home | Clear | Clear Formats**), we will see the actual whole number behind the cosmetic format. Note that we can also use the **General** number format to display the raw date in the cell. Excel works and stores dates as serial numbers in the background. The following screenshot provides a representation of cosmetic and raw date functions:

	A	B	C	D
1	Formatting applied	Function used	Without Formatting	Represented as
2	01/01/1901		367	whole number
3	31/12/9999		2958465	whole number
4	06/03/2022	=TODAY()	44626	whole number
5	06/03/2022 10:37	=NOW()	44626.44296	whole number.decimals
6				

Figure 11.1 – Representation of cosmetic and raw date functions

The date and time in cell A5 are represented as a *whole number* for the *date* portion of the function, and the *decimals* represent the *time* portion, as seen in cell C5 (raw data, without formatting applied).

If we wanted to display a date as text in a column, we would simply apply the **Text** format to the column that would align the data to the left of the cell, indicating that the data is not represented as a date. We could also indicate this using an ' (apostrophe) before entering a date into a cell to force it to the **Text** format in the cell, as illustrated in the following screenshot. The apostrophe is a silent character and will not show in the cell once you have pressed *Enter*:

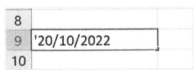

Figure 11.2 – Forcing a date to be displayed as text in a cell

We can use arithmetic to add and subtract days from dates easily or use various Excel functions in order to do so. So, to add a day to the date in cell A4 (**06/03/2022**), we would simply type **+ 1**, or **-1** to subtract a day from the date.

In the following section, we will learn all about how to construct date functions and become knowledgeable about when to apply different date functions in Excel.

Exploring date functions

In our previous book, *Learn Microsoft Office 2019*, we learned about the =TODAY()
and =DAY() functions. Throughout this chapter, we will use the type method to access
different date and time functions. Don't forget that we can also access all the **date and
time** functions, along with their explanations, by visiting **Formulas | Date & Time**, as
illustrated in the following screenshot:

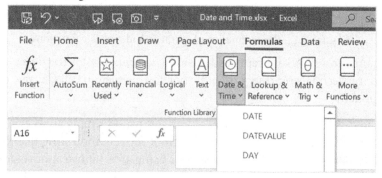

Figure 11.3 – Date & Time drop-down list, located on the Formulas tab

In the following table, we define a couple of date functions, some of which we will explore
in further sections.

Function	Explanation
=TODAY() or =NOW()	The current date in date format, and current date and time. Note: Time in Excel is represented as decimals. Tip: The keyboard shortcut for the date is *Ctrl + ;*.
=YEAR() or =MONTH() or =DAY()	Extracts the year from the date, the month from the date, and the day from the date.
=DATE()	Combines values to create a date.
=WEEKDAY()	Identifies the day of the week of a specific date.
=DAYS()	Finds the number of days between two dates.
=WORKDAY()	Returns the date for the specified number of working days entered from a specific date.
=EOMONTH()	Useful when needing to find out the last day of a month from the starting month after adding a specified number of months.
=EDATE()	This function adds or subtracts months from a given date. Equivalent day from another month.
=NETWORKDAYS()	Find the difference between two days showing the number of workdays only.
=DATEDIF()	This function is named a compatible function as it works out the number of days, months, and years between two dates.
=YEARFRAC()	Calculates the accurate number of days between two dates as a year fraction.

Table 11.1 – Date functions

When working with dates, always make sure that any dates imported into Excel are formatted correctly, and that cells are aligned correctly. #NUM! or #VALUE! errors can appear when this is the case.

Extracting the day, month, or year

We can extract various elements (day, month, or year) from a date into separate cells on the worksheet using the relevant function. There are many different scenarios in which you may want to achieve and extract the elements from a date—for instance, you are only interested in the year of a vehicle or may visually just need to filter the year in a separate column. As is the case with many features of Excel, there is always more than one method to achieve something, or the method could be dependent on a specific outcome you require. To extract an element from a date, proceed as follows:

1. Open the workbook named `Date and Time.xlsx`. Navigate to the **EXTRACT** worksheet.

2. On this worksheet, there is an existing **DATE of HIRE** column that includes the date of hire for each employee.

3. We will separate the *day*, *month*, and *year* from the existing date in cell G5 and place these in the respective columns on the worksheet (H5, I5, J5). We will use the following function syntax in order to do so: `=DAY(Serial_Number)` or `=MONTH(Serial_Number)` or `=YEAR(Serial_Number)`.

4. Click on cell H5, then construct the formula by pressing `=DAY(`.

5. Click on cell G5 to extract the *day* from the cell. Press *Enter* to confirm and display the *day* in cell H5. Do the same for the *month* and *year* cells, replacing the DAY function with either the MONTH or the YEAR function when constructing the formula. The process is illustrated in the following screenshot:

DATE of HIRE	Day	Month	Year
15-Apr-21	=DAY(G5)	4	2021
25-Jan-19			
01-Feb-90			

Figure 11.4 – The DAY function in action

6. Select cells H5:J5, and use the **AutoFill** handle to copy the formula to the rest of the employees on the worksheet.

> **Note**
>
> The day, month, and year data is dependent on the **DATE of HIRE** data in cell G5. If you no longer require the **DATE of HIRE** column and decide to delete the entire column, the formula in cells H5:J5 would display a #REF! error. Similarly, removing a date from a single cell in the **DATE of HIRE** column would display **0, 1, 1900** as the result in cell H5:J5. We will address this in the example that follows.

Formatting dates as values

To format dates as values, proceed as follows:

1. Following on from the previous example, we would now like to remove the **DATE of HIRE** column from the worksheet. As explained in the *Note* information box, we would return #REF! errors in the cells if we removed the entire column. Prior to doing so, we can format the dates to values so that they are static in the cell and not dependent on any formula.

2. Make sure you are on the **EXTRACT** worksheet (Date and Time.xlsx).

3. Select the cell range H5:J98.

4. Hover your mouse pointer, without clicking, to the outside border of the selected range.

5. Right-click, then hold down the mouse pointer and drag the range slightly off its placement cells, then back in position again.

6. You should now see a shortcut menu appear with several options to choose from.

7. Click to select **Copy Here as Values Only**, as illustrated in the following screenshot:

Figure 11.5 – Copy Here as Values Only

8. Delete the **DATE of HIRE** column.

9. The values remain in cells H5:J5 and are not affected by the deletion of the source column anymore.

We separated the contents of a single cell into three cells to display the day, month, and year independently of each other. How would we combine separate values to form a date in a single cell? Let's try the opposite now in the following topic.

Formulating a date from worksheet cells

We currently have the date, month, and year values in separate cells on the **EXTRACT** worksheet. Follow the next steps to combine them:

1. Make sure you have selected the **COMBINE** worksheet in the Date and Time. xlsx workbook.

2. Click into cell G5 as this is the cell in which we would like to construct our formula to pull through the day, month, and year values from the **EXTRACT** worksheet. We will use the DATE function. The DATE function syntax is =DAY(year,month,day).

3. Type =DAY(in the cell, then navigate to the **EXTRACT** worksheet.

4. Click on the **Year** value first in cell I5 followed by a *comma*, click on cell H5 followed by a comma, then—finally—click on cell G5, as illustrated in the following screenshot:

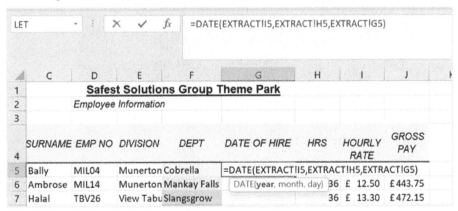

Figure 11.6 – The DATE function collecting the year, month, and date from another worksheet

5. Press *Enter* to see the result. Notice how the formula has referenced the different worksheets used to collect the year, month, and date.

6. Fill the contents of the cell down so that all dates are pulled through for each employee. Please note that any changes on the **EXTRACT** worksheet will amend the dates on the **COMBINE** worksheet unless you format these as values.

Now that you have learned to break dates apart and put them back together again, let's look at how to subtract or add months from a given date.

Subtracting months from a date

We can subtract or add months from a date to find out a future or past date. The EDATE function is perfect for projecting a payment due date for a term of purchase, or payment due date on a certain length of membership, or for finding out when the membership started by subtracting the length of the membership term. Here's how you can use this:

1. Make sure you are on the **EXAMPLES** worksheet in the Date and Time.xlsx workbook.

2. Firstly, we will work out the **New Date** value by subtracting the number of months in cell F3 from the **Date** value in cell E3. Once complete, we will autofill the results to *row 4*. The function we will use is EDATE. The EDATE syntax is =EDATE(start_date,months).

3. Click into cell G3, then start the formula by typing the =EDATE(function.

4. Click to select cell E3, the start_date value, press the comma to separate the arguments, then add the subtract operator and click on cell F3, which contains the number of months to subtract. The process is illustrated in the following screenshot:

E	F	G	H
	Subtracting or Adding Months		
Date	Months	New Date	
15/04/2021	12	=EDATE(E3,-F3)	
25/01/2019	24	EDATE(start_date, months)	

Figure 11.7 – Subtracting months from dates

5. Press *Enter* to see the **New Date** value.

6. If the cell is not formatted to a date format, the serial number will be displayed in the cell. Format the relevant date format to correct it. Autofill the formula result to cell G

7. Let's work out the second example by adding 6 months to the payment date to project the **Last Payment Due** date.

8. Click on cell F6, then type the =EDATE (formula, as illustrated in the following screenshot:

Payment Received	Last Payment Due	Membership Term
12/05/2022	=edate(E6,G6	6
26/07/1990	EDATE(start_date, **months**)	
12/06/2021		
30/12/1990		
05/06/2021		

Figure 11.8 – Adding months to dates

9. Click on cell E6, and add a comma to separate the arguments.

10. Click on select cell G6, which contains the **Membership Term** value. Note that we can type the value into the formula construction instead of using a cell reference, but if we want to change the **Membership Term** value at any time, we would want the formula to update automatically.

11. Press *Enter* to see the result, then autofill to the range F7:F10. If the **Membership Term** value changes, simply enter the new term value into cell G6 to update the values.

12. Now, let's see how we would add half a day to a particular date.

Adding half a day to a date

To add a day to a date, we would simply include + 1 in the formula. As we are working out for half a day, we would use 0.5. Here's how we'll do this:

1. In cell A10 of the **EXAMPLES** worksheet, we have entered the =NOW function to insert the current date and time.

2. In cell B10, we would like to work out the current date and time including half a day. Type the formula =A10+0.5 into B10 to find the answer, as illustrated in the following screenshot:

9	Adding half a day to the date	
10	19/03/2022 08:46	=A10+0.5

Figure 11.9 – Adding half a day to a date

3. Press *Enter* to see the future date/time.

At times, you may need to see the actual day name in a cell, alongside a full date. This helps with closing dates for property transactions, for example. We will learn how to pull the day from the date next.

Displaying the date day

We will now learn how to convert a short date to display the corresponding day in a column, as follows:

1. Open the workbook named `Date and Time.xlsx`.

2. Click to access the **DAY** worksheet. Column B consists of property dates. In column A (**Day**), we would like to automatically return the day, once the date is entered in column B (**Property Date**).

3. Select cell A2, then enter the formula =DAY(B2), as illustrated in the following screenshot. Press *Enter* to see the result:

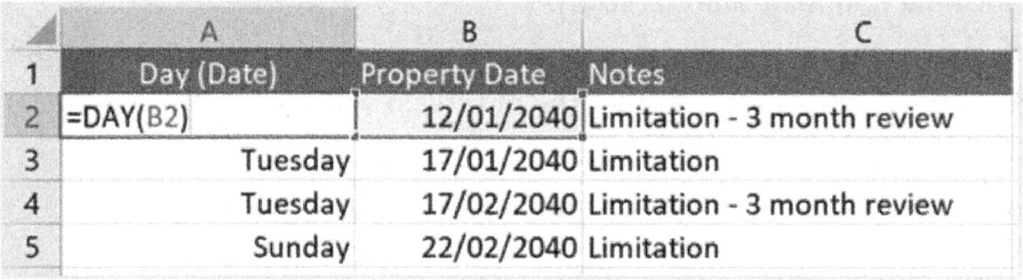

	A	B	C
1	Day (Date)	Property Date	Notes
2	=DAY(B2)	12/01/2040	Limitation - 3 month review
3	Tuesday	17/01/2040	Limitation
4	Tuesday	17/02/2040	Limitation - 3 month review
5	Sunday	22/02/2040	Limitation

Figure 11.10 – Converting the date to the name of the day

4. Notice that the result is not displaying the weekday name, only the day number. We will need to alter the format of the cell. Select cell A2 again, then visit **Format Cells**. Choose **Custom** to set the correct format. In the **Type:** field, enter dddd to display the date day. Look at the **Sample** box to see the format. The process is illustrated in the following screenshot:

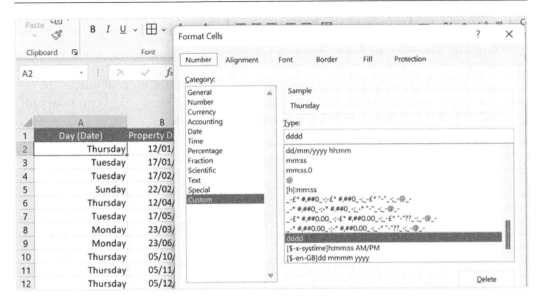

Figure 11.11 – Changing the custom format to reflect the day name

5. Click **OK** to confirm and display the name of the day in the cell.

6. Autofill the formula to cell A19. If you need to extend the selection from A2 all the way to A1048576 (the last cell in column A on the worksheet) as the worksheet data will grow over time, press *Ctrl*, *Shift*, and the down arrow.

7. Every time you enter text into column **B**, it will automatically convert the date to the **Day** value in column **A**.

8. If users edit the formula by mistake or enter in dates, and so on, simply drag the formula down again to correct it. You may prefer to lock the cells in column A so that the users cannot amend the day names. Use the =MONTH (function, then add mmmm as the **Custom Format** value.

If we have the name of a month in a cell and need to convert it to display the month number instead, we can use a combination of the MONTH and DATEVALUE functions. Follow the steps in the next example to explore this.

Converting the month name to a month number

To convert the month name to a month number, proceed as follows:

1. To return the month name to a month number, we simply use a combination of functions—namely, =MONTH(DATEVALUE(J2 & "1")); & "1" is necessary for the DATEVALUE function to comprehend that it is a date.

2. Try this out in cell K2 of the **EXAMPLES** worksheet (Date and Time.xlsx) workbook, as illustrated in the following screenshot:

J	K	L	M
Month name to Month number			
January	=MONTH(DATEVALUE(J2 & "1"))		
February	MONTH(serial_number)		
August	8		
September	9		
December	12		

Figure 11.12 – Converting the month name to the month number

3. The names of the months have been converted to the month number in K2.

    The following topic will explain how to quickly calculate a future date based on the number of days from the current date.

Working out the future date from the days specified

The WORKDAY function returns the date for a specified number of working days entered from a specific date.

Make sure you are on the **EXAMPLES** worksheet of the Date and Time.xlsx workbook. In cell A16, we have the **Start Date of Project** value, and in B16, we have listed the number of days till the end date of the project. We would like to find out the project end date. Here's how we do this:

1. In cell C16, start the formula by entering =WORKDAY(.

2. Click on the **Start Date of Project** cell (A16) then add a comma, and finally, add the number of working days. For the following example, we are using a cell reference that contains the number of working days in cell B16:

15	Start Date of Project	How many working days?	End Date		Star
16	29/03/2022	25	=WORKDAY(A16,B16)		
17			WORKDAY(start_date, days, [holidays])		
18					

Figure 11.13 – Working out the date from a specified number of days

3. Press the *Enter* key to see the **End Date** value in cell C16.

We can extend this function to add any holidays during the working day period specified, as follows:

1. In cells G16 and G17, we have entered two holiday dates we would like to include in the formula so that it works out the correct number of working days, taking holidays into account. Enter the formula as follows: =WORKDAY(E16,F16,G16:G17). You can see an illustration of this in the following screenshot:

Start Date of Project	How many working days?	Any Holidays	End Date
29/03/2022	40	15/04/2022	=WORKDAY(E16,F16,G16:G17)
		18/04/2022	WORKDAY(start_date, days, [holidays])

Figure 11.14 – Using the WORKDAY function to add holidays

2. Press *Enter* to see the **Project End Date** value.

Experiment with these functions and combine them to get the result you desire.

Finding the last day of a month after adding specified months

It is useful to find out the last day of a month from the starting month after adding a specified number of months. Let's investigate the EOMONTH function, as follows:

1. In cell J16 in the following screenshot, we have entered a **Start Date** value. In K16, you will see the number of months we will add to the existing start date. Let's build a formula in cell L16 to calculate the last day of the month, taking into account the number of months entered in K16:

Start Date	No. of Months	Result
26-Jan-21	2	=EOMONTH(J16,K16
05-Apr-21	-4	EOMONTH(start_date, **months**)
08-Aug-22	0	
18-Nov-21	5	

Figure 11.15 – Working out the last day of the month

2. Enter =EOMONTH (in L16. Click J16 to select the start date (*26-Jan-21*), then add a comma to separate the arguments.

3. Click on cell L16 to take into consideration the months entered in the cell.

4. Press *Enter* to see the result in cell L16. Note that the result is formatted as a serial number. To format as a date, use the relevant **Number Format** dropdown to select **Short Date**.

5. The date displayed in L16 is the last day of the month, 2 months from January 26, 2021.

6. Autofill the formula to the rest of the cells to fill in the relevant dates for each of the start dates.

The next couple of topics are for those interested in calculating the age of an employee or working out the date employees will retire.

Calculating the current age from a birth date

There are two common types of functions that calculate the age from a specified date. Let's investigate these in the next topics. Both the functions covered here are functions that every **human resources (HR)** employee should know.

Using the YEARFRAC function

The **YEARFRAC** function is used to calculate the accurate age of—for instance—an employee from their given birth date. Here's how you can use this:

1. Using the same workbook as prior topics, Date and Time.xlsx, we will click on the **EMPLOYEES** worksheet.

2. The worksheet contains employee information for the *Safest Solutions* theme park. Employee start dates are evident in *column I*, and birth dates in *column G*. Firstly, we would like to find out the employee's age in years in *column H*.

3. Click into cell H5 to construct the formula. We will be using the YEARFRAC function for this example. The YEARFRAC function syntax is shown here: =YEARFRAC(start_date,end_date,[basis]).

4. Type =YEARFRAC(, then click on G5 as this is our start_date value (birth date). Add a *comma* to separate the arguments, then type TODAY() as the end_date value as we are working out how old the employee is today.

5. End the formula off with another) to close the arguments and finish the formula. You can see the formula in the following screenshot:

DEPT	DOB	AGE	HIRE DATE	HRS / WEEK	HOURLY RATE
Cobrella	25/09/1973	=YEARFRAC(G5,TODAY())		40	£ 21.50
Mankay Falls	08/01/1962	YEARFRAC(start_date, end_date, [basis])		36	£ 12.50
Slangsgrow	03/05/1958		01/02/1979	36	£ 13.30
Shewe	01/06/1979		12/05/1999	40	£ 7.22

Figure 11.16 – YEARFRAC function to work out the age of employees

6. Press *Enter* to see the age of the first employee. If a date is presented in the answer cell, be sure to change the **Number Format** value to **General** so that it displays the age correctly. Autofill to the rest of the column.

7. If you would like to round down to the nearest integer, add the INT function at the start of the formula, as follows: =INT(YEARFRAC(G5,TODAY())). Remember to add an extra) at the end of the formula to include the function as you have three function arguments in your formula.

> **Note**
>
> The [basis] portion of the function syntax is an optional argument. This argument determines how the year must be calculated. However, if we don't choose a criterion, it will default to the 0 option (day count basis). Remember that we have used the TODAY() function in the example, so this will constantly update the age automatically as we go on in time.

We can also use the YEARFRAC function to determine the age of an employee at a specific future date. Here's how we'd go about this:

1. We will continue with the previous worksheet to work out the future age in cell I5 based on a specific date in cell I3—namely, 31/12/2025.

2. In cell I5, enter the following formula: =YEARFRAC(H5,$I$3).

3. Make sure cell I3 is referenced as *absolute* so that the reference does not move down when using the autofill to copy the formula to the rest of the cells.

4. Press *Enter* to see the age of the employee on **31/12/2025**. Copy down to the rest of the cells.

Let's look at the DATEDIF function in the following section.

Using the DATEDIF function

DATEDIF is a function that works out the age of the employee to display the year, month, and day in the cell. When working with the DATEDIF function, we will need to type the function into the cell to construct it from scratch. The DATEDIF function is not resident in the drop-down list of functions in Excel, and neither is the tooltip to guide you when constructing arguments. We will need to remember the function and construction arguments. Proceed as follows:

1. Using the same workbook as prior topics, Date and Time.xlsx, make sure you are on the **EMPLOYEES** worksheet.

2. Employee age is calculated in years in *column H*. If we wanted to work out the year, month, or day instead, we could need to use a different function. Let's calculate this in *column J* of the worksheet.

3. Click on cell J5 to construct the formula. We will be using the DATEDIF function for this example. The DATEDIF function syntax is shown here: =DATEDIF(start_date,end_date,unit). We will build this formula using different units to achieve the result.

4. Type =DATEDIF(then click on G5 as this is our start_date value (birth date). Add a *comma* to separate the arguments, then type TODAY() as the end_date value as we are working out how old the employee is today. Add a *comma* again to specify the last part of the formula.

    To find out more about the DATEDIF function, click on the blue DATEDIF link in the syntax, as shown here:

AGE	AGE based on fixed end date	AGE Y/M/D	HIRE DATE
	31/12/2025		
48	52	=DATEDIF(	13/06/1991
60	63	DATEDIF()	25/01/1990
63	67		01/02/1979

Figure 11.17 – The DATEDIF function

> **Note**
>
> To the right of the screen, in the **Help** pane, you will see information relating to the function, as well as the syntax. See the detail on each unit to help guide you in achieving the output you would like returned. Also, note that there are limitations with certain units in the list.

5. The first unit we require is the year, so we need to enter Y in the formula as the unit. Close the function bracket by adding).

6. As we would like to see the word *years* after the year unit, we need to include " years " after the function to expand the text string. Press the *spacebar*, then add another &.

7. Copy the first DATEDIF function and amend the *unit* to reflect "YM".

8. Add & to expand on the formula, followed by the *spacebar*, then include " months " after the function to expand the text string. Your formula should look exactly like this: =DATEDIF(G5,TODAY(),"Y")&" years " &DATEDIF(G5,TODAY(),"YM")& " months". You can see this displayed in the following screenshot:

DOB	AGE	AGE based on fixed end date	AGE Y/M	HIRE DATE	HRS / WEEK
25/09/1973	=DATEDIF(G5,TODAY(),"Y")&" years " &DATEDIF(G5,TODAY(),"YM")& " months"				
08/01/1962	60	63	60 years DATEDIF()	25/01/1990	36

Figure 11.18 – Formula to work out the age of employees

9. Press *Enter* to see the result and copy it down to the rest of the employees, as illustrated here:

	31/12/2025	
AGE	AGE based on fixed end date	AGE Y/M
48	52	48 years 5 months
60	63	60 years 2 months
63	67	63 years 10 months
42	46	42 years 9 months
43	47	43 years 9 months
56	60	56 years 8 months
39	42	39 years 1 months
48	51	48 years 0 months
31	35	31 years 9 months

Figure 11.19 – Employee age in years and months

You have now learned to apply the YEARFRAC and DATEDIF functions. In the next section, we will look at how to calculate retirement dates and the remaining retirement years for employees.

Returning the date of retirement

Let's work out the exact date our employees will retire using the EDATE function. Our employees reach retirement at 65. Follow the next steps:

1. Locate cell O5 on the **EMPLOYEES** worksheet. We will use the birth date of our employees to work out the date on which they will retire when reaching 65 years old. The syntax for the EDATE function is =EDATE(start_date,months).

2. Start the formula construction by entering the formula =EDATE(.

3. Click to select cell G5, which contains the first employee's birth date. Press the *comma* on the keyboard to separate the arguments.

4. Type *12* for the months of the year *multiplied by 65*—that is, **12*65**.

5. Press *Enter* to see the result for the first employee. Notice that a result is a serial number. Format the serial number in cell O5 to a short date. Autofill to the rest of the employees.

Now that we know how to calculate the actual date of retirement, there may be instances where we need to how many years until the employee reaches the retirement year. Let's work through this in the next section.

Working out years to retirement

To calculate the number of years to retirement, we can use the YEARFRAC function. In cell O5 of the worksheet, we have generated the retirement date. We will use the retirement date to aid our calculation. Proceed as follows:

1. Construct the formula in cell P5 of the worksheet. Type =YEARFRAC(then add the TODAY() function.

2. Add a *comma* to separate the arguments.

3. Click on cell O2 to include the actual retirement date of the employee, then enclose the formula with an ending), as illustrated in the following screenshot:

WEEKLY PAY	RETIREMENT DATE	YEARS TO RETIREMENT
£ 860.00	25/09/2038	=YEARFRAC(TODAY(),O5
£ 443.75	08/01/2027	YEARFRAC(start_date, **end_date**, [basis])
£ 472.15	03/05/2023	

Figure 11.20 – Working out the number of years till retirement

4. Press *Enter* to see the result.

5. Amend the formula to include the INT function so that it returns just the integer, like so: =INT(YEARFRAC(TODAY(),O5)).

6. Note that to calculate the last day of the retirement month, you would need to construct the following formula: =IF(DAY(G5)=1,DATE(YEAR(G5)+60, MONTH(G5),0),DATE(YEAR(G5)+60,MONTH(G5)+1,0)). You can see this formula in the following screenshot:

	G	H	I	J	K	L	M	N	O	P	Q
	DOB	AGE	AGE based on fixed end date	AGE Y/M	HIRE DATE	HRS / WEEK	HOURLY RATE	WEEKLY PAY	RETIREMENT DATE	YEARS TO RETIREMENT	LAST DAY OF RETIREMENT MONTH
	25/09/1973	48	52	48 years 5 months	=IF(DAY(G5)=1,DATE(YEAR(G5)+60,MONTH(G5),0),DATE(YEAR(G5)+60,MONTH(G5)+1,0))						
ls	08/01/1962	60	63	60 years 2 months	25/01/1990	36	£ 12.50	£ 443.75	08/01/2027	4	31/01/2022
	03/05/1958	63	67	63 years 10 months	01/02/1979	36	£ 13.30	£ 472.15	03/05/2023	1	31/05/2018
	01/06/1979	42	46	42 years 9 months	12/05/1999	40	£ 7.22	£ 288.80	01/06/2044	22	31/05/2039
ls	25/05/1978	43	47	43 years 9 months	27/07/2001	42	£ 16.75	£ 703.50	25/05/2043	21	31/05/2038
	23/06/1965	56	60	56 years 8 months	12/06/1997	40	£ 12.60	£ 504.00	23/06/2030	8	30/06/2025

Figure 11.21 – Working out the last day of retirement

7. Once you have formulated the function, be sure to change the date format.

In the next topic, we will find the number of days between two different dates.

Calculating days between two dates

The DAYS360 function accepts that there are 30 days in a month. Use this function to calculate the number of days between two dates. Proceed as follows:

1. Click to select the **EXAMPLES** worksheet in the Date and Time.xlsx workbook.

2. In B22 and C22, we have dates entered in the cells. Our task is to find out how many days are between the two dates.

3. We will construct the formula in cell D22.

4. Type =DAYS360(.

5. Click to select the date in B22, then separate the arguments by adding a *comma*.

6. Click to select the date in C22, then press *Enter* on the keyboard to confirm. The process is illustrated in the following screenshot:

	Date 1	Date 2	Days between
20			
21			
22	13/06/1991	05/01/1992	=DAYS360(E22,F22)
23	25/01/1990	05/02/1990	DAYS360(start_date, **end_date**, [method])
24	01/02/1979	08/08/1979	187
25	12/05/1999	07/06/1999	25
26	27/07/2001	26/08/2001	29
27	12/06/1997	11/08/1997	59
28	30/11/2005	19/12/2005	19

Figure 11.22 – DAYS360 function

7. The day between the two dates is displayed in cell D22. Fill down to the rest of the cells.

Now that we have explored date functions, let's have a look at some time functions.

Working with time

When working with time in Excel, we need to ensure that we format cells correctly. This is extremely important as Excel does not display hours over 24 (1 day), seconds greater than 60, or minutes greater than 60. Hours are always fractions of a day in decimal presentation, whereas dates are whole numbers. A whole number can never be interpreted using hours or minutes when working in Excel. Decimal numbers are units of time between 0 and 1—for example, 0.25; 0.5; 0.45; 0.35.

So, Excel by default does not display hours in the 24-hour format. When we need to display hours in the 24-hour format, we will need to change the format of the cells. Let's see how this is achieved in the following example.

Displaying hours as time

In the Date and Time.xls spreadsheet, we have entered **0.25** in cell B19 on the **TIME** worksheet. To display this value in the 24-hour format, we will need to format it to the **Time** number format, as illustrated in the following screenshot:

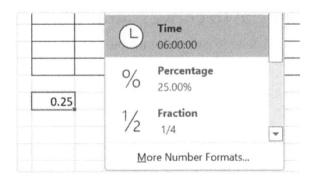

Figure 11.23 – Changing the display of values to the 24-hour format

The time is displayed as 6 hours as it is a quarter of the day (1 day = 24 hours; a half-day is 12 hours; a quarter-day is 6 hours). If you need to display hours over the 24-hour format, you will need to change the format so that it is customized to include a square bracket around the h format. Let's look at an example, as follows:

1. Open the workbook named Date and Time.xlsx and navigate to the **TIME** worksheet.

2. Cells **A1:G9** display time worked per employee on files within the business. The **Total Time** value is represented in column **G**. If we look closely at the sum calculation, we will notice that column **G** is not in time format.

3. Format cells G2:G9 to the **Time** format. Notice that it is still not displaying the time over the 24-hour period correctly.

4. Select G2:G9, then visit the **Custom** category in the **Format Cells** dialog box.

5. Type the following custom format into the **Type:** field as **[h]:mm**. Click on the **OK** button to confirm.

6. The cells are now showing the correct display for times greater than 1 day.

To display a whole number such as 29 as time, you would divide the number by 24 as follows: =29/24. This would present an answer of **1.208333333**. You would then format the cell as **Time** to display **05:00:00**.

Now that you have learned to understand how Excel interprets time, let's master a quicker method in the next section.

Using Paste Special to convert hours into time

Here is a quick and easy method to convert hours into time on the worksheet. Proceed as follows:

1. Open the `Date and Time.xlsx` workbook and navigate to the **PASTE** workbook.

2. In this workbook, we have a list of times employees and their time worked per file on the system. The values are entered as hours. We cannot apply the *time* format to the time worked, as this will result in 00:00:00 for every value. To fix this, we would need to divide the hours worked by 24 in order to format this correctly to reflect time as 1 day is equal to 24 hours.

3. Enter the value **24** in cell A11.

4. Select cell A11 and copy it so that it is retained on the clipboard.

5. Select the values on the timesheet—namely, D2:F9.

6. Click the drop-down arrow on the **Paste** button, then select **Paste Special…**, as illustrated in the following screenshot:

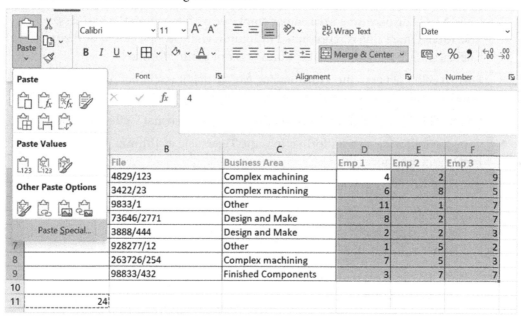

Figure 11.24 – Paste Special…

7. Choose **Divide**, to divide by the number of hours in a day (24), then click on **OK** to confirm.

8. Format the range D2:F9 as **Time**.

Here are a few time functions to boost your knowledge:

=HOUR() or =MINUTE() or =SECOND()	Used to extract hours, minutes, or seconds. Note that we cannot exceed 24 hours, 60 minutes, or 60 seconds as a result when using these functions. Note that you can test the hour, minute, or second function by using the =NOW() function in a cell.
=TIME()	This function converts hours, minutes, and seconds into a serial number in Excel.
=TIMEVALUE()	This function is applied to make sure cells are represented as time.
To enter the current time into a cell on a worksheet	The keyboard shortcut for the time is *Ctrl + Shift + ;*

Table 11.2 – Time functions in Excel

We will look at a few time functions in the following topics.

Separating time from date/time

If a date and a time are combined into a cell, we can extract the time from the date. In cell B23 of the **TIME** worksheet (Date and Time.xlsx), we have entered the =NOW() function to add the date and the time in one single cell. Carry out the following steps to extract the date or time, from the formula:

1. Click on cell C23—this is where we would like to build the formula to extract the date.

2. Type =INT(B23), then press *Enter* to confirm. INT means integer, so it will exact the whole number (the date) from the contents of cell B23. Format cell C23 in **Date** format so that it correctly displays the date in the cell, as illustrated in the following screenshot:

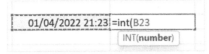

Figure 11.25 – The INT function

3. To display only the time, subtract the date from the cell that contains the date/time combination. Click into cell D23 (this is the cell in which you require just the time value).

4. Type =B23-C23, then press *Enter* to confirm. Format the cell to display the **Time** value, if necessary.

Let's learn how to change data imported as text into a time format.

Converting text to a time format

Sometimes, we may receive datasets that are in a text format or on import do not represent as a time format in Excel. We can fix this by using the `TIMEVALUE()` function. Here's how to go about this:

1. Open the workbook named `Date and Time.xlsx`.

2. Select the **TIME** worksheet. Note that the data in cells D12:D17 is aligned to the left of the cell, and therefore is not representing as time. The number format would display as **Text** or **General** format in this case.

3. To correct the format, let's change the format to **Time**. Notice in the following screenshot that the time is still positioned to the left of the cell:

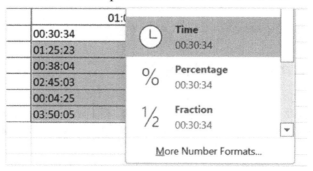

Figure 11.26 – Changing the format to Time

4. If we try to add up the time to find out what the total time would be, it would return a `00:00:00` time value to the right of the cell, as illustrated in the following screenshot. Excel is therefore still associating the data in cells D12:D17 as text:

00:30:34
01:25:23
00:38:04
02:45:03
00:04:25
00:00:00

Figure 11.27 – SUM value displaying as 00:00:00

5. To convert the text to time so that it is correctly interpreted as time in Excel, we can make use of the =TIMEVALUE() function. Click on cell E12 on the **TIME** worksheet, as illustrated in the following screenshot:

00:30:34	=TIMEVALUE(D12
01:25:23	TIMEVALUE(**time_text**)
00:38:04	

Figure 11.28 – TIMEVALUE function to convert text to time

6. Press *Enter* to confirm, then drag the formula down to fill in the rest of the time values. Be sure to format the cells as **Time**.

As mentioned in a previous topic, Excel does not take into account hours that exceed the 24-hour format. When adding time, this could be problematic and is often a cause of time being incorrectly calculated on a timesheet without even apprehending it!

Adding time

1. If you are working with time that extends the 24-hour format, it is important to change the format of your time entries to the **Custom** format. This way, you will ensure that all time is calculated correctly.

2. For this example, continue with the **TIME** worksheet in the workbook named Date and Time.xlsx.

3. Notice in the following screenshot that in cells G2:G9, the total time is not being calculated correctly for cells that are the 24-hour format:

C	D	E	F	G
Business Area	Emp 1	Emp 2	Emp 3	Total Time
Complex machining	07:00:00	08:37:00	10:00:00	01:37:00
Complex machining	00:36:00	08:00:00	02:34:00	11:10:00
Other	09:25:00	07:23:00	09:45:00	02:33:00
Design and Make	00:36:00	02:45:00	04:55:00	08:16:00
Design and Make	09:00:00	07:00:00	08:00:00	00:00:00
Other	02:00:00	02:00:00	00:25:00	04:25:00
Complex machining	00:18:00	07:00:00	00:45:00	08:03:00
Finished Components	03:36:00	02:33:00	03:34:00	09:43:00

Figure 11.29 – TIME worksheet displaying incorrect SUM value

4. To correct this, set the **Custom** format of the time in the **Format Cells** dialog box. Enter the following parameters in the **Type:** field: [h] :   mm; @, as illustrated in the following screenshot. Click on the **OK** button to apply the format to the selected range:

Figure 11.30 – Constructing a custom format to display time

5. The format is updated to display positive values over the 24-hour format. If you wish the format to be the same for the rest of the time data, simply apply the same format, as illustrated in the following screenshot:

	D	E	F	G
	Emp 1	Emp 2	Emp 3	Total Time
	07:00:00	08:37:00	10:00:00	25: 37
	00:36:00	08:00:00	02:34:00	11: 10
	09:25:00	07:23:00	09:45:00	26: 33
	00:36:00	02:45:00	04:55:00	8: 16
	09:00:00	07:00:00	08:00:00	24: 00
	02:00:00	02:00:00	00:25:00	4: 25
	00:18:00	07:00:00	00:45:00	8: 03
	03:36:00	02:33:00	03:34:00	9: 43

Figure 11.31 – Total time displayed using the [h]: mm;@ format

6. There are existing time formats in the **Custom** category we can apply, if preferred, such as [h]:mm:ss for hours—this format is already included as part of the custom formats in Excel, or add specific formats, such as the following:

   A. [m]:ss for minutes (for example, 08:16 will be displayed as 496:00).

   B. [ss] for seconds (for example, 08:16 will be displayed as 29760).

7. To sum the totals in cell G10, press the *Alt + =* keyboard keys, then press *Enter* to confirm and display the total in the cell.

8. If, for instance, **Emp 2** worked overtime, we can add these additional hours to the existing time to calculate a final total. When the overtime is less than the 24-hour period, we can formulate the following function: =E4+TIME(F4,0,0). You can see an illustration of this in the following screenshot:

E	F	G	
Emp 2	Emp 2 Overtime		Emp 3
08:37:00			
08:00:00			
07:23:00		5 =E4+TIME(F4,0,0)	
02:45:00		TIME(**hour**, minute, second)	

Figure 11.32 – Adding hours to time

9. If the overtime is greater than a day in hours, we can construct the formula as follows by dividing the number of hours by 24: =E7+(F7/24). You can see an illustration of this in the following screenshot:

07:00:00		
02:00:00	30 =E7+(F7/24)	
07:00:00		

Figure 11.33 – Overtime

> **Note**
>
> Do not forget that the calculations in *column I* would need to be updated due to the adjustments we have made to calculate additional hours. You may wish to change the layout completely in this case.

You should now have the skills to confidently work with time in Excel. In the next topic, we will recap PivotTables, as explained in our first-edition book, *Learn Microsoft Office 2019*, building on the foundation to learn more about PivotTables and any Excel 2021 enhancements.

Enhancing PivotTables

When creating a **PivotTable**, the data used to create the table remains as it is in the workbook—unchanged. A separate table is produced after creation where the data is manipulated to make it more understandable to the reader. There are a few things you should know before creating a PivotTable, in order to get the workbook data ready to get the most out of PivotTable reports.

The first point is that data needs to be organized vertically and contain column headings. The second point is to ensure that no blank rows are present in the data and that there are no additional descriptive notes or text in any of the cells or any additional formulas to the side or underneath the data. Another recommendation is that you format the data as a table before creating a table. The only reason for this is that any new data rows added to the table are included automatically in the range, adding them to the already defined dataset.

Let's get our data ready to generate a PivotTable, as follows:

1. Open the `MattsWinery.xlsx` workbook.

2. On the first sheet, **WINESALES**, you will see data relating to wine sales, per quarter, region, label, and year. Before we create a PivotTable from this data, we will format the data as a table.

3. Click into the data on the worksheet, then go to **Insert | Table**, or use the *Ctrl + T* quick key on the keyboard. The **Format as a Table** dialog box will be populated.

4. Ensure that the range is correctly assumed in the **Where is the data for your table?** field.

5. Check the box to indicate that you would like table headers to be included in the table, as illustrated in the following screenshot:

	E	F	G	H	
	Region	Date Sold	Cost Per Case	Cases Sold	
	North	14/02/2021 £	165.00	450	£
	North			550	£
	North			575	£
	North			650	£
	South			320	£
	South			325	£
	South			330	£
	South			350	£
	East			350	£

Create Table ? ✕
Where is the data for your table?
$A$1:$K$145
☑ My table has headers
OK   Cancel

Figure 11.34 – Create Table dialog box

6. Click on the **OK** button to format the selection as a table. Notice the **Table Design** tab at the end of the ribbon. Here, you can customize colors as well as name the table. We will call our table range **WineSales**. Enter this in the **Table Name:** field to the left of the ribbon, as illustrated in the following screenshot:

Figure 11.35 – Table Design tab displaying the Table Name: field

7. To create a PivotTable, go to **Insert | PivotTable**.

8. A **Create PivotTable** dialog box pops up, where you can specify the data range and where you would like to place the PivotTable in the workbook. Excel automatically assumes you are using the table and refers to it in the **Select a table or range** option at the top of the dialog box. Note that you can also use an external connection here.

9. We will choose to place the PivotTable on a new worksheet for this example.

10. The last step is to decide whether to add this data to the data model so that you can analyze more than one table, as illustrated in the following screenshot:

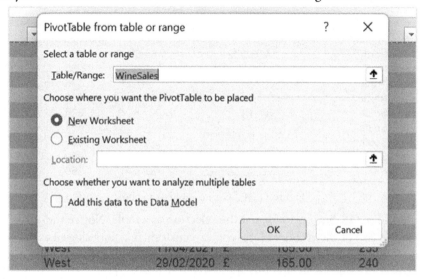

Figure 11.36 – Insert | PivotTable dialog box

11. Click on **OK** to confirm. A PivotTable is created on a new worksheet named **Sheet1**. Rename **Sheet1 Profit** and position it after the first sheet in the workbook.

If you are building a few reports or would like to bring a number of PivotTables together into a report **dashboard**, you could copy the **Profit** worksheet to create further worksheets on which to build your reports. Create another two worksheets by copying the **Profit** worksheet using the *Ctrl + click + drag* method so that we can build our different report dashboard views. You should now see the worksheets, as shown in the following screenshot:

Figure 11.37 – Worksheets in the MattsWinery.xlsx workbook

12. Let's continue on to the next section by adding fields to build our PivotTables.

Adding PivotTable fields

In the previous section, you followed the steps to create a PivotTable from the worksheet data. Now, we will learn how to construct a PivotTable report by adding fields from the worksheet columns, as follows:

1. Click to access the **Profit** worksheet. Be sure to have clicked on the PivotTable report so that the **PivotTable Fields** pane displays to the right of the window. This is where you add and customize field placements to produce a report.

2. If you click on the **Tools** icon to the right of **Choose fields to add to report**, you will see various options to change the layout of the **PivotTable Fields** pane. Let's change the view layout to **Fields Section and Areas Section Side-by-Side**, as illustrated in the following screenshot:

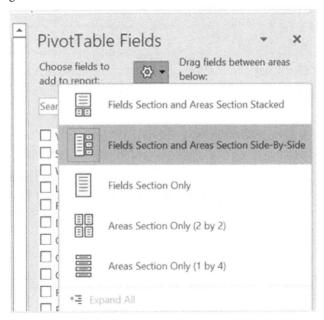

Figure 11.38 – PivotTable Fields pane

3. Drag the field names from the left into the areas you require on the right. For this example, we will drag **Region** to **Rows**, **Label** will move to **Columns**, and **Profit** will move to **Values**, as illustrated in the following screenshot. Experiment with your table fields to see how you would like to present the data in the PivotTable report by simply dragging and dropping fields into the relevant areas:

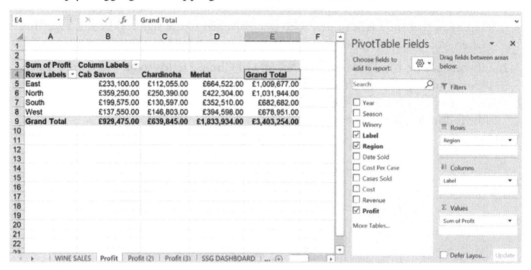

Figure 11.39 – PivotTable report and PivotTable Fields pane

4. Before we make customizations to our PivotTable report, set the **Report Layout** option to display in tabular format. Click on **Design | Report Layout | Show in Tabular Form**, as illustrated in the following screenshot. The reason we may want to do this is that field names will display as heading labels:

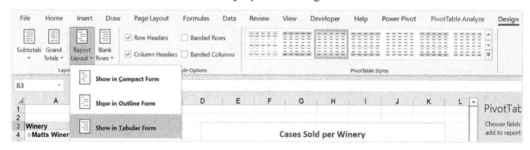

Figure 11.40 – Setting the Report Layout option to Show in Tabular Form

5. We can now highlight the values on the PivotTable report and right-click to **Show Values As**, and then choose **% of Grand Total**.

6. If you would like to sort your values, simply *right-click* in the **Grand Total** column and choose the **Sort** option. A submenu will be populated, where you can choose further options. Let's choose **Largest to Smallest**. Note that all the values are now sorted from biggest to smallest in value.

7. The second PivotTable report we will create will be to show *cases sold* by *year* and *season*. Remember you will need to click on the **Profit (2)** worksheet, then rename it **Cases**. Click into the PivotTable report, then drag the relevant fields into their position on the **PivotTable Fields** pane.

8. Select the values on your PivotTable report, then apply the desired number format. We will use the **Comma Style**, and **Remove Decimals**, as illustrated in the following screenshot:

	Winery	Season	Sum of Cases Sold
2			
3	Winery ▾	Season ▾	Sum of Cases Sold
4	⊟ Matts Winery	Autumn	8,135
5		Spring	8,513
6		Summer	7,210
7		Winter	8,342
8	Matts Winery Total		32,200
9	⊟ Prominent Wines	Autumn	4,580
10		Spring	4,668
11		Summer	4,509
12		Winter	4,536
13	Prominent Wines Total		18,293
14	Grand Total		50,493
15			

Figure 11.41 – Cases worksheet showing the populated PivotTable

9. Let's create another PivotTable. Rename the **Profit (3)** worksheet **Revenue**. Add **Label** (*rows*) and **Revenue** (*values*) to the PivotTable report.

10. After adding the relevant fields, change the column heading to read **Total Revenue**.

We have now added the relevant PivotTable reports to each worksheet. In the next section, we will focus on creating PivotCharts and customizing the *SSG dashboard*.

Creating dashboards

Dashboards are a visual way to represent data from worksheets in a dynamic format. In this topic, we will look at a few ways to make your data interactive. We'll proceed as follows:

1. As we are building an interactive dashboard after we have created the PivotTable reports, we will create one more report. Click back to the **WINESALES** worksheet, then choose **Insert | PivotTable** to create a new report on a new worksheet. Rename the worksheet **Date Sold**. Add **Cases Sold** and **Years** to build the PivotTable report, as illustrated in the following screenshot:

Years		Sum of Cases Sold
2019		4897
2020		20704
2021		21672
2022		3220
Grand Total		**50493**

Figure 11.42 – PivotTable report result

2. We are now ready to create PivotCharts for each of the PivotTable reports for the dashboard. We learned this skill we learned in our previous-edition book, *Learn Microsoft Office 2019*, so we will not recap the chart creation here.

3. Once you have created **PivotCharts**, *copy* each PivotChart and position it onto the **SSG Dashboard** worksheet. You will need to position, align, and resize the PivotCharts according to your requirements. Use your creative side to apply design colors of your choice.

4. Here is an example of our complete **SSG Dashboard** worksheet showing the four PivotCharts. We will recap by adding a timeline and slicers in another topic to complete the dashboard:

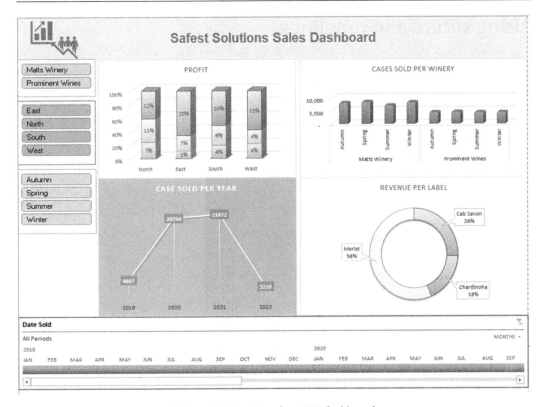

Figure 11.43 – Complete SSG dashboard

5. Before we look at slicers and timelines, we need to perform a few tasks so that the dashboard looks more professional.

6. Visit the **View** tab to customize the **Show** options so that the **Gridlines** and **Headings** options are removed from the workbook, as illustrated in the following screenshot:

Figure 11.44 – Gridlines and Headings options

We are now ready to customize the dashboard a little more so that it becomes dynamic and not static.

Using slicers and timelines

Using slicers and timelines is an excellent way of filtering data in a PivotTable. The difference between filtering and using slicers is that slicers are more visually appealing and also allow you to quickly retrieve data or update data. We can add slicers to PivotTables, as well as to data formatted as a table. Proceed as follows:

1. Click on the **Profit** PivotChart on the **SSG Dashboard** worksheet to select it.

2. Visit the **PivotChart Analyze** tab and click on **Insert Slicer** under the **Filter** group, as illustrated in the following screenshot:

Figure 11.45 – PivotChart Analyze tab to display the Insert Slicer option

3. Select fields to add to the dashboard. For this example, we will add **Region**, **Winery**, **Label**, and **Season**. Click on **OK** to add slicers.

4. The slicers are placed over the PivotCharts.

5. Click and drag each slicer to another location to position it neatly on the worksheet. Resize the slicers and align them, if required.

6. As we do not need the slicer headings, they can be removed from the slicers. Right-click on a slicer, then select **Slicer Settings**, which will take you to the screen shown here. Uncheck the **Display header** option. Click on **OK** to confirm. Repeat these steps for each slicer on the worksheet:

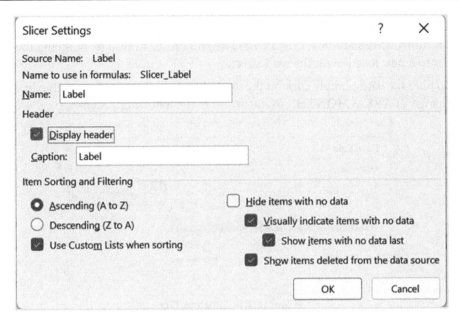

Figure 11.46 – Display header option

7. Slicers can be customized just the same as any other Excel element. Navigate to the **Slicer** tab to access **Slicer Styles** (see *Figure 11.47* in the next topic).

Now, we will look at the timeline feature.

Inserting a timeline

The timeline feature only works with date and time values and in tandem with the PivotTable tool. Timelines are not available to apply to a regular table dataset in a worksheet. Timelines are used to interactively filter dates. They operate in exactly the same way as slicers. Here's how to insert a timeline:

1. Click on the **Profit** PivotChart on the **SSG Dashboard** worksheet to select it. The workbook you are working on is named `MattsWinery.xlsx`.
2. Navigate to the **PivotChart Analyze** tab on the ribbon.
3. Choose **Insert Timeline** from the **Filter** group.

4. As we only have one date field in our dataset, select the **Date Sold** field from the list.

5. The timeline is placed over the PivotTable and can be moved by dragging the title bar to a new location on the worksheet.

6. To filter the dates, simply click on the drop-down arrow to the right of the timeline to change **YEARS** to **MONTHS**, as illustrated in the following screenshot:

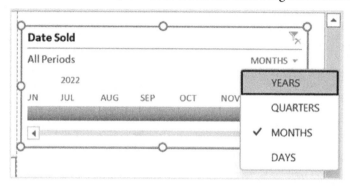

Figure 11.47 – Timeline filter

7. Resize and position the timeline on the dashboard, and change **Timeline Styles** by visiting the **Timeline** tab.

8. Select items along the timeline to filter the PivotTable data and see the visuals change across the PivotCharts.

    Now that we have learned how to create slicers and timelines, let's customize them so that they are updating all PivotCharts on the dashboard worksheet.

Setting up report connections

1. After adding slicers and timelines to a dashboard, you will notice that they only service the PivotChart you selected in order to add the slicer initially. You need to create dynamic **report connections** to all worksheet PivotCharts so that they all update at the same time, depending on the filter chosen in the slicer or timeline.

2. Using the same worksheet (**SSG Dashboard**) as the previous section, select a slicer by clicking on it.

3. Right-click on the slicer, then choose **Report Connections** or go to **Slicer | Report Connections,** as illustrated in the following screenshot:

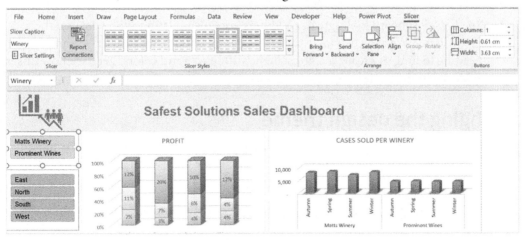

Figure 11.48 – Report Connections button on the Slicer tab

4. Ensure that all four connections are selected in the dialog box related to each sheet of the workbook so that the data updates visually as you filter using the slicer. Note that we can rename PivotTables from the default name given when creating them so that you are able to associate the PivotTable name with the required filter. This is especially important if you are developing or preparing report connections with colleagues. Once set up, it will make more sense to individuals working with you on the data. The **Report Connections** dialog box is shown in the following screenshot:

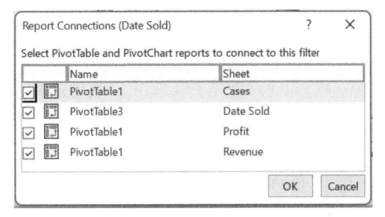

Figure 11.49 – Report Connections dialog box

5. Click the **OK** button to confirm.

6. Repeat this process for each slicer and timeline on the worksheet.

7. The SSG dashboard looks great, and filters are now updating all the data on the PivotCharts. We can customize the entire design in one single click if we are needing to find, or create, a color scheme with our brand colors. Let's see how this is achieved in the next section.

Changing the design theme

1. Now that we have altered styles independently for each element on the dashboard, we can save time using **Theme** templates to change every element at the same time.

2. Navigate to the **Page Layout** tab on the ribbon.

3. Select the **Themes** dropdown, after which a list of **Custom** and **Office** themes will appear. Click through the list to choose a theme to apply to your worksheet. Notice that all elements of the worksheet update to the new theme as you are clicking through the options. You are also able to customize **Theme Colors**, **Fonts**, and **Effects** options using the relevant buttons to the right of the **Themes** button.

4. Once you have customized a theme, you can click on the **Save Current Theme…** option at the bottom of the **Themes** drop-down list. Once a name is provided, this theme will become part of your **Custom** themes area at the top of the list, as illustrated in the following screenshot:

Figure 11.50 – Themes drop-down list

The dashboard is now complete and ready for other members of your company to interact with it. Let's see how we can share dashboards with others.

Sharing your dashboard with others

Once you have finished creating your dashboard, don't forget that you can share this with others using the **Share** button to the top-right of your Excel environment. Here's how to do this:

1. Click on the **Share** button, after which the **Share** pane will populate on the right-hand side of the screen.

2. Enter the email address of individuals with which to share the dashboard. Add a message, if required.

3. Make sure that the individuals you are sharing with can edit the dashboard so that they are able to interact with the filters.

4. Click the **Share** button to send an invitation to the individuals concerned, or use the **Get a sharing link** option to copy the address directly into an email or browser. We can also share dashboards by creating a group in Outlook, then add your dashboard to the group and create a pin to the dashboard so that it resides at the top of the group. We will look at creating groups in the Outlook chapter of this book.

There are so many different features and elements to dashboards that we could cover, but we hope that we have given you enough substance to be creative and explore this exciting topic applicable to your business needs.

Let's end this chapter with a few more PivotTable skills.

Additional PivotTable customizations

In our previous book, *Learn Microsoft Office 2019*, we learned to create PivotTables as an introduction to the tool. There are many features to explore to get the most out our of your PivotTable reports, a few of which are explained in the topics that follow.

Splitting data into separate worksheets

After you have created a PivotTable report, you can split the data into separate worksheets according to the category. Let's open the workbook named `SplitData.xlsx`. Proceed as follows:

1. Select the **Pivot** worksheet. Click on the PivotTable report to select it.

2. Navigate to the **PivotTable Analyze** tab and select **PivotTable | Options | Show Report Filter Pages…**, as illustrated in the following screenshot:

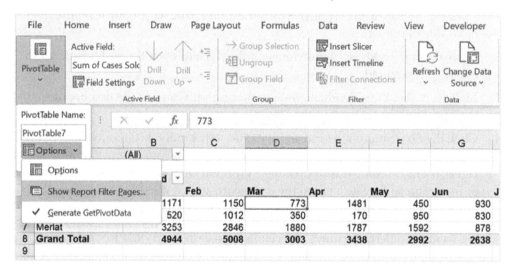

Figure 11.51 – Show Report Filter Pages… option

3. Choose the **Years** filter option.

4. Click on **OK** to confirm. The extra sheets are added to the workbook, splitting the data over each year.

In the next topic, we will learn how to change the settings of fields in the **PivotTable Fields** pane.

Changing value field settings

When we drag fields around the **PivotTable Fields** pane, the field might not take on the correct format of the data you require. Let's learn how to amend this, as follows:

1. Notice that the **Employer Cost** field in the **Values** area is reflecting the count of the value.

2. As we do not want the count of the ER cost, we need to visit **Value Field Settings….** Click the drop-down arrow to the right of the **Count of the ER Cost** field to see a list of options, as illustrated in the following screenshot:

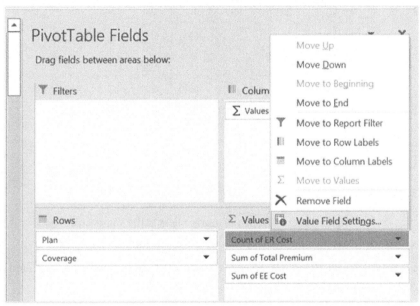

Figure 11.52 – Value Field Settings…

3. After selecting **Value Field Settings**, change the **Count** value to **Sum**, then click on **OK** to confirm. The PivotTable updates to reflect the change.

Let's learn how to change the percentage of a particular plan.

Counting employees

1. To count how many employees are enrolled in plans, drag the **Coverage** field from the **Field List** pane to the **Values** area, as illustrated in the following screenshot:

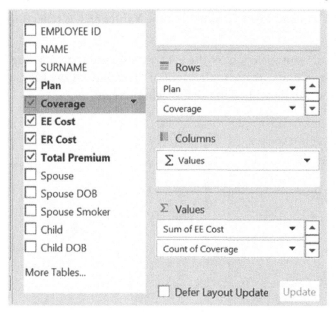

Figure 11.53 – Count of Coverage field in the Values area

The count of coverage is now evident in the PivotTable.

We need to change this value to see what percentage of people are enrolled in a plan versus a single level or family level of coverage.

2. Right-click on any of the values in the **Count of Coverage** PivotTable report.

3. Locate the **Show Values As…** option from the drop-down list, then slide right to select **% of Parent Total…**.

4. Select **Plan** from the **Show Values As (Count of Coverage)** box, then click the **OK** button to confirm.

5. The PivotTable data updates to reflect the percentage of coverage, as illustrated in the following screenshot:

	Row Labels	Sum of ER Cost	Sum of Total Premium	Sum of EE Cost	Count of Coverage
3					
4	⊟ Basic SSG		2320	2320	100.00%
5	Employee + Children		600	600	25.00%
6	Employee + Family		500	500	16.67%
7	Employee + Spouse		900	900	25.00%
8	Employee Only		320	320	33.33%
9	⊟ Extended SSG		4200	4200	100.00%
10	Employee + Children		1500	1500	28.57%
11	Employee + Family		2000	2000	28.57%
12	Employee + Spouse		600	600	28.57%

Figure 11.54 – Percentage of coverage

Now that we have amended the value to %, the heading does not quite fit the contents of the column. We will learn how to fix this in the next section.

Amending column headings

1. To update our column heading so that it reflects the percentage and does not count, we rename the field exactly as we would usually do on a worksheet. The only thing you need to be aware of is that the name you use may already exist in the PivotTable fields area/existing dataset. You will receive an error to state that the field name already exists if this is the case.

   If you need to use the same name, a space or underscore would need to be added so that it is not associated as a duplicate table field.

2. Double-click on the column header to amend it, then type the new headings into the **Custom Name:** field provided, as illustrated in the following screenshot. Click on **OK** to confirm:

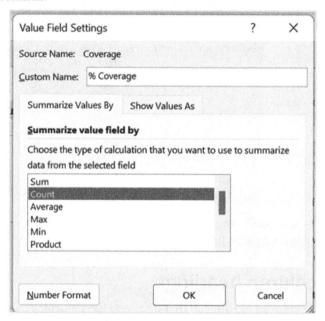

Figure 11.55 – Value Field Settings dialog to amend the heading

The column header is updated in the PivotTable report.

Let's learn how to move a PivotTable if you would like it positioned on the actual worksheet and not as a separate worksheet.

Moving PivotTable reports

If you would like to move the PivotTable next to your data and not display the report on a separate worksheet, follow these steps:

1. Click the **PivotTable Analyze** tab at the top of your ribbon, then select the **Actions** drop-down list. Choose **Move PivotTable**, as illustrated in the following screenshot:

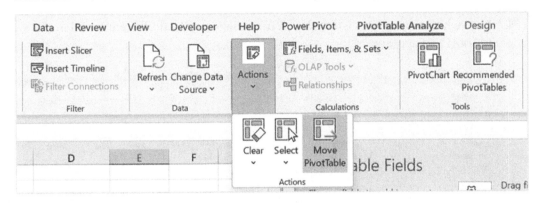

Figure 11.56 – Move PivotTable

2. Select whether you would like to move to an existing worksheet or a new worksheet.

3. Click on **OK** when you have chosen the desired option. The PivotTable is re-located.

Finally, we will learn how to use the GETPIVOTDATA function. This function is constructed to grab data (reference data) from a PivotTable cell.

Constructing the GETPIVOTDATA function

When working in a workbook that contains PivotTable reports, we may need to reference cells contained within a PivotTable report outside of the report on the worksheet. The GETPIVOTDATA function is great for this purpose. This function is available in the **Lookup & Reference** category in Excel.

There are a few constraints we need to be aware of when collecting PivotTable report references, which are discussed in the following steps:

1. Open the workbook named PivotFormula.xlsx.

2. Click to access the **Pivot** worksheet. Notice that the PivotTable report has already been created on this sheet in cells A1:M8. In cells A11:D14, we would like to populate data from our existing PivotTable report to use on the worksheet.

3. Click into cell B14 on the worksheet. Press the = key, then click on a cell you wish to reference in the PivotTable report. In this case, we want to populate the **Cases Sold in January per Label** data. Select cell B5 in the PivotTable report.

4. Notice here that the GETPIVOTDATA function is automatically referenced in the formula that appears:

| B5 | ▾ | ⋮ | ✕ | ✓ | *fx* | =GETPIVOTDATA("Cases Sold",$A$3,"Label","Cab Savon","Date Sold",1) |

◢	A	B	C	D	E	F	G	H	I
1	Years	(All) ▾							
2									
3	Sum of Cases Sold	Date Sold ▾							
4	Label ▾	Jan	Feb	Mar	Apr	May	Jun	Jul	Aug
5	Cab Savon	1171	1150	773	1481	450	930		2135
6	Chardinoha	520	1012	350	170	950	830	1360	208
7	Merlat	3253	2846	1880	1787	1592	878	2281	2490
8	Grand Total	4944	5008	3003	3438	2992	2638	3641	4833
9									
10									
11									
12									
13		Cab Savon	Chardinoha	Merlat					
14	Jan	=GETPIVOTDATA("Cases Sold",$A$3,"Label","Cab Savon","Date Sold",1)							
15	Feb								
16	Mar								
17									

Figure 11.57 – GETPIVOTDATA function in action

5. Press *Enter* to confirm.

6. As the GETPIVOTDATA formula is hardcoded into the cell, we cannot copy the formula across and down to the remaining cells without receiving a #REF! error. Let's fix the formula so that it enables us to autofill the values to other cells.

7. Double-click on cell B14.

8. Replace "Cab Savon" in the formula with the cell reference outside of the PivotTable report, by clicking on cell B13 (the **Cab Savon** heading). Be sure to apply absolute cell referencing to B13. The referencing would need to be applied to the row—that is, B$13.

9. We also need to amend the month reference so that it updates by grabbing the relevant month when copying down the column. Months in a PivotTable are referenced as hardcoded month numbers 1 (January), 2 (February), and so on. Let's replace the month number argument portion of the formula so that it updates for us.

10. Replace **1** at the end of the formula by entering the ROW(A1) function so that it will count the months automatically from 1 (which equates to January), and so forth.

11. Your formula is now constructed as follows: =GETPIVOTDATA("Cases Sold",$A$3,"Label",B$13,"Date Sold",ROW(A1)). You can see an illustration of this in the following screenshot:

TIME		:	×	✓	*fx*	=GETPIVOTDATA("Cases Sold",$A$3,"Label",B$13,"Date Sold",ROW(A1))		

▲	A	B	C	D	E	F	G
4	Label	Jan	Feb	Mar	Apr	May	Jun	Jul
5	Cab Savon	1171	1150	773	1481	450	930
6	Chardinoha	520	1012	350	170	950	830
7	Merlat	3253	2846	1880	1787	1592	878
8	**Grand Total**	**4944**	**5008**	**3003**	**3438**	**2992**	**2638**
9							
10							
11							
12							
13		Cab Savon	Chardinoha	Merlat			
14	Jan	=GETPIVOTDATA("Cases Sold",$A$3,"Label",B$13,"Date Sold",ROW(A1))					
15	Feb	GETPIVOTDATA(data_field, pivot_table, [field1, item1], [field2, item2], [field3, item3], [field4, ...])					
16	Mar	773	350	1880			
17							

Figure 11.58 – Completed GETPIVOTDATA formula

12. Autofill the formula to the right and down to fill in the remaining values.

> **Note**
>
> If you are unable to construct the GETPIVOTDATA function, it may be
> that the option is currently deactivated in Excel. Click into the PivotTable
> report, then visit **PivotTable Analyze | PivotTable | Options | Generate
> GetPivotData**. Make sure the option is enabled.

Summary

You have now learned valuable skills for visualizing and analyzing data in this chapter,
using powerful tools such as PivotTable to create slicers and timelines, and you can now
create dashboards and PivotCharts and customize your PivotTable reports. You are now
able to put your date and time functions into practice as you are equipped with all the
relevant functions applicable to each of these function categories.

In the next chapter, we will build on prior skills to work with math and trigonometry
and statistical functions using Excel 2021 and introduce some additional functions to the
mix. We will explore how to generate random numbers using RANDBETWEEN and RAND
functions. In addition, we will work through examples of PRODUCT functions, including
the SUMPRODUCT, MROUND, FLOOR, TRUNC, AGGREGATE, and CONVERT functions.

We will investigate the MEDIAN, COUNTBLANK, and AVERAGEIFS statistical functions in
the next chapter, with which you can experiment and apply to existing or new scenarios
when working with workbook data.

12
Useful Statistical and Mathematical Functions

Office 2021 includes a range of mathematical and statistical functions, some of which are considered important foundational skills to build more complex formulas.

We will build on prior skills to work with **Math & Trig** and **Statistical** functions using Excel 2021 and introduce some additional functions to the mix. We will explore how to generate random numbers using RANDBETWEEN and RAND functions. In addition, we will work through examples of PRODUCT functions, including the SUMPRODUCT, MROUND, FLOOR, TRUNC, AGGREGATE, and CONVERT functions.

In addition, we will investigate the MEDIAN, COUNTBLANK, and AVERAGEIFS statistical functions in this chapter, from which you can experiment and apply to existing or new scenarios when working with workbook data.

The following topics are covered in this chapter:

- Exploring mathematical functions
- Exploring statistical functions

Technical requirements

Prior to starting this chapter, you should be equipped with the knowledge of basic Excel formulas and skills and be able to save files and interact with the Office 2021 environment comfortably. If you have been through prior chapters of this book, you will have the necessary skills to tackle this chapter. The examples used in this chapter are accessible from the following GitHub **Uniform Resource Locator** (**URL**): https://github.com/PacktPublishing/Learn-Microsoft-Office-2021-Second-Edition.

Exploring mathematical functions

In previous Excel chapters of this book, we have introduced or built on some mathematical functions such as SUMIF and AVERAGEIFS, so we will not revisit these except to build on existing knowledge or look at other functions within the same family. Let's start the chapter off by having a look at a few functions to generate random numbers in the next section.

Generating random numbers

In this section, you will learn to understand and apply the RAND and RANDBETWEEN functions to generate random number lists and stop the result from updating in the workbook. We will also look at ways to customize the number range in workbook cells. This function is useful when you need to generate a dataset to test functions with, instead of using your own data. It is also great to generate a random list when training colleagues.

The RAND portion of the function name means *random*.

The main differences between these two functions are highlighted in the following table:

RAND	RANDBETWEEN
Located in the Math & Trig library in Excel.	Located in the Math & Trig library in Excel.
Used to generate random decimals between 0 and 1, by default.	Used to generate a random integer between the bottom and top values you specify.
Function syntax has an empty set of arguments within brackets.	Function syntax requires two arguments—a bottom value and a top value.

Table 12.1 – Differences between the RAND and RANDBETWEEN functions

We will now look at the syntax of each and how to apply the function in Excel. Proceed as follows:

1. Open Microsoft Excel.

2. On the first worksheet, select a cell, then start constructing a formula as you would normally.

3. Type =rand.

   The process is illustrated in the following screenshot:

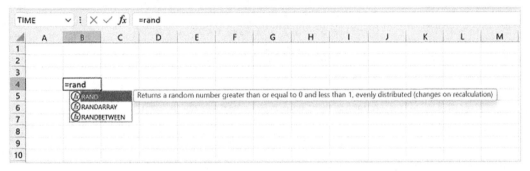

Figure 12.1 – Constructing the RAND function

4. Notice the function tooltip displayed on the screen, indicating the result will generate a random number greater than or equal to 0 and less than 1. It also mentions that the function will update when recalculated. This means that every time you update the workbook using the *F9* key, the function will update to a different decimal integer.

5. Select the RAND function by either double-clicking on RAND in the drop-down list offered or typing (to continue.

6. As we do not have to enter any arguments, simply press the *Enter* key on the keyboard to see the result.

7. When we press the *F9* keyboard key, for example, the formula will regenerate when we open the workbook or type into a cell.

8. Should you need a long list of random decimal numbers, simply use the autofill handle to drag the formula down or across to fill in these values. We could also select a range first and then fill the formula. Now that you are familiar with the function, let's continue with an example to generate a greater range of data.

9. Select cells B5:F14, then type =RAND (), as illustrated in the following screenshot, and press *Ctrl + Enter* to fill the cells:

B5		⌄ ⋮ ✕ ✓ *fx*	=RAND()			
◢	A	B	C	D	E	F	G
3						
4		0.390401				
5		0.883845	0.039216	0.317752	0.343313	0.941113
6		0.770718	0.899726	0.131034	0.315851	0.81194
7		0.06807	0.872962	0.08033	0.560043	0.588951
8		0.861014	0.415866	0.068008	0.200997	0.854263
9		0.253469	0.664422	0.151938	0.47075	0.05887
10		0.891632	0.382684	0.634277	0.055681	0.758425
11		0.085954	0.465749	0.63772	0.873947	0.845953
12		0.288258	0.427268	0.199569	0.075614	0.234326
13		0.737464	0.61019	0.264226	0.853487	0.305591
14		0.798645	0.138538	0.731156	0.344738	0.893167

Figure 12.2 – RAND function result

10. All the different combinations of decimal values between 0 and 1 are generated within the selected range.

> **Reminder**
> As the decimals update automatically within the cells on the workbook, it might be necessary to remove the formula from the generated values so that these remain static.

11. In view of the previous reminder and to make values static within the cells, simply select a range, then right-click and pull the range slightly to the right, then back again to its original position. You should notice a shortcut menu appear with a list of choices. Select **Copy Here as Values Only** from the list, as illustrated in the following screenshot:

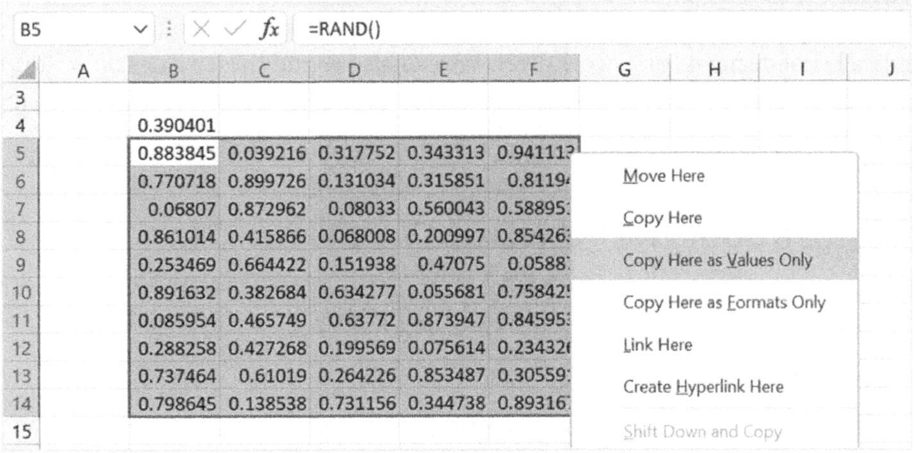

Figure 12.3 – Copy Here as Values Only

12. This forces the function to be removed from the cells, leaving behind just the raw data. You can now be confident that the data will no longer update automatically.

Let's learn how to provide a greater value range when dealing with the RAND function, as follows.

We can expand the range of values the RAND function generates by multiplying by the relevant value. Select cells I5:K5 on the worksheet, then type =RAND()*20. Press the Ctrl + Enter keys when done. Instead of values between 0 and 1 being generated, we can see from the following screenshot that a random list from 0 to 20 is now evident on the worksheet. Note that you can also use a cell reference to multiply by instead:

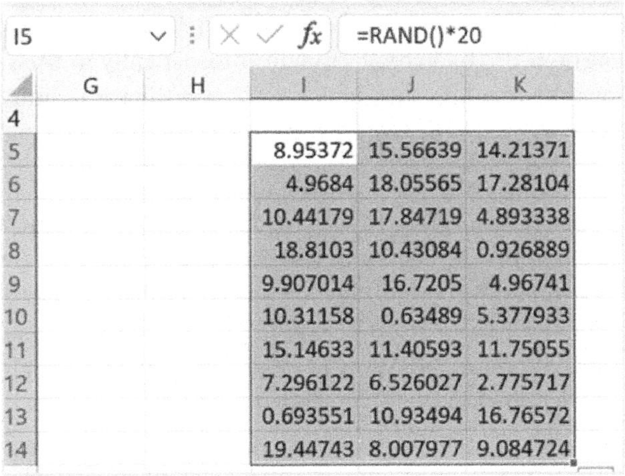

Figure 12.4 – Increasing the value of the RAND default

Whatever the purpose, the RAND function is a quick and easy solution to randomly generate a list of decimals on a worksheet. We can also round these values up or down depending on the requirements. This is covered in the ROUNDUP section in this chapter.

We will now look at one more function to generate numbers automatically.

Learning about the RANDBETWEEN function

The RANDBETWEEN function is like RAND, except it generates random integers within a bottom and top value constraint you provide. Let's look at an example, as follows:

1. Select cells B18:F26 of the workbook.

2. Start typing the formula as follows: =RANDBETWEEN(.

3. Notice in the following screenshot that the tooltip is indicating that the syntax requires a top and a bottom argument for this function:

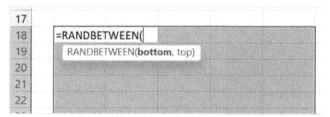

Figure 12.5 – RANDBETWEEN syntax

4. Type 45 for the *bottom* value, then add a *comma* to separate the arguments. Lastly, enter 580 for the *top* value.

5. Press *Ctrl + Enter* to generate a list. You will see a list of integers within the bottom and top values entered. The list will update automatically in the workbook. Don't forget to remove the formula should you not want the list to automatically update.

> **Note**
>
> If we provide a lower value greater than the top value in the arguments when using the RANDBETWEEN function, a #NUM! error will appear. Simply switch the value arguments within the formula construction and it will correct itself.

We will now move on to learn how to multiply ranges together to reach a product in Excel.

Working with PRODUCT functions

In this section, we will explore the PRODUCT and SUMPRODUCT functions.

The PRODUCT function

The PRODUCT function is a simple function that multiplies a given range, ignoring empty cells and any cells that contain text. To work out the **Revenue** value in the screenshot shown next, we would need to multiply the **Cost Per Case** value by the **Cases Sold** value:

1. To follow along with this example, open the MattsWinery.xlsx workbook. You can see the syntax here:

	G	H		I		K		L	M	N
	Cost Per Case	Cases Sold		Cost		Profit			Revenue	
	£ 165.00	450	£	40,500.00	£	33,750.00			=PRODUCT(G2,H2)	
	£ 165.00	550	£	49,500.00	£	41,250.00			PRODUCT(number1, [number2], [number3], ...)	
	£ 165.00	575	£	51,750.00	£	43,125.00				
	£ 165.00	650	£	58,500.00	£	48,750.00				
	£ 165.00	320	£	28,800.00	£	24,000.00				
	£ 165.00	325	£	29,250.00	£	24,375.00				
	£ 165.00	330	£	29,700.00	£	24,750.00				
	£ 165.00	350	£	31,500.00	£	26,250.00				
	£ 165.00	350	£	31,500.00	£	26,250.00				
	£ 165.00	360	£	32,400.00	£	27,000.00				

Figure 12.6 – Product syntax

2. Click on cell M2, then type =PRODUCT(.

3. Enter arguments to multiply the values in the respective cells—namely, G2 and H2—making sure that there is a *comma* separating the arguments in the formula. Press the *Enter* key when complete.

4. Copy the formula down to the rest of the range to work out the product for all rows in the worksheet.

This method is much easier than the traditional method of multiplying cells using an asterisk to separate arguments. Using the PRODUCT function alleviates any issues with blank cells in the arguments you supply. When we use the asterisk method, and values within the range are missing from the argument, the formula will return a 0 result.

Let's run through this by way of explanation.

When we use an asterisk to collect cells on the worksheet to multiply, it calculates the product of the cell references added. The process is illustrated in the following screenshot:

I	J	K
		Using the asterisk
2		=I18*I19*I20*I21*I22
4		
5		
12		
3		

Figure 12.7 – Using the asterisk method

When any of the referred references are empty, the formula returns a 0 result, as illustrated in the following screenshot:

I	J	K
		Using the asterisk
2		0
4		
12		
3		

Figure 12.8 – Empty cells causing the formula to return a 0 result

We can, however, use the PRODUCT function in such instances as the function allows cells to be empty as part of the function arguments, as illustrated in the following screenshot:

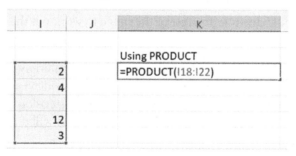

I	J	K
		Using PRODUCT
2		=PRODUCT(I18:I22)
4		
12		
3		

Figure 12.9 – PRODUCT function

When we remove one of the values from the arguments—for example, I20—the formula does not return 0. It will recalculate using the arguments considering the 0 value in I20.

Remember that the PRODUCT function can be implemented along with other functions in the same formula. We will now learn about the SUMPRODUCT function.

The adaptable SUMPRODUCT function

The SUMPRODUCT function can be used to multiply large datasets by multiplying each position in the array. When we use the SUMPRODUCT function, we can be sure that the function will work in any version of Excel. Array functions, as we are already aware, need to be created using the *Ctrl + Shift + Enter* keys to avoid any array formula output errors. The SUMPRODUCT function is used to create arrays without having to press the *Ctrl + Shift + Enter* key combination. The SUMPRODUCT function is way more flexible than using COUNTIFS or SUMIFS.

The SUMPRODUCT syntax is shown here:

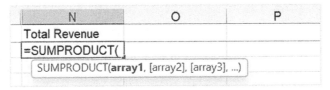

Figure 12.10 – SUMPRODUCT syntax

As you can see from the syntax in the preceding screenshot, the SUMPRODUCT function consists of an array of arguments. The first array argument includes the first range or array to multiply, then sum. The process is repeated for each array argument.

Let's work through the steps, as follows:

1. Open the MattsWinery.xlsx workbook.

2. On the first worksheet, the dataset relates to different wineries and sales data. We will work out the **Total Revenue** value in cell N2, using the **Cost per Case** and **Cases Sold** columns.

3. Click into cell N2, then type =SUMPRODUCT (.

4. Collect the first range from the worksheet—namely, cells G2:G145.

5. Add a *comma*, then select the next array range, H2:H145.

6. Press *Enter* to see the result of the formula in N2, shown in the following screenshot:

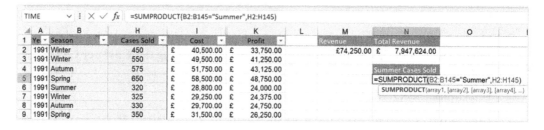

TIME		⌄ ⋮ ✕ ✓ ⨍	=SUMPRODUCT(G2:G145,H2:H145)						
	A	B	G	H	I		K		N
1	Ye ⌄	Season ⌄	Cost Per Case ⌄	Cases Sold ⌄	Cost ⌄		Profit ⌄		Total Revenue
2	1991	Winter	£ 165.00	450	£ 40,500.00	£	33,750.00		=SUMPRODUCT(G2:G145,H2:H145)
3	1991	Winter	£ 165.00	550	£ 49,500.00	£	41,250.00		SUMPRODUCT(array1, [array2], [array3], [array4], ...)
4	1991	Autumn	£ 165.00	575	£ 51,750.00	£	43,125.00		
5	1991	Spring	£ 165.00	650	£ 58,500.00	£	48,750.00		
6	1991	Summer	£ 165.00	320	£ 28,800.00	£	24,000.00		
7	1991	Winter	£ 165.00	325	£ 29,250.00	£	24,375.00		
8	1991	Autumn	£ 165.00	330	£ 29,700.00	£	24,750.00		
9	1991	Spring	£ 165.00	350	£ 31,500.00	£	26,250.00		
10	1991	Summer	£ 165.00	350	£ 31,500.00	£	26,250.00		
11	1991	Winter	£ 165.00	360	£ 32,400.00	£	27,000.00		
12	1991	Autumn	£ 165.00	370	£ 33,300.00	£	27,750.00		
13	1991	Spring	£ 165.00	375	£ 33,750.00	£	28,125.00		
14	1991	Summer	£ 165.00	230	£ 20,700.00	£	17,250.00		
15	1991	Winter	£ 165.00	235	£ 21,150.00	£	17,625.00		
16	1991	Autumn	£ 165.00	240	£ 21,600.00	£	18,000.00		

Figure 12.11 – SUMPRODUCT function

7. The result displayed in N2 should be 7947624 for the **Total Revenue** value.

Let's use the SUMPRODUCT function to sum the total cases sold for the **Summer** season:

1. Using the MattsWinery.xlsx workbook, locate cell N5.

2. The formula we are populating here is very similar to the examples you constructed before, but we will need to tweak the components a little to make it work for us. We will firstly create a formula incorrectly and then work through how to correct the result.

    As we are working out the total number of cases sold during the **Summer** season, we will be using those columns as arguments in our formula. In cell N5, enter the following formula: =SUMPRODUCT(B2:B145="Summer",H2:H145). You can see an illustration of this in the following screenshot:

TIME		⌄ ⋮ ✕ ✓ ⨍	=SUMPRODUCT(B2:B145="Summer",H2:H145)						
	A	B	H	I		K	L	M	N
1	Ye ⌄	Season ⌄	Cases Sold ⌄	Cost ⌄		Profit ⌄		Revenue	Total Revenue
2	1991	Winter	450	£ 40,500.00	£	33,750.00		£74,250.00 £	7,947,624.00
3	1991	Winter	550	£ 49,500.00	£	41,250.00			
4	1991	Autumn	575	£ 51,750.00	£	43,125.00			
5	1991	Spring	650	£ 58,500.00	£	48,750.00		Summer Cases Sold	
6	1991	Summer	320	£ 28,800.00	£	24,000.00		=SUMPRODUCT(B2:B145="Summer",H2:H145)	
7	1991	Winter	325	£ 29,250.00	£	24,375.00		SUMPRODUCT(array1, [array2], [array3], [array4], ...)	
8	1991	Autumn	330	£ 29,700.00	£	24,750.00			
9	1991	Spring	350	£ 31,500.00	£	26,250.00			

Figure 12.12 – SUMPRODUCT using SUMIF criteria

3. Press *Enter* to see the formula result. Notice that the result returned is 0. This is due to the first array being represented by true and false values; therefore, we need to force the first array to use 1s and 0s (numeric numbers) instead.

4. This is where the **double negative** comes into play. We need to force the evaluation of the array to convert from `true` and `false` to `0` and `1`. Double-click on cell N5 to amend it.

5. Type *two dashes* and `(` prior to the first array, like so: `=SUMPRODUCT(--(B2:B145="Summer"),H2:H145)`.

6. Press *Enter* to update the result. You should now see a result of `11719` in cell N5.

    Similarly, let's also sum the **Amount Owing** value for medicines using the `SSGPetFormat.xlsx` workbook.

7. Click into cell O2, then type the following formula, including the double negative to force the use of 0s and 1s instead of `true` and `false`: `=SUMPRODUCT(--(L2:L124="Medicine"),M2:M124)`.

8. The total amount owing for the **Medicine** category is displayed as £2498.

Use the preceding information to explore the SUMPRODUCT and PRODUCT functions even more by combining them with other functions in the function library. The next section will concentrate on the rounding of values.

Rounding with MROUND

In the previous-edition of this book, we introduced the ROUND, ROUNDUP, and ROUNDDOWN functions. When we use the increase and decrease decimal icons in Excel, we are formatting a cosmetic change to values by rounding them. This does not change the underlying raw data value in the cell.

To apply rounding to a value to use in calculations, we need to round by using a formula. We will now increase our knowledge by extending it to include the MROUND function. As a recap, the ROUND function allows us to round a number to a specific number of digits (decimal places). The MROUND function rounds numbers to the nearest multiple.

Note that the MROUND function will affect the result of formulas as it modifies cell data. Let's run through an example, as follows:

1. Open the `SSGPetFormat.xlsx` workbook to follow along.

2. Before we begin, let's insert a new column in between the **Amount Owing** column and the existing **Total Owing: Medicines** column.

3. As an introduction to the MROUND function, we will round the values in the **Amount Owing** column. The result of the formula will be in cell N2, as illustrated in the following screenshot:

	L	M	N	O
	Service	Amount Owing		
	Medicine	727.24	=MROUND(M2,5	
	Follow Up Consult	998.33	MROUND(number, **multiple**)	
	Pet Foods	108.05		
	Pet Winter Wear	254.6		
	Ear Spray	117.34		

Figure 12.13 – MROUND function to the nearest 5

4. Type =MROUND (then click on the value in M2. Add a *comma* to separate the arguments, then indicate the multiple types you require. For this example, we will round to the nearest 5.

5. Press *Enter* to confirm. You will see the following result:

	L	M	N	O
	Service	Amount Owing		
	Medicine	727.24	725.00	
	Follow Up Consult	998.33	1000.00	
	Pet Foods	108.05	110.00	
	Pet Winter Wear	254.6	255.00	
	Ear Spray	117.34	115.00	
	Leads and Jackets	822.9	825.00	

Figure 12.14 – MROUND function result

6. Notice the difference between the values in the two columns.

The FLOOR function is like the MROUND function, although it rounds down to the nearest multiple of significance to zero. Let's look at a practical example of this in the next section.

Rounding with the FLOOR function

Here, we will look at another method to round values. This time, we are rounding the nearest significant value to zero. Proceed as follows:

1. Continuing with the same workbook, click into cell O2.

2. Start to type the function, as follows: =FLOOR (.

3. Click on cell M2 as per the previous example, then add a *comma*.

4. For this example, we will also use 5 to locate the nearest multiple of 5 to 0.

5. Press *Enter* to see the result in cell O2. Copy the formula down the column, as illustrated in the following screenshot:

M	N	O
Amount Owing	**MROUND**	**FLOOR**
727.24	725.00	725
998.33	1000.00	995
108.05	110.00	105
254.6	255.00	250
117.34	115.00	115
822.9	825.00	820

Figure 12.15 – Difference between MROUND and FLOOR

6. Notice the difference between MROUND and FLOOR in column **N** and column **O**.

The opposite of the FLOOR function is the CEILING function.

7. Add another column in the worksheet so that we can explore this. Click into cell P2 to start the function.

8. Type =CEILING(M2,5) to find the closest multiple of 5. Press *Enter* to see the result. It should look like this:

M	N	O	P	Q
Amount Owing	**MROUND**	**FLOOR**	**CEILING**	
727.24	725.00	725	=CEILING(M2,5)	
998.33	1000.00	995	CEILING(number, significance)	
108.05	110.00	105	110	
254.6	255.00	250	255	
117.34	115.00	115	120	
822.9	825.00	820	825	
850.75	850.00	850	855	

Figure 12.16 – CEILING function

There are many methods for rounding values on a worksheet, and this section contains just a few of these methods. The next section will focus on the TRUNC function.

Returning integers

The INT and TRUNC functions have one similarity: they both return integers. INT rounds down to the nearest integer, basing it on the fractional part of a number, while TRUNC removes the fractional part of the number and truncates it to an integer. In layman's terms, it removes decimal places.

We will not go through this function step by step as the syntax is very similar to that shown in the previous sections. The following screenshot details the function and the result to display one decimal place only:

	M	N	O	P	Q	R
	TIME ⌄ ⋮ ✕ ✓ *fx*	=TRUNC(M2,1)				
1	Amount Owing	MROUND	FLOOR	CEILING	TRUNC	
2	727.24	725.00	725	730	=TRUNC(M2,1)	
3	998.33	1000.00	995	1000	TRUNC(**number**, [num_digits])	
4	108.05	110.00	105	110	108	
5	254.6	255.00	250	255	254.6	
6	117.34	115.00	115	120	117.3	
7	822.9	825.00	820	825	822.9	
8	850.75	850.00	850	855	850.7	
9	26.57	25.00	25	30	26.5	

Figure 12.17 – TRUNC function

Remember that any of these functions can be added to existing formulas to gain the result you require.

The next section concentrates on a function that enables a wide selection of mathematical functions within it to customize the output. The function is quite new, so if constructed in versions earlier than Excel 2010, the output will return a #NAME! error.

Working out how to use AGGREGATE

The AGGREGATE function is a useful tool to obtain, for instance, the maximum values in a range without including any error values in the selected range. The function can be constructed to ignore hidden rows and errors. It consists of required arguments from which you can choose further functions to base your result.

The syntax for the AGGREGATE function looks like this: =AGGREGATE(function_num, options, array, [k]).

The following table explains the relevant syntax arguments:

`function_num`	This is required. Choose from the list of functions available (19 functions) to apply to the function.
`options`	A number between 0 and 7 (which values are to be ignored when calculating).
`array`	The range (array) that the function must be applied to. A function is created to apply to vertical ranges, not horizontal ranges. Note that if the array contains a calculation, it will not ignore hidden rows.
`[k]`	Some functions selected in the first argument require this option to be filled in. This details the integer that denotes the position in the array.

Table 12.2 – AGGREGATE syntax

Although there are instances where we can use basic formulas to reach a result instead of the AGGREGATE function, this might not be as fluid as we need.

For instance, when we construct the AVERAGE function, the following constraints could impact the result:

- Any hidden column data is included in the result.
- Includes cells containing 0s in the formula result.
- Ignores logical values.
- Ignores numbers entered as text .

These constraints could return an incorrect result that could impact other formulas in the workbook.

The AGGREGRATE function arguments, although a bit of extra work for the end user, allow further customizations utilizing 19 functions with 8 options to choose from.

Let's work through an example, as follows:

1. Open the `Training Schedule.xlsx` workbook. Make sure you are on the **Overtime** worksheet.

2. The worksheet is set up to display overtime for trainers for remote training sessions per office. We will work out the sum of overtime per trainer in cell B13 as an example.

3. Start the formula by typing this into cell B13: =AGGREGATE (. You can see an illustration of this in the following screenshot:

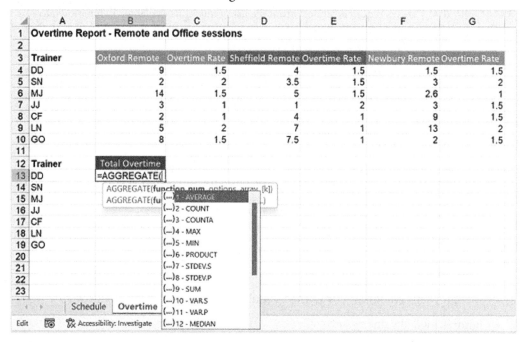

Figure 12.18 – AGGREGATE function syntax

4. A drop-down list will appear straightaway that houses 19 different functions to choose from. Double-click to select the SUM function from the list.

5. Insert a *comma*, after which the next argument will appear, displaying the eight options to choose from, as illustrated in the following screenshot:

Figure 12.19 – Argument options

6. This is the step where you could be more concise to refine the result of the formula so that calculations work effectively against your dataset. For this example, we will double-click option 5, as we may hide rows at some point as the dataset grows over time. This ensures that the formula will not include values from any hidden rows in the worksheet.

7. Insert a *comma* to move to the next argument and select a range (array) in the worksheet. Select cells B4, D4, and F4, as illustrated in the following screenshot:

	Oxford Remote	Overtime Rate	Sheffield Remote	Overtime Rate	Newbury Remote	Overtime Rate
3 Trainer						
4 DD	9	1.5	4	1.5	1.5	1.5
5 SN	2	2	3.5	1.5	3	2
6 MJ	14	1.5	5	1.5	2.6	1
7 JJ	3	1	1	2	3	1.5
8 CF	2	1	4	1	9	1.5
9 LN	5	2	7	1	13	2
10 GO	8	1.5	7.5	1	2	1.5
11						
12 Trainer	**Total Overtime**					
13 DD	=AGGREGATE(9,5,B4,D4,F4					
14 SN	AGGREGATE(function_num, options, **array**, [k])					
15 MJ	AGGREGATE(function_num, options, **ref1**, ref2, [ref3], ...)					
16 JJ						
17 CF						

Figure 12.20 – Array argument

8. Lastly, press *Enter* to see the result in cell B13. Copy the result to the rest of the column to see the result of total overtime for each trainer.

> **Important Note**
>
> If we hide row 6, the **Total Overtime** value for **MJ** will be 0 as this is not included as per the options set as part of the function arguments. If we used just the basic SUM function to add up the overtime values for each of the trainers and then hide row 6, the formula result would remain unchanged.

9. This function is a powerful function and something to consider as an alternative when using basic functions such as SUM and AVERAGE.

Just to mention here that the SUBTOTAL function is also part of the **Math & Trig** functions. The syntax is like that of the AGGREGATE function.

The AGGREGATE function is the most updated function with more option arguments than its predecessor, SUBTOTAL. The main difference between these functions is that with SUBTOTAL, we can choose to include or exclude manually hidden rows.

The next section concentrates on an engineering function. Although not directly part of the **Math & Trig** library, it is relevant and worth mentioning. Let's learn a little about this now.

Converting measurements with CONVERT

The CONVERT function is brilliant when needing to convert numbers to a different measurement system—for instance, **pounds (lb)** into **kilograms (kg)** or **feet (ft)** into **meters (m)**. This function is great to know as it applies to many aspects of life.

The CONVERT function only has three arguments, as presented here:

Number	This is the number you wish to convert.
from_unit	This is the current unit that the number is displayed in,
to_unit	This is the result that you wish to obtain.

Table 12.3 – CONVERT function syntax

If you do not locate the measurement in the drop-down list provided, when working through the function arguments, you will need to manually modify the unit accordingly to correct it. This is normally done when we are dealing with metric units.

Let's look at an example, as follows:

1. Open the `Convert.xlsx` workbook.

2. On the first worksheet, we have a **Miles** column and a **KM** column next to it. We would like to work out the **kilometer (km)** value for each **Miles** column entry.

3. Click onto cell B5.

4. Let's start to construct the formula as follows: `=CONVERT(`.

5. Click on cell A5 to collect the first value to convert.

6. Press the *comma* key on the keyboard to add it and to move to the next argument.

7. The `from_unit` argument drop-down list is now displaying on your screen. Select a unit of measurement that describes the number you are converting. Scroll down and select `"mi"` from the list, as illustrated in the following screenshot:

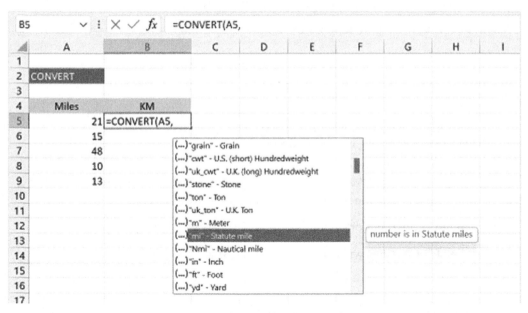

Figure 12.21 – "mi" selected as the second argument

8. Press a *comma* to move to the next argument.

9. As we scroll down the list, we do not see a "km" code in the list. This is where we need to do a little thinking about how a km is constructed. One km is equal to 1,000 m. In this case, we will need to double-click on "m" as this represents m in the list. Once this is selected, add k in front of m to force it to read "km".

10. Press *Enter* on the keyboard to see the result of the formula, then drag it down to the rest of the cells to fill in the results. The following screenshot illustrates this:

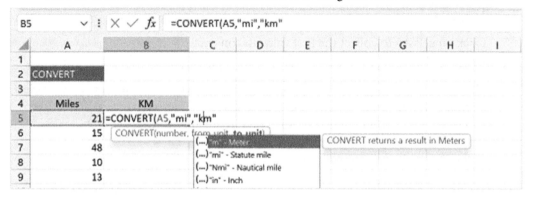

Figure 12.22 – "m" argument

> **Note**
>
> Similarly, with kg, we would need to select the "g" option, then change that so that it reads kg as 1 kg is 1,000 **grams** (**g**).

As you work with the CONVERT function more often, you will find the process quicker as you become familiar with amending units to achieve the desired result.

There are many more functions in the Maths & Trig category library for you to explore.

The next couple of sections will concentrate on the **Statistical** category.

Exploring statistical functions

In *Chapter 9, New Features, Filters, and Cleaning Data*, of this book, we learned about using the COUNTIFS statistical function. A list of statistical functions can be found in the Excel library. Click the **Formulas** tab, then click on **More Functions | Statistical** to see all types available, as illustrated in the following screenshot:

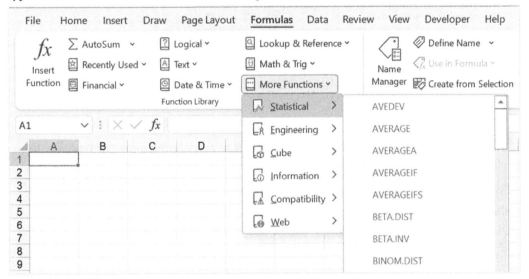

Figure 12.23 – Statistical functions

We will now learn about a few more statistical functions.

In the next section, we will discuss the MEDIAN function.

Finding the middle ground

The MEDIAN function is used to locate the average of the two middle numbers in a range of cells. MEDIAN is like the 19 function argument options listed in a previous function in the Maths & Trig section—namely, AGGREGATE:

1. Open the Training Schedule.xlsx workbook. Make sure you are on the **Median** worksheet.

2. Click into cell C2, then type the following formula: =MEDIAN(.

3. Select the range A2:A8 to find the average of the two middle values in the range, as illustrated in the following screenshot:

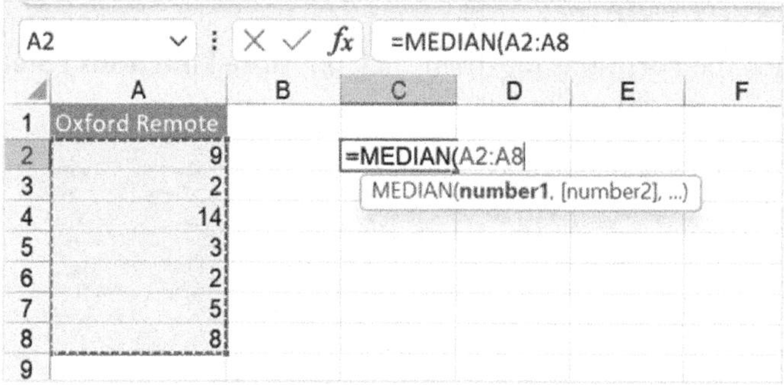

Figure 12.24 – MEDIAN syntax

4. Press *Enter* to see the result. In this case, the answer should be *5*. The best way to see if this is calculating correctly would be to sort the range.

In the next section, we will learn about the COUNTBLANK function. In the previous edition of this book, we introduced COUNT functions, and in earlier chapters in this edition of the book, we concentrated on statistical functions such as COUNT, COUNTIF, SUMIF, and SUMIFS.

Counting empty cells

In this function, the COUNTBLANK function only counts blank or empty cells in a range. The syntax is simple to construct. Let's work out which companies do not have any discounts applied next. Proceed as follows:

1. Open the SSGPet.xlsx workbook.

2. On **Sheet1**, there is a list of discounts in column **N**. Click into P2 to construct the formula.

3. Type =COUNTBLANK (then select the range N2:N124, as illustrated in the following screenshot:

	L	M	N	O	P	Q	R
	Service	**Amount Owing**	**Discount**		=COUNTBLANK(N2:N124		
	Medicine	727.24	10%		COUNTBLANK(**range**)		
	Follow Up Consult	998.33	25%				
	Pet Foods	108.05	5%				
	Pet Winter Wear	254.6	12%				
	Ear Spray	117.34	5%				
	Leads and Jackets	822.9	10%				
	Blankets and Foot Mat	850.75	25%				
	Shear and Nail Clip	26.57	40%				
	Teeth and Gums	788.04	5%				

Figure 12.25 – COUNTBLANK function

4.   Press *Enter* to see the result. 10 companies do not have discounts applied.

The next section will concentrate on the AVERAGEIF function. This function locates the arithmetic mean (the average) for a range specified by a condition or criteria.

Averaging using one condition

The AVERAGEIF function returns the arithmetic mean (average) of all cells in a range that meet a condition or criteria. In layman's terms, it calculates the average of cells meeting one criterion. Use the AVERAGEIFS function if you wish to calculate the average of cells meeting multiple criteria.

The syntax of the AVERAGEIF functions is described in more detail here:

range	This field must be filled in and needs to consist of one or more cells to average. If the range contains true or false, it will ignore these cells in the range when calculating. A range can contain numbers, names, arrays, and references containing numbers. Where are you looking for your criteria? In our example, we will be selecting the Winery range as this is where our criteria are located.
criteria	A required field. What is the criterion we are looking for in the range we specified in the first argument? The criterion in our example is Fortesque Vino.
average_range	If the criteria are met (if the criteria are located in the range specified), what do we want to return the average of? In our example, we will get the average of the Revenue range.

Table 12.4 – Syntax and explanation

Let's look at an example of the AVERAGEIF function to work out the average revenue for a particular winery. Proceed as follows:

1. To follow along, open the WinerySales.xlsx workbook.

2. This workbook consists of sales data for different wineries. Let's build the function.

3. Click into cell M4, as this is where we will build our calculation.

4. Start constructing the formula, as follows: =AVERAGEIF(.

5. For the first argument, select the range in which the criteria can be located. In the case of our example, we need to select the **Winery** range B2:B23. Press the *comma* key to move to the next argument.

6. Adding criteria is the next argument. We can use one of two methods to collect the winery name—either type the name directly into the criteria argument using *inverted commas* on either side of the winery name (that is, **"Fortesque Vino"**) or use a cell reference on the worksheet to collect the relevant winery criterion. The latter option is useful should you want to change the criterion at any time to make the formula more dynamic. For this example, we will use cell M2 to collect the winery name, **Fortesque Vino**.

7. The last argument is the range you wish to average should the criteria be successful. In this case, we will average the **Revenue** range, J2:J23.

8. Press *Enter* on the keyboard to see the result, which is displayed in the following screenshot:

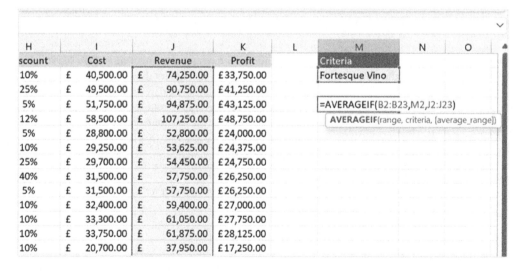

Figure 12.26 – AVERAGEIF function

9. Should you wish to see the average for any of the other wineries, simply type the company name into cell M2. Let's see what the average is for **Matts Winery**. Replace the text **Fortesque Vino** with **Matts Winery**, then press *Enter* on the keyboard.

10. Experiment with different scenarios using **wildcard characters** in the criteria argument. If we are interested in the average revenue for all wineries except **Prominent Wines**, we would build the formula using the *not equal to* sign, <>, as follows: =AVERAGEIF(B2:B23,"<>Prominent Wines",J2:J23).

When a situation arises where you want to include more than one single criterion as an argument, you can make use of the AVERAGEIFS function.

Averaging using more than one condition

The main difference between AVERAGEIF and AVERAGEIFS is noted here:

*   The AVERAGEIF function averages the number of cells within a range that meet a single condition you specify.

*   The AVERAGEIFS function counts the number of cells by evaluating different criteria in the same or different ranges.

In this example, we will look for the average profit for discounts applied over 25%, as well as the cases sold being equal to or greater than 250. Proceed as follows:

1. Using the same workbook as for the *Averaging using one condition* section, click into cell M8. We will build our function here.

2. For this example, we will use the **Insert Function** tool to help build our formula. The **Insert Function** tool is the **fx** button located to the left of the formula bar. Click the **fx** button to populate the **Function Arguments** dialog box.

3. The first part of the function syntax is to provide the Average_range value. Click into this area, then select the range K2:K23 on the worksheet. This range is the *profit* range as we will be finding the average profit according to a certain criterion.

4. Click into the Criteria_range1 area, then select the range G2:G23, then specify the "=250" Criteria1 detail to locate instances of cases sold greater than or equal to 250.

5. Finally, enter the second criteria by selecting the range H2:H23, after clicking into the Criteria_range2 area. Specify the Criteria2 detail "`>25%`" to locate discounts greater than 25%. The process is illustrated in the following screenshot:

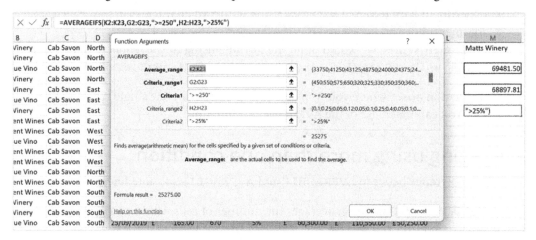

Figure 12.27 – AVERAGEIFS using the Function Arguments dialog box

6. The dialog box will report if there are any errors found. You will see a **Formula result** value at the bottom left of the dialog box. Click on the **OK** button to confirm and see the result on the worksheet.

7. Using the dialog box for more complex calculations aids you, as you can see the relevant worksheet data presented to the right of each selected range from the workbook.

We hope that we have covered enough ground here for you to experiment with different criteria to suit your specific requirements.

Summary

You now have the skills to work with Math & Trig and Statistical functions using Excel 2021. You have built on prior knowledge by learning valuable functions, such as being able to generate random numbers using RANDBETWEEN and RAND functions. In addition, you went through examples of working with PRODUCT functions and explored the SUMPRODUCT, MROUND, FLOOR, TRUNC, AGGREGATE, and CONVERT functions.

We also investigated the MEDIAN, COUNTBLANK, and AVERAGEIFS statistical functions in this chapter, from which you can experiment and apply to existing or new scenarios when working with workbook data.

This next chapter will take you through Outlook 2021 enhancements, where we will explore and configure objects such as mail, contacts, tasks, notes, and journals. You will set some advanced and language options in the interface and learn how to manipulate item tags and arrange the content pane.

In addition, we will apply some search and filter tools, and print Outlook items. You will learn best practices for sending email messages, as well as configure send and delivery options to improve productivity in the Outlook application. You will also learn to professionally format item content and attach content to an email.

Part 4:
Outlook 2021 and Useful Communication Tools

This part of the book will concentrate on Outlook 2021, providing an overview to update you on the new features of the Outlook 2021 environment. In addition, this part will introduce you to all the significant features to communicate and collaborate using online tools such as Microsoft Teams and Zoom. We will look at how to set up meetings within the Outlook 2021 environment, as well as how to join and manage meetings. You will learn about the different methods to present content using the Share icon within Teams and Zoom. There is also a topic on exploring the best method to work with meeting notes and how to present using PowerPoint Live.

In addition, we will discover the Teams app, pointing out useful features and top tips, and we will learn how to create and manage channels. A number of new tools will be introduced here, such as sharing emails directly to a Teams channel and enabling Teams meeting options. Brilliant tools such as OneNote, Tasks by Planner, approvals, and bookings are investigated, as well as learning how to collaborate in real time.

This part contains the following chapters:

13
Creating and Attaching Item Content

This chapter will take you through Outlook 2021 enhancements, where we will explore and configure objects such as mail, contacts, tasks, notes, and journals. You will set some advanced options and language options in the interface and learn how to manipulate item tags and arrange the content pane.

In addition, we will apply some search and filter tools and print Outlook items. You will learn best practices for sending email messages, as well as configure send and delivery options to improve productivity in the Outlook application. You will also learn to professionally format item content and attach content to an email.

The following topics are covered in this chapter:

- Investigating the Outlook environment
- Previewing Outlook items
- Manipulating Outlook program options
- Manipulating item tags

- Working with views, filtering, and printing

- Creating and sending email messages

- Creating and managing Quick Steps

- Attaching item content

Technical requirements

Although in our previous book, *Learn Microsoft Office 2019*, the basics of the email application were covered, we do not need any prior knowledge of this to learn how to use Outlook 2021 as a new user. Any examples used in this chapter are accessible from GitHub at `https://github.com/PacktPublishing/Learn-Microsoft-Office-2021-Second-Edition`.

Investigating the Outlook environment

You will take a tour around the Outlook 2021 interface and explore elements that are applicable to Outlook, such as the **Focused** inbox and the **To-Do Bar**, and learn how to view Outlook items. In the previous chapters of this book, we have already familiarized you with the generic interface options applicable to all of the Office 2021 applications.

Note that it depends on the subscription and platform of Outlook you are running on your system as to which features are visible or are deployed to the software. The interface icons and features depend greatly on whether you have Office 2021 desktop, Office 365, or Office for the web installed. Although we are concentrating on the desktop version of Office 2021 in these chapters, we will highlight important features from the other platforms.

In this chapter, you will also learn program options for all objects in the Outlook 2021 interface such as **Mail**, **Calendar**, **Tasks**, **Notes**, advanced options, and language options. We will cover the creating, formatting, and attaching of content to email messages, as well as how to set up **Quick Steps** to automate repetitive Outlook tasks. We will cover features such as **Instant Search**, **Translator**, and **Ink** functions, and touch on media features too.

Outlook is a better choice than web-based email for business- or work-related emails, tasks, calendars, and contacts, as you will have considerably more functionality and access to a productivity workflow. Multiple email accounts can be configured within Outlook, such as Gmail, Yahoo, and many more mail providers.

In addition, the ability to include **Teams** and **Zoom** meeting apps within the Outlook calendar offers a seamless approach to all your remote business needs. These features will be discussed in the Calendar chapters of this book.

The Outlook 2021 interface is upgraded with a slick design, and buttons are crisper and clearer than the Office 2019 interface.

Outlook 2021 has a choice between a **Simplified Ribbon** and a **Classic Ribbon**. The Simplified Ribbon is the default. To change the ribbon so that it displays more buttons and tabs, right-click over the existing ribbon area, then select the relevant option from the drop-down list, as illustrated in the following screenshot:

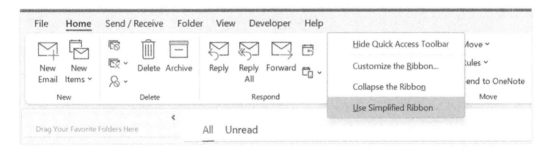

Figure 13.1 – Changing the ribbon from the Classic Ribbon to Simplified Ribbon

Accessing the Mini toolbar

The **Mini toolbar** is a formatting toolbar that pops up above selected text when editing an email message. It is automatically activated by double-clicking on a word, or after selecting a sentence or paragraph. If you move the mouse pointer away from a selected area of a message or click away from the selected text, the Mini toolbar will disappear. The Mini toolbar can be seen in the following screenshot, but is also evident in other Office applications:

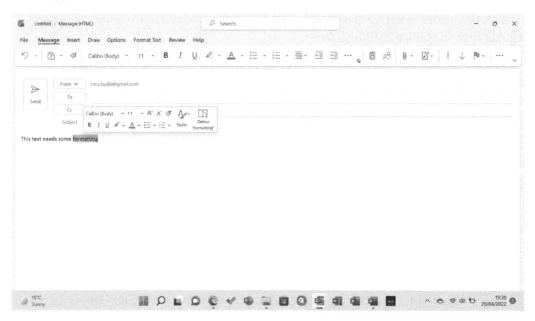

Figure 13.2 – Mini toolbar

This toolbar is an efficient way of changing text attributes, instead of moving the mouse pointer to the top of the Outlook screen to access the relevant format group. The toolbar also includes a **Define** button that, when clicked on, opens the *Search* pane to the right of the document window offering *Web*, *Media*, and *Help* features for the selected text.

Using the To-Do Bar

The **To-Do Bar** is formed of separate peek windows that can be populated to the right of the Outlook screen. The **To-Do Bar** can display the calendar, tasks, and people either all at the same time or separately. Note that when you add items from the **To-Do Bar** options, they will appear in order of selection to the right of the Outlook environment.

Only contacts you have marked as favorites will appear in the **Favorites** peek. Right-click on an existing email address to mark a contact as a favorite. The areas defined to the right of the Outlook screen are called **peeks**. To the right of each peek added to the Outlook environment, you will see a **Remove the peek** icon, as illustrated in the following screenshot:

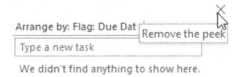

Figure 13.3 – Peeks appear to the right of the Outlook window

Change the **To-Do Bar** display properties by locating the **Layout** option on the **View** tab. Click the **To-Do Bar** icon to add or remove options. Use the **To-Do Bar** to create new tasks quickly by adding task details directly into the peek shown to the right of the Outlook environment, as illustrated in the following screenshot:

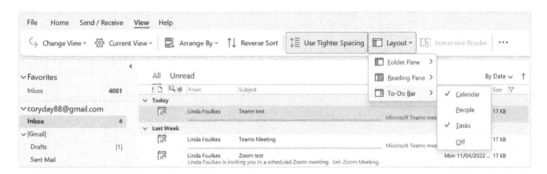

Figure 13.4 – To-Do Bar

You will also be able to view any emails that have been marked for action (flagged) in your mailbox on the **To-Do Bar**.

Outlook stores each type of information it manages in separate Outlook folders. A single piece of information is known as an **item**. An email message would be an item stored in the **Inbox** folder, and a single appointment would be an item stored in the calendar, and so on. It is also possible to create additional folders to store items.

Using the Message pane to display folder items

To view a folder, you need to click on the folder name to open it, after which Outlook displays the folder items in the Message pane of the Outlook window. Once the Message pane lists the contents of the current folder, the ribbon will change to reflect the options available to manage the information in the current folder. For instance, if I select the **Calendar** folder at the bottom left of the window, the **Home** tab will display calendar icons along with the ribbon, and so on.

The Navigation Pane

The Navigation Pane exists to the left of the Outlook screen. This allows you to select default folders in Outlook (**Inbox, Sent Items, Drafts**, and so forth). It is possible to drag an existing folder—for example, the **Inbox**—to the **Favorites** section of the Navigation Pane to enable quick access to the **Inbox** or other mail folders, as illustrated in the following screenshot:

Figure 13.5 – Dragging a folder to Favorites

Let's learn about the Peek feature in the next section.

The Peek bar

At the bottom of the Navigation Pane, you will find the **Peek bar** with default icons (**Mail, Calendar, Contacts, Tasks,** and an ellipsis). You are able to change the options on the Peek bar by visiting the ellipsis (three dots) to the right of it, after which a shortcut menu will open, allowing access to **Notes, Folders, Shortcuts,** and **Navigation Options…**, as illustrated in the following screenshot:

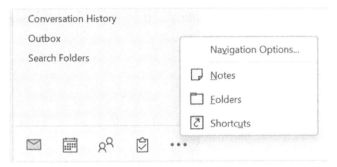

Figure 13.6 – Peek bar showing the ellipsis options

This bar is named Peek as it allows the user to hover over the icons on the bar to display a peek preview of an item. Users are able to create shortcuts to open favorite and most frequently used folders quickly.

Previewing Outlook items

You are able to set the number of lines to view per email message in the Message pane. This allows you to view the contents of an Outlook item without opening the entire item, by presenting the user with a view of the first few lines of a message on the main Outlook screen. Another way to view items is to set the properties of the **Reading Pane**, which shows the contents of an email without having to change the view with the mouse to open the entire message.

Previewing emails in the Message pane

Click on the **View** tab, and then locate the **Current View | Message Preview** icon. Select the drop-down list arrow and choose the desired number of lines to view per email message. You will receive a pop-up notification, asking whether you would like to change the preview setting for all mailboxes or just the current folder. Alternatively, turn off the preview altogether by selecting **Off** from **Message Preview**. When **Message Preview** is set to **Off**, then the text that is displayed in the **Subject** area will reflect the message subject only.

The default preview is set to display **1 Line** of text per email received, as illustrated in the following screenshot:

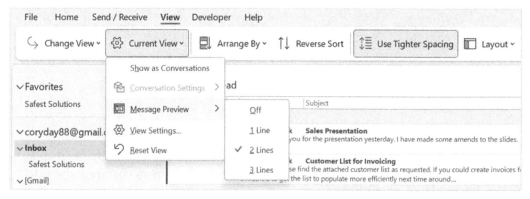

Figure 13.7 – Message Preview options

Using the Reading Pane

The **Reading Pane** allows the user to view the contents of an email message quickly without actually double-clicking on the email to open it. When set, you can use the down arrow on the keyboard (or click on each email message) to move from one email to another in the **Message Pane**, and each mail message will display its contents in the **Reading Pane**.

Options to position the **Reading Pane** to the right or bottom of the Outlook screen are available, or, alternatively, choose to turn it off completely. To use the **Reading Pane**, follow these steps:

1. Click on the **View** tab. Select the **Reading Pane** icon from the **Layout** option.

2. Choose where you would like the **Reading Pane** positioned on the Outlook screen (**Right** or **Bottom**), or click on the **Off** icon should you wish to not display it, as illustrated in the following screenshot:

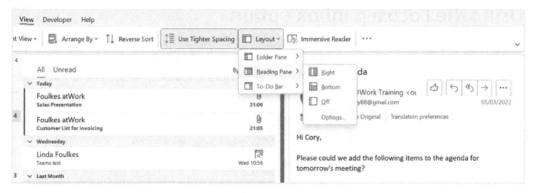

Figure 13.8 – Viewing the contents of an email using the Reading Pane

3. Click on the **Options...** icon to display a dialog box, where more changes to the **Reading Pane** are possible.

Manipulating Outlook program options

Outlook is a powerful information management application that allows you to do the following:

1. Use email (a mailbox) for communication

2. Use the calendar for time management and online meetings

3. Manage tasks, workload, employees, and projects

4. Put notes as reminders to yourself

5. Organize and track contacts and people you deal with every day by phone, email, distribution lists, or just reaching out

6. Create a timeline of actions for particular contacts using the journal

Once the Outlook installation is complete, the setup program will look for the user's profile (a group of settings that define the setup of Outlook for a specific user). The transport application called **Exchange** allows the flow of information and needs installing in order to use the email feature of Outlook.

Using the Focused inbox option

The **Focused** inbox is available for Office 365, Office, and Exchange accounts. It allows you to view the most important emails in a separate view. The **Inbox** is separated into two tabs, one for the **Focused** items and one for **Other** items, as illustrated in the following screenshot:

Figure 13.9 – Focused Inbox on Office 365

The **Focused** tab is set as the default. Should you wish to alter these settings, visit the **Settings** button on the ribbon. Scroll down and click the button to deactivate the **Focused** inbox setting.

Investigating mail options

Mail options in Outlook have the greatest range of settings in the program. There are so many ways to configure message options using this dialog box. As you work through the chapters on Outlook 2021, we will cover items from this dialog box. When composing email messages, the body of the email uses a Word 2021-based editor. This gives you a huge amount of functionality from the Office 2021 Microsoft Word program. You can set the importance of a message, set delivery receipt options, and set expiry dates for messages. Some of the settings can be seen in the following screenshot:

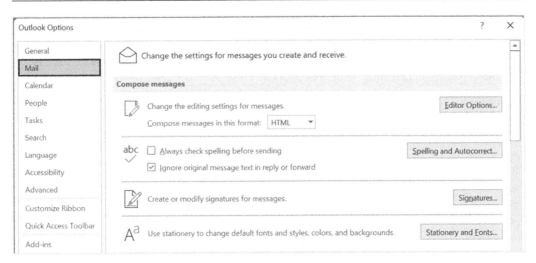

Figure 13.10 – Outlook Options dialog box

To access interface options, click on the **File** tab, then select **Options** from the drop-down menu provided. Select a category on the left of the dialog box—namely, the **Mail**, **Calendar**, **Tasks**, and **Advanced** options, which are all listed in the **Outlook Options** dialog box in separate categories.

Another method to access options for all items within Outlook is to right-click on an item on the Peek bar, located at the bottom of the Navigation Pane. Choose **Options...** from the shortcut list to launch the **Outlook Options** dialog box, as illustrated in the following screenshot:

Figure 13.11 – Options... button on the Peek bar

The following table shows a list of some of the **Options...** categories and their descriptions:

Calendar options	This category in the dialog box allows the setting up of start and end times for working hours and calendar reminders, colors, and resource scheduling.
Tasks options	Options relating to setting and assigning tasks to others using Outlook are located in the Tasks menu in the Outlook Options dialog box. Task colors and reminder settings are of importance here.
Advanced options	Advanced options in the Outlook Options dialog box include settings for reminders and sounds, and for customizing different parts of the Outlook environment (screen layout). It is possible to add additional languages to edit documents in Outlook. To change language settings, visit the Language menu in the Outlook Options dialog box.

Table 13.1 – Example of Outlook options and their descriptions

In the next section, we will take a look at email notifications and how to manage the mailbox.

Turning off email notifications

When managing our mail and our working environment, we may (or may not) want email notifications to constantly distract us, especially if we have an extremely busy mailbox. In addition, when meeting with clients remotely in a Teams meeting, email notifications—either through sound or banners—when sharing screens could be sensitive in their nature.

To customize such notifications, we would need to visit the **Settings** option on our Windows environment. If you are not sure where to locate such settings, simply search for **Settings** using the magnifying glass on your Windows taskbar. In the screenshot that follows, you will notice that Outlook is set to display **Banners, Sounds**. Click the slider to change the option to **Off**, or customize settings individually by clicking on the arrow to the right of the button:

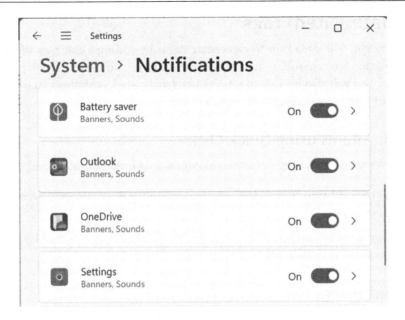

Figure 13.12 – Outlook notification settings on Windows 11

It is also possible to customize these settings with the Outlook application by navigating to **File | Options | Mail | Message arrival**.

Another method to alleviate emails coming through when you are trying to get other tasks completed during the day would be to turn your Outlook 2021 mail to **Offline,** just while you attend to your other tasks—no distractions. Click on the **Send / Receive** tab and then select **Work Offline**, as illustrated in the following screenshot:

Figure 13.13 – Work Offline feature

Let's take a look at how we would categorize mail items using color coding in the next section.

Manipulating item tags

In this section, you will learn how to categorize items by adding a color, as well as go through the options to rename, assign categories to items, and remove a category from an Outlook item. You will also be able to set a Quick Click, work with flags, mark items as read or unread, and view message properties.

Categorizing items using Quick Click

To understand what categorizing items means, you would need to understand the following:

- **What is meant by an item?**: An item is an email message, a task, a calendar entry, a contact, or a note.

- **What is meant by categorizing?**: Categories are keywords assigned by a color that help you keep track of items.

Categorizing using color

Categorizing items allows you to filter, sort, and group with ease according to categories. The most efficient method to add a category color to an email item would be to do the following:

1. Click into the outlined square block placeholder to the left of the **Categories** column for an email in the mailbox, as illustrated in the following screenshot:

Figure 13.14 – Inbox showing the Red Category applied to an email

2. Double-click to open the email in order to change the category color or to amend the category name.

3. Right-click on the **Red Category** name, then choose a different category to assign to the email. To clear the existing category, click on **Clear "Red Category"** from the drop-down list, as illustrated in the following screenshot:

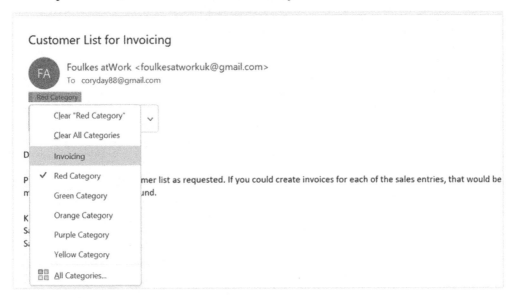

Figure 13.15 – Assigning new categories to an email

4. To amend category names and colors, click on the **All Categories…** option.

5. Click on the **New…** button to create a brand-new category and color, or select an existing category on the left and click the **Rename** button on the right to change the name of the category.

6. To change a category's color, select the category to amend, then visit the drop-down list under the **Color:** heading and select a new color, as illustrated in the following screenshot:

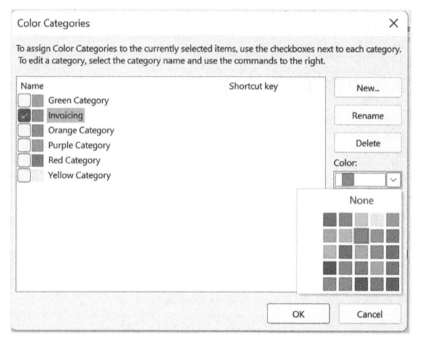

Figure 13.16 – Color Categories dialog box

7. Click on the **OK** button to confirm.

8. Note that we can assign shortcut keys to categories. This makes it easier to add a category to an email message using the shortcut keys on the keyboard. Use the **Shortcut Key:** drop-down list to assign a shortcut key to a selected category. Once assigned, simply select an email, then press the associated keyboard shortcut to assign a category. Be careful with this option, though. If you have keyboard shortcuts already assigned with the same keystrokes, or existing program shortcuts, they will be replaced. The process is illustrated in the following screenshot:

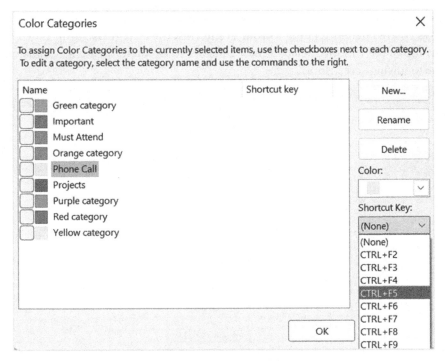

Figure 13.17 – Category shortcut key

Category names can be changed to suit your working environment and the nature of the emails you deal with daily. Here's how you can do this:

1. Click on **OK** to return to the email. Note that the email message now has a category color assigned in the message header section.

2. You can assign more than one category to one email message. Remember to click on a category to remove it from the email message if you decide to change to a different category color.

3.   Color categories can also be applied to calendar events in Outlook web. Once you have entered details relating to your event, click the **Categorise** drop-down list at the top of the window. Select a color category to assign to the item, as illustrated in the following screenshot:

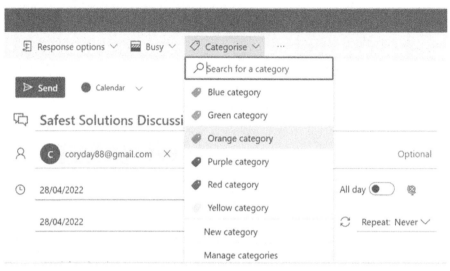

Figure 13.18 – Assigning categories to calendar appointments

4.   By adding calendar category colors this way, we can focus on important—or urgent—must-attend events in our calendar.

Searching for specific categories

We can use the new **Instant Search** feature to locate items by category. This is a great tool to use to locate items in your mailbox or commands you regularly use. Here's how to start using this new feature:

1.   At the top of the Outlook screen, in the title bar, click into the **Instant Search** field.

2.   Notice that the **Search** tab automatically appears on the ribbon.

3.   Click on the **Search** tab.

4.   Locate the **Categorized** drop-down list, then select a category to search by, as illustrated in the following screenshot:

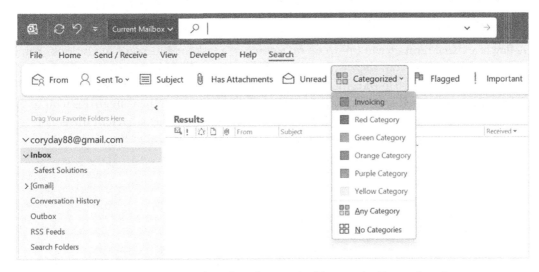

Figure 13.19 – Drop-down list of categorized items using Instant Search

5. All mail assigned with the category is displayed as a search result.

6. Notice in the following screenshot that the **Instant Search** field now contains code for the search you performed. This is stored in the drop-down list so that when you click into the **Instant Search** field again, it will remember the search command for you:

Figure 13.20 – Instant Search field displaying code

7. Click on the **Close Search** button along the ribbon to exit the search results and return to your mailbox.

Setting flags

A **flag** is a visual reminder to follow up on a contact, a task, or a message in Outlook. You are able to customize your flags with specific dates. Once a flag is assigned, it appears in the email view, the **To-Do Bar**, the **Daily Calendar Task List**, and the **Tasks View**. The default flag color is red and, when assigned, it will appear next to the **Categories** icon to the right of the email message. In the following screenshot, the flag is seen in the email and in the task list (located to the right of the screen positioned under the calendar):

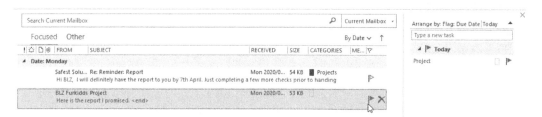

Figure 13.21 – Red flag assigned to an email and in the task list

If you assign a flag to an email message that must follow up on a task on the same day, then the time that the reminder will pop up on your screen will depend on the workday default settings in Outlook.

Consult the Outlook **Help** feature for an explanation of how default dates work for follow-ups.

Click on the **Help** tab, then select **Help** again, after which the **Help** pane will open to the right of the Outlook window. Type the following into the search area provided: how do dates work for follow ups. Press the *Enter* key on the keyboard to display information on follow-up default reminder settings.

In the next section, we will look at options to add flags to messages and contacts.

Adding a flag to a message and contact

To add a flag to a message and contact, proceed as follows:

1. To the right of an email message (in the Message pane), you will notice little white flag outlines. Click on the flag to add a reminder to the message for a follow-up.

2. By default, the flag is assigned for **Today** and will remind you an hour before the end of the working day (as set in Outlook). The flag turns red once assigned.

3. To add a flag to a contact, open the **Contacts** pane located at the bottom left-hand corner of the Outlook window.

4. Click to select a contact, as illustrated in the following screenshot:

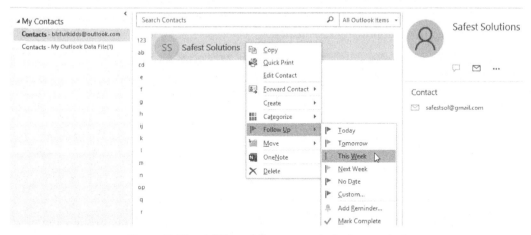

Figure 13.22 – Adding a follow-up reminder to a contact

5. Right-click on the contact to add a follow-up reminder using the **Follow Up** option.

Marking mail items as read/unread

At times, you may read an email, or click on it to open it, and would like to refer to it later. Until you refer to it again, you might want it to appear in your **Inbox** as unread. This option gives the user information at a glance, as new email messages are always highlighted in bold text. Here's how we do this:

1. Click on a message you wish to mark as unread. Locate the **Tags** group on the **Home** tab. Click on the **Unread/Read** icon.

2. This icon is a toggle icon; press once for unread and once again for read.

> **Note**
> Right-clicking on a message to mark it as unread is another way to achieve this.

Checking for new messages

To check for new messages, proceed as follows:

1. Click on the **Send/Receive All Folders** icon on the Quick Access Toolbar, located in the very top-left corner of the Outlook environment, to check for new mail, as illustrated in the following screenshot:

Figure 13.23 – Send/Receive All Folders icon

2. You can also use the *F9* function key to refresh the **Inbox** to bring through any new messages. In the following topic, we will learn how to work with content views, as well as the filtering and printing of Outlook items.

The next topic will cover content on the content page—such as changing the view type—and we will also take a look at the **Reminders Window**.

Working with views, filtering, and printing

Here, you will become confident in using built-in search folders, and search and filter facilities. In addition, you will learn to print attachments, calendars, multiple messages, contact records, tasks, and notes.

Changing the view type

A few main built-in views are located within the **View** tab that can be managed or saved as a new view in order to customize the layout of your Outlook application. As a default, you may see **IMAP Message**, **Hide Messages**, **Group Messages**, and **Preview**. Here's how you can change the view type:

1. To change the current view, click on the **View** tab and select **Change View**, as illustrated in the following screenshot:

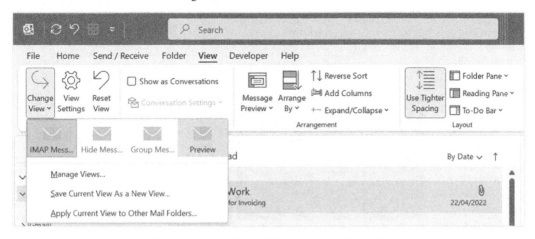

Figure 13.24 – Change View option in Outlook

2. From the drop-down list, select a view to see the change on the screen. Each view has a certain arrangement of fields that can be modified using the **Manage Views…** icon. Explore this option to find the view that works best for you. The **View Settings** icon will drive the views you see listed in the **Change View** area, as you are able to customize what you see as columns, filters, and sorts in your mail view. Use **Other Settings…**, for example, to customize the column and row font size of email messages, or the message preview font too.

Using the Focused Inbox option

If you are using an Exchange Server mailbox or an email that flows through a Microsoft account, you will see the additional **Focused Inbox** option in Outlook. This allows you to view the most important emails in a separate view. The **Inbox** is separated into two tabs, one for **Focused** items and one for **Other** items, as illustrated in the following screenshot:

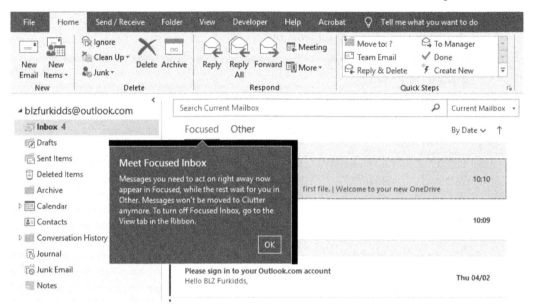

Figure 13.25 – Focused Inbox

Show Focused Inbox is set as the default, but you can toggle the **Show Focused Inbox** icon off and on to suit your requirements.

To move important messages into **Focused Inbox**, simply right-click on the message you would like to move from the **Other** folder, then choose the **Move to Focused** option, as illustrated in the following screenshot:

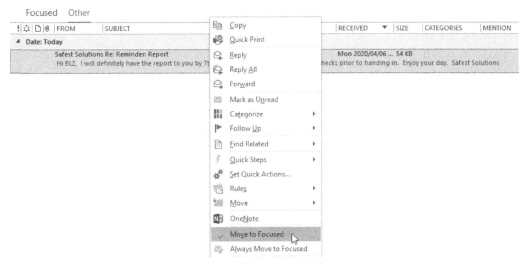

Figure 13.26 – Moving items to Focused Inbox

3.   The message is moved to **Focused Inbox**.

Using the Reminders Window

The **Reminders Window** opens (pops up on screen) while you are working to remind yourself of important meetings and/or tasks you need to attend to. The **Reminders Window** can be manually opened by visiting the **View** tab and clicking on the **Reminders Window**, located under the **Window** group. These reminders are set on an item when creating a reminder flag for an item by right-clicking on an item. The **Reminders Window** button is located to the right of the **View** tab ribbon.

Once the **Reminders Window** pops up on your screen, you can open an item to view its content, snooze the item for a further selected time period, or dismiss the reminder, as illustrated in the following screenshot:

Figure 13.27 – Reminders Window

> **Note**
> Reminders are also displayed along the Outlook Status Bar.

We will now look at ways to locate and filter for Outlook content in the next section.

Applying search and filter tools

To quickly find items in Outlook, you can use the **Instant Search** facility, which is a built-in search. This facility is available at the top of the Outlook environment along the Title Bar. We can search our *current mailbox, current folder, subfolders*, or on every one of our *Outlook items*. Here's how to do this:

1. Click on a folder in the Navigation Pane in which to search—for instance, **Mail**, **Calendar**, **Tasks**, or **People**. In the **Instant Search** text area, enter the information you are looking for. Notice that there is a drop-down list to the right offering customization of search criteria. To the left of the **Instant Search** text area, there is a further dropdown where you can specify items to search. The **Instant Search** textbox can be seen in the following screenshot:

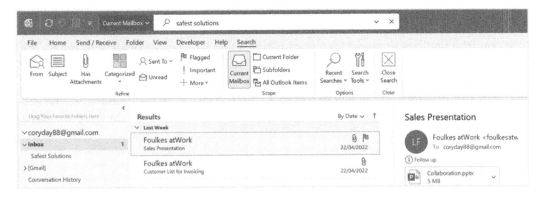

Figure 13.28 – Instant Search for "safest solutions" in Current Mailbox

2. Once you have entered the search term—for example, `safest solutions`, as per the previous screenshot—press *Enter* to start your search.

3. The search results are highlighted in yellow in the Message pane. Notice that the ribbon has changed to reflect options to refine the search. The **Search** tab is now visible on the ribbon. Experiment with these options.

4. The **Recent Searches** icon along the ribbon allows you to reuse a previous search. The **Search Tools** icon must also not be ignored as you will be able, for instance, to have located items displayed in a color other than yellow. Note that you will need to restart Outlook if you change these options for them to take effect. The **Recent Searches** icon can be seen in the following screenshot:

Figure 13.29 – Recent Searches, Search Tools, and the Close Search button

5. To clear a search, click on the **X** sign located on the right side of the **Instant Search** box or click on **Close Search** at the right of the ribbon.

Printing Outlook items

You can print Outlook items such as attachments, calendars, tasks, contacts, or notes. The procedure for each option is very similar to choosing the **Print** facility within the relevant icon on the **Backstage** view. When working through this topic, please keep in mind that we only print when it is absolutely necessary to do so. Most work environments today are practicing paperless offices, so this feature is available, but it's not something we would not normally do.

Printing attachments

To print an attachment, proceed as follows:

1. Open the email containing the attachment, then click on the drop-down arrow to the right of the attachment. In the case of this example, we have an Excel document as an attachment. Notice the **Attachments** tab at the top of the window is now evident with a host of options.

2. Choose **Quick Print** from the shortcut menu, after which you will receive a trust notification warning, highlighting the importance of opening only trustworthy attachments. Click on **OK** to print the document to the default printer. If you prefer to save the attachment first to the computer and then print using the relevant application options, choose **Save As** from the drop-down list instead, or upload the file to an online storage facility such as OneDrive, as illustrated in the following screenshot:

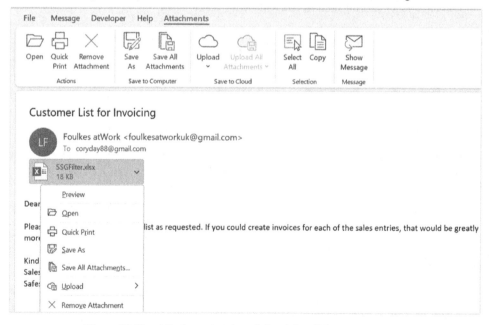

Figure 13.30 – Attachments tab and the right-click menu options

3. Please note that this option will use the current default printer as well as the default options, and will send the attachment straight to the printer without previewing the document or allowing you to set printing preferences.

Printing calendars

To print calendars, proceed as follows:

1. Click on the **Calendar** icon located at the bottom of the Navigation Pane. Click on the **File** tab to access the **Backstage** view.

2. Choose the **Print** icon from the menu. From the **Backstage** view, select a style for the **Calendar** printout.

3. To access more options, click on the **Print Options** button, where you can customize the **Print style** to edit a particular print style if you would like to customize it and keep the changes for the next time the calendar is printed using the same style.

Printing tasks, notes, and contacts

Click on the relevant task, note, or contact icon on the Navigation Pane to open the item. Select items using the *Ctrl + click* method. Click on **File | Print** from the menu. In **Preview**, select multiple pages so that you can see all tasks in the **Preview** pane. Set **Print Options**, and print as usual.

You will discover more about each one of the preceding items in the chapters that follow.

Creating and sending email messages

In this section, you will learn how to specify a message theme, and understand the use of the **Bcc** field when sending mail. We will delve into configuring message delivery options. We will look at how to set voting and tracking options, and also proofing and sorting mail messages.

Specifying a message theme

A theme helps you create professional-looking emails. When themes are applied to documents, their fonts, styles, backgrounds, colors, tables, hyperlink colors, and graphics are all affected. Here's how to specify a message theme:

1. Click on the **New Email** icon to create a new message. On the **Options** tab, select the **Themes** group to apply to the email message, or set the **Colors**, **Fonts**, and **Effects** types yourself by using the relevant icons, as illustrated in the following screenshot:

Figure 13.31 – Themes drop-down list

2. The **Page Color** type is also changeable via the drop-down arrow. You would need to click into the body of the message (the white-space area under the **Subject** of the email message) to activate the **Page Color** button.

Showing/hiding the From and Bcc fields

The **To** and **Cc** fields are displayed on a new mail message by default. The **Bcc** field is not part of an email message by default. This option needs to be activated to appear in email headings. The **Bcc** field is located by clicking on the **Options** tab in the new mail message dialog box. This applies to the **From** field as well as the **Bcc** field. To show/hide these fields, proceed as follows:

1. Click on the **Bcc** field to send a copy of the email to the person specified in the **Bcc** field without the main recipient of the email knowing, as illustrated in the following screenshot:

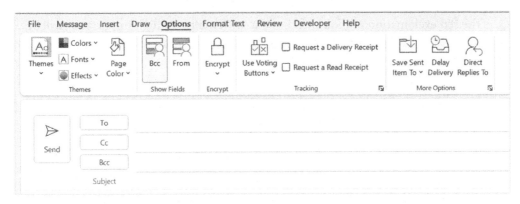

Figure 13.32 – Options tab showing Bcc and From fields

2. Click on the **From** field icon to select the email address of the person you would like to send the email to. This only works if you have delegated access to that person's account.

Configuring message delivery options

In this topic, we will learn how to set the importance option for an email message to highlight to a recipient that the message is urgent.

Setting the level of importance

Setting the level of importance of a mail message identifies to the recipient, when receiving the message in the **Inbox**, how important the contents of the message are and how promptly they are expected to respond to the message. The example in the screenshot indicates that the message is of high importance (with a red exclamation mark). This also helps to sort email messages by importance in the message list.

To set this option, follow these steps:

1. Click on the **New Email** option to create a new message. Select the **Message** tab and locate the **Tags** group.
2. Click on **High Importance** to set the level.

3. The red exclamation mark indicating that the email is of high importance will be visible in the **Inbox** or **Sent Items** folders, as illustrated in the following screenshot:

Figure 13.33 – Email message showing high importance as a red exclamation point

4. You can also set a delivery receipt to show when a recipient has read or received your email. Use the **Options** tab to set this in the **Tracking** group.

5. Click on **Request a Read Receipt** to request a notification when the message has been read by the recipient.

Configuring voting and tracking options

Creating a poll in Outlook 2021 is a stunning feature that allows you to quickly gather replies to a question sent to recipients via an email message. It is, however, always best to make sure that all recipients are using the same version of Office as you are. Here's how you can use this feature:

1. Click on the **New Email** message icon. From the **Options** tab, select the **Use Voting Buttons** icon from the **Tracking** group.

2. Select one of the default tracking buttons or click on **Custom…** to create your own, as illustrated in the following screenshot:

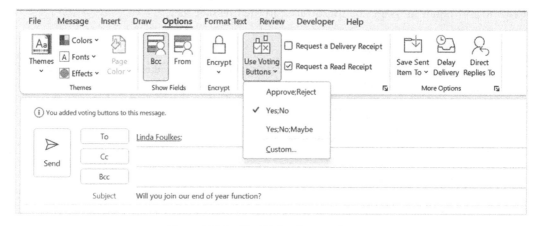

Figure 13.34 – Use Voting Buttons feature

3. In the **Properties** dialog box, make sure you have located the **Voting and Tracking options** heading. Click on the **Use Voting Buttons** checkbox to make it active.

4. Type your own custom text into the space provided. In the following example, I have used **Mon; Tues; Wed** as I would like to obtain a poll on when colleagues could attend a training session. Remember to put a semicolon in between each voting choice and not a comma, as illustrated in the following screenshot. Click on **Close** to confirm:

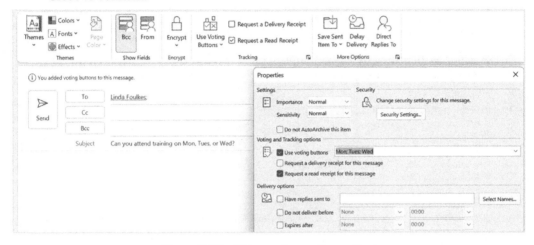

Figure 13.35 – Using custom voting options

5. Your email header will now display an information bar with the text **You added voting buttons to this message**.

6. The recipient will receive an email with voting buttons in the message header, on which they will click to select a day that suits them for the training, as illustrated in the following screenshot:

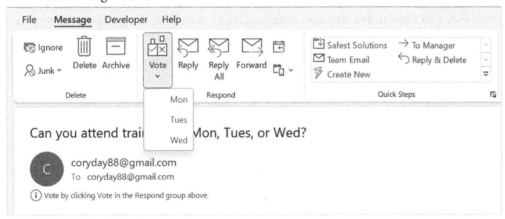

Figure 13.36 – Replying to a voting email using the Vote drop-down list

7.   A response is then sent to the sender.

Sending a message to a contact group

To send a message to a contact group, proceed as follows:

1.   Click the **New Email** icon to create a new message.

2.   In the message header, click on the **To** icon to access the address list, or type the contact group name into the **To** text area. From the **Address Book** drop-down list, select **Contacts**. Click on **OK** to add group information to the email message.

3.   A group is identified by a two-people icon and will display a bold attribute, as illustrated in the following screenshot:

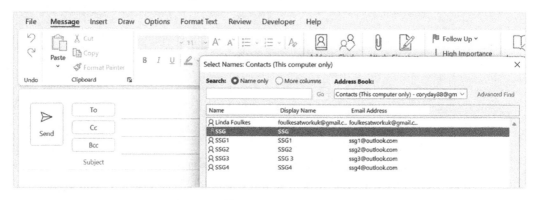

Figure 13.37 – Adding contacts to an email message

4.   Select a group to send the email to by double-clicking on the group name—for example, **SSG**, as in the preceding screenshot.

5.   The group name will appear at the bottom of the dialog box in the **To** heading. Once you have added all your recipients, click on the **OK** button to return to your email message.

6.   A contact group will also display a + sign next to the contact's name in the email address area, indicating that it is a group.

Moving, copying, and deleting email messages

Copying or moving information from one email to another is exactly the same concept as in any other Microsoft Office application. Select an element to cut or copy, then use the right-click method over the selected element to cut or copy. Move to the destination email message and right-click once again to paste the information into the email. To delete an email from your **Inbox**, simply click on the email and press the *Delete* key on the keyboard.

Replying to and forwarding email messages

To reply to and forward an email message, proceed as follows:

1. Select an email message in the **Inbox**. Click on the **Reply**, **Reply All**, or **Forward** options to respond to the message you have received, as follows:

   A. **Reply**: To only the person who sent you the email

   B. **Reply All**: To the sender and all other recipients in the message

   C. **Forward**: To send the email message to someone else for them to action

2. Edit the subject, if necessary, and then send the email.

Creating and managing Quick Steps

You will be proficient at performing Quick Steps by creating, editing, deleting, and duplicating Quick Steps after completing this topic. Quick Steps help you to quickly manage your mailbox by selecting multiple options to apply to mail messages at once. An example would be if you frequently send emails to certain folders or forward emails to a certain person regularly. You are also able to formulate and customize your own Quick Steps for actions that need to be done quickly. There are some default Quick Steps available to get you started. Here's how to proceed with this:

1. Locate the **Quick Steps** group on the **Home** tab.
2. There are a number of default Quick Steps, some of which are outlined here:

   A. **Move to Folder...** moves a new mail message to another folder and then marks the message as read.

   B. **To Manager** will forward an email to the manager specified in the dialog box that populates.

C. **Team Email** moves the message to a specified folder and marks it as read and complete.

D. **Reply & Delete** opens a reply to the selected message and deletes the original message.

Some of the aforementioned options can be seen in the following screenshot, with the addition of a custom Quick Step named **Safest Solutions**, which moves the selected read email to the **Safest Solutions** folder:

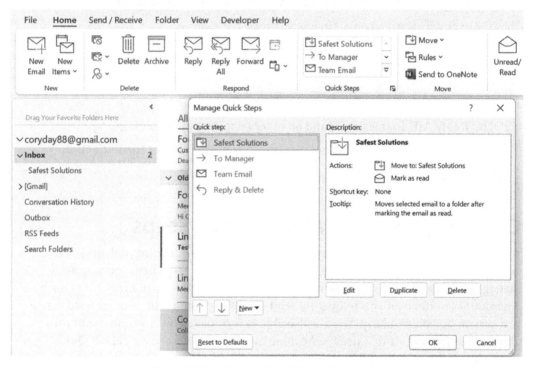

Figure 13.38 – Manage Quick Steps dialog box

3. Be careful of the **Reply & Delete** option. It happens so fast that you hardly see it and realize it's deleted the original!

4. To apply a **Quick Step**, click on the mail message to apply the step to. The first time you use a Quick Step, it will ask you to enter the details to set up the Quick Step. Thereafter, it will not prompt you again until you right-click and edit the step.

5. Enter the name of the manager you wish to use as the Quick Step. In this case, we will enter the manager's name as BLZ Furkidds.

6. Click on **Save**, as illustrated in the following screenshot:

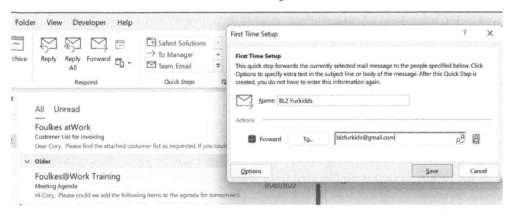

Figure 13.39 – First Time Setup dialog box for the To Manager Quick Step

7. Once the Quick Step has been edited, you will notice that the item has been updated in the **Quick Steps** group, as illustrated in the following screenshot:

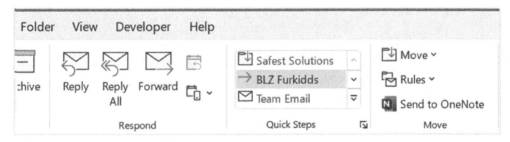

Figure 13.40 – BLZ Furkidds Quick Step

8. When you next use the Quick Step, simply click on the **BLZ Furkidds** Quick Step to forward the selected email to this manager.

Attaching item content

By the end of this topic, you will have learned how to attach an Outlook item and various external file types to an email.

Attaching an Outlook item

At times, it might be required of you to attach another email message, task, calendar item, or contact to a message you are sending. Here is the quickest way to attach multiple items of this nature:

1. Open a **New Mail** message. From the **Insert** tab, locate the **Include** group, then click on **Outlook Item**.

2. From the **Insert Item** dialog box, locate the folder to search (this could be an item from a **Task**, **Contact**, **Calendar**, or **Email** types), then the item you wish to attach to the existing email message. Alternatively, use the **Business Card** dropdown to insert a contact as an email attachment from the **Include** group on the **Insert** tab. The former option is highlighted in the following screenshot:

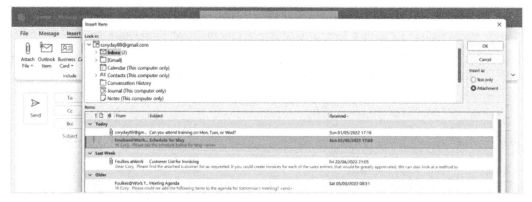

Figure 13.41 – Insert Item dialog box

3. Click on the item, and then click on **OK** to insert the item into the mail message.

4. In the email message, the inserted item will appear in the **Attached** area in the message header, as illustrated in the following screenshot:

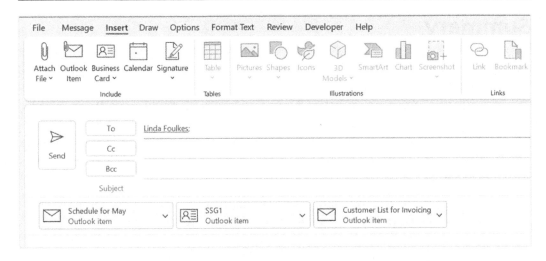

Figure 13.42 – Outlook items attached to an email

5.   Don't forget to click on **Send** once you have added the recipients and attached the item content to the email.

Attaching external files

To attach an external file, proceed as follows:

1.   Open an existing email or a **New Mail** message to add an attachment. From the **Message** tab, locate the **Include** group.

2.   Click on the **Attach File** icon. You will see a drop-down list populate, containing most recently worked-on files, as well as a **Browse this PC...** option to locate the file you wish to add to the email.

3.   Once you have located the file attachment on the PC, click on **Open** to place the document into the email message. The file is inserted below the **Subject** line, into the **Attached** section. To remove an attachment, if you have inserted it in error, simply click on the drop-down arrow at the end of the inserted filename attached, then select **Remove Attachment**.

Summary

Throughout this chapter, you have collected skills to create and send email messages within the Outlook 2021 application. You are able to attach item content from different items in Outlook, and can confidently add and remove file attachments and content. Quick methods to enhance productivity have also been learned, and you will now be able to apply Quick Steps and item tags and set a message as being of high importance. You will also be able to set a message so that the sender receives a notification that the message has been read by the recipient. We have also learned how to search, print, and filter mail messages in **Inbox**.

In the next chapter, we will cover best practices while working with message attachments and will learn about keeping your mailbox clean and streamlined. You will learn how to set up rules and manage junk-mail options and create or modify signatures within the Outlook application. The next chapter will also teach you how to set up and manage contacts and contact groups.

14
Managing Mail and Contacts

This chapter will introduce you to the best practices while working with message attachments, to keep your mailbox clean and streamlined. You will learn how to set up rules and manage junk mail options, as well as how to create or modify signatures within the Outlook application. This chapter will also teach you how to be proficient at creating business cards for contacts, as well as how to set up and manage contacts and contact groups.

The following topics will be covered in this chapter:

- Cleaning up your mailbox and managing rules
- Managing junk mail and automatic message content
- Creating contact information and groups

Technical requirements

To work through this chapter, you need to have prior knowledge of navigating the Outlook 2021 interface and setting options. In addition, you will need to be confident in creating, sending, and managing your mail environment. You should be able to insert and attach item content to elements within the interface, as well as format email content, just as you have learned in the previous chapters of this book. The examples in this chapter can be found on GitHub at `https://github.com/PacktPublishing/Learn-Microsoft-Office-2021-Second-Edition`.

Cleaning up your mailbox and managing rules

Keeping your mailbox clean is a task you should do regularly. With the amount of digital correspondence and attachments that come into your mailbox daily, you must manage your workflow. In this section, we will learn how to clean up our mailbox and where to locate our mailbox's size. We will also learn how to work with message attachments and save a message in an external format. Finally, we will learn how to ignore conversations and use the cleanup tools available in Outlook 2021.

Many solutions are implemented in the workplace to reduce the size of employee mailboxes, including additional software such as Mimecast, which enables employees to utilize large file send features. It also acts as a mailbox backup online.

Here, we will learn how to access the rule options in Outlook and create a basic rule, then apply the rule to a selected email message. We will also cover deleting, modifying, and running a rule on a specific folder.

Cleaning up the mailbox

Our mailboxes often get extremely cluttered with messages from subscriptions to sites, which are delivered daily, weekly, and monthly. This can get out of control very easily, and we normally only start to worry about this once we are reaching our full mailbox capacity. Let's learn how to view the mailbox size in Outlook 2021.

Viewing the mailbox size

1. Click on **File | Tools**.

2. Locate the **Mailbox Settings** heading, just to the right of **Tools**, as shown in the following screenshot:

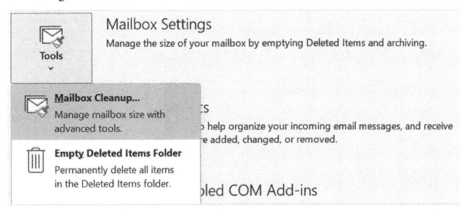

Figure 14.1 – Mailbox Cleanup… settings

Here, you will see the mailbox capacity and the amount of free space available. The slider shown in the preceding screenshot will depict this graphically.

Another way to keep your mailbox's size at a reasonable size is to delete email attachments since these take up a huge amount of space in your mailbox. We'll learn how to tackle this in the next subsection.

Saving message attachments

It is important to keep your mailbox's size down by saving email message attachments to your computer, instead of leaving them attached to email messages in your inbox. This will reduce your mailbox's size considerably.

1. Open an email that contains an attachment to download, then click on the attachment to open it.

2. The **Attachment Tools** contextual menu will open. Click on **Save As** to save the file to a location on your computer.

3. To return to the message, simply click on **Back to message** or use the **Show Message** icon at the end of the ribbon, as shown in the following screenshot:

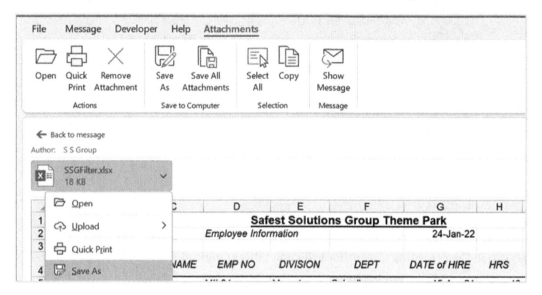

Figure 14.2 – The Save As feature and the Attachments tab

4. A **Remove Attachment** option is also available, and the **Save All Attachments** option allows you to save attachments to a specific location if the message contains more than one attachment. Note that, if connected, you can also use the **Upload** icon in the **Save to Cloud** group to save attachments to an online location (such as *OneDrive*).

Saving a message in an external format

1. Open a message you wish to save to an external format, then click on **File | Save As**. In the **Save As** dialog box, select the drive and folder where you wish to save the message, then enter a filename in the relevant text area. The default save option in Outlook is **Outlook Message Format - Unicode (*.msg)**, as shown in the following screenshot:

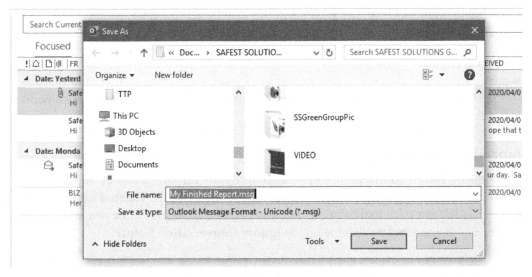

Figure 14.3 – The Save As dialog box to save an email message

2. Click on **Save**. Saving in this message-type format will open the email message in Outlook when the user double-clicks on the My Finished Report.msg file after saving it.

3. Other options are available under the **Save as type:** drop-down list, such as **Text Only**, which saves the message as a .txt file and removes any pictures, graphics, and formatting from the message. The **Outlook Template (*.oft)** option works the same as a Word template in that it allows you to save the formatting of a message. This allows you to apply this message template to a new email at a later stage. The **HTML (*.htm; *.html)** option saves the message in web format (with the code, images, and text in a separate file to accompany the message) and opens in a browser once it's been saved and opened. Finally, the **MHT files (*.mht)** option is a web page archive file format that also opens in a web browser.

All these options can be seen in the following screenshot:

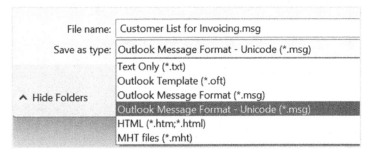

Figure 14.4 – The Save as type: formats when saving email messages

4. If you prefer, you can save your email in `.pdf` format for safekeeping on your computer.

With that, you have learned how to save messages in external formats for safekeeping. This is purely a personal choice, and many companies will have policies on how your inbox is stored. Alternatively, they will have additional software that you can integrate with your Outlook mail application.

Ignoring a conversation

The **Ignore Conversation** feature can be used to remove unwanted conversations in your inbox. Please note that an ignored conversation will end up in the **Deleted Items** folder, and if you delete it from that location, you won't be able to recover it. Be careful to select the correct message before clicking on the **Ignore Conversation** feature:

1. Click on the message's header (but do not open the message). Click on the **Home** tab, then choose the **Ignore Conversation** option from the **Delete** group.

2. A dialog box will appear on your screen with the following warning:

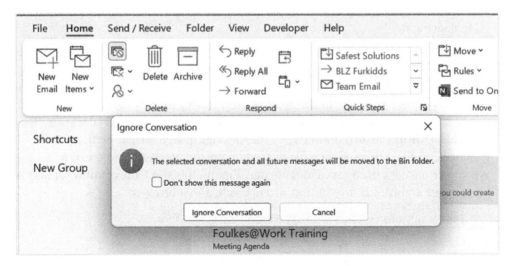

Figure 14.5 – Ignore Conversation

3. Click on **Ignore Conversation** to confirm. This feature is also available for open emails but is located via the **Message** group instead.

    If you decide to stop ignoring a conversation, do the following:

    I.   Locate the email in the **Deleted Items** folder, then double-click to open the email.

    II. Click on the **Ignore Conversation** icon on the **Message** tab, after which a dialog box will appear on your screen.

    III. Click on **Stop Ignoring Conversation**, as shown in the following screenshot:

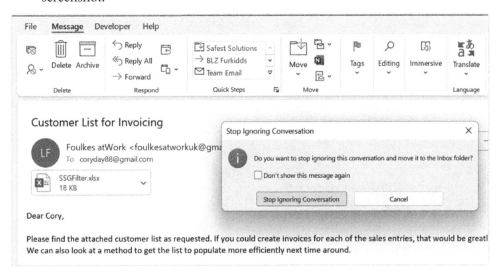

Figure 14.6 – Stop Ignoring Conversation.

The email will return to your inbox.

Using cleanup tools

Mailbox cleanup tools are located on the Backstage view. You can use this option to find out the size of your mailbox and the folders within it. Other features under this heading enable you to empty the **Deleted Items** folder and archive old items to the Outlook Data File (*.pst) archive.

1. Click on **File | Tools | Mailbox Cleanup…** to view your mailbox's size.

2. The **Mailbox Cleanup…** dialog box will launch with a range of options, as shown in the following screenshot:

Figure 14.7 – Mailbox Cleanup options

3. In this dialog box, you can view your mailbox's size, categorized by Outlook item, and find items based on the number of days and size. **AutoArchive** will move all old items to the Outlook Data File, which is normally located in the `Documents\ Outlook Files` folder on your hard drive. You can also empty the **Deleted Items** folder and delete versions of items from this dialog box.

Creating and managing rules

Messages can be managed by creating rules for them automatically, every time an email is received or sent. When creating a rule, it can be based on your own rules, templates, or an existing message.

1. On the **Home** tab, locate the **Move** group, then click on **Rules**.

2. Choose **Create Rule…** or **Manage Rules & Alerts...** to edit an existing rule, as shown in the following screenshot:

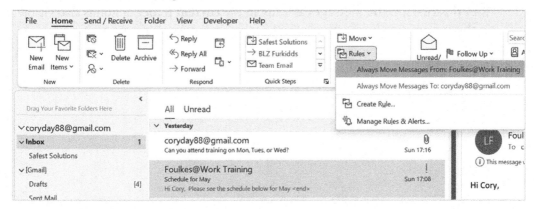

Figure 14.8 – Rules drop-down list

3. In the **Create Rule** dialog box, set the conditions for the message. For this exercise, we will set up a rule that sends all emails that are received from **Foulkes@Work** to a folder named **Safest Solutions** in my inbox. You can click on **Advanced Options...** to set further conditions if required. To create a folder for all the **Safest Solutions** emails, click on the **Select Folder...** option at the bottom of the dialog box, then click on **New...** to create a new folder called **Safest Solutions** in your inbox, as shown in the following screenshot:

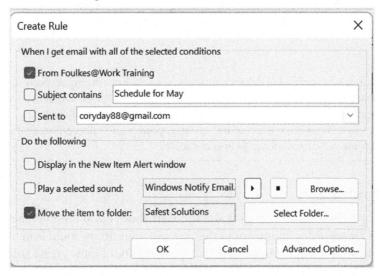

Figure 14.9 – The Create Rule dialog box

4. Click **OK** to set up the rule.

5. You will see a message on your screen, indicating that the rule has been created. The **Run this rule now on messages already in the current folder** option is also visible in this information box, as shown in the following screenshot:

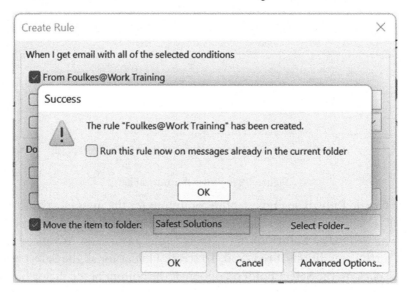

Figure 14.10 – Run this rule now on messages already in the current folder

6. Click on the **Run this rule now on messages already in this current folder** checkbox, then click on the **OK** button to see the results.

> **Note**
>
> When a rule is applied, all delivery receipts, read receipts, voting responses, and automatic replies are also based on the criteria upon which the email message is sent. When they're received, they are acted upon automatically by that applied rule. Tracking is affected by voting responses and tally responses if the email is moved automatically to another folder.

Modifying rules

There are many rules to choose from under the **Edit Rules** option. Remember that setting too many rules on incoming messages in your inbox could lead to confusion, and you may miss very important emails that need attention! Only create rules when they are necessary and can help you with your productivity or workflow.

1. Go to **Home | Rules | Manage Rules & Alerts** and click on **Change Rule** at the top of the dialog box.

2. Choose **Edit Rule Settings**.

3. From the **Rules Wizard** dialog box, adjust the settings by selecting a new condition, or click on the blue highlighted underlined words to change the criteria to suit your requirements. In this case, we will choose **with specific words in the body** for **Step 1: Select condition(s)**, and **with Report in the body** for **Step 2: Edit the rule description (click an underlined value)**.

4. Click on **Next**, then **OK**, as shown in the following screenshot:

Figure 14.11 – The Rules Wizard dialog box

5. Click on **Next >** until you have finished making any relevant changes. Then, click on **Finish**.

Deleting rules

1. Click on **Home | Rules | Manage Rules & Alerts**.

2. Select the rule you wish to remove, as shown in the following screenshot:

Figure 14.12 – Using the Delete button to remove rules from Outlook

3. Click the **Delete** button to remove the rule.

Changing rule order

Rules are run on incoming messages in your inbox according to how they were set in the list when they were created. We can change the priority of which rules will run first by reordering their position in the **Rules** area. Follow these steps:

1. To reorder rules, go to **Rules | Manage Rules & Alerts…**.

2. Simply click on a rule you wish to move from the **Rules and Alerts** dialog box, then click on the **Move Up** or **Move Down** arrow to reorder it.

Note that you can also **Stop processing more rules** by selecting this option via the **Rules Wizard** dialog when creating a rule. This will allow rules to be stopped if more than one rule is applied to the same email.

Managing junk mail and automatic message content

In this section, you will learn about the junk mail options, such as allowing a specific message to not be junk; filtering junk mail with an option that never blocks the sender; viewing a list of safe senders; and learning how to block a sender.

You'll learn how to create and manage signatures; assign a signature to an email message manually; specify font options for new HTML messages; set options for replying to and forwarding mail messages; and, lastly, set a default theme for all HTML messages.

Allowing a specific message (not junk)

Sometimes, email messages are sent to the **Junk Email** folder by mistake. To mark the message as not junk, do the following:

1. From the **Navigation** Pane, click on the **Junk Email [1]** folder, as shown in the following screenshot:

Figure 14.3 – The Junk Email folder in Outlook

2. From the **Message** pane to the right, click a message that you want to mark as not junk. Then, click on **Home | Junk | Not Junk**.

3. A dialog box will notify you that the message will be moved back to the **Inbox** folder and that messages from that recipient will always be trusted, as shown in the following screenshot:

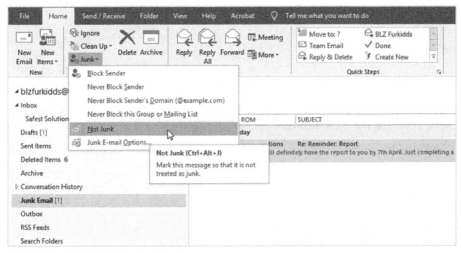

Figure 14.14 – Specifying messages as Not Junk

An email message that is sent to the Junk Email folder is saved as plain text, and all the links contained in it are removed. Moving a message out of the Junk Email folder restores the message to its format and links.

Filtering junk mail with Never Block Sender

It is possible to mark a recipient in your inbox as a safe sender. If you do not want to allow just a single email address from a large company and would prefer to allow receipt of all user addresses from a company, then use the **Never Block Sender's Domain** option (for example, @packt.com). In addition, if you belong to a mailing list, you can add this to the safe senders' list too. The steps are the same for each of these options, and are illustrated here:

1. From the **Message** pane, click on a message that's been received from a recipient you trust. Click on **Home | Junk | Never Block Sender**, as shown in the following screenshot:

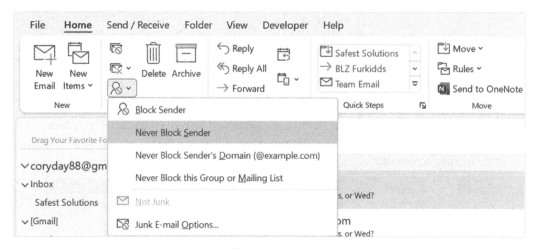

Figure 14.15 – The Never Block Sender feature

2. A dialog box will appear, informing you that the sender of the chosen message has been added to the **Safe Senders** list.

3. Click on **OK** to confirm.

Viewing the Safe Senders list

1. Click on **Home | Junk Email Options...**.

2. In the dialog box that appears, select the **Safe Senders** tab, as shown in the following screenshot:

Figure 14.16 – The Safe Senders tab

3. The addresses of safe senders will be shown in the list. You can add and edit the list from there.

Blocking senders

If you receive messages in your inbox that look suspicious or are spam, you can ensure that you don't receive such messages in the future by marking the recipient as blocked. Follow these steps:

1. From the **Navigation** Pane, click on a message from a recipient you trust. Then, click on the **Home | Junk | Block Sender** option

2. A dialog box will appear, informing you that the sender of the selected message has been added to the blocked senders' list and moved to the Junk Email folder.

3. Click on **OK** to continue.

Managing signatures

A personal business card can be added automatically to every email message you send, or manually to the messages you choose. This is called a **signature**. It contains contact information that will appear in the body of each new email message you create in Outlook 2021.

Creating a signature

1. Open a new email message, then click on **Signature**. You will see any existing signatures.

2. To create a new signature, choose **Signatures…** from the drop-down list, as shown in the following screenshot:

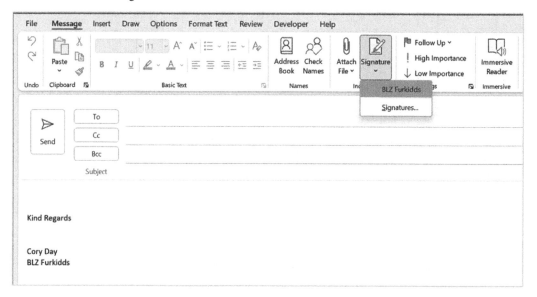

Figure 14.17 – The Signature feature in Outlook

3. Click on the **New** icon to create a new signature. In the textbox that appears, enter a name for the signature. The name of the signature is not going to appear in the email; it is just a name that's given to the signature to identify it.

4. Click on **OK** when you're done.

5. In the **Edit signature** text body area, type in the relevant contact details and format the text using the options provided. Note that you can also insert a picture and a hyperlink, as well as a business card. These options can be seen in the following screenshot:

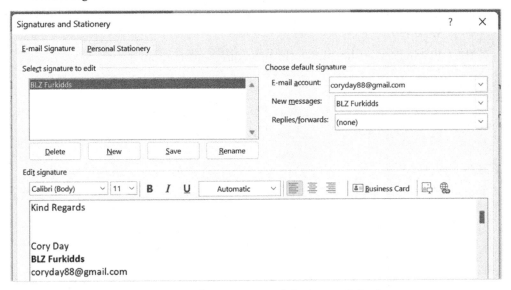

Figure 14.18 – The Signatures and Stationery dialog box

6. To the right of the dialog box, you will see the **Choose default signature** heading. If you do not want to add the signature you have just created to every new email message you compose, then you will need to change the option in the drop-down list next to **New messages:** to **(none)**. This can also be changed by going to **File | Options | Mail | Signatures**. You can set a separate signature for the **Replies/ forwards:** option as well.

7. Click on **OK** to confirm.

Specifying the font for new HTML messages

You can specify the fonts for traditional-style documents – namely, the HTML-type message as a default in Outlook 2019. By traditional-style documents, we mean those that contain bullet points, fonts, colors, and images. Plain text messages are also available but, of course, will not support bold, italics, or any formatting.

1. Click on **File | Options**. Then, in the **Outlook Options** dialog box, make sure you are on the **Mail** category to the left to access the available options.

2. Under the **Compose messages** heading, click the **Stationery and Fonts…** button.

3. Click on the **Font…** icon under the **New mail messages** heading to specify the font for new HTML messages.

4. In the **Font** dialog box, choose the formats you would like to apply to every new mail message by default. In this example, the font face and font color have been changed. For reference, font face refers to the font type that you choose from the **Font:** drop-down list.

    The following screenshot shows the preceding information:

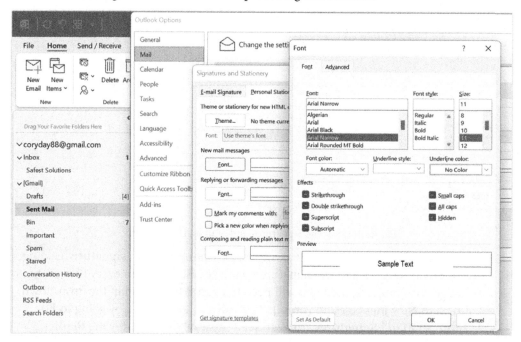

Figure 14.19 – The Font… button for New mail messages

5. Click on **OK** to confirm, then **OK** again, and once again to exit the dialog box. The sample text will be updated in the preview window, and, when typing in a new mail message, the changes will be noted.

Specifying options for replies and forwards

You can set a different font and attributes for replying to and forwarding messages as follows:

1. Click on **File | Options**. Then, in the **Outlook Options** dialog box, make sure you are on the **Mail** category to the left to access the available options.

2. Under the **Compose messages** heading, select the **Stationery and Fonts…** button.

3. In the **Signatures and Stationery** dialog box, locate the **Replying or forwarding messages** heading.

4. Click on the **Font…** button to change the attributes. Then, click on **OK** when you're done. Note that two other options in the dialog box are related to replying to and forwarding messages.

Setting a default theme for all HTML messages, stationery, and fonts

1. Click on **File | Options | Mail | Signatures and Stationery**.

2. In the **Signatures and Stationery** dialog box, locate the **Theme…** icon on the **Personal Stationery** tab.

3. In the **Theme or Stationery** dialog box, select a theme to apply to all messages by default. Choose whether you wish to display background graphics at the bottom left-hand corner of the dialog box. Click on **OK** to confirm your choices. This is shown in the following screenshot:

Figure 14.20 – Theme or Stationery options

4.   Click on **OK** to confirm.

Creating contact information and groups

In this section, you will learn how to create a contact business card and modify it. You will also learn how to forward and update a contact in the Outlook address book. We will look at creating contact groups and how to manage the contact group's membership, show notes about a contact group, and delete a contact group. In addition, we will look at the search features that are available to search for a specific contact or group to send a meeting to that contact or group.

Modifying a default business card

A business card provides contact information for a contact within Outlook. Follow these steps to learn how to modify a default business card:

1.   From the **Navigation** pane, select the **People** icon located on the **Peek** bar.

2.   Double-click on an existing business card to edit it. Edit the business card by clicking in the relevant text area to type new information or edit existing information.

3.   Click on **Save & Close** when you're finished.

> **Note**
>
> Once an email has been opened, you can right-click on the sender's email address to save the contact to your address book, or drag the message from your inbox to the **People** icon on the **Peek** bar at the bottom of the **Navigation** pane to create a new contact.

Forwarding a contact

1.   Click the **People** icon on the **Peek** bar at the bottom of the **Navigation** pane.

2.   Locate the **Share** group on the **Home** tab, then select **Forward Contact**, as shown in the following screenshot:

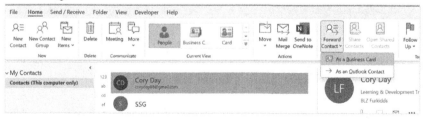

Figure 14.21 – Forwarding a contact as a business card

3. Choose the relevant option from the drop-down list, as follows:

    ▪ The **As a Business Card** forwarding option will insert the business card into a new mail message and attach a `* .vcf` file to the email.

    ▪ The **As an Outlook Contact** forwarding option will attach the business card to the message.

    ▪ You can also **Share Contacts** using the icon on the **Share** group. This option grants other users access to your contact list in Outlook and/or permission to access other people's contact lists.

Creating and manipulating contact groups

When emailing contacts regularly for a specific purpose – such as conference attendees, a list of parents, or a list of meeting attendees – it is much simpler when you have a group of contacts set up. That way, when you're emailing all of the contacts, you can just use the group name as the recipient, and each contact listed in the group will receive the email message that's been sent.

Creating a contact group

Let's create a contact group using the **People** icon, as follows:

1. At the bottom of the **Navigation** pane, locate the **People** icon.

2. Click on **New Contact Group** from the **Home** tab, as shown in the following screenshot:

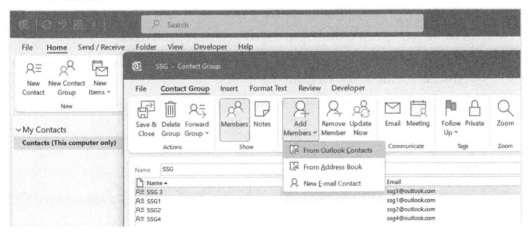

Figure 14.22 –New Contact Group

3. In the dialog box, name your new contact group in the **Name** text area. For this example, let's create an **SSG** group.

4. To add the email addresses of all the members of the group, click on the **Add Members** icon.

5. Choose **New E-mail Contact**, **From Address Book**, or **From Outlook Contacts**

6. For this example, we will use **New E-mail Contact**. In the dialog box, enter a display name in the text area, and type the contact's email address in the space provided. Click on **OK**.

7. Keep on adding contacts in this way until all the required members are in the group. Click on **Save & Close** when you're done.

8. In the **Contacts** window, the new group called **SSG** (in the case of this exercise) should be visible.

Managing contact group membership

You can manage a group with ease by using the ribbon. All the relevant icons are displayed for ease of use. Using these ribbon options, you can do the following:

-   Add new members using the **Add Members** icon (members can be added from emails, the address book, or the Outlook contact list).

-   Remove any member from the list by clicking on their display name and then choosing **Remove Member** from the ribbon.

-   Update the group by clicking on **Update Now**, if you have made changes.

-   Add **Notes** about the distribution list.

-   Categorize your group according to a specific category and color.

-   Use the **Private** lock at the end of the ribbon to mark the group as private so that no one else can see the details thereof.

-   Set a **Follow Up** reminder to remember to do something related to the contact group.

Now, let's learn how to work with the **Notes** feature.

Showing notes about a contact group

1. In the **People** contacts window, locate the contact group that you want to create a note for.

2. Double-click on the group's name to open it. We will open SSG, which we created earlier in this chapter, for this example.

3. On the **Contact Group** tab, click inside the **Notes** area of the contact. Add a note for the current group by typing text into the notes area. We will add a note that states **This client is one of our acquisitions for September**, as shown in the following screenshot:

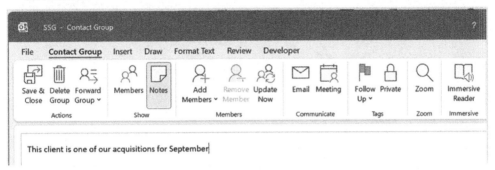

Figure 14.23 – The Notes button on the Contact Group tab

4. Click on **Members** to return to the contact group email list. To view the notes for the group, click on the **Notes** icon again.

5. Click on **Save & Close** when you're finished.

Deleting a contact group

1. Open the contact group, as shown in the preceding subsection. From the **Contact Group** tab, click on the **Delete Group** icon to move it from the list.

2. A dialog box will ask if you are sure you want to delete the group.

3. Click on **Yes** to confirm this.

Sending a meeting to a contact group

1. At the bottom of the **Navigation** pane, click **People**.

2. Locate the contact group you would like to invite to a meeting. Open the contact group by double-clicking on it.

3. Locate the **Meeting** icon on the **Contact Group** tab

4. A new meeting request will be opened, where you can confirm the date(s) and time of the meeting request, as shown in the following screenshot:

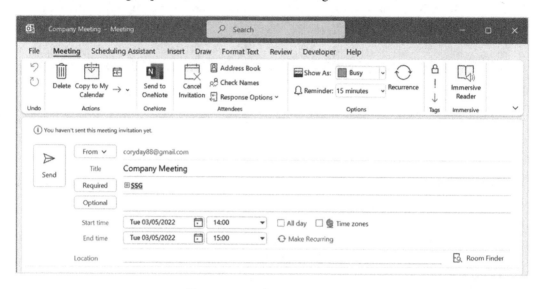

Figure 14.24 – Creating a meeting

5. Fill in the details, then click on **Send**.

> **Note**
> You can also check your calendar, copy the meeting to your calendar, use the **Scheduling Assist** feature to check for availability, send your meeting to OneNote, or add an online meeting location to the appointment. We will discuss these options later in this book.

Searching for a contact

1. Navigate to **People** from the bottom of the **Navigation** pane.

2. Locate the search box at the top of the contacts list. Type the name of the contact you wish to find in the search text area:

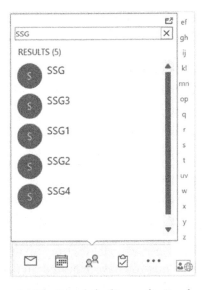

Figure 14.25 – Search facility on the People pane

3. Note that you can also click on the **People** peek to navigate directly to the **Contacts** area, then select the search facility at the top of the screen to open the **Search** tab and view the relevant options.

4. Click on **All Outlook Items** to view the drop-down list of search destinations, as shown in the following screenshot:

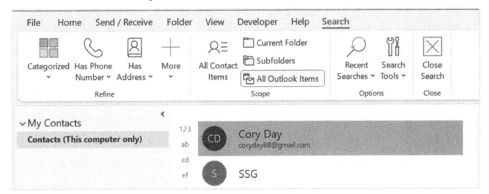

Figure 14.26 – The Search tab showing All Outlook Items on the Scope group

5. The search will return the results from the criteria you entered. Note that the ribbon contains several search options, including a list of **Recent Searches**, as well as **Search Tools** to investigate. When you have finished searching, click on **Close Search** at the end of the ribbon, or click on the **X** button located at the end of the search entry text area.

Summary

In this chapter, you learned how to keep your mailbox clean, where to check your mailbox's size, and how to add messages to the safe senders or blocked senders list. You can now set and manage rules on your mailbox and folders and work with the various junk mail options. You have also mastered how to set up signatures when sending new email messages, as well as when replying to and forwarding emails. Specifying font options for new HTML messages, as well as setting up fonts when replying to and forwarding emails, are also skills you have acquired. In addition, you can set up a theme for all HTML messages and work with contact groups in Outlook 2021.

In the next chapter, we will work with calendars, appointments, and events. We'll learn how to set meeting response options and arrange calendars and calendar groups. We will also learn how to create tasks and assign them to other Outlook users, as well as track them via the **Status Report** tool. We will also cover **Journal**, where we will learn how to create items such as telephone calls and use this method to record the time particular tasks took to complete using Outlook 2021.

15

Calendar Objects, Tasks, Notes, and Journal Entries

In this chapter, you will learn how to work with calendars, appointments, and events, as well as how to set up meeting response options and arrange calendars and calendar groups. Additionally, you will learn how to work with tasks and how to assign them to other Outlook users and track them via the status report tool.

This chapter also includes a section on journal entries, which you can use to create and track items such as telephone calls, tasks, and documents relating to a specific client on a timeline. This is particularly useful if you need to record the time spent on certain tasks in Outlook.

In this chapter, we will cover the following topics:

- Working with the calendar, appointments, and events
- Modifying meeting requests and manipulating the calendar pane
- Creating and managing tasks
- Creating and manipulating notes and journal entries
- Setting out-of-office options

Technical requirements

To work through this chapter, you need to have prior knowledge of the Outlook 2021 interface and settings options. In addition, you need to be confident in creating and sending mail and managing the mail environment. You should be able to insert, format, and attach items to elements within the interface. All of the examples used in this chapter can be accessed at `https://github.com/PacktPublishing/Learn-Microsoft-Office-2021-Second-Edition`.

Working with the calendar, appointments, meetings, and events

This section will cover the process of setting up appointments (including events and meetings) and options, forwarding and printing appointments, scheduling a meeting with a message sender, and sharing a calendar.

Difference between meetings, events, and appointments

Let's outline the differences between meetings, events, and appointments so that you understand the use of each within the calendar:

Type	Explanation
Meetings	A meeting can be created when you want to involve other people in addition to yourself. It could involve participants who are invited during a blocked-out period in your day. Also, meetings normally contain booked venues, such as a meeting room location, alongside other resources.
Events	When we double-click on a day in the calendar, it will create an event and display the **Event** tab on the ribbon. Usually, events are created when an appointment time exceeds 24 hours. Events are displayed at the top of your Day view and not as blocked-out time on your calendar.
Appointments	An appointment is a block of time that has a start time and an end time, normally within a 24-hour period, for example, from 09:00 to 10:00. It exists as an outlined block for a specific timeframe within your day. Normally, appointments don't have participants invited to them, although the functionality is available to do so. An appointment is normally created for one person.

Table 15.1 – The differences between meetings, appointments, and events

We hope that you understand the differences between the three elements, as compared in the preceding table.

Creating and manipulating appointments or meetings

In this section, we will look at how to set up an appointment and use the **Recurring Appointment** option. Additionally, we will learn how to print your appointment details, invite participants, and forward an appointment to another recipient.

Setting the appointment options

1. Locate the **Calendar** icon in the peek bar at the bottom of the Navigation Pane. As you place your mouse pointer over the **Calendar** icon, you will see the calendar peek detailing any meetings you have scheduled for the rest of the day:

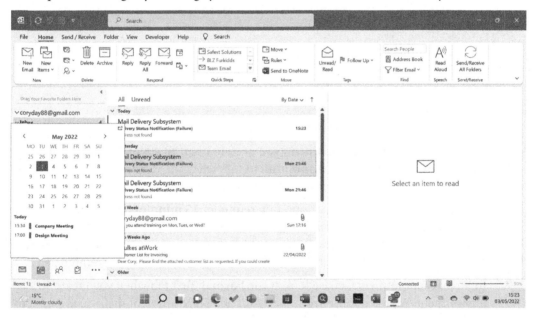

Figure 15.1 – The Calendar button

2. From the **Home** tab, locate the **New** group. Click on **New Appointment**. Note that you can right-click or double-click directly on a day in the calendar to create a new appointment. If you are creating a meeting, click on **New Meeting**.

3. To enter the start time and the end time of the appointment, make sure that **All day event** is not active (remove the tick from the option). Be careful to watch the A.M. and P.M. time slots, as you could end up setting your appointment to the wrong hour of the day. If your appointment will occur at the same time on certain days of the week for a certain period of time, then the recurring appointment option is perfect.

4. Click on **Recurrence** on the **Appointment** tab to set the recurring appointment options. Click on **OK** to confirm the changes:

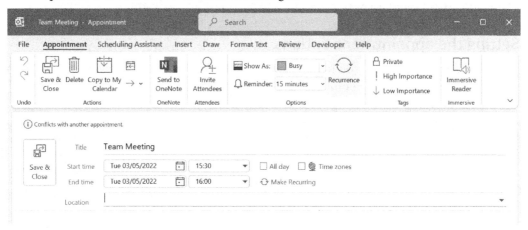

Figure 15.2 – Creating appointments

5. To remove a recurring appointment, you need to open an appointment where the recurrence occurs. From the **Appointment** tab, select the **Recurrence** icon. At the bottom of the dialog box, choose **Remove Recurrence**.

6. For **Reminders**, you will receive a pop-up reminder **15 minutes** before an appointment begins. This reminder can be turned off or set for a longer period of time. You would probably miss someone's birthday party if you only have 15 minutes to get there or buy a gift! Additionally, you can assign a sound to your reminders.

7. To format appointments, take a look at the **Format Text** tab when you create an appointment. All the options from the Word 2021 environment that you are used to can be accessed from here. **WordArt** can be inserted alongside files, Outlook items, tables, charts, pictures, clip art, **SmartArt**, screenshots, textboxes, drop caps, and objects. In addition, the horizontal line icon is available here. Remember to click inside the body of the email message prior to clicking on the **Format Text** tab.

8. Note that at the end of the **Appointment** ribbon, there is a button named **View Templates**. This button is a great feature to formulate and house quick email responses (templates) to add to appointments or meetings, saving you lots of time:

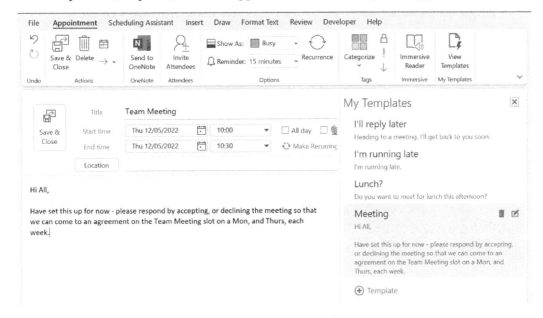

Figure 15.3 – Viewing templates

9. Simply click on the template you would like to apply to the body of the appointment or meeting. The template is added to the message body. Note this is useful if you are using the **Inviting Attendees** option for the meeting or appointment.

10. Click on **Save & Close** to add the appointment to the calendar.

Inviting participants to a meeting or appointment

1. Open an existing meeting or appointment in your calendar or create a new appointment or a new meeting.

2. Make sure you are in the **Appointment** tab, then click on **Invite Attendees,** after which the appointment will turn into a meeting. If you are creating a meeting, you can simply add the participants into the **Required** or **Optional** fields.

3. As you start to enter the participants' names, the application will try to complete the names for you. This is especially useful if the participants already exist in your address book. To check whether the names you have typed into the field are correct, click on the **Check Names** icon, which is located in the **Attendees** group:

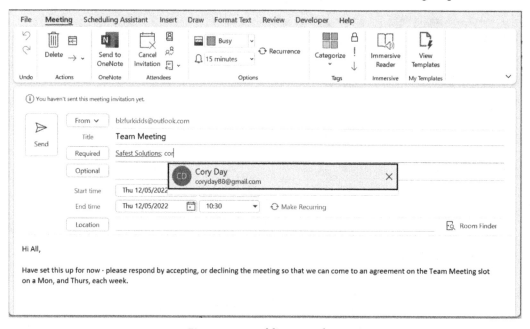

Figure 15.4 – Adding attendees

4. Once you have filled in all the required fields, you can click on the **Send** button to send the meeting request to the attendees. The meeting request will arrive in their mailbox along with several buttons (**Accept, Decline, Tentative**, or reply to **Propose New Time**). It will also appear in their personal calendar:

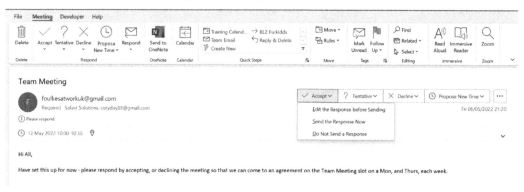

Figure 15.5 – Responding to a new meeting request

5. When we add attendees to our meeting, we can use the **Scheduling Assistant** tab to view the availability of all the attendees to find an available time slot during which to hold the meeting.

6. The **Scheduling Assistant** tab contains a number of buttons to **Add Rooms** (resources), **Add Attendees**, and various categories along the bottom of the window detailing the different categories and color-coding settings:

Figure 15.6 – The Scheduling Assistant screen

In the next section, we will learn how to forward an appointment to others.

Forwarding an appointment

If you have been invited to a meeting, and think a co-worker can benefit from attending, it can be forwarded to others:

1. Navigate to the calendar. Then, click on an appointment to select it.

2. From the **Appointment** tab, click on the **Forward** icon:

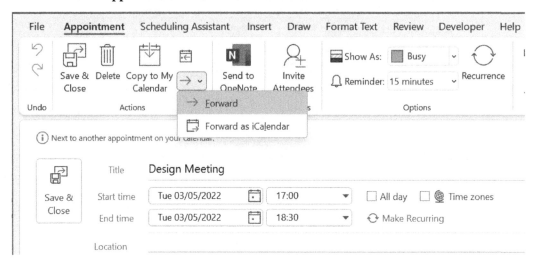

Figure 15.7 – Forwarding appointments

3. A new email will open, listing all the information about the meeting:

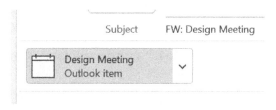

Figure 15.8 – Adding the meeting as an attachment to forward to others

4. Enter a recipient in the **To:** text area. Click on the **Send** icon to forward the message.

   When we are creating a new meeting using Microsoft 365 or Outlook for the web, we can stop the forwarding of meetings to others.

5. Create **New Meeting** and then click on **Allow forwarding** to deselect it and stop the recipients of the meeting from forwarding it on.

6. Complete the meeting details and then **Send** the meeting as usual:

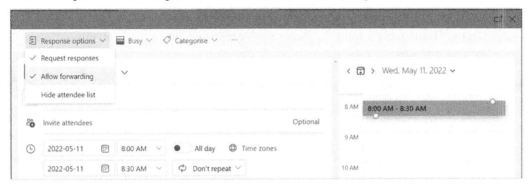

Figure 15.9 – The Office 365 Outlook meeting detailing Response options

In the next section, we will run through the steps for printing the appointment details if required.

Printing the appointment details

Although we can print the appointment details, this might not be something that is encouraged in a business or at home. Today, we have so many opportunities to work online, using our mobile phones, and gain access to remote meetings on the go when we travel or are at the office:

1. Double-click on an appointment to view its details.

2. From the **File** tab, choose the **Print** menu item.

3. The appointment is displayed in **Memo Style**. Look at the preview pane to see the appointment details.

4. Check that you are happy with the print settings and always check that you have the correct printer selected. A business could make use of specific printer software, such as PaperCut, to manage the print process. Click on the **Print** icon to send it to the printer.

Scheduling a meeting with someone who sent a message

1. If you receive an email message from someone, for example, asking you for a coffee catch-up, you can create a meeting directly from the message. Double-click on the message to open it.

2. On the **Home** tab, click on the **Reply with Meeting** icon to create an appointment in your calendar:

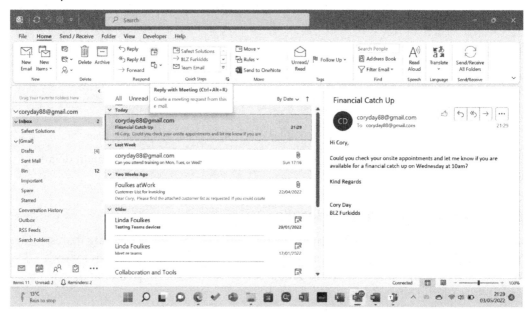

Figure 15.10 – The Reply with Meeting button

3. The name of the recipient will automatically be inserted into the **To:** text area. Click on **Send** to add the appointment to your diary and send the meeting request to the recipient (that is, the person who sent you the email message in the first place).

Sharing a calendar

It is possible to share your calendar with other contacts and ask permission to gain access to their calendars. When sharing a calendar, we can choose to only share certain details, such as the **Availability Only**, **Limited Details**, or **Full Calendar** details. Outlook accounts can share calendars, but not IMAP accounts. This is only achieved if the account is added as a Microsoft Exchange account to Outlook:

1. Open the calendar by clicking on the **Calendar** icon at the bottom of the Navigation Pane.

2. Click on **Share Calendar** in the ribbon.

3. Enter the name of the contact that you would like to grant access to your calendar:

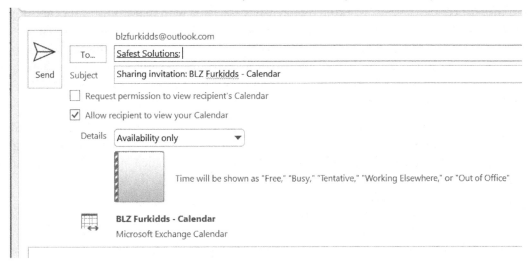

Figure 15.11 – Sharing Outlook calendars

4. Choose a sharing option from the **Details** drop-down list—either **Availability Only**, **Limited Details**, or **Full Details** access. For this example, we will choose **Availability Only**.

5. When you have finished, click on **Send**:

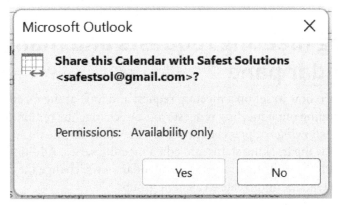

Figure 15.12 – Clicking on Yes to share your calendar

6. A notification will pop up on the screen asking whether you are sure you want to share the calendar with the permissions you have granted. Click on **Yes** to continue.

Scheduling remote meetings

In the past couple of years, working remotely has escalated with many businesses choosing a blend of office and home working. We have the ability to schedule **Zoom**, **Teams**, and **Skype** meetings through our Outlook calendars. Currently, Microsoft Teams and Zoom are the two most popular tools available. Skype could be the default in your application, depending on whether you have this enabled or disabled if you are using the Microsoft 365 environment.

Outlook will display the Teams and/or Zoom meeting icons on the calendar's **Home** tab and in the **New Appointment** screen you are creating. If you do not see the **New Teams Meeting** icon in your Outlook environment, it could be that you are not signed into the Teams app on your desktop or the Teams add-in for Outlook has not been installed correctly:

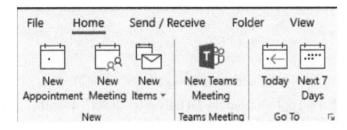

Figure 15.13 – The New Teams Meeting icon on the Home tab

In the next section, we will concentrate on meeting options and responses.

Modifying meeting requests and manipulating the calendar pane

Now, you will learn how to set up a meeting request and look at the meeting response options. After sending out a meeting request, you can change the options to update or cancel a meeting, allowing recipients to propose a new time for the meeting. Next, we will look at how to view the tracking status and edit a meeting series. Additionally, this section will equip you with the skills to arrange your calendar views, change the calendar formats, display or hide calendars, and create a calendar group.

Setting the response options

Before sending a meeting request, you can set the response options. If you would like the recipient to be prompted to accept, reject, or tentatively accept the meeting request, then you need to check whether those options have been selected. Also, you can request a new time slot if the meeting time does not suit you. By default, both of these options should be activated in the Outlook program:

1.   Open your calendar and then select **New Meeting** from the **New** group. Once you have filled out the meeting details, you can set the response options:

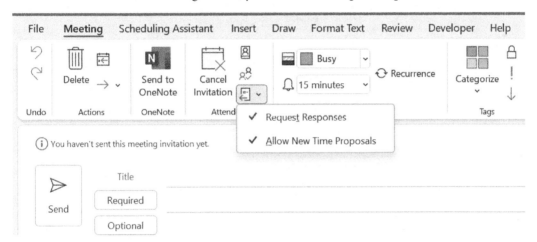

Figure 15.14 – The meeting response options

2.   From the **Attendees** group, select **Response Options**. You can choose **Request Responses** and/or **Allow New Time Proposals**. Both of these options are turned on by default.

Updating a meeting request

To update a meeting request, double-click on the appointment in your calendar. Once the appointment is open, change the details to update them. Once you are done, you need to click on the **Send Update** icon to resend the meeting to all of the recipients so that their calendars adjust accordingly.

Canceling a meeting or invitation

1. Open the meeting that you need to cancel from your calendar.

2. Click on the **Cancel Meeting** icon under the **Meeting** tab. Don't forget to click on **Cancel Meeting**. Then, click on the **Send Cancellation** button to send an update to the recipients:

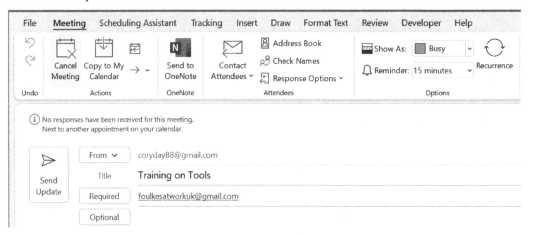

Figure 15.15 – Canceling a meeting and notifying the recipients

Next, let's learn how to suggest another time slot for a meeting.

Proposing a new time for a meeting

If you are unable to make the time of a meeting request, a new time can be proposed and sent to the sender:

1. Open the meeting request from your inbox.

2. Click on the **Propose New Time** icon on the **Meeting** tab or from the **Respond** area of the meeting.

3. Choose either **Tentative and Propose New Time** or **Decline and Propose New Time** to select a time that you are available:

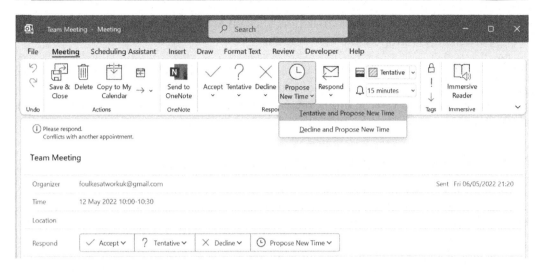

Figure 15.16 – Proposing a new time for a meeting

4. Once you have selected a new proposed time using the drop-down arrows next to **Meeting start time** and **Meeting end time**, or you have used the **AutoPick Next >>** button to find the next available time slot, click on **Propose Time** to reply to the meeting request:

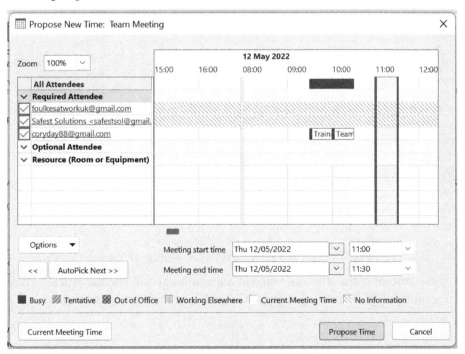

Figure 15.17 – Proposing a new time slot

5.   Once you have checked the invitation, click on **Send** to forward the email to participants to propose the new time slot.

The next section is extremely valuable if you are working with calendar appointments, meetings, and events for the majority of your day. Even though the Teams and Zoom platforms allow you to view an online attendance record, it is good to see, at a glance, who has responded to your meeting request.

Viewing the tracking status of a meeting

If you have sent a meeting request to a number of attendees and would like to see whether they have responded without having to check your email countless times, the **Tracking** feature is a wonderful tool to use:

1.   Click on the meeting entry in your calendar.

2.   Locate the **Tracking** tab to view the individual responses from recipients of the invite:

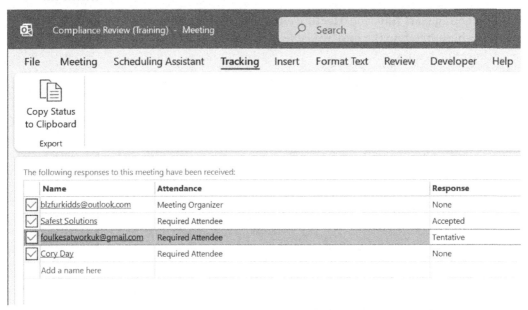

Figure 15.18 – The Tracking tab when viewing a meeting

3.   At the bottom of the window, you will see a summary of who has and who hasn't responded to your meeting request. Close the pane when you are finished.

> **Note**
>
> Note that you can also take a screenshot of the tracking detail by clicking on the **Copy Status to Clipboard** button and then pasting it into an Excel worksheet if required. This way, you can keep a record of meeting attendance. Remember that when working with online platforms, such as Teams and Zoom, we can download or access attendance reports after the meeting. We will concentrate on these, and more, features in the online meeting chapters that follow in this book.

Now, let's learn how to edit a series of meetings in one go.

Editing a meeting series

If you have set a recurring appointment and wish to edit the entire series, simply open the appointment. A dialog box will prompt you to choose whether you would like to edit the series or just the appointment you clicked on:

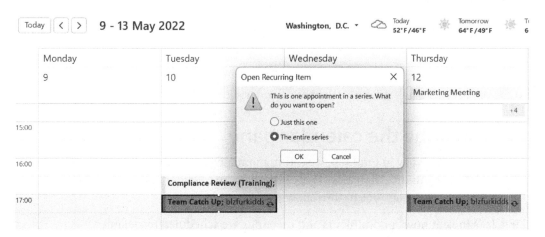

Figure 15.19 – Editing a recurring item in the calendar

Click on **The entire series**. Then, make the changes to the appointment. Click on **Save & Close** once you are done to update the series.

In the next section, we will look at how to quickly add participants or contacts to meetings.

Using the @ mention feature

To quickly add contacts to an email or meeting, simply type the @ sign followed by the name of the contact. A drop-down list will appear with matching contacts. Press *Tab* on the keyboard to automatically populate the contact. The contact is then automatically added as an attendee to the meeting:

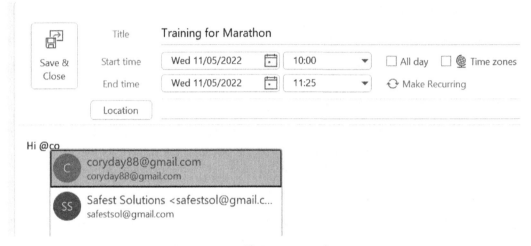

Figure 15.20 – The @ mention feature

In the next section, let's investigate some calendar settings.

Manipulating the calendar pane

Just like any other view in Outlook, we can manipulate the calendar's elements, such as the font settings and the color, and arrange the way the calendar entries are displayed. Let's investigate these options in the following sections.

First, let's look at how appointments and meetings are scheduled by default.

Setting the default meeting and appointment duration

We can set the default duration for meetings and appointments in Outlook. The default setting is set to 30 minutes. To change this setting so that all appointments and meetings are created with a 1-hour duration, visit the **File | Options | Calendar** settings in Outlook. Navigate to the **Calendar options** heading and then change the **Default duration for new appointments and meetings** setting to **1 hour**. Click on the **OK** button to commit to this change.

Create a new appointment in the calendar—note that the default duration is now set to 1 hour.

Microsoft 365 also offers the ability to **End appointments and meetings early** by adjusting the meeting time to allow meeting durations of less than 1 hour, or longer than 1 hour, to end earlier:

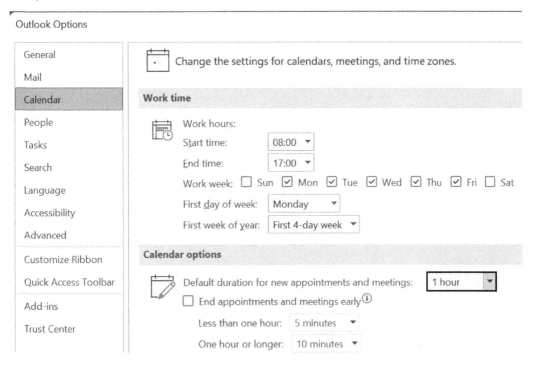

Figure 15.21 – The Outlook calendar options

This is a perfect setting to adjust when booking calendar appointments for conferences, for example, to allow participants to move to the next venue with enough time to make the next meeting.

This option is located just below the **Default duration for new appointments and meetings** option. Click on the **End appointments and meetings early** checkbox, then enter the appropriate duration into either the **Less than one hour** or **One hour or longer** drop-down list.

Once this setting has been applied, the appointment details for all activities in the calendar will update to the new *end time* accordingly. Take a look at the following screenshot:

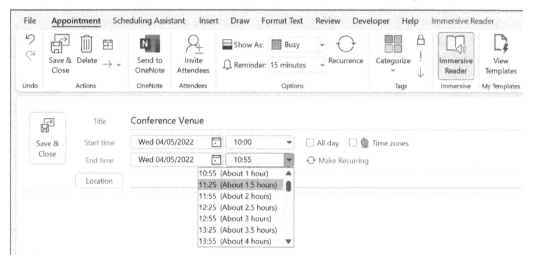

Figure 15.22 – Ending appointments and meetings early

In the next section, we will concentrate on learning about further calendar options.

Arranging the calendar view

The default calendar view in Outlook is set to **Month**. When you open the calendar from the bottom of the Navigation Pane, you will notice that the **View** tab is available for the Calendar arrangement. Click on **Day**, **Work Week**, **Week**, **Month**, or **Schedule View** to display the calendar in your preferred format.

Schedule View displays the calendar horizontally. You can use **Schedule View** when viewing multiple calendars, as this view allows more space on the interface window. The calendar arrangement options are also available under the **Home** tab.

Changing the calendar color

Applying color to the calendar elements is easy; simply use the **Color** button on the **View** tab. In addition, **Conditional Formatting** can be applied for more color-specific calendar changes. Let's look at both of them:

1. Click on the **Calendar** icon at the bottom of the Navigation Pane to access the calendar.

2. From the **Color** group under the **View** tab, select the **Color** icon. A drop-down list of colors will appear. Select a color to apply to your calendar.

3. The calendar will update to the chosen color. Additionally, the color of the calendar can be set in the Outlook **Options** dialog box.

Changing the calendar's font settings

To change the calendar's font settings and the other **Day**, **Week**, and **Month** view settings, click on the **View Settings** icon when viewing the calendar. Choose **Other Settings...** from the **Advanced View Settings: Calendar** dialog box that appears on your screen. From the **Format Calendar** dialog box, choose **Font...** to apply changes to the font and size attributes. Note that you can also set **Time scale** for **Day and Week View**:

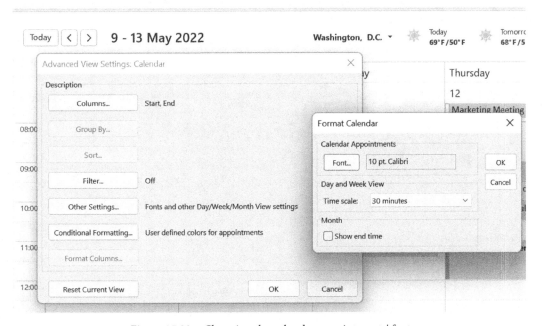

Figure 15.23 – Changing the calendar appointments' font

In the next section, we will look at how to display and hide calendars.

Displaying or hiding calendars

It is extremely useful to be able to hide or show calendars when working with others from the same or external organizations. If you have access to someone's calendar, you can show or hide it in your calendar view. You can send an invitation to others so that they can access your calendar in the contacts list within Outlook. This is only possible with an Exchange, Microsoft 365, or Outlook.com account:

1. At the bottom of the calendar folder pane, you will notice a number of different calendar headings. The first is **My Calendars**, the second is **Other Calendars**, and the third is **Shared Calendars**. In the following screenshot, **Calendar - blzfurkidds@ outlook.com** is visible because that particular calendar has been selected:

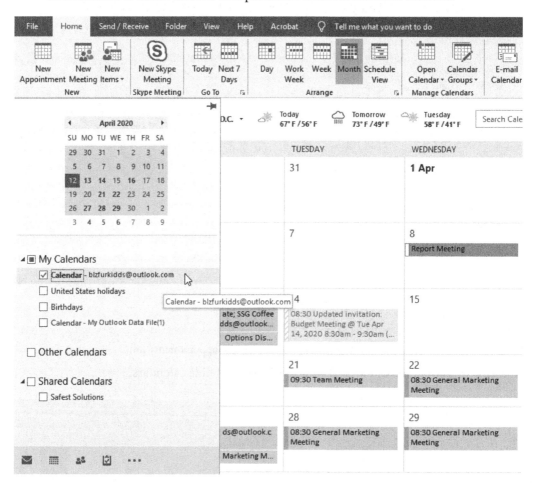

Figure 15.24 – The calendar categories in the Outlook Calendar view

2. To view another calendar alongside your personal calendar, click on it from the **Shared Calendars** folder to view it. You will notice that you also have access to the **Safest Solutions** calendar, as it is listed under **Shared Calendars**:

Figure 15.25 – Shared Calendars

3. Once you check a calendar to add it (in this example, **Safest Solutions**), the calendar is shown on the right-hand side of your personal calendar. At times, the calendar might be placed in **Overlay** mode.

4. To hide the selected calendar, click on the **x** icon at the end of the **Calendar** tab, right-click on the tab, and choose **Hide This Calendar**. Alternatively, click on the name of the calendar under **Shared Calendars** to hide it from view:

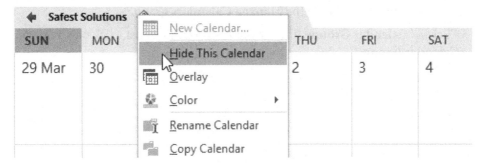

Figure 15.26 – The Hide This Calendar feature

5. Calendars can also be set to **Overlay**. This is very useful when you want to view multiple calendars at the same time in one calendar view. Right-click on the **Calendar** tab and then choose **Overlay**.

6. If you can't see a calendar that you need under the **Shared Calendars** heading on the left-hand side of the calendar view, click on **Open Calendar** from the top-level ribbon. You can choose to open a calendar using the **From Address Book...**, **Create New Blank Calendar...**, **From Room List…**, **From Internet…**, or **Open Shared Calendar...** options:

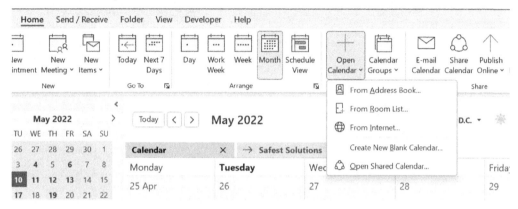

Figure 15.27 – The Open Calendar drop-down list

Note that certain calendars will require permission from the owner to open them.

Creating a calendar group

1. Open the calendar view by clicking on the icon at the bottom of the Navigation Pane.

2. From the **Home** tab, locate the **Manage Calendars** group.

3. Click on **Calendar Groups**. Then, from the drop-down list, click on **Create New Calendar Group**:

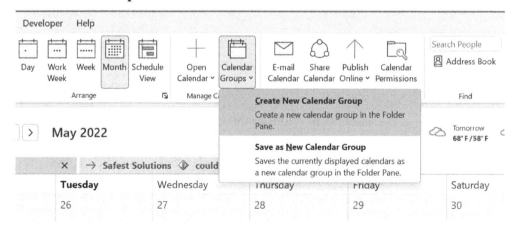

Figure 15.28 – The Create New Calendar Group option

4. In the dialog box, type a name for the new calendar into the text area that is provided. For this example, we will create a calendar group called `SSG Calendar`. When you are done, click on **OK**:

Figure 15.29 – SSG Calendar

5. Select **Contacts** from the address book to view all of the available contacts. Double-click on each contact to add them to the **Group Members** section at the bottom of the dialog box. Click on **OK** when done.

6. The calendar information will display on your screen. If someone from your group has not shared their calendar, then you will not be able to view it. Click on the **Send a sharing request to see more details for this Calendar** icon in the bottom-right corner of each of the contacts in the calendar to see more details in the calendar:

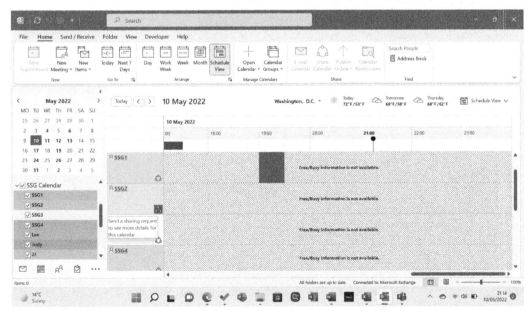

Figure 15.30 – The Send a sharing request button

Each person is displayed in a different color on the calendar, and you can hide or display individual calendars using the group list on the left-hand side under the folder pane.

Creating and managing tasks

In this section, you'll learn how to create and manage a task so that you receive a reminder of items you need to complete by a certain date and a status report. Additionally, we will cover how to mark tasks as complete and assign a task to another Outlook user. Accepting and declining task assignments will also be covered in this section.

Creating tasks

1. Click on the **Tasks** icon at the bottom of the Navigation Pane:

Figure 15.31 – The Tasks button on the navigation bar

2. In the task window, you will see any follow-up messages you have received, along with any outstanding tasks or to-do list items.

3. Click on the **Home** tab and then select the **New Task** icon:

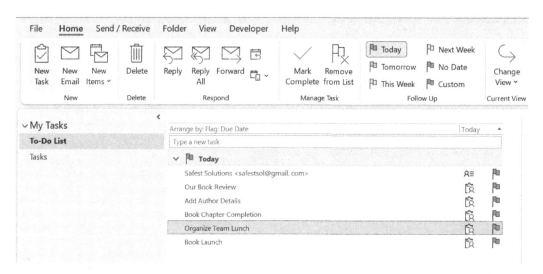

Figure 15.32 – The New Task button on the Home tab

4.   Fill out the details of the task:

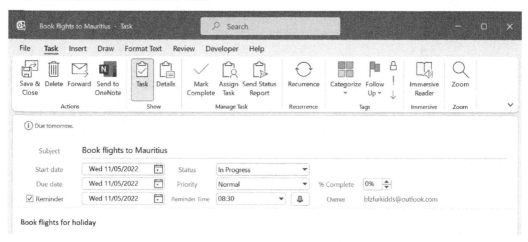

Figure 15.33 – A new task pane

5.   Click on the **Save & Close** icon.

> **Note**
>
> Outlook items can be dragged to the **Tasks** icon in the Navigation Pane to create a task from the item. This is the quickest way to create a task as it fills in all required information from the Outlook item. Also, you can set a reminder for a task as you would with appointments.

Managing the task details

1.   Open a task to view its contents. Take a look at the **Task** and **Details** options in the **Show** group of the **Task** tab. This area is used to enter any secondary information about the task or to update the task.

2.   Click on the **Save & Close** icon to update and close the task.

Sending a status report

Sending an email to someone to let them know how far you have got with a task is really simple. Perform the following steps:

1. Open the task, then select the **Task** tab.

2. Click on the **Send Status Report** option in the **Manage Task** group:

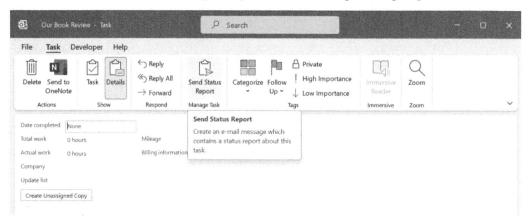

Figure 15.34 – Send Status Report

3. A new email is created with **Task Status Report: Our Book Review** as the subject (in this case, **Our Book Review** is the name of the task).

4. In the body of the message, the task details are listed, indicating the percentage of completion. Note that the **% Complete** option will not work unless you diligently update the task as you work on it. Enter a recipient into the **To…** text area. Click on **Send**.

Now, let's look at how we would assign a task to others.

Assigning a task to another Outlook contact

It is really easy to assign tasks to others within the business or another contact within your Outlook address book. Perform the following steps:

1. Create a task to assign to a colleague.

2. Click on the **Assign Task** icon under the **Manage Task** group, which is located on the **Task** tab:

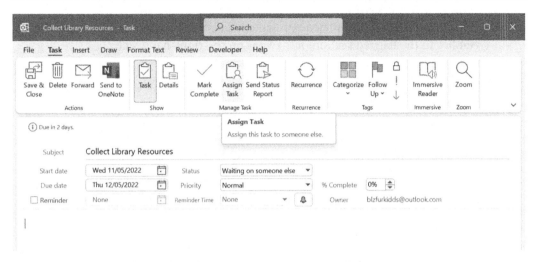

Figure 15.35 – The Assign Task option

3. In the **To…** text area, type in an address to send the task to or click to populate the address book to select a contact. Make sure the task details have been filled in correctly. Click on **Send**.

Marking a task as complete

1. Open the task that you want to update.

2. Under the **Task** tab, locate the **Mark Complete** icon and click on it. Alternatively, select the task in the **Tasks** pane and then click on the **Mark Complete** icon:

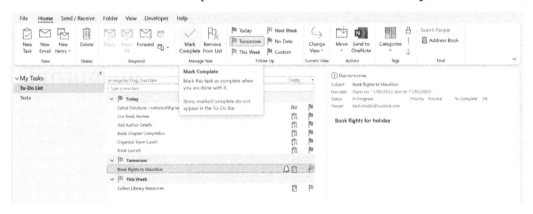

Figure 15.36 – Marking a task as complete

3. The task is marked as complete with strikethrough lines in the **Tasks** pane and a *green tick* in the flagged section of the view on the right-hand side:

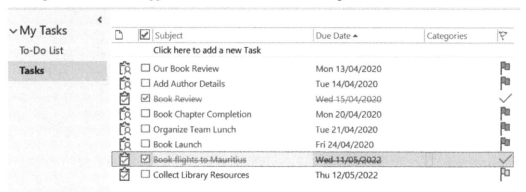

Figure 15.37 – The Tasks pane showing a strikethrough in the completed task with a green tick

4. Note that the task was automatically moved from the **To-Do List** pane to the **Tasks** pane when marked as complete.

Accepting or declining a task assignment

When we assign tasks to other users, they can decide to accept or reject the task. Let's run through the steps:

1. In your inbox, open a task that you have received.

2. Click **Accept** or **Decline** using the icons under the **Respond** ribbon.

Now we will take a look at notes and journal entries.

Creating and manipulating notes and journal entries

In this section, you will learn how to create a note, change the current view, and categorize notes.

Creating a note

A **note** is a useful space in which to jot down thoughts and ideas within Outlook 2021. You can drag notes from Outlook 2021 to your Windows desktop so that they are always visible, even when you are not in the Outlook application. Notes can be categorized in the same way as any other item within Outlook. **OneNote** is the master application that we can use, as this integrates with all of the Microsoft applications—we will concentrate on the OneNote features in the following chapters of this book:

1. Click on the three dots at the bottom of the Navigation Pane to access the **Notes** option:

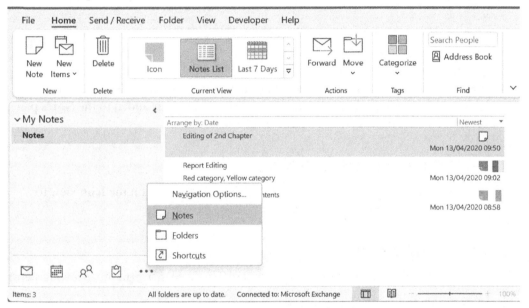

Figure 15.38 – The Notes window

2. The **Notes** window will open. Click on the **New Note** icon to create a new note.

3. The **New Note** icon opens at the top of the Outlook window in a separate window and can be moved to the desktop while Outlook is open:

Figure 15.39 – Creating a new note

4. Once you have typed some text into your new note, close the note using the **X** symbol in the upper-right corner of the screen. The note is added to the **Notes** pane. The first line of the note's text becomes its title.

Changing the current view

Notes can be viewed in icons, lists, and the last 7 days' view. Click on the **Icon** view to change the view in the **Current View** group.

Categorizing notes

Notes are categorized just like other items in Outlook. To do so, perform the following steps:

1. Select the note you want to categorize.

2. Click on the **Categorize** icon under the **Home** tab.

3. Select an existing category or click on **All Categories…** to assign a different category to the new note.

Working with journal entries

In this section, we will look at how to manipulate journal entries by recording Outlook items and folders and how to edit a journal entry. A journal records actions you choose that relate to different contacts and enters the information into a timeline. The journal can track meetings and email messages, along with other Office program files. The timeline shows all the items that have been sent, received, created, saved, or opened, as well as items that you have made changes to.

Tracking Outlook items and files

1. Click on the three dots in the lower-right corner of the Navigation Pane.

2. Choose **Folders** and then locate **Journal**. In this view, you will see any previously tracked items, and you will be able to create new ones:

Figure 15.40 – Navigating to the journal using the Folders button

3. Click on the **Home** tab. Then, select **Journal Entry** from the **New** group to create a new entry. Enter a subject for the journal entry. Add details about the journal entry, such as **Entry type** and **Start time**.

4. **Start Timer** is a very useful tool to track the amount of time a task takes—for example, you might track a client business call so that you can bill the client for your time:

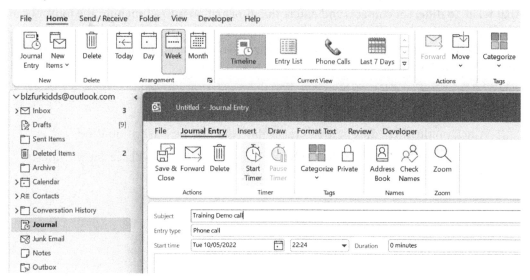

Figure 15.41 – Journal Entry

5. Click on **Save & Close** to view the entry in the timeline. You can change the view to display the entries in a list by clicking on the **Entry List** icon under the **Current View** group:

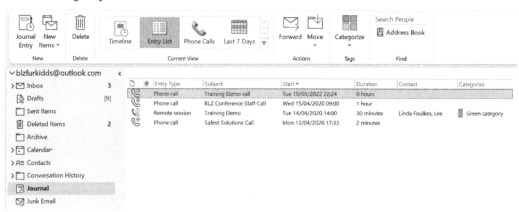

Figure 15.42 – The Journal Entry List view

6. To edit a journal entry, simply double-click on the entry in the **Timeline** view or the **Entry List** view. Make changes to the entry and then click on the **Save & Close** icon again to update it.

Setting out-of-office options

If you are going to be away from your desk or office for a long period of time (for example, if you are going on holiday or to a conference), you can set up an automatic reply that notifies others that you are unable to respond to incoming email messages. To do so, perform the following steps:

1. Click on **File**. Then, choose **Automatic Replies** from the Backstage view.

2. In the **Automatic Replies** dialog box, click on **Send automatic replies**. Make sure that **Only send during this time range:** is selected if you are only going to be out of the office for a set amount of time—for example, for annual leave or maternity leave.

3. Enter the **Start time** and **End time** criteria. Then, add an explanatory note in the space provided under the **Automatic replies** section. Note that you can format your message using the formatting options located on the **Automatic replies** tab. Click on **OK** to set the automatic reply:

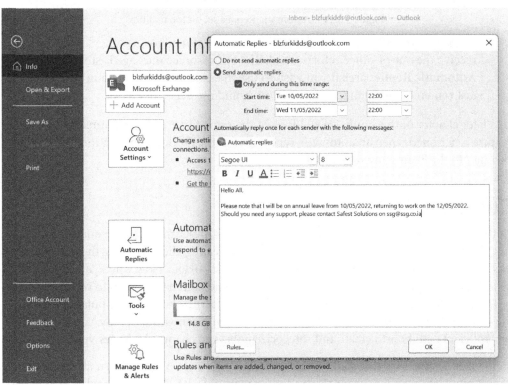

Figure 15.43 – Setting an out-of-office reply

The automatic reply is set and all messages that you receive are automatically responded to with this message, highlighting that you are away from the office and for how long.

4.   When you visit your inbox, you will see a yellow notification, just under the ribbon, indicating that you have an automatic reply set on your mailbox:

Figure 15.44 – Automatic Replies set on the mailbox

5.   Click on **Turn off** to remove the setting from your mailbox so others no longer receive the out-of-office return email. The out-of-office message is stored in the **Automatic Replies** area if you wish to use the same message again in the future— just remember to change the dates, times, and message.

In a later chapter of this book, we will look at the same feature in the **Teams** app. This feature is actioned when an automatic reply is set in the Outlook application and will pull through to the Teams environment.

Summary

In this final chapter, you mastered working with notes, tasks, the calendar, and the journal in Outlook 2021. You should now feel confident in creating and managing these items and working with the different views and options that are available. Now when you are out of the office, you understand how to set up the option to send automatic replies to recipients and how to turn this setting off on your return. You have learned how to manipulate calendar views, change the calendar color, and set up a calendar group. Additionally, you should now be proficient with how to create and categorize notes and change the **Notes** view.

In the next chapter, we will concentrate on online meetings. We will learn all about the Teams application and discover top tips when working with Teams channels, learn how to collaborate with others, and learn how to work with files within the Teams environment. Additionally, we will concentrate on the remote meeting space and learn how to present with PowerPoint in a Teams meeting.

16
Creating and Managing Online Meetings

Many working environments have altered in one way or another over the past 2 years with a focus on remote working, so the aspects of this chapter are very relevant and being enhanced within the workplace and industry.

This chapter will introduce you to all the significant features you can use to communicate and collaborate using online tools such as Microsoft Teams and Zoom. We will learn how to set up meetings within the Outlook 2021 environment, as well as how to join and manage meetings. We will also learn about the different ways to present content using the **Share** icon within Teams and Zoom, as well as the best way to work with meeting notes.

In addition, we will discover the Teams app and point out useful features and top tips for creating and managing Channels. We will also look at brilliant tools such as OneNote and Tasks by Planner, as well as learn how to collaborate in real time. Finally, we will introduce the **Bookings and Approvals** app.

In this chapter, we will cover the following topics:

- Adding remote meetings to Outlook
- Creating and managing Channels

Technical requirements

Prior knowledge of the Teams/Zoom environment is not necessary. It is, however, imperative that you have the relevant software available to practice and work through this chapter. It is advantageous to have prior knowledge of the Outlook 2021 email application and be familiar with creating appointments in the Calendar view. The examples for this chapter can be found in this book's GitHub repository at `https://github.com/PacktPublishing/Learn-Microsoft-Office-2021-Second-Edition`.

Adding remote meetings to Outlook

Remote meeting tools are available as add-ins if you have access to Microsoft 365 and your business supports a meeting platform, such as **Teams** or **Zoom**. The primary user must ensure that at least one Exchange mailbox has been set up in their Outlook profile to schedule Teams meetings or Zoom meetings using the add-in (the client needs to have Exchange set up in the background).

> **Note**
>
> We can also create remote meetings using the Zoom and Teams platforms directly. For instance, Zoom meetings can be scheduled using the Zoom website or the Zoom app instead. **Internet Message Access Protocol** (**IMAP**) or **Post Office Protocol** (**POP3**) email accounts can schedule meetings using the Outlook web app. A Gmail address would be an example of an IMAP account.

IMAP ensures that all your mail is available on all your devices when it's accessed through the Outlook client. For example, if I download an email through Outlook on my laptop, then it will be available on my phone too. IMAP talks back and forth with the mail server to sync data. Emails are always kept on the mail server.

POP, on the other hand, accesses mail from the server and downloads it to the client (Outlook 2021 on your laptop) only. POP does not make the downloaded mail available through accounts on your devices automatically (no data syncing happens).

The **Skype Meeting add-in for Microsoft Office**, although not as popular as Teams and Zoom today, is also available by going to **File | Options | Add-ins** in Outlook 2021. If you would like to use this tool, make sure it is enabled in this area.

The Zoom and Teams add-ins can be deployed to users in a business via an admin user through the Microsoft 365 admin center. The add-ins that are deployed to users can be selected from either the store or as a custom add-in. This setting can take up to 12 hours to deploy:

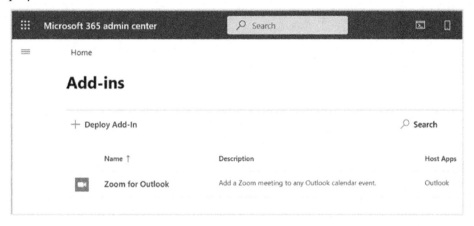

Figure 16.1 – Zoom for Outlook deployed through the Microsoft 365 admin center

If your mail hasn't been configured through Exchange but you wish to use the Outlook app, you can deploy the **Zoom for Outlook** add-in by visiting the **Microsoft Store**, after which you can sign in using your Outlook credentials.

The following screenshot shows a new remote meeting in **Outlook on the web** showing the *Teams meeting* location as the default, with the option to **Add a Zoom Meeting** from the ribbon:

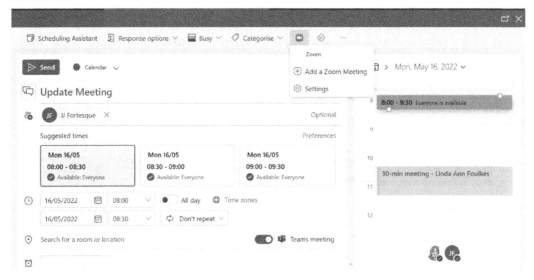

Figure 16.2 – The Add a Zoom Meeting button

Microsoft Teams is configured and customized through the Microsoft 365 admin center if it is part of the plan you have purchased. You may need to download Teams on the client if it's not already installed.

Learning about Teams and Zoom meeting add-ins

In this section, we will discuss both the Zoom and Teams meeting add-ins and learn how to create Team and Zoom meetings. We will also discuss a few troubleshooting tips.

Creating meetings using the Zoom meeting add-in

Adding a Zoom meeting to an appointment in Outlook is a simple process. Follow these steps:

1. Open the Outlook 2021 application.

2. Double-click on the **Calendar** icon to create a new meeting.

3. Locate the **Add a Zoom Meeting** icon at the end of the ribbon:

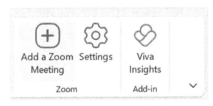

Figure 16.3 – Add a Zoom Meeting

4. Sign in to your Zoom account or sign up for the Zoom service. If you prefer, before creating Zoom meetings within Outlook 2021, you can sign up for the service at `http://zoom.us`.

5. Once you have signed into Zoom, the meeting's details will appear in the meeting body in Outlook. Note that the details here are dependent on the type of plan you have signed up for with Zoom as you would not receive audio conference dial-in via phone audio with a Basic Plan. The *Basic Plan* is a free plan that allows for 40-minute meetings to take place.

6. Enter the meeting's details, invite attendees, and check the date and time. The meeting link is included in the body of the message detail, along with the *Meeting ID* and *Passcode*:

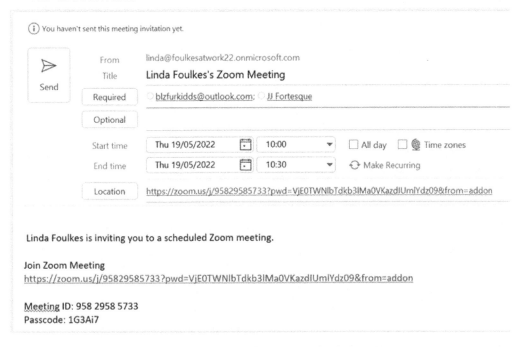

Figure 16.4 – Zoom meeting details in a calendar appointment

7. Click on the **Send** button to forward the remote meeting to recipients.

> **Tip**
>
> Once the Zoom meeting's details have been added to the body of the meeting, the **Join Zoom Meeting** link is often not formatted as a hyperlink. A quick tip is to always include a space after the link so that it turns into a hyperlink. This will help your meeting participants a lot as they can just use the *Ctrl + click* shortcut to access the meeting.

In addition to the Zoom add-in, the Zoom plugin can be downloaded, which provides a different set of online meeting icons on the Outlook ribbon. Let's investigate this option next.

Zoom Outlook plugin

After signing up for a Zoom account online, the option to download the **Microsoft Office plugin** for Zoom becomes available. Follow these steps:

1. Click the **Download** link to install the plugin for Outlook:

Figure 16.5 – Microsoft Outlook Plugin

2. This will enable the **Zoom** group in the Outlook ribbon, along with the **Schedule a Meeting** and **Start Instant Meeting** buttons:

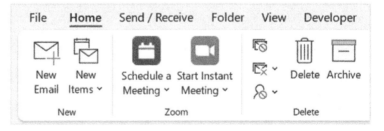

Figure 16.6 – The Schedule a Meeting and Start Instant Meeting buttons

3. Click the **Schedule a Meeting** icon to create a remote meeting.

4. The **Zoom – Schedule Meeting** dialog box will populate, allowing you to set various meeting options. Options such as setting the **Participants** video to **On**, and whether you wish to only allow users that have been admitted by the host to join the meeting, are just a few settings here. The number of options also depends on which Zoom plan you have signed up for:

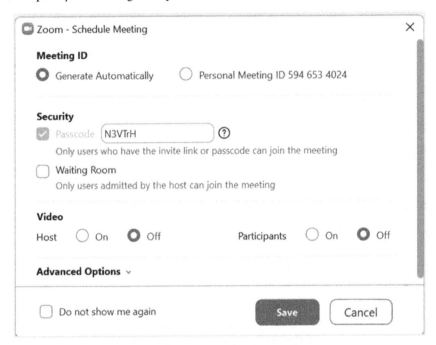

Figure 16.7 – The Zoom – Schedule Meeting dialog box

5. Click the drop-down arrow to the right of the **Advanced Options** heading for further settings. A useful option to remember in this area would be the ability to add additional hosts to take over the meeting if the original host is unavailable at the time to take the meeting. This option is only available on paid plans.

Zoom's buttons and settings are very similar to those in the Teams platform. Now, let's learn how to create a Teams meeting.

Teams meeting add-in

It is important to investigate whether you are signed into Microsoft Teams on your desktop before creating any remote meetings in the calendar. This ensures that the **New Team Meeting** icon is visible in the calendar. If this icon is missing, the first thing to check is that you are signed into Microsoft Teams.

Let's create a meeting within the Outlook 2021 calendar:

1. Open Outlook 2021, then use the navigation pane to open the Calendar.

2. A **New Teams Meeting** icon, along with the **Meet Now** icon, will be visible on the Calendar ribbon, as well as the **Teams Meeting** icon within the appointment screen:

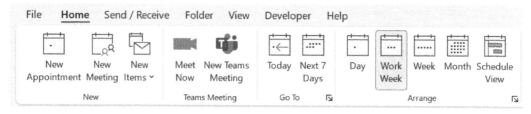

Figure 16.8 – The New Teams Meeting and Meet Now icons on the Calendar ribbon

3. Click on the **New Teams Meeting** icon to create a new remote appointment for a future date and time or use the **Meet Now** icon to meet immediately with others.

> **Note**
> Double-clicking on the Calendar is another way to create a new remote meeting.

4. Fill out the details for the meeting by entering the **Required** participants into the relevant field, adding a **Title**, and checking the **Start time** and **End time** details.

5. Note that the **Microsoft Teams meeting** detail to join the meeting is automatically added to the body of the email. You can navigate to the web using the **Meeting options** link below the **Microsoft Teams meeting** detail in the body of the message to customize the meeting options (you will need to authenticate your account using the Authenticator app or method of your choice). The same set of options is available on the **Meeting Options** ribbon, which is located in the **Teams Meeting** group:

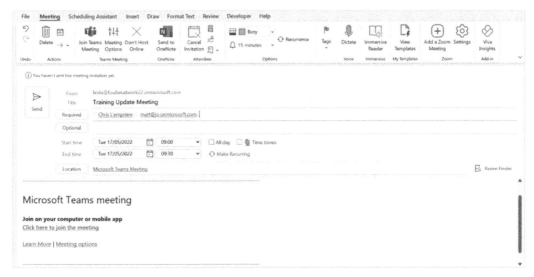

Figure 16.9 – Microsoft Teams meeting detail

6. Once all the details have been added to the **Meeting** tab, click the **Send** button. The recipients can then accept or decline the meeting.

Now, let's look at a few troubleshooting tips you should run through, should you have trouble trying to connect the Teams and Zoom apps to the Outlook 2021 environment.

Troubleshooting the Teams Meeting icon

There are a handful of reasons why the **Teams Meeting** icon may not be visible in the Outlook 2021 calendar. The first troubleshooting tip would be to log out of the Teams app and Outlook 2021, then restart Teams before Outlook. This should enable the **Teams Meeting** icon in the Outlook calendar. Let's look at a few further troubleshooting techniques.

Registering Teams as a Chat app

Follow these steps:

1. Open the **Microsoft Teams** app on your desktop.

2. Click on the *ellipsis* to the left of the profile image at the top of the screen.

3. Click on **Settings**:

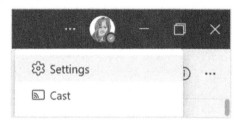

Figure 16.10 – The Settings icon in the Teams app

4. The **General** options are visible by default. Scroll down to access the **Application** heading, then ensure that **Register Teams as the Chat app for Office (requires restarting office applications)** is selected:

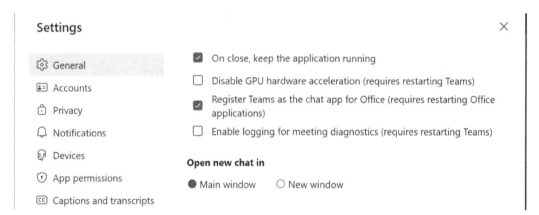

Figure 16.11 – Registering Teams as the chat app for Office

5. Exit Microsoft Teams, then right-click on the *Teams* icon on the status bar and select **Quit**:

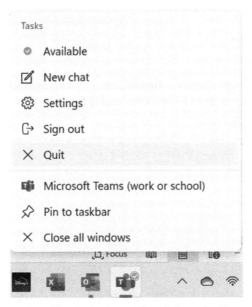

Figure 16.12 – The Quit option after clicking the Teams icon

6. Open Microsoft Teams, then exit Outlook 2021 and open it again.

If the Teams icons are still missing from Outlook, try one of the options provided in the next few sections.

Checking for updates

Always ensure that you have the latest updates for Microsoft Office and Windows installed as this could attribute to not seeing the **Teams Meeting** icon in the Outlook calendar.

Another resource to check would be the Teams Meeting policy in the Microsoft 365 admin center to **Allow Outlook Add-ins** if you're rolling Teams out to your business.

Enabling add-ins

Both the Zoom and Teams platforms require the relevant add-in to be installed in the Outlook 2021 application. If these add-ins are not enabled, it could cause the icon not to display in the Outlook Calendar.

To enable the add-in, follow these steps:

1. Go to **File | Options**.

2. Click the **Add-ins** category.

3. In the following screenshot, **Microsoft Teams Meeting add-in for Microsoft Office** has been enabled, as well as **Zoom Outlook Plugin**:

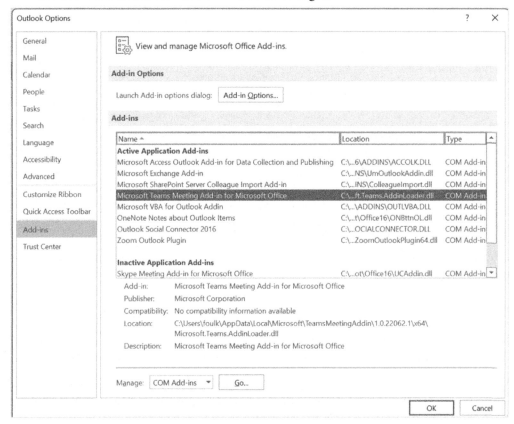

Figure 16.13 – Outlook Options dialog box showing add-ins

4. If an add-in is not enabled, go to **COM Add-ins** drop-down list and select **Disabled Items**. Click the **Go...** button to see a list of available disabled items. Select the item that is disabled, then click the **Enable** button at the bottom left of the dialog box to add it:

Figure 16.14 – The Disabled Items drop-down list

We hope that these troubleshooting tips come in handy when meeting add-ins are missing from your Outlook 2021 ribbon. In the next section, you will learn how to join and leave meetings.

Joining and leaving meetings

In this section, you will learn how to access a meeting and leave once the meeting is complete. There are numerous ways to access Zoom and Teams meetings. Here is a list of a few of those methods:

- Via the Calendar Teams app (Zoom and Teams meetings)
- By using the Zoom app within the Teams app
- From your Outlook 2021 calendar
- Via Webmail calendar access via the browser
- Using the Zoom app
- From the meeting notification on your Windows environment
- Using a device, such as a tablet or your mobile phone

One thing to consider would be where you access online meetings on your computer or laptop. Often, organizations will make use of local desktop and/or **remote desktop protocol** (**RDP**) connections. RDP connections generally have issues connecting to video in online meetings, and similarly, the audio could be affected. The reason for this is that it loses the ability to recognize the peripheral device.

Normally, a notification will pop up on-screen when your meeting is about to start. You can join directly from this link. This would, of course, depend on whether you have Zoom and Teams notifications set up in your Windows environment:

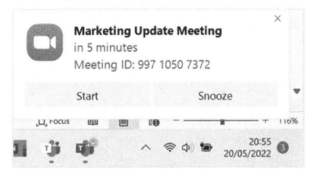

Figure 16.15 – Joining a Zoom meeting from the desktop

Other than Windows notifications, the most common way to access meetings would be through the **Teams app**. Once launched, the Teams app consists of several apps down the left-hand side of the window. Whether you can access these apps would depend on the plan you have purchased, or whether you have been granted permission to certain apps through the Microsoft 365 admin center.

The following screenshot shows an example of the Teams app when signed in with a business account (work or school account). This account has a host of features compared to that of a free account or standalone version of the Office 2021 suite:

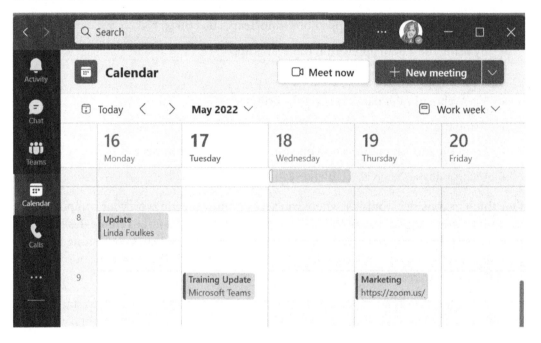

Figure 16.16 – The Microsoft Teams app (business account)

Here is an example of the Teams app signed in with a free account or a Microsoft Office 2021 standalone plan:

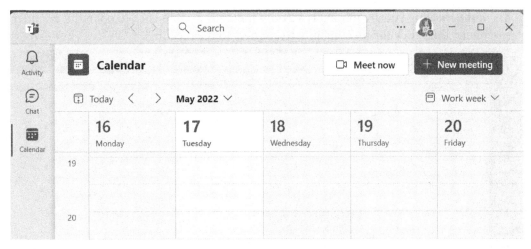

Figure 16.17 – The Microsoft Teams app

Now, let's learn how to join meetings once the invite has been accepted.

Joining meetings

Once you have accepted a calendar invite, the meeting will appear in your Outlook 2021 calendar. The meeting will include the join meeting link, which you can click on to join the meeting through the calendar.

There are many ways to join a meeting, as outlined in the previous section. The most common way would be through the Microsoft Teams app. We can join Teams and Zoom meetings directly from within the Teams Calendar app. Follow these steps:

1. Open the **Microsoft Teams** app on your desktop or through your Microsoft 365 online account.

2. Click the **Calendar** app on the left-hand side of the window.

3. If the meeting you are joining is a Teams meeting, you can simply click the calendar invite and select **Join** to connect to the meeting. Note that you can also chat with participants before the start of the meeting using the **Chat with participants** link. This is handy if you are the host and need to let the participants know that you will be 2 minutes late, for instance.

4. If the meeting you are joining is a Zoom meeting, double-click to open the calendar invite, then click the meeting link to connect to the meeting:

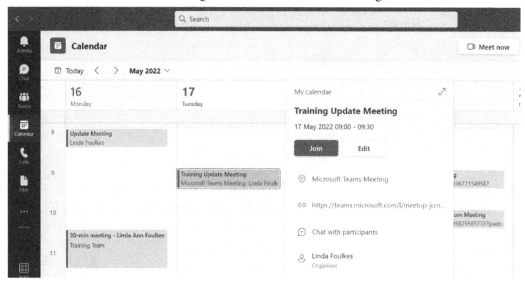

Figure 16.18 – The Microsoft Teams Calendar app showing the Join button

5. Once we click the **Join** button or click on the link, the meeting will load on the desktop. This screen allows you to check your video and audio settings before entering the meeting. If you are using a headset, the settings should automatically update:

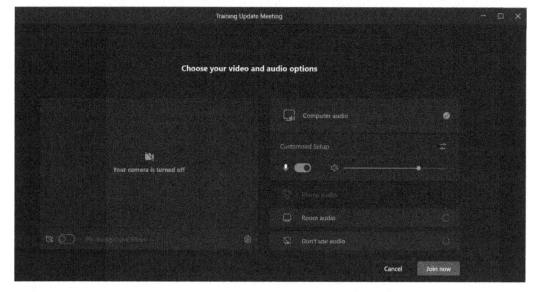

Figure 16.19 – Joining a Teams meeting

6. Click the video slider at the bottom left-hand corner of the window to activate the video. You will now see your video on the screen. If you prefer to hide your video background, the **Background filters** options are a great alternative to peruse.

7. Click on the **Join now** button to enter the meeting.

Later in this chapter, we will explore the Teams meeting options. Now, let's learn how to join a Zoom meeting:

1. When we join Zoom meetings from the Teams app, we must click on the meeting in the calendar. The popup screen comprises a meeting link, which you can copy and paste into a browser to join the meeting:

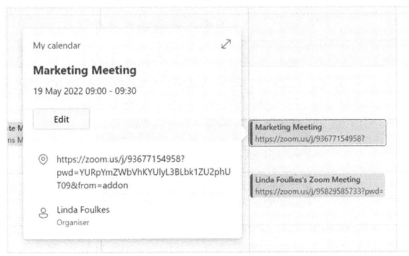

Figure 16.20 – Zoom meeting popup detail

2. Alternatively, click the **Edit** button to open the meeting detail, then click the link to populate the Zoom meeting:

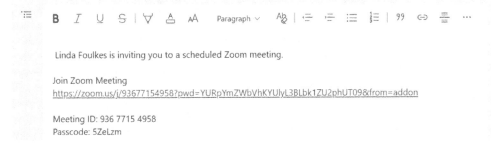

Figure 16.21 – Zoom meeting link

3. The Zoom popup notification screen will appear over the browser. Click the **Open** button to join the meeting. You may be asked to sign in to your Zoom account if you have not done so already:

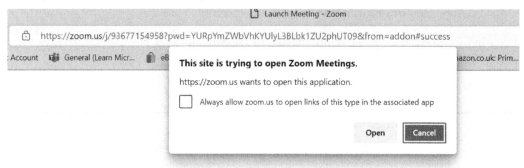

Figure 16.22 – Zoom notification popup

4. The Zoom meeting will launch. If your video is turned off at the start of the meeting, you can click the **Start Video** button to activate it:

Figure 16.23 – Using the Start Video button to activate your video

5. The Zoom meeting options will be discussed later in this chapter.

When you are in a Teams meeting, the Teams app will indicate this via a red circle to the top right of the Teams icon on the Windows taskbar:

Figure 16.24 – The Teams app icon on the Windows taskbar

The Teams app will also indicate that you are busy by placing a red dot on your profile image at the top of the window:

Figure 16.25 – Teams profile picture showing that you're busy

Now, let's learn how to exit meetings.

Leaving or ending meetings

When the meeting is over, you can click on the **Leave** button or the **End Meeting** button at the top-right corner of the Teams meeting. These buttons will differ, depending on whether you are an attendee or the host. If you leave the meeting, the other participants will remain in the meeting. When you are the host and have indicated to all participants that the meeting is over, you can use the **End Meeting** button to exit the meeting for everyone involved. This ensures that the meeting, as well as all the participants, are disconnected from the call. The host is the only participant who will see the **End Meeting** button in the meeting:

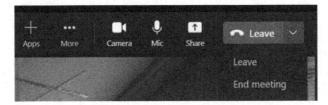

Figure 16.26 – The Leave and End meeting buttons in Teams

The Zoom meeting controls are at the bottom right of the meeting window, which is the opposite of the Teams meeting environment:

Figure 16.27 – The Leave Meeting and End Meeting for All buttons in Zoom

Click the **Leave Meeting** button to leave the meeting (the other participants will remain in the meeting) or use the **End Meeting for All** button to end the meeting for everyone.

There are numerous options to explore in the Teams and Zoom apps. Let's investigate a few next.

Customizing meeting options

Teams and Zoom are very similar in terms of their meeting options, as shown here:

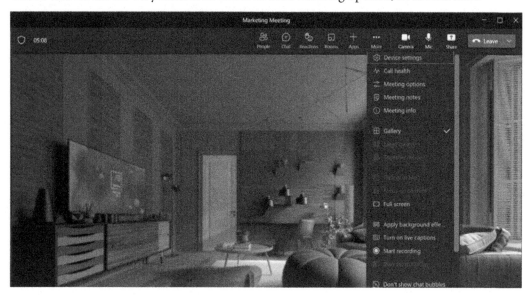

Figure 16.28 – Teams meeting options

Let's look at the different features that are available and explain them:

Feature	Explanation
People	Clicking on this option will open the **Participants** pane to the right of the window. In this pane, we can manage permissions, download attendance list, lock meeting to prevent others from joining, and share invites by copying a meeting link. The **Spotlight** for everyone feature is also available in this pane, which we will discuss a little later.
Chat	Use this button to open the Chat pane to send messages to meeting participants and to download an attendance report.
Reactions	This tool allows participants to react by clicking on various emojis or raise hand if they would like to notify the host that they have a question:
Rooms	This is the fantastic *Breakout Room* feature, which allows meeting participants to be split into defined groups to partake in discussions in breakaway rooms, and then regroup again with all the participants.
Apps	Various apps can be added to the meeting to collaborate, live stream, and so on.
... **More**	Here, we can take meeting notes, apply background effect, set gallery options, turn on live captions, and start recording the meeting, to name a few options.
Camera and **Mic**	These options allow you to enable or disable video and audio.
Share	With this option, you can share your screen with others, include computer sound, choose an applicable Presenter Mode, use Microsoft Whiteboard to collaborate, and present using PowerPoint Live. These will be explained later in this chapter.

Table 16.1 – Teams meeting options

As mentioned in a previous section, the Zoom and Teams meeting functionality is very similar. In terms of Zoom, the buttons are located at the bottom of the Zoom window instead:

Figure 16.29 – Zoom options

Click the arrow at the right-top corner of the **Start Video** button to navigate to **Video Settings…** and customize the **Video Settings...**, **Choose Virtual Background...**, and **Choose Video Filter...** options.

Zoom has additional functionality, named **Zoom Studio Effects**, which is a separate bar along the bottom of your screen for adding touch-ups to facial features and applying filters:

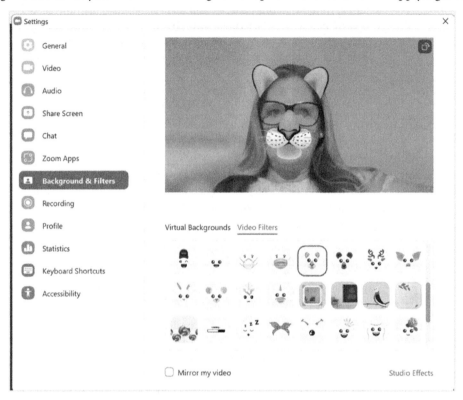

Figure 16.30 – Zoom Studio Effects

We can have a lot of fun with the different effects as well as the share screen options, which we will explore later in this chapter.

When we work with the Teams app, we may find it easier to create teams. Let's investigate the teams side of the Teams app.

Creating and managing Channels

A **Team** is a group of people (called members) who gather to collaborate on a project, a specialist area, or within a department, to name a few examples. Within a team, we can create **Channels**. Channels are created within a specific Team. We use Channels to have conversations with others, work on project tasks and milestones, take meeting notes, collaborate on a specific part of a project, and invite only those members. The list of possibilities is endless.

Creating Channels

We can set up teams in the Teams area within the Teams app. For instance, we could create a Team for our business, named *Safest Solutions*. Channels can be created within the Teams app on a remote desktop connection or local area. Normally, we would collaborate using the **remote desktop (RDS)** as this is our daily workspace, but there are some constraints. One is the ability to use our camera when in meetings, while another is that our audio is affected by feedback or breaking up. We can work on teams inside and outside of an RDS since any updates sync automatically. Follow these steps:

1. Open the **Teams** app.

2. Navigate to the **Teams** button on the left-hand side of the navigation pane.

3. At the bottom of the window, click on **Join or create a team**:

Figure 16.31 – Join or create a team

4. Click **Create a team** or enter a code to join an existing team. When using **Join a team with a code**, you will receive the code via email or can send a code via **Settings** when managing a channel.

5. When we choose the **Create team** option, two options will appear – to create **From a group or team** or create **From scratch**. You can also **Select from a template**, which is a great way to start from a skeleton template where you can build a team. Depending on the template chosen, you will see several custom apps and Channels that have been automatically created for you. We have selected **Onboard Employees** as an example. Click **Next** to continue.

6. Choose whether the team will be **Private** or **Public**, then enter the details related to your Team and check the Channel's details:

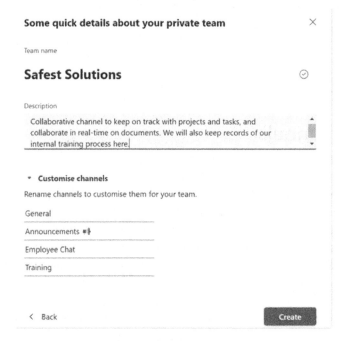

Figure 16.32 – Entering details about your private team

7. Click **Create** to populate the team once you have filled out the required information. A few moments later, the team will appear.

8. Directly under the Team name, you will see a few Channels. The first is **General**. The General channel's name cannot be amended, but other channel names can be changed.

Now that we know how to create a Channel, let's learn how to customize the Team and the Channels within it.

Managing Channels

In this section, you will learn how to manage Channels by investigating some of their options.

Channel activity

If a Channel is in bold, this means that there is an activity in the Channel that you have not looked at yet:

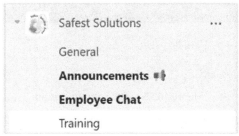

Figure 16.33 – Channels in bold mean new activity

Click the Channel's name to see any new activity.

Channel notifications

It could become quite annoying if you keep receiving notifications while you work, so knowing where to customize this activity is beneficial.

The main notification customization area is at the top right of the Teams app (profile picture). Follow these steps:

1.   Click your profile image, then select the drop-down arrow next to **Available** to see a list of status defaults that can be amended to suit your requirements:

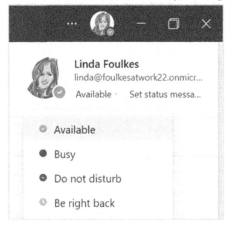

Figure 16.34 – Status within the Teams app

2. To set further customizations, you can click the *ellipsis* to the left of your profile image, then access **Settings**:

Figure 16.35 – The Settings option

We will highlight some of the main features that are available in the **Settings** area in the following sections.

Setting an out-of-office greeting

When you're on annual leave or away from your Teams space, you can set an **out-of-office greeting** (just like we can in Outlook). Anyone trying to contact you will see the out-of-office notification in the Chat area, for example. This works in conjunction with your **Out of Office** setting in Outlook, so make sure that is set before you select this option. Follow these steps:

1. Make sure you are on the **General** category on the left of the **Settings** screen.

2. Scroll down to select **Calls** on the left. Then, locate the **Voicemail** heading and select **Configure voicemail**.

3. Scroll down to **Out of office greeting**, then click the checkbox next to **When I have an Outlook auto reply**:

Figure 16.36 – Out of office greeting options

4. At the top of the screen, you can **Record a greeting** to play when someone tries to call you through the Teams app.

You can also set notifications for Teams within the **Settings** area, or customize notifications on each Channel separately if required.

Setting Teams and Channel notifications

Let's look at where we can find Teams notifications settings:

1. Click on **Settings | Notifications**. Then, scroll to **Teams and channels** and customize your notifications using the options provided:

Figure 16.37 – Notification settings for Teams and Channels

2. To set individual channel notifications, select the *ellipsis* to the right of the channel name, then select **Channel notifications**. Choose an option from the list provided:

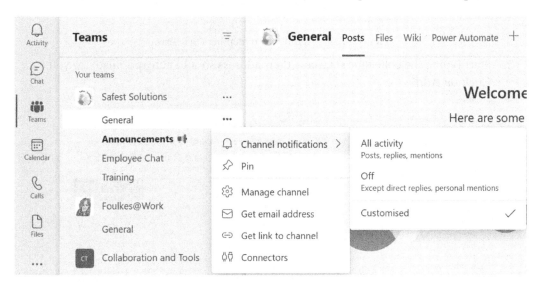

Figure 16.38 – Setting Channel notifications

3. We can turn notifications **Off** completely, see **All activity**, or select **Customised** to set mentions, including all replies and post activity.

In the next section, you will learn how to add members to your Team.

Adding Team members

Follow these steps:

1. Click on a **Team**, then select the *ellipsis* to the right of the team's name. Choose **Manage Team** or **Add member**:

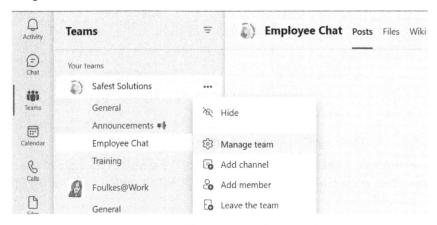

Figure 16.39 – Adding team members to a Team

2. Start typing the colleague's name – their address should auto-populate for you. Click on **Add**:

Figure 16.40 – Adding members to a Team

3. When adding members to a team, you can add the email address of someone outside your organization to add them as a guest, after which a request will be sent to them:

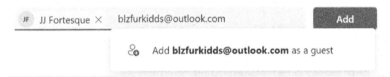

Add members to Safest Solutions

Start typing a name, distribution list, or security group to add to your team. You can also add people outside your organisation as guests by typing their email addresses.

Figure 16.41 – Adding external people to a Team

4. External guests will show as an icon at the top right of the Team or to the left of the Channel **Meet** button, indicating that you have included members that are not part of your organization:

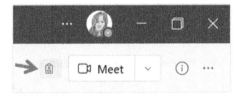

Figure 16.42 – Icon displaying that individuals have been included from outside the business

At times, it is easier to send a code to individuals to join the team directly. The next section will take you through the steps to do so.

Sending a Team code to individuals

Follow these steps:

1. We can also send a code to individuals to request that they join the Team.

2. Click on the three dots (*ellipsis*) next to the Team name, then choose **Manage Team**.

3. Select **Settings** from the options provided. Choose an option to customize, such as **Team code**:

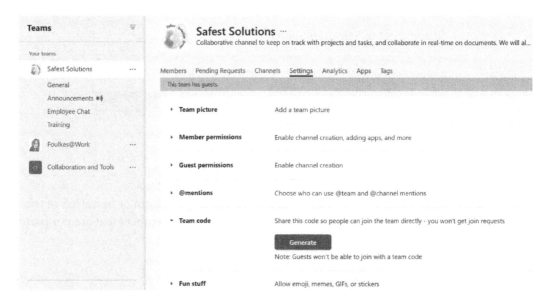

Figure 16.43 – Generating a Team code

4. Click on **Generate** to access the code. Note that guests outside the business cannot join via this code.

5. Send the code via email, chat, or verbally. The recipient will enter the code into the **Join or create a team** area, as explained previously.

You won't see any join requests when you share a Team code. Now, let's look at how to move Teams.

Reordering Teams

To change the order in which Teams are presented in the **Teams** pane, simply click on a Team name, then drag it to another position (either up or down the list). Once you let go of your mouse, the Team will be reordered.

Hiding and showing teams

If you have been invited to a few teams and have started creating your own teams, then you may find that the environment becomes a little busy.

Once a Team is hidden, it will become part of the **Hidden teams** list at the bottom of the Teams panel:

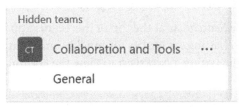

Figure 16.44 – The Hidden teams list

1. Click on the *ellipsis* to the right of the Team name, then select **Hide**.

2. To remove the team from the hidden list so that it appears in the Teams list once again, simply choose **Show** from the *ellipsis* options.

Meeting with Channel members

Instead of sending a Teams Outlook calendar invite, you can set meetings or meet directly from within a created Team or Channel.

Click the drop-down list to the right of the **Meet** button (just below your profile) to access the **Meet Now** or **Schedule a meeting** option:

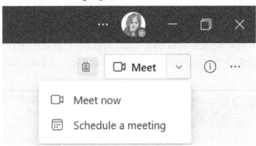

Figure 16.45 – The Meet now and Schedule a meeting options

When setting a meeting within a Channel or Team, it will be visible to all within the channel.

> **Tip**
> Do this on your local area to ensure you have access to video and audio. The remote desktop session has its constraints when working with video/audio calls.

Quick ways to communicate or set options

Time is everything, so the *Search* bar at the top of the Teams app is fantastic for reaching colleagues by calling and chatting, as well as for quickly amending settings. Have a look at the list that's available by typing a *backslash* to view the commands in a drop-down list within the Search bar:

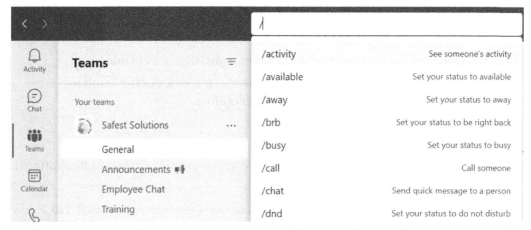

Figure 16.46 – Search bar commands

Instead of selecting a Channel, or initiating a **Chat**, we can call a colleague directly using the /call command, after which you can start typing the name of the colleague you wish to reach. However, note that on pressing the **Send** button, Microsoft Teams will launch an active call immediately:

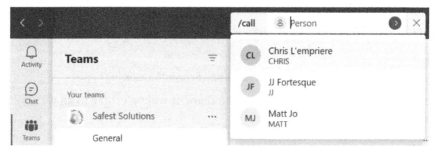

Figure 16.47 – The /call feature

We can also use **@mention** to start a chat with someone, instead of trying to locate a Chat from the left-hand side of the Teams pane:

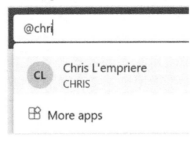

Figure 16.48 – @mention

Now, let's learn how to create custom tags so that we can **@mention** more than one colleague at a time.

Creating Channel Tags

Channel **Tags** are useful when you need to use the **@mention** feature to notify a group of colleagues at the same time, such as a team at a specific office within a business Channel such as **SSOxford**, or a couple of individuals in a specific department, such as **SSMarketing**:

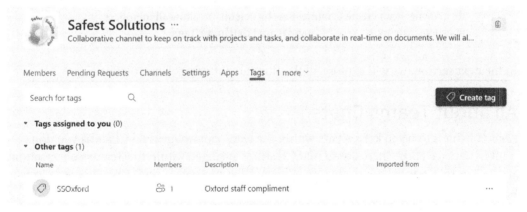

Figure 16.49 – Tags

To use the Tag, simply type @SSOxford into a chat, conversation, or meeting detail, or just type the @ sign to bring up the list of available **Suggestions** to select from:

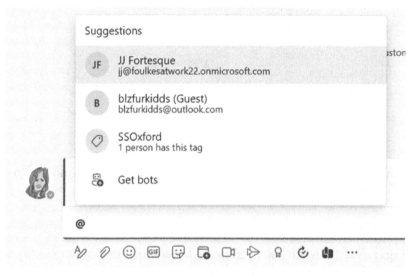

Figure 16.50 – Suggestions

> **Note**
> Team owners can create Channel tags by default. To allow all members to create tags, you must go to **Manage team | Settings | Tags**.

In the next section, we will explore all the functionality chats have to offer.

All about Teams Chats

A good habit is to try to keep Chats within the team, but not general Chats as you don't want to manage both. There are so many features available within the Teams conversation area (**General Channel**, for example). When a Chat message is sent, you will see a circle with a tick icon, indicating that the message has been sent. Once the message has been read by the recipient, the icon will turn into an eye icon:

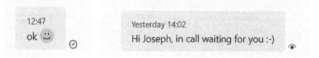

Figure 16.51 – The Sent and Read icons

The following screenshot shows the options that are available along the bottom of the **New Conversation** area:

Figure 16.52 – Chat features in Teams

Let's look at some of these features.

Using the Praise icon

This icon needs to be managed through Teams Admin. The **Praise** icon is situated at the end of the Chat icons. It is a great way to encourage teamwork by giving praise to individuals.

Using New conversation

Instead of typing a quick message using the **New conversation** button, the **Format** button opens numerous options in the Chat. This is especially useful if you want to create a professional chat or announcement.

Click on **New conversation**, then select the **Format** icon (the first icon beneath the chat) to set various options, such as limiting replies and **Post in multiple channels**. We can add tables and so much more:

Figure 16.53 – Creating a professional chat or conversation

In the next section, we will look at other formatting options.

Creating announcements

We can turn a chat into an **Announcement** with more prominent features. You can also give it a headline and add color. After sending the message, it will appear in the Channel with the notification icon to the right of the message:

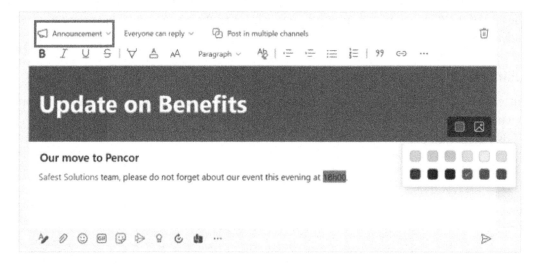

Figure 16.54 – The Announcement feature

At times, we need to mark a message as **Important**. We'll go through this in the next section.

Marking a message as Important

Using the **Mark as important** option by clicking on the *ellipsis* at the end of the ribbon allows you to assign importance. The border of the message will turn red and some text stating *IMPORTANT* in red will appear as the message's subject line.

Pinning messages

Use the *ellipsis* to the right of a conversation to **Pin** the conversation. Doing so will make it more visible with a green border and green icon. Note that everyone who is part of the Channel can view pinned messages:

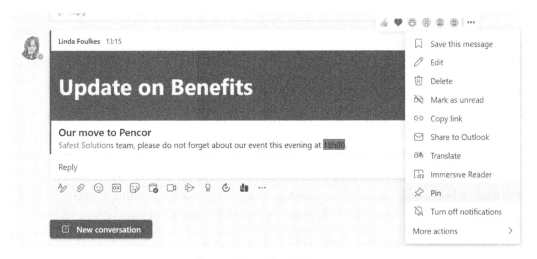

Figure 16.55 – The Pin feature

Pinned messages, however, will get lost as the Channel Chat builds. If this happens, you can click on the *Information* icon to **Show channel info** at the top right of the window to see any pinned posts down the right-hand side panel. The Channel info pane displays more activity regarding members and updates:

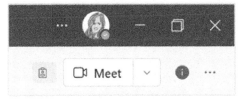

Figure 16.56 – The Show channel info button

The **Pinned posts** area will now appear in the right-hand information pane:

Figure 16.57 – Pinned posts

Pinned posts will display within the Chat with a green pin icon at the top right of the post.

Sharing posts to Outlook

The option to **Share to Outlook** can be set up by your Admin team if it's missing from the *ellipsis* drop-down menu. This option is extremely useful for sending chats to Outlook directly from within Teams. This alleviates you from having to copy and paste the contents of an email:

Figure 16.58 – Share to Outlook

After clicking the **Share to Outlook** option, the email will populate the necessary fields. Then, click the **Send** button.

Investigating the Immersive Reader feature

Immersive Reader is a feature that was added to all the Office apps. It aids accessibility by adding a range of features such as **Translate**, **Read aloud**, **Reading by line focus**, and so much more. The **Read aloud** feature aids those who would like to sit back and listen to correspondence, including additional accessibility options. To access the feature, use the *ellipsis* to the right of a Chat, then select **Immersive Reader**.

Amending the Sticker options

You can add emojis, gifs, and stickers to a Chat. You can even customize the text on the images! Select **Stickers**, then choose a category. Edit the text, then click **Done** to post it to the Chat:

Figure 16.59 – The Sticker feature

> **Tip**
> When we create a Chat or conversation, we sometimes make the mistake of hitting the *Enter* button on the keyboard before finishing our message. To avoid this from happening, simply press the *Ctrl + Shift + X* buttons on your keyboard when in a Chat or conversation. This will activate the compose box so that you can use the *Enter* key freely without accidentally sending the message before you've finished typing it.

Let's look at another fantastic app for adding value to productivity in the workplace.

Approving requests

The **Approvals** app is a great workflow to add to your Chat or Teams environment. We can use this tool to approve leave requests, sick notes, community hours, training, or workflows, such as a training checklist or project plan. To add **Approvals** to the Teams environment, simply add the tool as an app. For example, click the ellipsis to the right of the Chat, then search for **Approvals** to add it to the Chat. The respective icon will appear at the bottom of a conversation, along with all the other default options:

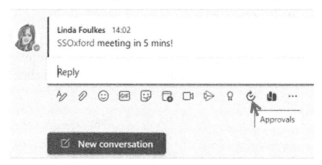

Figure 16.60 – The Approvals feature

Click the **Approvals** button to create a **New approval request**. Choose from the **Basic request**, **e-Sign**, and **Template** options. Fill out the details of the request, attach any supporting documentation, and then press **Send** to forward it to the approver.

We can add the **Approvals** app to the sidebar of the Teams environment so that we can **Approve** or **Reject** requests from teammates and see an overview of the process:

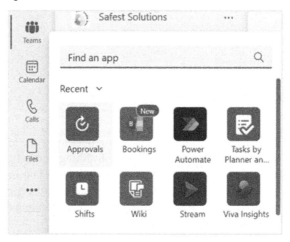

Figure 16.61 – Adding the Approvals app to Teams

The approver will be notified of the new request via the **Activity** bell in Teams, or a desktop notification popup. The approver can also navigate to the **Approvals** app on the Teams sidebar, then click on the request and select either **Accept** or **Reject**:

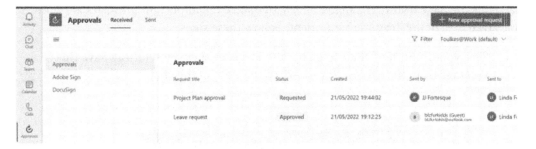

Figure 16.62 – The Approvals app

Here, you can see all the **Sent** and **Received** approvals and the **Status** details of each in the Approvals app.

Now, let's learn how to send an email from Outlook directly to a Teams Channel in Microsoft Teams using the **Get email address** feature. This feature needs to be activated within the admin portal to push to the organization if it's not available in your Teams app.

Locating Chat files

Any files that are shared in a Chat will be available in the **Files** section of your Team Channel, as well as in the **Files** app to the left of the Teams pane. We will look at this later in this chapter.

Hiding Chats

You can hide chats and bring them back when required by following these steps:

1. To hide a chat, click the *ellipsis* icon and select **Hide**.

2. Use the **Search** feature at the top of the window to unhide chats by searching for the individual's name or anything else to do with the Chat discussion. The results of the search will display as a drop-down list at the top of the Teams window. Select the applicable Chat to unhide it and open it in the Chat area.

Saving important Chats

We can use the **Pin** feature to pin Chats so that we can revisit them. The only issue with this is that the pinned items move down, and we tend to forget about them. Using the **Save this message** feature is a better alternative since the important messages are added to the **Saved** area of the Teams environment. Follow these steps:

1. Save your important chats to go back to at a later stage by selecting **Save this message** from the *ellipsis* drop-down to the right of the chat:

Figure 16.63 – Save this message

2. The Chat message will now be saved in the **Saved** area of Teams.

3. Click your profile picture at the top right of the Teams app.

4. Select **Saved** from the drop-down list:

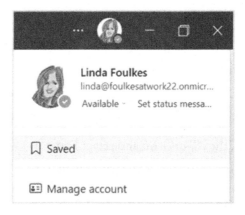

Figure 16.64 – The Saved option

5. All the saved important messages will appear to the left of the window:

Figure 16.65 – The Saved area in Teams

6.   Click the maroon marker to remove the item from the **Saved** list.

Emailing a Teams Channel from Outlook

A great feature within Teams is being able to send an email to a Teams Channel for discussion. Follow these steps:

1.   Select the Channel you wish to email.

2.   Use the *ellipsis* to the right of the channel's name, then click on **Get email address**:

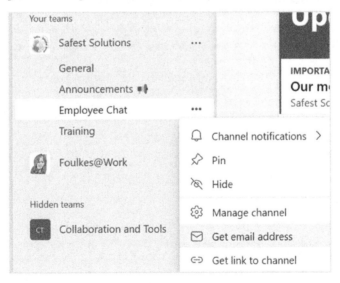

Figure 16.66 – The Get email address feature

3. Click **Copy** to place the email address on the clipboard or visit **Advanced settings** to customize the link's settings:

Figure 16.67 – The Get email address feature

4. Navigate to **Outlook 2021**, then create a **New Email** message.

5. Use the right-click and paste method or *Ctrl + V* to paste the email address for the channel into the **To** field. Add a **Subject** and message body and attach the relevant documents, if required:

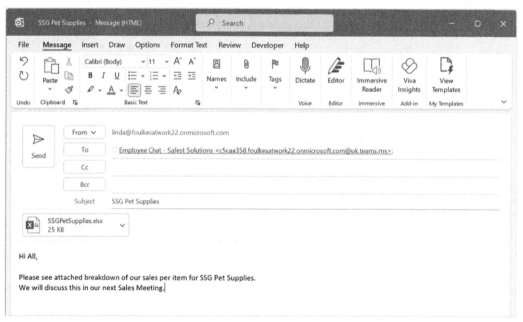

Figure 16.68 – New email message in Outlook

6. Send the email to the Channel. The email will appear in the Channel, along with the attachment.

All files and their associated emails are stored in the **SharePoint Files** folder within the Teams app. Each Team has a SharePoint folder. Files in groups or private chats are stored in **OneDrive**.

Summary

In this chapter, you learned how to communicate and collaborate using Microsoft Teams and Zoom. You learned how to set up, join, and manage meetings. We also investigated add-ins and how to troubleshoot issues that may arise.

At this point, you should be confident in making decisions regarding presenting content using the Share icon within Teams and Zoom, as well as all the Presenter modes. We also learned the best way to work with meeting notes.

In addition, you went through the Teams app and learned some top tips for using it and how to create and manage Channels. You also learned about brilliant tools such as OneNote and Tasks by Planner, Bookings, and Approvals, to name just a few. You also explored all the functionality within Teams meetings. You can now collaborate in real time and work with version control and the **New Sheet View** feature.

In the final chapter, we will see how to present and collaborate with our teams online.

17
Presenting and Collaborating Online

In the previous chapter, we introduced all the significant features of communicating and collaborating using online tools such as Microsoft Teams and Zoom. We concentrated on joining and managing meetings using the Outlook 2021 Calendar and the methods to present content using the Share icon within Teams.

In this chapter, we will discover the Teams app while pointing out useful features and understand the different locations we can save to in the online space. In today's climate, it is important to learn about features that are advantageous to hybrid working. In this chapter, we will explore the best ways to share and present PowerPoint slides using PowerPoint Live, as well as the new Presenter modes. We will look at important features to become familiar with such as Spotlight, attendance reports, raising a hand, recording videos, and meeting notes. Finally, we will address collaborating and file sharing using Teams and learn about versions and Sheet View.

The following topics will be covered in this chapter:

- Differences between OneDrive and SharePoint
- Overview of Teams apps
- Presenting during online meetings
- Collaborating and file sharing

Technical requirements

Prior knowledge of the Teams/Zoom meeting environment is advantageous. It is, however, imperative that you have the relevant software available to practice and work through this chapter. The examples for this chapter can be found on GitHub at `https://github.com/PacktPublishing/Learn-Microsoft-Office-2021-Second-Edition`.

Differences between OneDrive and SharePoint

Before we start collaborating in real-time and working with files in the online space, we need to understand a little more about the different locations to save data.

Let's investigate the difference is between **OneDrive** and **SharePoint**:

1. OneDrive is an online document/file storage platform. Typically, it is used by individuals and business teams who require a centralized location to store and access files.

2. SharePoint is a collaboration tool for businesses, which allows multiple individuals and teams to work on documents and products at the same time. The following table shows the difference between OneDrive and SharePoint:

OneDrive	SharePoint
Personal and Private	Team and Shared

Table 17.1 – The difference between OneDrive and SharePoint

The next feature we will explore is quite vast, with many skills we can learn for each app we select within the Teams environment. We will cover only a few as an introduction.

Apps within Channels

There are several apps we can use within a Team or Channels within a Team. Teams is a one-stop location for all collaboration requirements.

The following table outlines some of the apps we can add to our Teams environment:

App Name	Explanation of the Value of the Tool
OneDrive	This is a great personal tool for storing files in one central location. It can act as a transfer tool from one desktop connection to a remote desktop, or for large file transfers. This tool enables collaboration and file sharing and downloading. You can also use this tool to grab files to use within meetings.
SharePoint	This is Teams-focused, so files that are collaborated on in Teams are saved automatically to the SharePoint online area.
OneNote	This app is one of my favorites and is used widely for meeting notes, audio, video, dictation, to-do lists, and so much more. It connects with so many areas of the Teams environment, including Teams meetings.
Forms	You can use this app to create and generate Microsoft Forms within your channels for editing or distributing to others.
Tasks by Planner	This tool allows for team interaction, updating tasks, and tracking. It has many different analysis views and is great for team project collaboration.
Zoom	You can add this app to access Zoom meetings easily through the Teams environment.
Calendar	You can use this app to create a Teams calendar showing tasks and meetings.
Whiteboard	You can use this app to collaborate within meetings or Teams Channels to explore ideas and create boards.
Milestones and Employee Ideas	These are two great apps to explore and add to Channels for employees to add milestones and ideas
Power Automate	With this tool, you can promptly activate scheduled flows using the Flow bot in Teams and mechanize business activities, thus saving you lots of time.
Bookings	You can use this app to schedule appointments using multiple calendars and resources.

Table 17.2 – The apps that are available in Teams

We hope that this gave you a general overview of the apps that are available in the Teams environment. You can always delve into those you think would suit your requirements in the Teams app.

In the next section, we will concentrate on how to present PowerPoint slides within a meeting, as well as collaborating in real time.

Presenting during online meetings

In this section, we will concentrate on how to present PowerPoint slides within a meeting.

When it is time to present slides to an audience in a remote meeting, we can use several **Share** options through Teams. Let's investigate them.

Presenting PowerPoint options

The **Screen** option allows you to share content from multiple desktops or areas on your computer. Follow these steps:

1. Join the meeting from your Teams calendar, or directly from within your Teams Channel.
2. Click the **Share** button from within the Teams meeting to see the available options.
3. Notice the **Screen** and **Window** options in the **Share content** side panel.
4. Choose **Screen** if you would like to have control over whether you share a local desktop or remote desktop and would like to move from one area to another with ease (this is popular when moving from a local desktop to a remote desktop).
5. Select **Window** if you would like to select a specific window to share only and have control over what you share with your audience. When in doubt, select **Screen**:

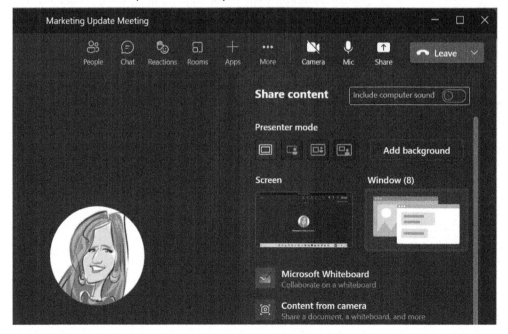

Figure 17.1 – Teams meeting Share options

6. For this example, we will select **Window** as we only want to share content from the desktop and be able to navigate to another area (the server) if we need to. Everything you have open currently will be displayed in the **Window** area. Notice that the preceding screenshot shows that **(8)** windows are currently open. Select one of the windows to share with your audience.

7. Once you are sharing your desktop, open the file you wish to share with your audience or navigate to the presentation if you already have it open.

8. If you're sharing PowerPoint, be sure to choose **Slide Show | From Beginning** so that your audience enjoys the presentation in **Slide Show** view and not **Edit** mode:

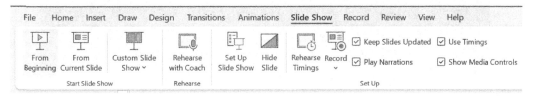

Figure 17.2 – PowerPoint 2021's Slide Show | From Beginning option

9. Once the presentation is open to your audience, you can change the host presentation view to show in **Presenter View**. This helps you take control of the presentation as a host and allows you to see the working view, including your speaker notes to aid your presentation. Right-click on the slide background, then select **Show Presenter View**. The view will load differently for the presenter:

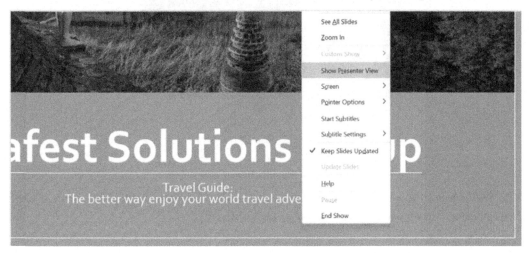

Figure 17.3 – Show Presenter View

> **Note**
>
> When using Presenter View, be sure to test this out beforehand on your system, especially if you are using a remote desktop, as this view change could present both to your audience and the presenter, which would be a little embarrassing.

10. Once you have finished the presentation and are ready to return to the meeting, minimize any open remote desktop connections (normally, there will be a bar at the top of the screen you can click to minimize) and return to the meeting. Here, you can select the **Stop presenting** button at the top of the screen:

Figure 17.4 – The Stop presenting button in the Teams meeting

If you are presenting from your desktop, click on the **Stop sharing** button on the minimized meeting on the progress screen to end the screen share and return to the meeting:

Figure 17.5 – Meeting in progress screen

The next presenting option is the best by far as it allows you to see your slide notes, use the laser pointer, and view the audience. Let's check this out!

Presenting using PowerPoint Live

This option allows you to access a presentation using either the **Browse...** option to collect files from your computer or your OneDrive online storage account. Follow these steps:

1. Join the meeting from your Teams calendar, or directly from within your Teams Channel.

2. Click the **Share** button from within the Teams meeting to see the available options.

3. Glance down to the bottom of the screen. You will notice the **PowerPoint Live** heading. Directly under the heading, you may see some PowerPoint files listed. Select one of the PowerPoint files, if applicable, or use the **Browse OneDrive** or **Browse my computer** option to locate the relevant file to present.

4. If you are using the **Browse my computer** option, make sure that the PowerPoint presentation you want to show your audience is on your local desktop area if you are working on a remote session setup. You cannot navigate to a remote session using this option. Alternatively, **Browse OneDrive** and select the file you wish to present. For this example, we will choose the `Safest Solutions Travel.pptx` file:

Figure 17.6 – Locating the presentation on OneDrive

5. Click the **Share** button at the bottom of the window to share the presentation with your audience.

6. The selected presentation will open in Presenter mode. The audience, however, will see only the slide preview. As a presenter, you can do the following:

    I.   View your currently shared slide.

    II. See a thumbnail of the presentation along the bottom of the window.

    III. Refer to any slide notes you need to elaborate on during your presentation, or so that you don't forget certain points. You can adjust the font size of the notes too.

    IV. See the participants (**People**) to the right of the presentation.

V. See any comments from the audience by being able to visit the **Chat** area during the session and respond to the audience.

VI. Adjust your video so that you are displaying content and hosting the video by selecting **Standout** mode so that you retain engagement with the audience:

Figure 17.7 – PowerPoint Live

VII. Create Breakout Rooms using the **Rooms** button to break the participants up into groups so that they can discuss elements of the presentation and provide feedback. Another great reason to use Breakout Rooms is for trainers to assign tasks to their trainees and collaborate in group discussions and brainstorming sessions.

VIII. Apply cursor, laser pointer, and highlight options.

IX. Use the *eye* icon at the top of the screen to prevent participants from moving through the presentation independently.

10. The audience can **Take control** of the presentation, should they wish to demonstrate something to the audience or presenter, or it may be time for the next host to explain a section of the presentation. The following screenshot shows the **Take control** button on the slide view, which the audience can press to take control:

Figure 17.8 – The Take control feature

11. The audience can take control of the presentation by pressing the **Take control** button. Once this is selected, the presenter will receive a notification at the top of the Teams meeting to indicate that a user has taken control and can **Take back** the control, if necessary:

Figure 17.9 – Take back

In this section, we looked at some of the options to explore within the meeting environment. In the next section, we will look at the different **Presenter Modes** that are available when using the Share feature in Teams.

Exploring Presenter Modes

When we share content with an audience, we can present it using multiple Presenter Modes. These modes offer more engagement possibilities when sharing content through meetings. The following modes are available:

- Content only
- Standout
- Side-by-side
- Reporter

Let's learn about these options while we walk through the steps to activate them:

1. Join the meeting as usual, then click on the **Share** button at the top of the meeting.

2. In the **Share** content drop-down, notice the **Presenter mode** heading. Underneath this heading are four views, as explained at the beginning of this section.

    The first view is **Content only**, which is the default view. Always ensure this option is selected if you don't want to show your video to the audience while presenting:

Figure 17.10 – Presenter mode

The second button is for **Standout** mode. This mode will place the video over the slide content to the right.

The next is **Side-by-Side**, followed by **Reporter** mode. We can select the relevant mode from the **Share** drop-down list, or after we have chosen the relevant **Window** or **Screen** from which to present.

3. Once we are viewing the presentation to the audience, we can select the relevant mode to present from the meeting controls at the top of the screen. Move your mouse pointer to the top of the screen to view the meeting controls.

4. The following screenshot shows the different modes at the top of the screen, as well as an **Edit your view** mini screen over the presentation. Only the presenter can see this mini screen. Use the mini screen view to customize the options for the mode you have selected, such as its size and position. The presenter can minimize the mini screen.

5. Click each of the modes at the top of the screen to see how they will be displayed to the audience:

Figure 17.11 – Presenter modes and the mini screen to set options

6. Once you are done presenting, click the **Stop presenting** button at the top of the screen, or select the **Stop sharing** button on the mini-meeting controls to the bottom-right of your Windows desktop. You will then return to the meeting to engage with the audience.

7. Note that should you wish to show a video with sound while in Presenter mode, be sure to click the required audio when presenting, and click the **Include computer sound** button on the meeting controls:

Figure 17.12 – The Include computer sound button on meeting controls

In the next section, we will learn a little more about meeting options.

Functionality in Teams Meetings

The Teams environment is a great learning curve with lots of options to customize. In this section, we will look at a few more customizations you may want to consider adding to the mix when you are regularly using the meeting feature in Teams.

Activating Spotlight

Adding **Spotlight for everyone** to a meeting allows the participant or host video to be the main video that everyone sees when presenting. The host can action this for different participants as they need to be in the spotlight. To activate this, click on the **People** icon when the meeting starts, then navigate to the participant in the *Participants pane* to the right. Click the ellipsis, then choose **Spotlight for everyone**. Click on **Spotlight for everyone**.

Downloading attendance

We can download the attendance list from the **Participants** area before leaving the meeting. Click the ellipsis next to the **Participants** heading, then click **Download attendance list**. The list will download to the Downloads folder on your local computer or to a default location specified by your organization:

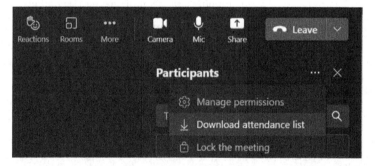

Figure 17.13 – Download attendance list

Meeting attendance can also be downloaded through the Teams app's Calendar. Click to access the meeting, then click **Edit** to open its contents. Select **Attendance** at the top of the screen, where you can view its details, or click on **Download attendance**:

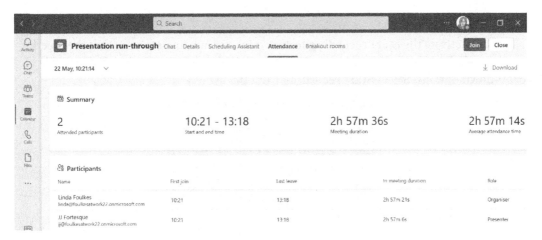

Figure 17.14 – The Calendar app showing the Attendance tab

The Meeting **Attendance Report** will appear in the Channel, as well as the meeting appointment in the Teams Calendar, which is also available in the meeting chat. The Attendance Report will be downloaded in `.csv` format, after which it can be saved as an Excel workbook.

Raising a hand

When participants use the **Raise hand** feature, the host is notified on-screen but is also able to get back to those participants who have raised their hands to ask a question in the order they were asked. Being fair when responding to questions in a meeting is important, especially if you have many participants:

Figure 17.15 – The Raise hand feature with the order displayed

Hosts can identify the order in which participants raised their hands and respond accordingly.

Recording video

Hosts can activate the **Start recording** feature once the meeting starts so that the meeting is recorded. Click on the **More…** action at the top of the meeting to view the available drop-down options. Select **Start recording** from the list:

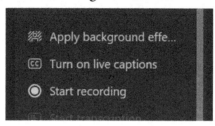

Figure 17.16 – Start recording

Be sure to let everyone in the meeting know that you would like to record the meeting. The record button will be displayed at the top left of the screen. Recordings are also displayed in the meeting's Chat and on the **Participants** screens. To stop the recording, go to the **More…** option and select **Stop recording**. The recording will download and be displayed in the meeting's Chat and as a **Recordings** folder in the Teams Channel **Files** area.

Be sure to check out the **Start transcription** feature, as well as the ability to **Turn on live captions**. This is a great feature to use if audio is an issue.

Taking meeting notes

It is important to be able to take notes before, during, or after your meeting. You can also take meeting notes using the transcription feature.

While in a meeting, select the **More…** button at the top of the meeting screen. Select **Meeting notes**:

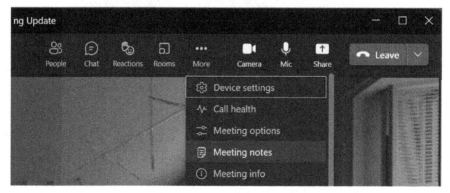

Figure 17.17 – Meeting notes

The **Meeting notes** pane will open, after which you click on **Take notes**.

The Teams app will open and include the **Meeting Notes** tab at the top of the relevant Channel. Click into the **Notes** area to start the note-taking process. Notes are saved automatically:

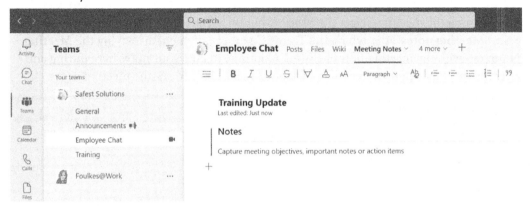

Figure 17.18 – Meeting Notes in Channel

We can also use **OneNote** to take meeting notes. This is a wonderful app bursting with features to explore. Open a meeting or create a new meeting using your Calendar in Microsoft Outlook 2021. From the **Meeting** tab, click **Send to OneNote**.

You can choose to **Take notes on your own** or **Share notes with the meeting** participants. Select the option you prefer, after which the link to the notes will be inserted into the meeting body. Send the meeting to participants as usual:

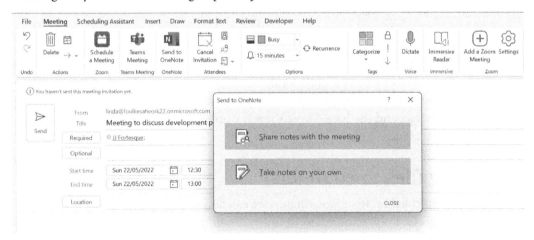

Figure 17.19 – Sharing notes with the meeting options

The **Meeting notes** pane will open, after which you can click on **Take notes**.

The Teams app will open and include the **Meeting Notes** tab at the top of the relevant Channel. Click into the **Notes** area to start the note-taking process. The notes will be saved automatically.

After joining the meeting, select the **More…** button at the top of the meeting screen. Select **Meeting notes**, after which the Teams Channel will open, displaying the **Meeting Notes** tab with the meeting notes below it. Continue to take your notes here during and after the meeting. All members of the Channel will be able to see the meeting notes:

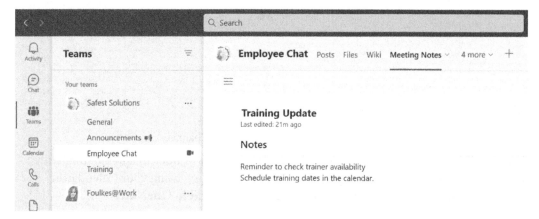

Figure 17.20 – Meeting Notes

Take time to explore OneNote's options as this is a very powerful application. In the next section, we will focus on real-time co-authoring with others.

Collaborating and file sharing

In this section, we will explore the collaborative side of the Teams app. We will learn how to upload and work with files in the Teams environment and understand the difference between default views and the **New Sheet View** feature in Excel. Finally, we will touch on version control document history.

Uploading files to channels

When we want to collaborate on documents, we can add them to a Channel. Any files that are shared via Outlook or attached to conversations are visible in the **Files** area of the channel. Follow these steps:

1. Click on a Channel within the Teams environment.

2. Click the **Files** option at the top of the channel.

3. Choose **Upload | Files** or **Upload | Folder** to browse your computer and collect documents or folders to upload:

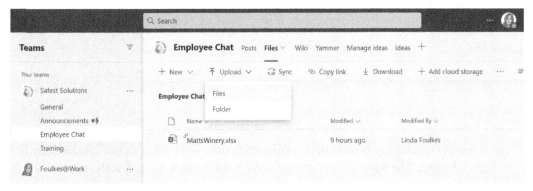

Figure 17.21 – Uploading files to a Channel

4. Choose the relevant file location, then select the file or files to upload.

5. Click the **Open** button to add the files to the Teams Channel.

6. To open the file and begin collaborating with others, simply click on the file within the **Files** area of the channel.

7. We can share comments and conversations, and see who is editing the document in real time with others. Note that every time you open, update, save, and close a document, a new version is created. Versions will be explained later in this chapter.

8. When we collaborate in real time on a shared workbook, we will see amendments that have been made by others immediately. Look out for the user marker in the document (shown in the following screenshot) to indicate that the collaborator is amending the file:

	E	F	G	H
	Region	Date Sold	Cost Per Case	Cases Sold
	North	18/05/2020	£ 165.00	450
	North	02/08/2020	£ 165.00	550
	North	14/12/2020	£ 165.00	575
	North	15/02/2020	£ 165.00	650
	South	02/11/2021	£ 165.00	320

Figure 17.22 – Collaborating in real time

9. The **Open in Desktop App** option may present itself in the notification area just below the ribbon. When you're working in the full version of the app (the desktop app), and before any amendments can be actioned, we need to click on **Edit Workbook** at the top of the screen:

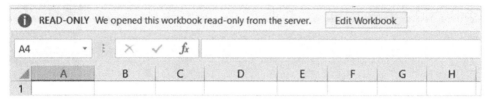

Figure 17.23 – Edit Workbook

10. After the amendments have been made, click the **Save** button to update the copy in the Channel. The **Save** button is a web save button that's located at the top left of the Excel environment:

Figure 17.24 – Using the Save button to update author amendments

11. There are several buttons at the top right of the document. These buttons allow you to copy a link to the document, add/view comments, catch up on colleague amendments, start a conversation, download the document, or view the document in your browser:

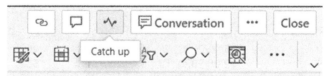

Figure 17.25 – Buttons located at the top right of the workbook

12. Click through each of these buttons to see how they can support your collaborative workflow.

In the next section, we will explore the **New Sheet View** feature in Excel.

Working with New Sheet View

When we are working collaboratively, it could become frustrating when, for example, filters are applied to workbooks. Every time you access the file, it could be filtered or manipulated by others who have access to the collaborative workflow. There is a solution named **Sheet View**. Sheet View allows each collaborator to set up custom views that contain, for instance, a filtered set of data that's only applicable to you. So, you can sort and filter to your heart's content without disrupting the original dataset.

Note that the normal cell edits will update the original data. We can only use Sheet View when a document is filed to OneDrive or SharePoint. Everyone collaborating on the file can access your Sheet Views, so they are not locked to one individual.

Follow these steps to create a **New Sheet View**:

1. Open the file you wish to work on using either SharePoint or OneDrive.

2. Click on the **View** tab, then select **New Sheet View** from the **Sheet View** group:

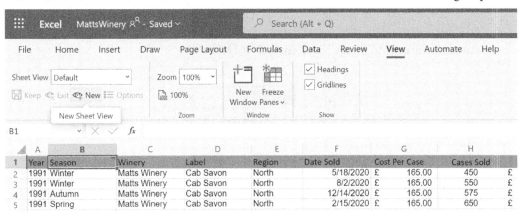

Figure 17.26 – New Sheet View

3. Notice that the border (rows and columns) of the workbook have changed to the black fill to indicate you are now working in a **New Sheet View**. Filter and sort the workbook to meet your requirements, then click the **Keep** button in the **Sheet View** group to save the view so that you can view the customized filter and sort it at any time. Notice that the default name for the view is **Temporary View**. You can rename this to suit the sort and filter that's been applied:

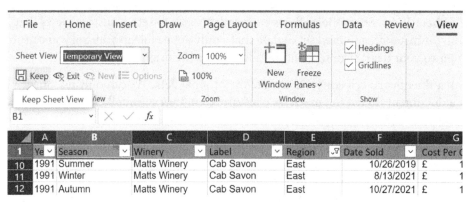

Figure 17.27 – Keep Sheet View

4. To return to the default view, and exit the **New Sheet View** feature, click the drop-down arrow next to **Sheet View** and select **Default**:

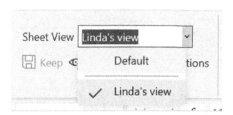

Figure 17.28 – Default workbook view

5. To return to your custom view, simply repeat this process.

In the next section, we'll look at document versions.

Working with versions

Versions are the history of document amendments that have built up over time. Each time amendments are made by the same or different individuals, the document is updated to reflect the latest version. We can revisit or restore previous versions of a file over time. Follow these steps:

1. Every time we open, update, save, and close a file, a new version is created.

2. To access the version history of a document, open a document in **SharePoint**. To do so, select the file, then click on the ellipsis to show the drop-down list of options. Then, click **Open in SharePoint**:

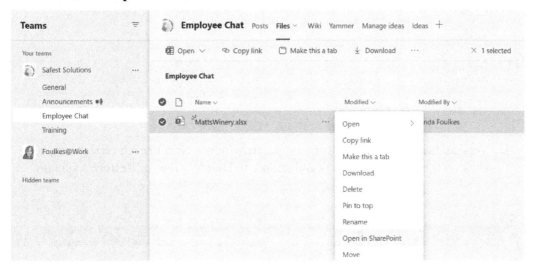

Figure 17.29 – Open in SharePoint

3. When in SharePoint, use the ellipsis to show the **Version history** properties of a document:

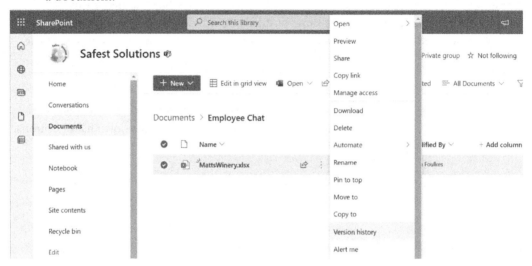

Figure 17.30 – Version history

4. **Version history** will populate in a separate window. Next to each version, we can click on the drop-down arrow and choose to **Delete**, **View**, or **Restore** a version:

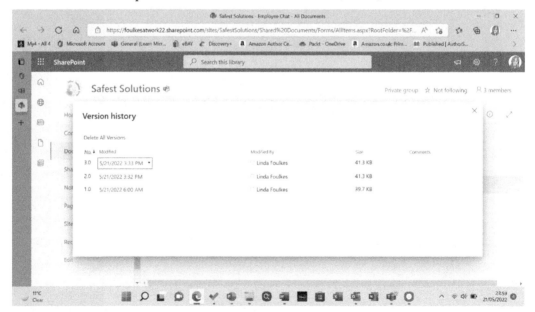

Figure 17.31 – The Version history pane

There are a few things to take into consideration when working with versions in SharePoint, as shown in the following table:

Version Numbers	The number that's been assigned to a version is not renamed if a version is deleted.
Deleted Versions	Versions are moved to the recycle bin with the version number intact. You can restore deleted versions to their original position within the version history of a document.
Restoring Versions	We can restore deleted versions to the latest version.
Comparing Versions	Original versions can be reviewed and compared in the desktop application with revised versions, or versions can be restored to become the latest version of the document history.

Table 17.4 – Working with versions

Follow these steps to learn how to delete and restore versions:

1. Open a document in SharePoint and make sure you are viewing its **Version history**. Refer to the previous section for instructions, if required.

2. Click the drop-down arrow next to the version you wish to remove, then click the **Delete** button:

Figure 17.32 – The Delete button in the drop-down list

3. The **Version history** window will now update to reflect only two versions. Notice that the version numbers are still intact, namely 3.0 and 1.0, and that version 2.0 is now in the recycle bin:

Figure 17.33 – The Version history pane has been updated

4. The deleted version will move to the SharePoint **Recycle bin**. Click the **Recycle bin** icon to the left of the window to access it:

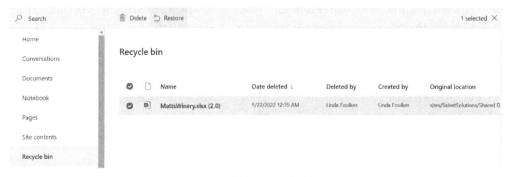

Figure 17.34 – Recycle bin

5. Notice that the version number is still intact at the end of the filename – that is, MattsWinery.xlsx (2.0).

6. To restore the version so that it becomes part of the version history, click the file you wish to restore, then select the **Restore** button at the top of the window.

7. The version will be restored to its original position in the version history.

We hope that this chapter has touched on enough content to stimulate interest and helped you explore the host of available features – they all have so much more to offer.

Summary

In this chapter, you learned how to present and collaborate using Microsoft Teams. We hope that you now understand the difference between OneDrive and SharePoint for saving files and that you have an overview of Teams apps. You learned how to share PowerPoint slides using PowerPoint Live and apply Presenter modes. We also investigated several features in the Teams meeting space and learned how to upload files to Teams Channels to collaborate in real time, as well as how to work with version control and the **New Sheet View** feature.

As this is the last chapter of this book, we hope that you have learned a wealth of knowledge that you can apply to all aspects of your professional and personal life.

Index

Packt.com

Subscribe to our online digital library for full access to over 7,000 books and videos, as well as industry leading tools to help you plan your personal development and advance your career. For more information, please visit our website.

Why subscribe?

- Spend less time learning and more time coding with practical eBooks and Videos from over 4,000 industry professionals

- Improve your learning with Skill Plans built especially for you

- Get a free eBook or video every month

- Fully searchable for easy access to vital information

- Copy and paste, print, and bookmark content

Did you know that Packt offers eBook versions of every book published, with PDF and ePub files available? You can upgrade to the eBook version at packt.com and as a print book customer, you are entitled to a discount on the eBook copy. Get in touch with us at customercare@packtpub.com for more details.

At www.packt.com, you can also read a collection of free technical articles, sign up for a range of free newsletters, and receive exclusive discounts and offers on Packt books and eBooks.

Other Books You May Enjoy

If you enjoyed this book, you may be interested in these other books by Packt:

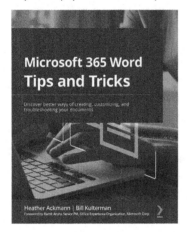

Microsoft 365 Word Tips and Tricks

Heather Ackmann, Bill Kulterman

ISBN: 9781800565432

- Track a document's changes as well as comment on and review changes by others, both locally and remotely
- Use Word's navigation and view features to improve productivity
- Generate more consistently formatted documents with Styles
- Perform common tasks through simple formatting techniques, Quick Parts, customizing AutoCorrect/AutoFormat, and memorizing keyboard shortcuts
- Troubleshoot the most frustrating formatting problems experienced by Word users
- Create more universally accessible documents by adding Alt Text using the accessibility checker and other Word features

Work Smarter with Microsoft OneNote

Connie Clark

ISBN: 9781801075664

- Understand how to create and organize notes in your notebooks
- Discover how to turn handwritten notes into typed text
- Explore how to access your content from anywhere even if offline
- Uncover ways to collaborate with your team or family and stay in sync
- Understand how to insert your emails, documents, or articles from the web
- Find out how to integrate with other Microsoft products such as Outlook or Teams

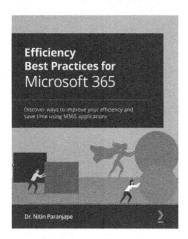

Efficiency Best Practices for Microsoft 365

Dr. Nitin Paranjape

ISBN: 9781801072267

- Understand how different MS 365 tools, such as Office desktop, Teams, Power BI, Lists, and OneDrive, can increase work efficiency
- Identify time-consuming processes and understand how to work through them more efficiently
- Create professional documents quickly with minimal effort
- Work across multiple teams, meetings, and projects without email overload
- Automate mundane, repetitive, and time-consuming manual work
- Manage work, delegation, execution, and project management

Packt is searching for authors like you

If you're interested in becoming an author for Packt, please visit authors.packtpub.com and apply today. We have worked with thousands of developers and tech professionals, just like you, to help them share their insight with the global tech community. You can make a general application, apply for a specific hot topic that we are recruiting an author for, or submit your own idea.

Share Your Thoughts

Now you've finished *Learn Microsoft Office 2021*, we'd love to hear your thoughts! Scan the QR code below to go straight to the Amazon review page for this book and share your feedback or leave a review on the site that you purchased it from.

https://packt.link/r/1803239735

Your review is important to us and the tech community and will help us make sure we're delivering excellent quality content.

Made in the USA
Las Vegas, NV
29 November 2022

60682023R00359